THE
Instrumental
RESOURCE

for Church and School

A Manual of Biblical Perspectives
and Practical Instruction
for Today's Christian Instrumentalists

Compiled and Edited by
Julie Barrier and Jim Hansford

Mark Johnson, Coordinating Editor

CHURCH
STREET
PRESS

Church Street Press
Nashville, Tennessee

ISBN 0-6330-04901
Dewey Decimal Classification: 784
Subject Headings: INSTRUMENTAL MUSIC

Printed in the United States of America

LifeWay Church Resources
LifeWay Christian Resources of the Southern Baptist Convention
One LifeWay Plaza
Nashville, Tennessee 37234

To order additional copies of this resource:
WRITE LifeWay Church Resources Customer Service,
One LifeWay Plaza, Nashville, TN 37234-0113;
FAX order to (615) 251-5933; PHONE 1-800-458-2772;
EMAIL to CustomerService@lifeway.com;
or visit the LifeWay Christian Store serving you.

The following is a list of Scripture translations used in this book.

Scripture quotations marked (CEV) are from the *Contemporary English Version*, Copyright © 1991, 1992, 1995 American Bible Society. Used by permission.

Scripture quotations marked (KJV) are from the Holy Bible, King James Version.

Scripture quotations marked (MES) are from *THE MESSAGE.* Copyright © by Eugene H. Peterson, 1993, 1994, 1995. Used by permission of NavPress Publishing Group.

Scripture quotations marked (NASB) are from the *New American Standard Bible,* © Copyright The Lockman Foundation, 1960, 1962, 1963, 1968, 1971, 1972, 1973, 1975, 1977, 1995. Used by permission.

Scripture quotations marked (NIV) are from The Holy Bible, *New International Version,* copyright © 1973, 1978, 1984, by International Bible Society. Used by permission.

PRODUCTION STAFF

Mark Johnson, *coordinating editor/ministry specialist*
Julie Barrier, Jeff Cranfill, Jon Duncan, John G. Gage, Jim Hansford,
Camp Kirkland, Terry Terry, *contributing editors*
Jere Adams, Connie Powell, Terry Terry, *editors*
Wendell McGuirk, *graphic designer*
Jim Gibson, *director, music publishing and recording*
Rhonda Edge Buescher, *managing director, music publishing and recording*
MUSIC PUBLISHING AND RECORDING OF LIFEWAY CHURCH RESOURCES

Acknowledgements

The Publisher wishes to acknowledge the contribution made by the writers and production staff in the formulation of this text. Their desire has been to create a definitive resource for churches, colleges and seminaries, and Christian schools to use as they strive to teach, instruct, and include instrumental music as a vital part of all that it means to be a viable witness for Christ through the medium of music. A book of this scope would not be possible without the additional assistance of some persons who might not otherwise be recognized. To that end, we express our gratitude to the following:

To members of these Tucson, Arizona, groups for serving as models for photographs:
- Orchestra of Casas Adobes Baptist Church;
- Band of the Ironwood High School, Mark Hodge, Director; and
- Band of the Mountain View High School, Ellen Kirkbride, Director.

To Roland Corporation U. S. and Yamaha Corporation of America for supplying photographs of instruments.

The Publisher

Contents

Preface, *Camp Kirkland* viii

Introduction, *Julie Barrier* x

SECTION 1
A Philosophy of Instrumental Worship

1. Biblical Foundations for Instrumental Music Ministry,
Jon Duncan 13

SECTION 2
The Instrumental Conductor and Arranger

2. Conducting: The Silent Art, *Jim Hansford* 27

3. Arranging for Instruments, *Camp Kirkland* and *Jeff Cranfill* . . 52

SECTION 3
The Instruments of the Orchestra

Introduction, *John G. Gage* 63

Woodwinds

Introduction, *Christopher Bade* 64

4. The Flute and Piccolo, *Rebecca Danner Remley* 65

5. The Oboe and English Horn, *Jon S. Remley* 74

6. The Clarinet and Bass Clarinet, *Robert F. Wall* and
Christopher Bade. 86

7. The Bassoon, *Ruth Shelley Unger* 100

8. The Saxophone, *Edson Dickinson.* 104

Brass

Introduction, *John G. Gage* 112

9. The French Horn, *Jeffrey H. Girdler* 113

10. The Trumpet, *Douglas Smith* 119

11. The Trombone, *Douglas Yeo* 127

12. The Euphonium and Baritone Horn, *Gerald P. Armstrong* . . 138

13. The Tuba, *Charles A. Krause* and *Jim Hansford* 146

Percussion

Introduction, *Steve Kirby* 155

14. Percussion, *Michael Katterjohn* 156

Strings

Introduction, *Terry C. Terry* 171

15. The Violin, *Celeste Myall* 172

16. The Viola, *Terry C. Terry* 185

17. The Cello, *Timothy H. Cierpke* 190

18. The Double Bass, *Lloyd Mims* 196

19. The Harp, *Carol McClure* 204

SECTION 4

The Instrumental Music Minister

Developing and Administrating a Church Music Program

20. Recruitment and Development of Volunteer
    Instrumentalists, *Bob Williamson* and *Julie Barrier* 213

21. Auditioning and Evaluating Players, *Brad R. Matheson* 217

22. Developing an Instrumental Feeder Program,
    Carter Threlkeld 222

23. Worship Planning with the Instrumentalist in Mind,
    Ed Callahan 230

24. Practical Consideration of the Preservice Rehearsal
    and Worship Service, *Larry Mayo* 242

25. Programming and Special Events for the Church
    Instrumental Program, *Brad R. Matheson*
    and *Billy Payne* 248

26. Hiring Professional Musicians, *Jack Wheaton* 254

27. **Rhythm Sections: Nuts and Bolts,** *Bob Barrett,*
David Winkler, and *Julie Barrier* 258

28. **Integrating Keyboards with the Church Orchestra,**
David Winkler. 269

29. **Optional Instrumental Ensembles From Within Your**
Sanctuary Orchestra, *Terry McNatt* 277

30. **The Conservatory of Music: Its Development and**
Implementation, *Terry McNatt* 280

31. **Selecting Appropriate Literature,** *Camp Kirkland.* 291

32. **Creatively Complementing the Vision Statement**
of a Church, *James E. Helman* 297

33. **Developing an Orchestra Handbook,** *John G. Gage* 300

34. **Budget and Fund-raising,** *Eddie Fargason* 304

35. **Officers and Section Leaders,** *John G. Gage* 307

36. **Communication,** *John G. Gage* 313

37. **Developing and Maintaining a Music Library,** *Ruth Gage* . . 315

38. **Using Technology to Enhance the Instrumental Program—**
Computers, Multimedia, and Video, *Larry Brubaker.* . . . 319

SECTION 5

The Christian School
Instrumental Music Educator

39. **Christian School Bands,** *Jeff Cranfill, Jim Hansford,*
Max Cordell, Mel Wilhoit, and *Mark Bailey* 323

• Benefits of Having a Band Program 324

• Motivation. 325

• Discipline 327

• Curriculum Development and Program Structure 327

• Assessment and Evaluation. 329

• Scheduling 331

• Instrumentation 332

• Literature Selection 334

- Organization and Administration 336
     Auditions, Recruiting and Retention, Student Leadership,
     Seating, Equipment Needs and Strategies for Procurement

- Support for the Band Program, Communication 342
     Parent Booster Organizations, Budgeting, Fund Raising,
     Handbooks, Publicity, Chapel Services, Community Performances

- Concert Attire and Protocol. 349

- Group Protocol and Stage Etiquette 351

- Marching Band 354

- Conclusion 357

- Resources. 357

40. Christian School Instrumental Ensembles,
     Mark Bailey, Jim Hansford, and Mel Wilhoit 363

41. Cooperating with the Other Arts, *Mel Wilhoit*. 372

SECTION 6
What's Next?

42. Wave of the Future: Contemporary Worship Trends
     Julie Barrier. 375

Appendix
     Range and Transposition Chart. 386

Index 388

Scripture Index. 398

Preface

by Camp Kirkland

Assembling and writing a book with this quantity of information is a staggering task. The list of topics is broad-based and comprehensive. Each section could be a book of its own. All of the contributing authors are extremely experienced and knowledgeable about their topics. Each contributor is actively involved in working with instrumental groups in either a church or school setting. Also, the writers consulted educators, performers, and countless written resources in each of the instrumental areas addressed.

The task of preparing this book is certainly a unique one. Church instrumental groups do not all conform to a standard instrumentation. Christian school instrumental groups strive to conform to a standard of excellence, but they are often left to perform literature that exceeds their resources. Interestingly, many principles for growing and maintaining these groups are consistent. In the preparation of this book, it was amazing to hear the commonality of techniques and concepts used by many to achieve common goals. Many of the ideas contained here are "nuts and bolts" concepts. However, in the ministry to the group and the individual as discussed here, spiritual principles are integral to formulating philosophy and practice. The individual player should never be labeled just "a trombone player." The label should always be "John Jones, a vital member of the instrumental group who plays the trombone."

God has honored the use of instruments in worship of Him for thousands of years. His word is filled with accounts of this testimony. A favorite is in 2 Chronicles 5:11-14.

"The priests then withdrew from the Holy Place. All the priests who were there had consecrated themselves, regardless of their divisions. All the Levites who were musicians—Asaph, Heman, Jeduthun and their sons and relatives—stood on the east side of the altar, dressed in fine linen and playing cymbals, harps and lyres. They were accompanied by 120 priests sounding trumpets. The trumpeters and singers joined in unison, as with one voice, to give praise and thanks to the Lord. Accompanied by trumpets, cymbals and other instruments, they raised their voices in praise to the Lord and sang: 'He is good; his love endures forever.' Then the temple of the Lord was filled with a cloud, and the priests could not perform their service because of the cloud, for the glory of the Lord filled the temple of God" (NIV).

Another is Psalm 150: "Praise ye the Lord. Praise God in his sanctuary: praise him in the firmament of his power. Praise him for his mighty acts: praise him according to his excellent greatness. Praise him with the sound of the trumpet: praise him with the psaltery and harp. Praise him with the timbrel and dance: praise him with stringed instruments and organs. Praise him upon the loud cymbals: praise him upon the high sounding cymbals. Let every thing that hath breath praise the Lord. Praise ye the Lord" (KJV).

Certainly, the purpose of this book is to offer guidance to those who wish to fulfill a desire to begin and grow an instrumental music ministry. The role of instruments in churches and Christian schools has changed greatly through the centuries. At the publication of this work, there has never been a more sustained growth of instrumental groups in both church and school. The evolution of these groups has led to an unprecedented variety of instrumentations and styles of music used. Every effort has been made to consider most of these in this text. The ultimate goal of the writers and publisher is that God is honored through the creation of this compendium.

"Let the word of Christ dwell in you richly as you teach and admonish one another with all wisdom, and as you sing psalms, hymns, and spiritual songs with gratitude in your hearts to God" (Col. 3:16, NIV).

Camp Kirkland's musical career includes teaching high school band, college band, music theory, and low brass. He has also performed on trombone or euphonium with a number of professional orchestras and bands, including the Jacksonville Symphony Orchestra and the River City Brass Band. In 1976 he was the first full-time church orchestra director. He served as a church orchestra director for 17 years. He is now a freelance composer, arranger, and clinician. He has over 1,000 published choral and instrumental works. Mr. Kirkland also serves as the instrumental product development consultant for Lifeway Christian Resources. He lives in Jacksonville, Florida.

Introduction

by Julie Barrier

God has created within the heart of man the desire to express passion for his Creator with "groans that words can not express" (Rom. 8:26, NIV). This cathartic heart-cry of pain and ecstasy, of fear and faith, exceeds simple words. The authors and editors of this volume agree that instrumental music is a God-given tool for man to commune with his Heavenly Father. The writers also believe that it is impossible to describe God's inscrutable power and majesty, His supernatural intervention into human lives, with simple words. All great instrumental music is numinous—it has the Divine touch in a mundane world. When the imprint of the Almighty is heard and felt by the listener, it is life transforming. Men and women consecrated to God and worshiping Him with their instruments can reach hearts across cultures in worship. Instrumental music foreshadows the perfect praise that will penetrate the halls of heaven in the throne room of the King.

The vision, consequently, is clear: place in the hands of Christian musicians the tools they need to create powerful instrumental worship. *The Instrumental Resource for Church and School* is designed to be a toolbox. It may be studied in the college or seminary classroom as a broad-based introduction to instrumental education and ministry from a Christian perspective. This compendium may also be a trusted reference for music ministers and Christian instrumental directors currently serving in churches and Christian schools.

Upon perusal, the reader will discover that each chapter is unique in style and organization. This diversity is intentional. The authors of these chapters are experts in their respective fields, and topics were assigned to capitalize upon their individual musical and educational strengths. By giving the writers the freedom and creativity to generate the chapter information in their own unique writing styles, the personality and the philosophy of the individual authors is reflected in the text.

The book is divided into six main sections:
- **The Philosophy of Instrumental Worship**
- **The Instrumental Conductor and Arranger**
- **The Instruments of the Orchestra**
- **The Instrumental Music Minister**
- **The Christian School Instrumental Music Educator**
- **What's Next? Wave of the Future: Contemporary Worship Trends**

Section 1 assists the instrumental music director in developing a vision that is biblically based and culturally relevant. Chapter 1 discusses historical and theological concepts of instrumental worship.

Section 2 articulates essential information a conductor needs to communicate effectively and musically with his or her ensemble. The instrumental arranger provides practical precepts for creating a musical score for any ensemble. Arranging is addressed to the church orchestra director. The ranges and capabilities of the instrumentalists in a church orchestra are carefully considered so that the musical scores are playable and appropriate for worship.

Section 3, an introduction to the instruments, is a comprehensive description of each of the band or orchestral instruments most often used in schools and churches. The authors have written brief histories of the instruments, basic playing techniques, pedagogical helps, procurement and repair of instruments, and comprehensive resource lists for each instrument. Symphony players, music professors, and experienced teachers have been consulted to assure that these chapters are solid in pedagogy and practicality.

Section 4 equips the instrumental music minister to create and develop an effective instrumental program in the church. The authors selected are experienced, highly successful instrumental directors with cutting-edge ministries in local churches. The first half of the ministry section discusses how to develop a church music program. Creating a vision statement, recruiting and developing volunteers, auditioning and evaluating players, feeder groups, creative worship planning, and concert programming are all discussed at length. Other practical topics include working with a rhythm section, developing a music conservatory, and hiring professional players. The last portion of this section addresses administration of a church instrumental music program.

Section 5 of *The Instrumental Resource for Church and School* is written for Christian school instrumental music educators. Experienced educators have compiled extensive information about creating an instrumental program for the Christian school. The philosophy for Christian music education, the motivation and discipline of students, the development of appropriate curricula, the grading and evaluation of student performance, and the scheduling and programming of performances provide valuable guidelines for the instrumental school educator.

Section 6 challenges the reader to examine several criteria for developing powerful, authentic relevant worship in today's culture. The instrumental worship leader and pastoral staff should ask three questions in planning worship in the next millenium: **1.** Who comes to church? **2.** Who should be there? **3.** Who came and did not return? The post-modern church must go beyond rational, presentational, and formulaic services to an experiential, mystical, relational, spontanious encounter with God.

This compendium should sharpen the skills of the Christian instrumental director. It should create a solid foundation of knowledge for the Christian college or seminary student called to the instrumental music ministry. It should inspire the Christian music educator to be innovative, efficient, and engaging in the classroom. No reader will agree with every philosophy or methodology proposed by the authors, but he or she will be challenged to solidify his or her unique vision for ministry. Men and women who are called to "praise the Lord with stringed instruments and organs" (Ps. 150:4) should touch the lives of others more deeply with the presence and power of God through instrumental music ministry.

Julie Barrier holds degrees in music from Baylor University and the University of Arizona. She is currently Associate Minister of Worship at Casas Adobes Baptist Church in Tucson, Arizona. Julie currently serves as an adjunct professor with the Golden Gate Baptist Theological Seminary in Mill Valley, California, and as a conference speaker for Intimate Life Ministries in Austin, Texas.

Introduction

SECTION 1

A Philosophy of Instrumental Worship

Biblical Foundations for Instrumental Music Ministry

by Jon Duncan

Who are the leaders of worship? Much attention will be given, in the material to follow, to defining worship and the roles participants are to fulfill. A question must be asked, however: "Who are the leaders of worship?" Another way to ask would be, "Who are the facilitators, equippers, encouragers, stimulators, and models for corporate worship?" Worship leaders are to be concerned with all of these aspects of influence. This includes the instrumentalists. It is common to only consider the pastor or minister of music as "worship leader." This is a narrow concept. The instrumentalist is involved in creating an atmosphere that draws the individual and corporate body to a realization of Christ's presence. In addition, the instrumentalist takes part in the proclamation ministry of the church through facilitating and inspiring the congregation's confession. As a result of these vital roles, it is important for the instrumentalist to fully realize his or her responsibilities and the level of commitment that is required. The instrumental ministry reflects a microcosm of the church. Many diverse parts join together to produce a unified heart of praise to the Creator–Redeemer–Lord. Such modeling always leads to imitation. Through God's grace, He has chosen ordinary people to reflect His very image through the indwelling of the Holy Spirit. Such modeling inspires the church and draws the unchurched. Even before tuning, the instrumentalist is a worship leader.

Biblical Worship

Awakened to Worship
In the best-seller nonfiction book *Awakenings,* Oliver Sacks discovered a temporary remedy for patients who for years had been in a "sleeping" or semi-comatose state.[1] In other words, their physical condition was basically good, but they couldn't respond to the world around them. The medicine introduced by Sacks "awakened" them to the outside world. Part of the therapy included taking the

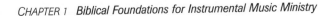

patients on a field trip. The physicians considered taking them to the theater or the museum; however, the group's response was limited. In short, they didn't want to watch or observe; rather, they desired an experience. Part of the therapy included singing and dancing.[2] The therapy was highly successful. This analogy applies to the worship experience of many people. According to a recent George Barna survey, few "church goers" ever experience a personal encounter with God in worship.[3] Their eyes may be open, but they are actually "asleep" to the opportunity that worship provides. As the Mount Carmel Hospital case illustrates, many today are faced with the same choices of therapy—a show or museum. God's people need to be "awakened" to experience real worship.

Jesus also dealt with this issue. In His visit with the Samaritan woman in John 4, Jesus also described the nature of powerful worship. The woman said to Jesus, "Our fathers worshiped on this mountain, but you Jews claim that the place where we must worship is in Jerusalem." Jesus responded, "…a time is coming when you will worship the Father neither on this mountain nor in Jerusalem.…a time is coming and has now come when the true worshipers will worship the Father in spirit and truth, for they are the kind of worshipers the Father seeks" (John 4:20, 21, 23, NIV).

The mountain Jesus talked about was Mt. Gerizim. This worship context was highly emotional but lacking in content. It was all show. Jesus also expressed concern for Jewish worship. Jesus said the religious leaders were full of "dead men's bones" (Matt. 23:27, NIV). In other words, the worship of Jerusalem was a barren and lifeless museum.

Real worship is not hype, and it is never boring. Real worship celebrates the truth through the Spirit. The truth is that God sent His Son to be the Savior of the world, and worship should be Christ centered. Worship is also Spirit driven. As believers, the Holy Spirit prompts worship within the human spirit. When believers are "awakened" to His presence in genuine worship, lives are changed and God is honored.

Defining Worship

A sound definition of worship for this discussion is:

Biblical worship is the believer's sincere and Spirit-empowered response to the redemptive act of God in Christ Jesus.

• Real Worship Is Biblical

The Bible is the source for issues related to worship content. Sensitivity to culture and tradition is important, but these concerns should not drive worship. In God's Word, the worshiper discovers the model for worship (Isa. 6), the content of worship (John 4), and the attitude of worship (Heb. 10). The Bible also identifies false worship in Amos 5:21-23. The Lord says, "I hate, I despise your religious feasts; I cannot stand your assemblies. Even though you bring me burnt offerings and grain offerings, I will not accept them. Though you bring choice fellowship offerings, I will have no regard for them. Away with the noise of your songs! I will not listen to the music of your harps" (NIV).

During the reign of Jeroboam, the children of Israel were observing right worship practice. They observed the solemn assemblies and the feast days.

They even prepared the offerings according to Levitical law. Their worship, however, was rejected. Their hearts were far from God. They were doing the "right thing," but they were doing it in the "wrong way." The Word of God is the believer's source for worship content.

• Real Worship Is for Believers

Biblical worship is based on relationship. Hebrews 10:19-25 emphasizes this critical point: "So friends, we can now—without hesitation—walk right up to God, into 'the Holy Place.' Jesus has cleared the way by the blood of his sacrifice, acting as our priest before God. The 'curtain' into God's presence is his body. So let's *do* it—full of belief, confident that we're presentable inside and out. Let's keep a firm grip on the promises that keep us going. He always keeps his word. Let's see how inventive we can be in encouraging love and helping out, not avoiding worshiping together as some do but spurring each other on" (MES).

Because of Christ's atoning sacrifice, the redeemed have rightful access to the throne of God. It is the privilege and responsibility of believers to wholeheartedly participate in corporate worship. Worship is the goal of redemption. Life's purposes are fulfilled when man truly worships His Creator.

• Real Worship Is Sincere

Nothing is more devastating to worship than pride. In revisiting Amos 5, the focus of worship was on form only. They were going through the motions. Sin had infiltrated the Israeli camp: "You people hate judges and honest witnesses; you abuse the poor and demand heavy taxes from them. You have built expensive homes, but you won't enjoy them;...I am the Lord, and I know your terrible sins. You cheat honest people and take bribes; you rob the poor of justice" (10-12, CEV).

In contrast, during Hezekiah's reign, worship was reformed. The focus was on the heart rather than the form. Passover had not been observed during Ahaz's reign. The house of the Lord had been repaired and purified, however, there were not enough priests prepared to serve God as the Law specified. Passover was to be observed on the first month (Ex. 12:2); however, Hezekiah needed more time. So the leaders moved the observance to the second month. God didn't order Hezekiah to halt, but rather to move forward. The people confessed their sins and were cleansed. They even celebrated seven more days than was permitted under Levitical law—"and God heard them, for their prayer reached heaven, his holy dwelling place" (2 Chron. 30:27, NIV). God's pleasure is found not through methodology, but through a repentant heart.

• Real Worship Is Empowered Through the Holy Spirit

The Holy Spirit enables worship to happen. Because the Holy Spirit resides in every believer, it would be impossible to experience authentic worship apart from the Holy Spirit. Through the dynamic of the Holy Spirit's revelation of Christ, God's presence is communicated to the worshiping community. The

Spirit convicts people of sin, while He simultaneously encourages the worshiper to confession of sin. In addition, the work of the Holy Spirit sanctifies the believer and interprets God's Word for his or her daily life. The Spirit motivates and inspires praise, prayer, teaching, preaching, and ministry.[4]

• Real Worship Tells the Story of Redemption

The worship of Israel was rooted in the Exodus event. The theme of Hebrew worship has always been deliverance. Although the worship practices changed through the centuries, the content remained consistent. Believers' worship is also event oriented. The theme of Christian worship is Christ's redemption. This was the vision of John the Revelator. This is the vision for believers today. This kind of worship is not "goal driven," but "Christ driven." Robert Webber states: "Worship represents Jesus Christ through re-presentation. Worship tells and acts out the living, dying, and rising of Christ. Worship celebrates God's saving deed in Jesus Christ."[5]

In worship, the community of faith retells the story of redemption.

• Real Worship Is Dialogue with God

In his *Doxology,* Geoffrey Wainwright views worship as a dialogue.[6] God initiates dialogical worship through grace.

The believer then responds through praise, prayer, confession, and commitment. This approach is modeled in Scripture. Isaiah's "dialogue" began with God's revelation of His attributes (Isaiah 6).

"I saw also the Lord sitting upon a throne, high and lifted up, and his train filled the temple. Above it stood the seraphims: and one cried unto another, and said, Holy, holy, holy, is the Lord of hosts; the whole earth is full of his glory" (1-3).

The discovery of God's holiness caused Isaiah to see himself, as he really was—a person in need. The revelation of God's distinctive nature started a worship dialogue. Isaiah's response was to confess his and his people's sin before the Lord.

"Then said I, Woe is me! for I am undone; because I am a man of unclean lips, and I dwell in the midst of a people of unclean lips; for mine eyes have seen the King, the Lord of hosts" (v.5).

His confession then led to a response from God. God forgave, cleansed, and restored Isaiah.

"Lo, this hath touched thy lips, and thine iniquity is taken away, and thy sin purged" (v.7).

The forgiveness of God placed Isaiah in a new position. He was now in a position to hear the Word of the Lord.

"Whom shall I send, and who will go for us" (v.8)?

Isaiah responded with "Here am I; send me." The dialogue continues. As a result of Isaiah's changed and willing heart, God commissions him to "Go, and tell this people" (v.9). Isaiah would be asked to be God's voice to people that would not receive His message. He was charged to be God's voice until the "cities be wasted without inhabitant, and the houses without man, and the land be utterly desolate" (v.11).

This worship dialogue is a model for the church. God initiates worship through grace as He reveals Himself through the Holy Spirit. The church is led to recognize God's attributes of power, majesty, and holiness, which lead to self-examination. Upon confession, there is forgiveness, which places the worshiper in a position to hear the Word of God. The Holy Spirit communicates the message to the cleansed heart by which a response of obedience leads to commission. The worshiper departs empowered to serve God and fulfill His mission.

• Real Worship Is Centered in Christ

The focus of worship is Jesus Christ. Redemption requires an encounter with Jesus Christ. Worship is made possible as a result of the Christ event. Segler states, "All true worship is Christocentric, for only in Christ can we find God."[7]

It is at this point that style issues become major concerns. Style is a communication vehicle, upon which rides content. It is vital that worship content is clearly communicated. The Christ event should never be portrayed amidst confusion, disorder, or apathy. Styles (of any nature) that are embraced for the sole purpose of providing an appreciative response from an entertained crowd is anthropocentric and a distraction from the focus of worship—Jesus Christ.

This is not to say that worship should be detached from a changing world. Worship should be open to change. For many, it is critical that stylistic changes be realized in order to clearly communicate redemption's story in biblical worship. Biblical worship practices indicate different methods to communicate the same central truth. The worship of Abraham was patriarchal, or family-involved. It proclaimed the covenant of redemption that was to come. The worship of Moses witnessed the rise of the Levitical order as redemption was acted out through the tabernacle sacrifices. Davidic worship witnessed dramatic change as the monarchy became strongly involved in corporate worship. King David moved the tabernacle, added choirs and instrumental groups, and involved the people in different ways. Worship in the temple was festive and elaborate. In contrast, worship during the exile was intimate and emphasized instruction and prayer. Some sources suggest the synagogue was established during this period. According to Ralph Martin, the early church was strongly influenced by the synagogue practice.[8] Through its praise, prayer, proclamation, Eucharist observance, and fellowship, the early church dynamically portrayed the Christ event.[9]

Although biblical models relate change in practice, the message is always consistent. All scriptural worship points to Christ. A style or methodology that points to any direction other than Christ is out of place in biblical worship. Biblical worship is initiated by God, focused in Christ, and empowered by the Holy Spirit.

Worship and the Use of Instruments

Scripture provides affirmation for the use of instruments in worship. The Old Testament presents many examples of using instruments in worship. The New Testament also affirms the use of instruments, although it is less specific. Because the use of instruments is not specifically commanded in New Testament Scripture, some (a small minority) believe this is a reason to forbid instruments in Christian worship. For the most part, these traditions follow the "regulative" principle of exegesis, which simply means if Scripture is silent on a matter, it is forbidden. For these, instrument use in the Old Testament was under God's command in direct connection with sacrificial offerings under ceremonial law. Because the New Testament is silent regarding the use of instruments and Christ's atoning sacrifice is complete, some proponents believe there is no need to add anything.[10]

The problem with the "regulative" principle lies in its inconsistency. What pleases God in the Old Testament should not be considered "forbidden" in the New Testament. The New Testament's silence is the strongest affirmation for its continued usage. Although stated by others, few have said it better than W. Hines Sims:

"If God the Father recognized and received the praise and worship connected with singing and the playing of instruments in accepted forms all through the Old Testament, He also, as God the Son and God the Holy Spirit in the New Testament, endorses such use in New Testament churches, for He is One and unchanging and cannot be incompatible with Himself. The fact that instruments were an accepted part of worship in the Old Testament makes clear the thought that had God wished that churches not use instruments, He would have, through the medium of His inspired writers, specifically said so."[11]

A close look at Ephesians 5:19 presents New Testament affirmation for instrumental usage in worship: "Speaking to yourselves in psalms and hymns and spiritual songs, singing and making melody in your heart to the Lord."

The word "melody" comes from the Greek word *psallo,* which literally means to "sing with the harp" or to play on a stringed instrument. Paul also uses the same word "psallos" in Romans 15:9 and 1 Corinthians 14:15 as he encourages the practice of singing with instrumental accompaniment.

Scriptural references not only specify the types of instruments used, but also the purpose of their usage. In Scripture, instruments were not used for individual self-expression, but served instead to celebrate the life of the people of God.

The term *kelim* is used to indicate instruments that accompanied singing (1 Chron. 16:42; 2 Chron. 29:26; Neh. 12:36; Amos 6:5). The term is also used in other references denoting weapons, utensils, and even "baggage" (1 Sam. 10:22). Richard Leonard relates that instruments had a utilitarian nature in the biblical perspective. Leonard is speculating when he interprets this as insight into the functional use of instruments within the life of the covenant people as opposed to their sole usage for individual self-expression.[12] This is an important concept for believers today. Proper (biblical) usage of instruments is not self-serving. Musical gifts are to be used in service to God and others.

Scripture References for Instruments Used in Worship
1 Samuel 10:5
2 Samuel 6:5
1 Chronicles 13:8; 15:16, 28
Psalms 81:2-3; 92:3; 150:3-5

Instruments Associated with Banquets
Isaiah 5:12

Improper Use of Instruments by the Ungodly
Job 21:12

Improper Use of Instruments Related to Idolatry
 Daniel 3:5, 7, 10, 15
Instruments Used in Relation to Judgment
 Revelation 18:22
Instruments Used as Metaphor
 1 Corinthians 14:7-8
Instruments Used to Sound Warning or Announcement
 Leviticus 23:24
 Numbers 29
 1 Corinthians 15:52
 1 Thessalonians 4:16
 Revelation 8:2, 6[13]

Why Have an Instrumental Ministry?

Why is it important to develop an instrumental ministry? The simple answer is that God's Word instructs believers to give their total life in sacrificial service to the Lord:

"Therefore, I urge you, brothers, in view of God's mercy, to offer your bodies as living sacrifices, holy and pleasing to God—this is your spiritual act of worship" (Rom.12:1, NIV).

Worship is a lifestyle. All human talents, gifts, and abilities are under God's authority. Because Christians are adopted as sons into God's family, the natural response is a consecrated life joyfully offered to the Father. It is tragic that some believers will offer their best for a secular concert, but will refuse to offer that same gift of excellence in corporate worship.

In addition to the scriptural mandate for instrumental music, it should be included for practical reasons. Instrumental music inspires participation in worship. It also provides an atmosphere that assists the worshipers in encountering the living God personally. Instrumental music that is presented with sensitivity can be used by the Holy Spirit to move biblical truth deeper into the life of the believer. If people are inspired, uplifted, and nurtured through instrumental music, then it should be used. When adding instruments to the music ministry of the church, a new and refreshing approach to worship is offered. Many new people can be brought into the music ministry that may have never been involved before. In addition, an instrumental group gives variety in the church's musical life. In short, an instrumental ministry is a practical means of touching the lives of people.

There is also a theological dimension for the use of instrumental music. If Christians are stewards of what God has given (and God has given all), then what has been entrusted to His children must be used for the glory of God. In Paul's first letter to the Corinthians, he addresses the issue of Christian freedom. He states that everything man does should be an offering to the Lord: "whatever you do, do it all for the glory of God" (1 Cor. 10:31, NIV).

Responsible Christians should be motivated to use every means available to praise and serve God. If He has given such a musical gift, then a faithful servant will glorify God, because all things are His. "Through him all things were made; without him nothing was made that has been made" (John 1:3, NIV).

Instruments in the Bible

The instruments of the Bible fall into three families: percussion, winds, and stringed instruments.

Bronze cymbals, Ptolemaic Period (about 200 BC).

Percussion

Cymbals. The common Hebrew word for cymbals is *meziltayim* (1 Chron. 15:16; 16:42; 25:1; 2 Chron. 5:13). The word *zelzelim* is used in Psalm 150:5 and, according to Richard Leonard, could be onomatopoeic (representative of the clashing sound the instrument makes).[14] The word means "tingling," "ringing," or "clanging."[15] According to Josephus, the zelzelim was a large bronze plate played with both hands. This would model Egyptian cymbals with their broad, flat rim and large bulge in the center that helped to enhance the resonance.[16] First Chronicles 15:19 indicates that the sanctuary cymbals were made of bronze and joined with winds and strings in its praise.

The Greek word *chalkos* mentioned in 1 Corinthians 13:1 is used metaphorically. Paul is most likely referring to the two kinds of cymbals already discussed.

Roman Age sistrum

Sistrum. The term *shalishim* found in 1 Samuel 18:6 refers to a shaken instrument. The word is connected with the Hebrew *shalosh* (three). Research points to an instrument with three rods, or a rod with three rings. Although evidence varies, it would seem the term is onomatopoeic, which would indicate that it would be a shaking or rattling instrument. In 2 Samuel 6:5, the term *mena'an'im* is used for a similar instrument. Sendrey states that it signifies a shaking instrument, like the sistrum, though maybe not so richly adorned.[17]

Drums. The *tof* is an onomatopoeic term of the common hand drum. Leonard suggests the term also includes tambourines. Sendrey states that evidence is not available to suggest the inclusion of metal discs to the *tof,* producing a type of tambourine prior to the 13th century.[18] What is known is that the instrument consisted of a wooden or metal hoop covered with an animal skin.

Bells. *Pa'amonim* relates to the bells attached to the lower seam of the high priest's purple garment (Ex. 28:33-34). The function of the bells may be tied to a simple utilitarian function in order that the priest would be heard when he entered and left the "holy place." Some sources indicate that the bells

could have had a superstitious origin as a means to keep away evil spirits.

The word *mezillot,* found in Zechariah 14:20, was probably a larger type of bell that was hung upon horses. Similar to the pa'amonim, it is possible that the bells were utilized as protection for the animals in keeping away evil spirits.

The Winds

The Bible mentions three types of wind instruments: horns, trumpets, and pipes. Psalm 150:3 gives reference to the family of wind instruments—*ugab.* This family consists of the *keren, shofar, yobel, hazozerah,* and *halil.*

Shofar

The Horn. The *keren,* mentioned in Leviticus 4:7, 18, 25 and 1 Chronicles 25:5, refers to a hollowed animal horn (usually a ram's horn) with a mouth hole. Since the word *keren* is considered synonymous with the *shofar,* English Bible versions do not make any distinctions. Like the *shofar,* the *keren* served as a signal instrument, since the biblical text never connects the words with a worship service.

Another term for the horn is the *shofar,* as mentioned in Exodus 19:16; 1 Chronicles 15:28; and Psalms 81:3; 98:6. The instrument received its name from the material from which it is made—*shapparu,* or "wild goat." According to Sendrey, the original form was curved. Later, curved and straight horns were employed to signal temple ceremonies.[19]

The *yobel* mentioned in Leviticus 25:9, Exodus 19:13, and Joshua 6:5 refers to a composite of materials. The characteristic feature of the *yobel* was a detachable metal sound bell—a type of megaphone—which made it a powerful instrument. This was the instrument referred to at the destruction of Jericho. The various terms are used interchangeably, as in Joshua 6:5. The ram's horn had a limited number of pitches, and it is more often mentioned as an instrument of warning, assembly, or announcement rather than as an instrument for music. Scripture indicates that the instrument was used in the temple in announcing various sacrifices and festive days and in signaling the Year of Jubilee (Lev. 25:9).

Trumpets. The trumpet of the Bible—*hazozerah*—was originally made from silver, according to Numbers 10:2. Richard Leonard indicates that ancient coins show the instrument as a straight metal tube, similar to the herald trumpet.[20] Unlike today's valve trumpet, the biblical type could play only a limited number of notes. The usage of the instrument was similar to other horns in order to signal or summon the people. Scripture also mentions both the ram's horn and the trumpet as sounding instruments to herald the coronation of a king (1 Kings 1:39; 2 Kings 9:13; 11:14). The instructions for the Feast of Trumpets (Lev. 23:23-25) literally call for a "memorial of shout" *(t'ru'ah)* rather than a call for trumpets.

Pipe

Pipes. The *halil* (*aulos*—Greek equivalent) was an instrument with fingering holes. Although the *halil* or *aulos* is usually called a "flute" in English versions, evidence suggests that it had a double reed mouthpiece and represented a primitive type of *shawm*—the forerunner of the oboe. Originally it was cylindrical, but later acquired a conic shape. Jeremiah refers to the "wailing" or "moaning" sound of the instrument (Jer. 48:36). It is also mentioned as an instrument associated with festivals and coronations (Isa. 30:29; 1 Kings 1:40). Jesus refers to the use of the *aulos* to accompany dancing (Luke 7:32) and in the customary rites of mourning for the dead (Matt. 9:23). The *halil* had a limited function in worship. The superscription of Psalm 5 directs the use of the *nahilah,* a related word, in performance.

A youth playing a double-pipe.

Stringed Instruments

Kinnor. The *kinnor* is mentioned more frequently than the harp and seems to have been a more popular instrument in common life as well as in the worship life of the Hebrews. Sources differ regarding the *kinnor's* shape. Some indicate a lute-like instrument while others relate it to a type of harp or lyre. The closest relative, however, would probably be the *kithara*. The Greek instrument had many variations, including a version with nine strings stretched across a frame from a bar supported by two necks. The Psalms frequently refer to the *kinnor* (Pss. 43:4; 71:22; 98:5; 137:2; 147:7; 149:3), and it appears elsewhere in Scripture (Gen. 4:21; Job 30:31; Isa.

This spendidly crafted lyre discovered in the royal tombs at Ur bespeaks the love of fine music by the ancients. This instrument has eleven strings and a bowed sound box and dates to 2400 BC.

This wooden harp has a spade-shaped sounding board and five strings

Ancient bas-relief showing musicians with stringed and wind instruments

5:12; Ezek. 26:13). The superscriptions of Psalms 6 and 12 direct their performance with instruments "upon the *sh'minit*," perhaps an eight-stringed version. The *kinnor* is frequently mentioned together with the *nebel* (1 Kings 10:12; Pss. 57:8; 81:2; 150:3). Rabbinic tradition indicates that nine or more *kinnors* were always used in the worship of the sanctuary. The *kinnor* was David's instrument (the translation "harp" is incorrect), and with it he soothed Saul's mental depression (1 Sam. 16:16, 23). Together with the harp and other instruments, the *kinnor* is associated with the activities of prophetic bands that frequented the sanctuaries (1 Sam. 10:5). When the central sanctuary was established, its musicians, led by Jeduthun, prophesied to the accompaniment of the *kinnor* (1 Chron. 25:3). The prophets of Israel were musicians who customarily uttered or sang their oracles, apparently with stringed instruments. Elisha called for a string player or "minstrel" *(m'naggen)* when the king asked him to prophesy (2 Kings 3:15).

Nebel. Twenty-seven times Scripture refers to the *nebel*. The Hebrew term refers to a bulging shape. It is quite possible the term indicated utensils or bulky vessels might have been applied to the instrument. The prophet Amos describes it as an instrument that is plucked. Based on the accompaniment functions of the *kinnor* and *nebel* it is likely that the latter is a smaller and higher pitched version of the former.

Asor. The word *asor* appears three times in Psalms 33:2, 92:3, and 144:9. The word is connected with its root meaning of "ten." Sources point to an instrument of 10 strings. Curt Sachs indicates it is a type of zither.[21]

Sabbeka. The *sabbeka* is mentioned as an instrument used in King Nebuchadnezzar's court. Although sources indicate a variety of possibilities, most point to the instrument as having strings that were stretched over a wooden sound box.

Pesanterin. Mentioned in Nebuchadnezzar's court, the *pesanterin* was most likely a dulcimer prototype. Pictures from antiquity indicate an instrument of eight strings over a wooden, slightly-arched box with sound holes. The strings are most likely struck with a type of hammer.

Kathros. Another instrument played in Nebuchadnezzar's court is the *kathros* or *kithros.* The instrument was most likely a four-stringed type of lute or lyre.

The Sanctuary Orchestra

When the ark was brought up to Mount Zion, it was accompanied by horns, trumpets, cymbals, harps, and lyres (1 Chron. 13:8; 15:28). David established permanent Levitical orders whose duty it was to play the various instruments used in the continuing worship on that site (1 Chron. 15:16-24; 16:4-7; 25:1-7). The instruments were used orchestrally in the praise of God. They sounded simultaneously to call the assembly to worship (Ps. 98:6). This appears to have been the custom in pagan cults as well, as the instruments summoning the people to bow down to the gold image of Nebuchadnezzar (Dan. 3:4-6) seem to be playing together. There is no indication that independent parts were employed. Some sources indicate that the stringed instruments and pipes played the modalities being used in the psalm being sung, with perhaps some pattern of ornamentation provided by the horns, trumpets, and cymbals.[22] The selah of the Psalms may have been an instrumental interlude or a general "lifting up" of sound or change of mood by both singers and instrumentalists.[23]

Careful study of the Scriptures will provide the instrumental director with a vision for instrumental worship that is God-centered and God-directed. A devoted believer will always long to express love and gratitude to the Creator in a multitude of ways. It is the duty of the instrumental music minister to search the Scriptures and discover his or her model for instrumental worship as the Holy Spirit directs.

[1]Oliver Sacks, *Awakenings* (New York: Harper-Collins, 1990), 367.

[2]Ibid., 125.

[3]Barna internet.

[4]Franklin Segler, *Christian Worship,* revised by Randall Bradley (Nashville: Broadman and Holman, 1996), 53.

[5]Robert Webber, *Blended Worship* (Peabody, MA: Hendrickson Publishers, 1998), 39.

[6]Geoffrey Wainwright, *Doxology* (New York: Oxford, 1990), 18-21.

[7]Segler, *op. cit.,* 50.

[8]Ralph Martin, *Worship in the Early Church* (Grand Rapids: William Eerdmans, 1975), 18.

[9]Ibid.

[10]Bruce Steward, *Churches That Refrain from Use of Instruments in Worship,* Volume 4, *Library of Christian Worship* (Nashville: StarSong Publishing, 1994), 439.

[11]W. Hines Sims, *Instrumental Music in the Church* (Nashville: Broadman, 1947), 16.

[12]Richard Leonard, "Musical Instruments in Scripture," *The Encyclopedia of Christian Worship* (Nashville: StarSong Publishing, 1993), 234.

[13]Ibid., 236.

[14]Ibid., 234.

[15]Alfred Sendrey, *Music in Ancient Israel* (New York: Philosophical Library, 1969), 375.

[16]Ibid.

[17]Ibid., 384.

[18]Ibid., 373.

[19]Ibid., 346.

[20]Leonard, 236.

[21]Curt Sachs quoted in Sendrey, 291. Sach's History, 126.

[22]Ibid., 237.

[23]Notes, *The Scofield Reference Bible,* Psalm 3:2.

Jon Duncan has served as Worship and Church Music Specialist, Baptist General Convention of Oklahoma, since 1991. In 1992 he founded the Oklahoma Baptist Symphony, which is made up of auditioned lay musicians from dozens of Baptist churches in Oklahoma. The 80-member symphony has been on several mission tours and performs many times each year. A native of Oklahoma, Duncan holds a B.M. from the University of Oklahoma, M.M.E. from Phillips University, M.M. from Southwestern Baptist Theological Seminary, and Doctor of Ministry in Worship Studies from Northern Baptist Theological Seminary in Chicago, Illinois.

SECTION 2

The Instrumental Conductor and Arranger

CHAPTER 2

Conducting:
The Silent Art

by Jim Hansford

Conducting is one of the primary tools which helps worship leaders communicate with musicians. It forms the basis of how vocalists and instrumentalists will interpret the music for a worship service, concert, or other performance opportunity. Although the revival of orchestral instrument use in churches is only a few decades old, conducting has traditions and developments that span several centuries. Church instrumentalists often have experience in a wide variety of musical venues and will frequently have high musical and leadership expectations that must be met by the instrumental conductor.

Good conducting skills are essential to the church instrumental leader who will preform classic musical works as well as contemporary Christian literature. Recorded music, radio, the Internet, television, and other media have brought all types of music to the largest audience ever in history. The increased sophistication of listeners means that the public will know many musical works well and expect them to be faithfully and skill- 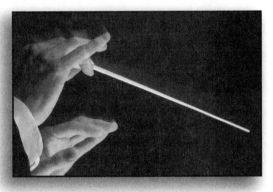 fully recreated in church settings. Poor preparation skills on the part of the conductor can greatly endanger the sucess of the works performed and their ability to create an atmosphere where worship can thrive. Whether the goal is to sucessfully unite musicians in a medley of hymns and praise choruses or to perform an entire oratorio, the instrumental conductor must continually strive to develop and refine his conducting skills.

The silent art of using physical gestures to communicate musical ideas that has become known as conducting is a relatively modern notion. The standard image of a conductor working from a podium with a baton became a general practice only in the mid-19th century. The earliest manifestations of conducting—chironomy or hand signals to illustrate the motion of melody—may date back as far as 2800 B.C. in Egypt.[1] From the Middle Ages through the Baroque period, various time-beating gestures were used by the organist or harpsichordist to assist rhythmic precision. Illustrations from this period indicate it was popular to use a stick, a roll of paper, or even a staff for tapping on the floor to provide a pulse. Jean-Baptiste Lully (1632-1687) may have been one of the first to assume the role of violinist/conductor and establish beat patterns to keep the musicians together. Musical interpretation was not likely a priority for conductors at the time. During the late Baroque and early Classical periods the musical leader was often the court composer/keyboard director who provided musical guidance when there was a combination of vocal and instrumental performers, as in opera. In the case of purely instrumental music, the responsibility often rested on the shoulders of the violinist-leader. The art of conducting and orchestration developed at the same time. Ludwig Spohr arrived in England in 1820 and conducted with a stick. A new breed of conductor-composers, including Mendelssohn, Liszt, Wagner, and Berlioz, set the stage for the modern conductor as we know him today. Hans von Bulow (1830-1894), remembered as the greatest conductor of Wagner's music, was highly respected for his ability to create an emotional impact on musicians and as one of the first conductors to dispense with the use of the score.[2] Although many aspects of conducting were in the process of being standardized prior to the 20th century, many refinements continue to be made. Conducting, in its broadest sense, is an art form which is never completely learned but is constantly being analyzed and altered for more efficient communication.

Michael Haithcock
Director of Bands and
Professor of Conducting,
University of Michigan

"Conducting is indeed a silent art! The true conductor must be able to hear the music in total silence with only the sound of the score alive in the inner ear. Also, the true conductor must be able to physically portray the musical images in the score utilizing a gestural language that illuminates that which cannot be spoken or notated. Understanding these silent truths and blending them with discipline to study and practice in total silence are the necessary ingredients in the recipe of artistic conducting."

Delimitations

The information in this chapter is written based on the assumption that the reader has learned the typical fundamental conducting skills, techniques, and general musical understandings taught prior to or during the first half of a beginning university conducting course. There is also the presumption that the reader has at least one reputable conducting textbook with myriad photos and conducting diagrams. In a brief survey of popular conducting texts, one will observe that standard conducting beat patterns tend to differ very little among the experts. The primary objective here is to give a brief overview of the basic skills, then focus on some intermediate and advanced techniques and concepts. Other areas addressed include roles of the conductor as a music educator; further considerations beyond the podium; and manual technique, including score study and rehearsal matters. This chapter does not, in any way, serve as or intend to replace, a comprehensive text on conducting technique.

Conducting: What Is It?

In its highest form, conducting is indeed an art—a silent art. Through gesture and without the luxury of words, the conductor must convey the musical intent (the very essence of the music) to the ensemble members and to the listeners in a concert setting. These gestures with arms, fingers, hands, face, mouth, and the complete torso are vital components of basic technique. The total anatomy and aura are critical tools employed by the competent conductor. Elizabeth Green states in *The Modern Conductor* that "impulse of will" is a necessary ingredient to unifying the musicianship of an ensemble into one secure interpretation. Although she never specifically defines impulse of will, it is evident that she is describing the positive atmosphere, air, and environment surrounding a conductor that communicates security and clarity of intent to the musicians. This energy, confidence, and ability to sensitize the ensemble members to conductorial gestures is the bottom line in determining the effectiveness of the conductor. In fact, the total effectiveness of a conductor is determined by the musical response of the ensemble. Performers create the sound; conductors shape it.

The Basics

Stance

The first visual attribute of the competency of a conductor is the atmosphere that is created once he or she steps on the podium. This stance or posture is critically important to the overall effectiveness of the conductor. The feet should be placed not more than shoulder width apart and the hips need to be squared toward the ensemble. If more balance can be achieved by placing one foot slightly forward of the other, then do so. The torso and head should be slightly stretched to make the body fully erect as if one had a string attached to the top of the head with someone pulling up on it. (What instrumental teacher has not used this to encourage good posture from young instrumentalists?) The body should be relaxed and convey a sense of openness to the ensemble. It is the desire of the conductor to invite the ensemble to join in a collaborative effort of music making, and podium posture should express such. Dropping the head, slumping at the waist, slouching on one leg, or raising the shoulders should all be avoided. Muscular tension in the ankles, knees, hips, shoulders, and neck can restrict motion and in some cases cause dizziness.

Stance must include the ready position of the arms and hands prior to the downbeat. As the arms are lifted to a horizontal position, the elbows should be moved slightly outward and forward as if preparing to shake hands, but with the right-hand palm facing downward, or almost downward. Be careful not to twist the forearms unnatu-

Photo 1

Photo 2

rally to achieve the palm-down position. Moving the elbows slightly further away from the torso can help achieve this. In the absence of a baton, the fingers should be extended (not spread), relaxed, and slightly curved (not allowing the thumb to stick out too far). Some conducting teachers advocate placing the thumb on the tip of the index finger for proper appearance. Each person, with the assistance of a colleague or teacher, must formulate the most appropriate hand and finger position to fit his or her needs and appearance. (See photo 1 and photo 2.)

Conventionally, performers expect the beat to be given with the right hand. Although one will occasionally see a "left-handed" conductor, this writer does not consider it optional as to which hand should be used for giving the beat. The goal of the conductor is to develop independence between the hands. As soon as the left-handed person learns to maintain good beat patterns with the right hand it will become obvious that left-handed students possess a decided advantage over their right-handed colleagues when it comes to developing left-hand agility in cueing and expressive gestures.

The Baton

The technical instrument of the conductor is the baton. Whether to use a baton or not is an ongoing controversy. Although a majority of instrumental conductors tend to use the baton and a minority of choral conductors actually use one, conductors should learn and polish basic baton skills. Following are a few reasons to consider:

• Since most instrumentalists are accustomed to the baton, the batonless choral conductor is at a disadvantage when performing joint choral and instrumental works.

• It is generally agreed that the tip of the baton provides more clarity and precision of the beat.

• When working with a pit orchestra, the baton is critically important in providing visually effective cues to stage singers.

• Those conductors who use the baton will likely be more marketable, versatile, and even more effective in a variety of musical situations.

Batons come in many sizes and shapes and can range in length from about 10 inches to over 18 inches. A white baton of about 12 to 14 inches will suffice for most situations. They can range in cost from the inexpensive fiberglass stick with a cork handle often used in beginning conducting classes, to the more expensive, polished and varnished exotic woods with a variety of handle shapes. The best batons are lightweight and well balanced. The well-balanced baton will have a balance point no more than an inch beyond where the handle joins the stick. It is a good idea to have several batons of different sizes that feel comfortable and are appropriate whether conducting a small chamber group or the combined forces for a large oratorio.

The Grip

Those who have observed many professional conductors will have noticed that there is little or no unanimity regarding a specific baton grip. Elizabeth Green, in *The Modern Conductor,* points to some basic tenets of baton grip that have emerged through the years. She cites several internationally recognized conductors, such as Sir Thomas Beecham, Pierre Monteux, Eugene Ormandy, Herbert von Karajan, Bruno Walter, and George Szell, who subscribed to it. Many of Elizabeth Green's protégés in the wind-band conducting world also subscribe to those basic tenets. She admits the grip is not eternal and that it should be a point of departure. This author has used the following basics of baton grip in conducting classes for 25 years. They are from Green's basic tenets.

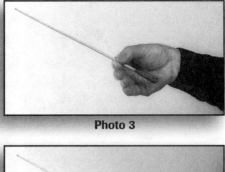

Photo 3

1. Hold the stick between tip of thumb and side of the index finger between the middle joint and the thumb nail. (See photo 3.)

2. Thumb should be bent outward and relaxed, contributing to a relaxed wrist. (See photo 4.)

Photo 4

3. The heel of the stick should rest at the base of the thumb in the hollow of the palm. (See photo 5.)

4. The palm of the hand should face downward. (The wrist joint works with more flexibility in this position.)

5. The tip of the baton should point forward (or slightly to the left).

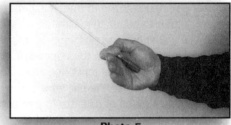

Photo 5

As the baton is anchored between the thumb tip and index finger with the heel of the stick resting at the base of the thumb in the palm of the hand, the fingers are lightly curled around the handle and the stick, with the ring finger making contact at the heel of the handle. Remember to bend the thumb to release pressure and assist wrist relaxation.

Photo 6 (incorrect)

The baton is an extension of the conductor and it should aid in communication with the ensemble. It can be effective only if it appears natural and comfortable and looks like an extension of the body. The occasional baton user who has never really mastered a skillful baton is in real danger of appearing awkward if the baton is used on the

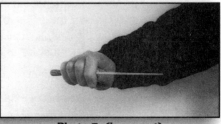

Photo 7 (incorrect)

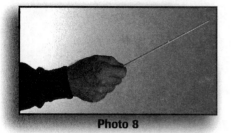

Photo 8

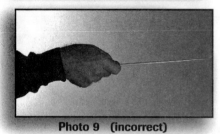

Photo 9   (incorrect)

spur of the moment for a one-time performance. Occasionally conductors will hold a baton so that the focal point is in the hand and the energy and clarity of precision is not extended to the tip of the baton. In these instances the baton actually becomes a distraction.

Following are some pitfalls to avoid regarding baton grip:

1. Do not allow the heel of the stick to float in the palm of the hand.

2. Index finger should not rest on top of baton. (See photo 6.)

3. Heel of baton should not slide to a position at the base of the little finger or protrude beyond the palm of the hand causing the baton to point to the left. (See photo 7.)

4. Do not unnaturally turn the wrist to the right in an effort to perfectly line up the baton with the arm. Instead, adjust the stick under the thumb. It is better to have the stick pointing slightly to the left than to cause this extreme wrist tension. (See photos 8 and 9.)

Just as hand positions are critically important issues to the violinist and clarinetist, so it is to the conductor. Although there are some basic tenets of grip, each individual must find what is natural and comfortable within these guidelines. At first, the use of a baton will feel awkward and unnatural, but with a few months of daily use it can become a skillful device for music making.

The Preparatory Beat and Downbeat

Once proper stance and a general ready position have been established, including good eye contact with the musicians, it is time to execute a preparatory beat, the most important technical skill of the conductor. This preparatory beat must signal some basic musical necessities to the musicians as follows:

1. tempo (speed)—must be in the exact tempo of the piece,

2. style (character, force, articulation),

3. dynamic level (volume, intensity),

4. the beat on which the work begins.

Ascertain that the musicians are indeed ready to begin before initiating the preparatory beat. A quick overview of the ensemble, making eye contact with various individuals, is advisable. It is at this moment that the conductor must be assertive as the leader of the group and assist the ensemble in feeling musically secure. Do not surprise the ensemble or "sneak up on them." Once the preparatory beat has begun it is impossible to retrieve. Many ambiguous and ragged ensemble beginnings can be attributed to an insecure and slipshod preparatory beat by the conductor.

Begin
Prep.

1   FIGURE A

The proper preparatory beat for a work commencing on beat one should move the hand from the ready position in a slightly downward curve and up to the beginning of beat one at the top of the beat pattern. **(See Figure A.)** Ensure that the preparatory beat does not move downward to the bottom of the conducting plane before swinging back up in preparation for beat one. Performers can interpret this downward swing as a downbeat and a disastrous entrance can occur, especially if there is any movement in the hand just prior to that downward move. **(See Figure B.)** There should not be even the slightest movement in the hands prior to initiating the preparatory beat. This extra movement is often called the "double prep" and can be extremely confusing.

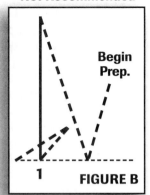

For music starting on a beat other than one, the preparatory beat will be the beat prior to the first play-ing beat. For example, in ⁴₄ meter if the piece starts on beat three, the preparatory would be the second beat of the measure but with a slight upward arc of beat two before moving right to beat three.

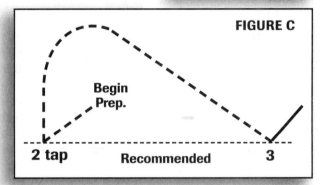

(See Figure C.) The preparatory beat and downbeat sequence ends at the bottom of the downbeat pattern (often called the conducting plane) when the sound begins as a result of the baton rebounding. This beat point or **ictus**, is totally controlled by the conductor and clearly defined gestures are crucial. A slight bounce or click of the wrist (as if bouncing a ball with the finger tips) is beneficial in producing an effective ictus or pulse point. The rebound should occur at, or near, a point where the forearm is parallel to the floor, and it should not rebound higher than halfway up the path of the downbeat. As the conducting pattern continues, this rebound serves as the connecting motion to the next beat.

Two other important aspects of the preparatory beat include inhaling in tempo during the execution, then exhaling on the downbeat, and embodying confidence, assurance, courage, and security to ensure the ensemble that you are in charge of this musical moment.

Common Problems of the Preparatory Beat

1. The "double prep"—extraneous movement in the arm or hand just prior to the primary preparatory beat.

2. Dropping the hand too low to the conducting plane causing the prepar-atory beat to appear as the primary beginning beat. This is especially a prob-lem if there is extra movement just before the preparatory beat.

3. Hesitating at the top of the preparatory beat before following through with the downbeat. There should be a continuous and smooth flow from the start of the preparatory beat to the ictus of the downbeat.

4. Slowing down or speeding up the tempo after the preparatory beat. Remember: the preparatory beat must be in the exact tempo of the music to follow.

5. Inhaling before the preparatory beat or having the ensemble do so, requiring conductor and ensemble to hold their breath during the preparatory motion. The conductor should open his or her mouth and inhale with the ensemble during the preparatory beat.

For preparatory beats that enter on a beat shorter than the pulse of the work, a fractional beat (that is, a pickup note such as an eighth note in $\frac{4}{4}$ meter), the basic duration of the preparatory beat does not change, regardless of the beat on which it may occur. In most cases, this pickup will represent a subdivision of one pulse and can be readily detected by the ensemble. There may be a rare occasion when the pickup note, if it is near a tempo change or part of a very difficult rhythmic figure, can be prepared with a double preparatory beat. A flick of the wrist for the first preparatory beat followed by the standard preparatory beat will often suffice. (The eighth note pickup at the beginning of the $\frac{6}{8}$ march, "The Jack Tar March" by Sousa, is one example.) Although a mature ensemble can sense the quick pickup note, there is a certain degree of security that the extra flick of the wrist gives to the ensemble.

The ***preparatory beat,*** whether it be the initial one to start the work or one that occurs at the end of a section or after a fermata, is probably ***the most important technique*** to be developed by the young, beginning conductor. The metric subdivisions must be heard in the conductor's mind before the actual preparatory beat is initiated. Remember: the preparatory beat may be a passive (nonresponsive) gesture to the ensemble, but it is an active gesture for the conductor, always showing clear intent.

Negotiating the Fermata

Along with the preparatory beat, the fermata tends to be an area where young conductors often experience the most confusion and uncertainty, most frequently with interpretation rather than physical gesture. The fermata is a musical symbol that denotes the indefinite elongation or extension of a note. How long should one hold a fermata? The composer could easily stipulate how long to sustain any note by simply tying it over for the desired number of beats, but the implication of the fermata is for the conductor to make that decision. Interpretation is influenced by the historical context of the work, the basic style, and the emotion and drama of the musical moment. The ambiguity is in regarding how the fermata should be ended and how one should proceed after it.

With regard to execution, it is generally understood that there are three basic methods of terminating a fermata:

1. A complete cutoff and stop—(a caesura [//]—or a rest following the fermata); a total cessation of both the sound and the pulse. This type will need another preparatory beat to start the next note.

2. A complete cutoff but continuing immediately—sometimes a breath mark might be present, but often there will be no additional markings except the fermata. The cutoff to this fermata will be the preparatory beat for the next entrance.

3. Continue with no break in sound. This fermata is connected to the next note by a slur and no cutoff is required; only the preparatory beat is needed to continue.

In reality, there are numerous situations in the great wealth of literature available today in which fermatas occur in ways that may not always fit the "book solution." If one can comfortably negotiate fermatas in one of the three ways mentioned above, then it will be a matter of studying the specific musical situation and applying the basic rules to arrive at the most satisfying interpretation which preserves the musical integrity of the work.

The biggest issue regarding the fermata is that too many conductors do not observe it. Remember that each fermata has its own attributes and character and how it is negotiated is determined by the specific musical context and performance situation.

Helpful Hints for Conducting a Fermata

1. Fermata means "stop" or to cease the rhythmic pulse. Do not beat time during a fermata. In fact, the conductor's rhythmic pulse should also cease.

2. Fermatas should not be held for a predetermined number of beats. They should always last longer than the written note; the length being determined by the emotion of the musical moment. (The only exception to this is with some music from the classical period in which the fermata is held twice its written value and in Bach chorales when the fermatas are basically treated as phrase endings.)

3. Keep the hand(s) moving slowly (usually in a horizontal direction) during the fermata to assist in sustaining the sound and to display energy.

4. Plan ahead for the direction of the cutoff to be properly prepared for the next beat.

5. Fermatas over rests do not lengthen the notes on either side of the rest unless other tempo marks are present.

6. Do not disregard fermatas! HOLD THEM! They abound in music and provide momentary pauses to add drama and excitement to the composition.

Cueing and Use of the Left Hand

When the beginning conductor has established a reasonable degree of independence with the right hand, it is time to begin training and activating the left hand. It will become evident as to how much of a habit the basic beat patterns have become once the left hand enters the picture. Practice activating the left hand from a position of naturally hanging at your side in simple gestures such as touching the top of your head or chin; raising it to chest level and making a fist; or try turning the pages of a book while executing the basic beat patterns (¼, ¾, ¼). ***Basic autonomy of the left hand should be one of the first goals in developing left hand conducting skills.*** Working in front of a mirror cannot be overemphasized at this point.

When used appropriately, the left hand signals the performers that something special is about to occur. Cueing is suggesting, reminding, intimating, encouraging, insinuating, or implying through gesture. It can be very subtle or quite direct depending on the particular musical moment. In many situations the left hand is adding emphasis to, not replacing, what your right is signaling. Following are some appropriate uses of the left hand for cueing:

- Signal an entrance, especially after a section has rested for a lengthy period
- Sudden (*subito*) changes of all kinds—tempo, dynamics, style, meter, etc.
- Releases
- Dynamics—crescendo and diminuendo
- Phrase shaping
- Entrances of a particularly tricky nature
- Solo entrances
- Isolated notes, chords, or a cymbal crash
- Balancing parts
- Serve as a warning "not" to play or to prevent an early entrance

Photo 10

Proper appearance of the left hand during the various gestures is of optimum importance. Its graceful and fluent shape is just as important to the conductor as similar hand gestures are to stage actors and dancers. In general, the fingers should retain the same graceful curve as they do when the arm is hanging in a relaxed position at your side. The fingers should not be spread out, and simply pointing with the index finger while the rest of the hand is in a fist (or in a pistol grip) is something that should be avoided, as a rule. Fingers extended and curved forming a "V" or "U" with the thumb is an acceptable position. In this case, the hand may be in a "palm in" position in a gesture of invitation or it may be in a "palm out" position indicating a lessening of volume. Another acceptable position is one in which the thumb touches the side of the index finger near the nail and the remaining fingers are gently curled in touching, or almost touching, the palm. (See Photo 1.) Everyone must find the optimum hand position that works well for them within the confines of what is appropriate and does not distract from the overall musical presentation.

The problem of activating the left hand is a challenge in the early stages of development. What does one do with the left hand when it is not being used? Obviously, the left hand is not needed all the time, and one must decide where to put it when it is not active. There are several acceptable options supported by many conducting teachers. The left hand may hang naturally at the side. Often, young students tense up the arm or even stretch it away from the side of the body. Other options include bringing the left hand to a relaxed position near the belt buckle, abdomen, or at the bottom of the sternum. Do not place the open palm on the abdomen (indicating an aching stomach), but rest the thumb near the tip of the index finger and curl the fingers in toward the palm in a relaxed position. From this position in front of the torso the left hand can be swiftly activated to give required cues. (See Photo 10.) Do not place the left hand in a pocket, under the belt, or hook the thumb in a belt loop. These are unsightly and inappropriate.

Remember: An effective cue must be prepared one beat before the event actually occurs and should convey, not only when, but how to attack and the volume level.

Developing effective and appropriate left-hand expressive gestures requires practice and dedication. In the early stages the young conductor should strive to develop this independence by practicing initiating cues on different beats of the measure in all the standard beat patterns. Conduct an imaginary orchestra or band and cue various sections in a variety of styles and tempos. Most conducting textbooks contain exercises that can be used for practicing cueing.

Mirror conducting—moving both hands in the same time-beating gesture simultaneously—is often a problem for amateur conductors. This is a duplication of effort and should be avoided. There might be occasion to mirror conduct when conducting an opera or a musical from an orchestra pit when lines of sight from the stage to the pit present a special problem or if the orchestra is extremely spread out from side to side with poor lighting conditions. These situations tend to be infrequent and conductors should resist the urge to mirror conduct, an unwanted mannerism in the profession.

It is generally agreed that there are three basic methods of giving cues:

1. With the baton hand as part of a time-beating gesture in the specific direction of the section or soloist,

2. With a special gesture by the left hand to the specific section or individual,

3. With the face or head—a nod or a facial gesture with the eyes or eyebrows is effective.

Melding and "The Disappearing Ictus"

Sometimes called phrasal conducting, melding is merging, linking, fusing or combining two or more beats into one smooth motion. This is an advanced technique that comes after one has solidly established the standard beat patterns and can move away from them and return without losing one's place (sometimes called shadow conducting). The simplest type of melding occurs when all members of an ensemble have a whole note. There is no need to conduct four beats in a measure such as this. Keep the hands moving in a smooth straight line or in an arcing motion throughout the measure indicating some type of dynamic nuance as you begin preparing for the kind of release required. Other simple types of melding opportunities include a quarter note followed by a dotted half (conduct an ictus on beat one and two and meld beats three and four) or a quarter followed by a half followed by a quarter (conduct an ictus on one and two, meld beats two and three and conduct an ictus on four). Phrasal conducting and melding are the first steps away from being a "time-beater" and striving to create musical shapes and images with conducting gestures. It is a skill that requires practice and an uninhibited desire on the part of the conductor to let the emotion of the musical phrase flow through the body and communicate to the musicians.

Asymmetrical and Changing Meters

The development of asymmetrical, irregular, or unbalanced meter conducting patterns at one time were considered an advanced technique in undergraduate conducting classes. With a plethora of contemporary music using asymmetrical rhythmic devices, even for younger ensembles, it is now a technique that must be addressed early in one's conducting study.

Irregular or unbalanced beat patterns are those that combine duple and triple beat groupings within the same measure causing the beat pattern to be unbalanced in the beat point placement right and left of the vertical conducting plane. The most popular asymmetrical meters are those using fives and sevens, although one will encounter meters of eight, nine, ten and eleven organized in various groupings of duple and triple combinations.

Slow tempos. When conducting a measure with five or seven primary beats at a moderate or slow tempo, it is necessary to decide how the pulses are subdivided and craft your beat pattern based on that information. In a five-beat measure the pulses will be grouped or subdivided in a 2 + 3 or a 3 + 2 configuration. In a 2 + 3 situation one can simply use a standard $\frac{4}{4}$ beat pattern with an added beat on the right side of the vertical plane. If pulses are divided 3 + 2, then a basic $\frac{6}{8}$ pattern might be used with the last beat deleted. (A $\frac{4}{4}$ pattern will also work in this situation by adding a beat to the left side of the vertical plane.) With a seven-beat measure, the $\frac{6}{8}$ beat pattern can again be used by crafting the beat points based on whether the measure is divided 3 + 4 or 4 + 3 and placing the extra beat on the appropriate side of the vertical plane. The five- and seven-beat patterns need to be practiced in all configurations, at a slow tempo, in order for them to be mastered.

Fast tempos. When complex meters occur at a bright tempo the beat pattern must be altered to accommodate the rapidly moving pulses, similar to what is done when a $\frac{6}{8}$ passage is conducted with two beats per measure. For example, in $\frac{5}{8}$ meter (or $\frac{5}{4}$) the basic $\frac{2}{4}$ beat pattern is used, and depending on how the measure is divided one must "stretch" (or float) the beat that receives the three eighth notes (or quarter notes). (This means the baton will move faster on the beat that receives two pulses than it will on the stretched beat that receives three. The distance in space covered will be the same.) Apply this same principle when conducting in $\frac{7}{8}$ (or $\frac{7}{4}$) meter but utilize the basic $\frac{3}{4}$ conducting pattern and stretch the appropriate beat. Basic beat patterns can be adapted to fit a variety of complex meters including unusual grouping of $\frac{8}{8}$, $\frac{9}{8}$, $\frac{10}{8}$, and $\frac{11}{8}$.

When dealing with changing meters one must first decide if the basic pulse unit (eighth, quarter, half, etc.) remains the same or if the basic unit changes. Most frequently in a work that alternates between various combinations of $\frac{2}{4}$, $\frac{3}{4}$, $\frac{4}{4}$, or $\frac{5}{4}$, the quarter note will remain constant and the only changes the conductor must make is a change in the beat pattern from measure to measure. These situations present no particular problem and are relatively easy to execute.

A common meter change that often presents problems for young conductors is the meter change from $\frac{4}{4}$ to $\frac{6}{8}$. Most frequently in these cases the eighth note will remain constant and the conductor must alter his primary pulse to keep the eighth note moving metronomically through the measures. (See Example 1.) The mistake most often made in a transition from $\frac{4}{4}$ to $\frac{6}{8}$ is that the conductor will keep the basic quarter note pulse moving through the $\frac{6}{8}$ measure and perform the two groupings of three eighth notes like they were two groups of triplets in a $\frac{2}{4}$ bar. The best way to practice conducting this situation is to set the metromone on an eighth-note pulse (about 180 bpm) and conduct through a series of alternating measures ($\frac{4}{4}$-$\frac{6}{8}$-$\frac{2}{4}$-$\frac{6}{8}$ etc.), ascertaining that the eighth-note pulse stays constant and the beat pattern matches the required meter. Mastery of this concept is mandatory for the modern conductor.

EXAMPLE 1

frequently used

Many composers will insert a helpful aid over the barline to assist performers in determining the intent.

EXAMPLE 2

often misleading and confusing

Careful attention and study is required to determine the composer's intent in Example 2. There seems to be no standard method of presenting the information. Some composers use the first note to refer to the upcoming measure and others use the first note to apply to the present measure. It is prudent to examine the musical passage and decide which system the composer chose to use or determine an appropriate interpretation if there is no helpful insert. There are numerous options for changing meters, more than can be examined in this chapter. There are many textbooks that present specific exercises for practicing this technique, some of which are listed at the end of this chapter.

Divided Beat Patterns

Divided beats (sometimes called subdivision) should be used only when the tempo is too slow to maintain an even or steady, consistent flow of the main pulses. Do not resort to conducting the rhythm of the notes, regardless of how slow the tempo gets; stick with the beats. These divided beats should be as precise and proportional as the primary beats and should be reserved to show some musical subtlety or a delicate change in the rhythmic flow of the music.

Divided beat patterns are most commonly crafted on the standard beat pattern. The divided strokes should be small and remain relatively close to the main beatpoint. One good option is to strike the primary beatpoint with a standard rebound, then retap the same beatpoint (lightly) with a shorter rebound to show an accurate division. This technique works well in all situations except with an ultra-legato or a tenuto musical line that has a broad, sweeping lyrical phrase. In this case, a more expansive divided beat pattern with beat points farther apart is advised. One other option is advisable in a staccato or extremely marcato musical phrase. This divided beat will be very controlled and mostly "in the wrist." No rebound is required and the pattern is very angular.

Remember:

• Use a divided beat only when it is absolutely necessary; there should be a specific musical reason.

• Do not get into the habit of showing every rhythmic event with a beat division; this can easily develop into a gesture that is constantly shaking.

• Too much subdivision is distracting both to the musicians and the audience.

• Never abruptly shift to a slower tempo simply by immediately using a divided beat. The conductor should begin the ritard with the primary beat pattern and as the tempo slows, the divided conducting gesture joins the already slowing subdivided pulses and takes control of the ritard. There should be a smooth transition between the primary beats and the divided beats or precision will be lost.

Score Study

Once the conductor has determined, after a brief overview of the score, that a work is indeed musically and technically appropriate for the ensemble, it is time to begin the initial act of serious score study. In some cases, depending on the complexity of the music and the maturity of the ensemble, it might require more than a "brief overview" of a score to ascertain its appropriateness for a particular ensemble. For more complex and challenging works, many conductors will purchase a score only for extended study before finalizing the decision concerning a probable performance. It is advisable for young and inexperienced conductors to request assistance from a mentor teacher or another experienced director in determining the appropriateness of a particular work based on the performance level of the band or orchestra.

The key to learning a score well is to live with it over a period of time on a daily basis. Erich Leinsdorf, former conductor at the Metropolitan Opera and the Boston Symphony Orchestra stated in his book, *The Composer's Advocate:* "The prerequisite to conducting any work well is an intimate knowledge of the score." [3] The goal is to achieve an aural concept of the work in one's inner ear. (Edwin Gordon, renowned psychologist and music researcher coined the word "audiation" for this concept.) An experienced conductor knows that when he or she enters a rehearsal, the standard guide for preparing a work is the ideal aural image one hears in the inner ear, a model that is compared with the sound that is actually being played by the live group. As the score is being studied, the conductor should actually practice conducting this aural interpretation and shape the expressive conducting gestures based on this imaginary mental (aural) image.

Musical Merit

Beyond the criteria of being musically and technically appropriate, one must ascertain the basic artistic merit of a work, that is, whether or not the work is of good musical quality. In today's musical market there is a plethora of poorly conceived music being used in some school systems under the guise of being "training music." Music worthy of reading or performing in rehearsal should be likewise worthy of being performed in a concert. All concert pieces do not have to be masterpieces, but consideration should be given to the aesthetic, artistic, and expressive qualities of the music.

- Is the composer or arranger known to have produced quality work?
- Does the music exhibit the expressive quality of tension and release?
- Is it a traditional work that has stood the test of time?
- What kind of craftsmanship does the composition exhibit?
- Will the music "wear thin" after a few hearings or is there opportunity to develop a deep appreciation for its musical subtlety?

These are but a few things the director should consider when judging the merit of a work. Obviously, one should not be limited to performing only works by well-known composers. One must remember that well-known composers had to get their start somewhere. The ultimate decision rests with the musical maturity and experience of the conductor.

Primary Score Overview

Following are things the conductor should consider in the early stages of score study:

- What is the instrumentation of the work? Are there voice parts or added instruments such as piano, harp, or organ? Is there a requirement for the less ordinary instruments such as $E\flat$ soprano clarinet, English horn, $B\flat$ contrabass clarinet, contrabassoon, soprano saxophone or any less common percussion instruments? The conductor must decide if these instruments are indeed necessary for a musically acceptable performance.

- Who is the composer and what do you know about his or her compositional style? Are program notes available? Research may be necessary to answer these questions.

- What is the basic harmonic structure of this work? Is it composed in a traditional, conventional style or is it more contemporary?

- Scan the work for primary melodic material. What is the appropriate or marked tempi for these melodies? Sing the melodies and decide basic phrasing and style. Are there countermelodies or contrapuntal lines?

- Are there repeated sections? Sketch out a big picture of the formal presentation for study. Is the work in movements or sections? What is the basic form? Dissect this big picture later for a more thorough analysis.

- Survey the work for key signature changes, unusual meter, and any special rhythmic metric relationships that may be present for special effect.

• Review all transpositions, clefs, and unfamiliar foreign or technical terms. (Have a music dictionary nearby.)

• Note how and where dynamics are used to present musical climaxes. Is there any special coloristic use of dynamics (*sforzando*, etc.)? Check especially the percussion parts for unusual dynamic effects.

• Depending on the keyboard skills of the conductor, it is advantageous to work through the composition at the piano even if one is only able to realize a couple of lines at a time. Listening to recordings can help one in gaining a rapid overall concept of the work. (This is addressed in more detail below.)

Obviously, this list is not all inclusive for a complete, in-depth analysis of a score. More exhaustive study will include a full harmonic analysis indicating cadence points; a thorough classification of the overall form (binary, ternary, fugue, theme and variation, rondo, sonata allegro, etc.); an investigation of the motivic development and evolution; a realization of the manner in which the work grows and progresses, including kinds of thematic development; a determination of phrase types and use of rubato; and an understanding of important instrument doublings or unusual instrument combinations for reasons of timbre or texture.

Additional Considerations for the Worship Service Leader

• The road map. What repeats are used? Will additional repeats be added? Woodwinds first verse; brass second verse; Tutti on final chorus, modulations, etc.

• How vocalists interact? Will the instrumentalists need to adjust their volume levels or should the number of persons playing be reduced to make certain that the text is understood?

• Will there be a need for cued or substitute parts to be used for missing instrumental lines that are crucial?

• Where, within a worship service, will this piece be performed? Do adjustments need to be made based on when it occurs in the service?

• Does this work show the strengths of the performing group? Are there ways to better minimize the weaknesses of the group?

There are reasons other than formal musical analysis for proper score study. One is to allow the conductor to locate and anticipate possible difficult conducting spots including fermatas, caesuras, subito changes in style and dynamics, abrupt tempo or meter changes, special cues, or fractional pickup notes. Some conductors have an elaborate color-coded method of marking the score with various colored pins and highlighters. If a score is to be marked that extensively, purchase two scores, one for study which can be covered in marks and comments and another to use in rehearsal and performance. Erich Leinsdorf says, "What can be found in scores previously used is often startling. Large penciled letters are used to make a ritard or an accellarando more easily discernible, cues are underlined, and huge numerals remind the reader that here we must beat four and there eight. And all of this is written in a variety of colors, more closely resembling a map for a myopic boy scout than a score for a fully prepared conductor."[4]

The point here is that a properly and well-prepared conductor will not need all these markings to ensure that he or she does not get lost or that a tempo or meter change is not forgotten during a rehearsal or a performance. Be prudent and sensible in keeping the markings on the performance score to only those that are genuinely valuable, ensuring that one is not depending on all the marks as a "crutch."

There are conductors and teachers who do not endorse the idea of listening to recordings as part of the score study process because it might overly influence one's interpretation of a work. Listening to quality recordings conducted by skilled and competent musicians can serve as great models, especially to the novice conductor. Learn more about style, nuance, and interpretation by listening to recordings and attending live performances. On the other hand, do not replace thorough score study by listening to a recording. Listening to an inspired performance can often serve to get the "creative juices" flowing and, in addition to saving time, it can aid the conductor in obtaining a good aural image of the composition.

In addition to obtaining an overall musical concept of the work and searching out areas that might present conducting problems, there is one other good reason for a complete score analysis—that is to locate areas that will present problems for the ensemble. These are things that will need to be addressed in rehearsal and, depending on the maturity and experience of the ensemble, it could include such things as key signatures, articulation, rhythmic challenges, fingerings, bowings, dynamics, stylistic elements, intonation, blend and balance matters, unusual meters, and probable places that will present specific technical challenges. Experienced school directors can spot these places quickly and have an alternate fingering recommendation, or some piece of advice ready ahead of time to share with the students to help alleviate the problem. This should be the goal of every aspiring young public or Christian school director.

Memorizing the Score

There are many varying opinions regarding the necessity of score memorization. No universal law or prescription exists governing the approach to this process and there are about as many views on the subject as there are conducting teachers. Score memorization is an easier process for some conductors than others. There are famous conductors, past and present, who conduct from memory (some who actually rehearse without a score) and report that they can see the score in their mind's eye as they conduct and know what note is being played by any specific instrument. This writer has witnessed retired Air Force band conductor, Colonel Arnold Gabriel, rehearse and conduct on a number of occasions without a score and it was obvious he had fully ingested the score. Toscanini, when asked how he memorized the score, expressed that he really did not know. There are also some conductors who, reportedly, have a photographic memory.

Score memorization also allows the instrumental conductor greater freedom to facilitate worship.

When is a score considered memorized? Elizabeth Green says, "a score is memorized when one can think it through accurately in tempo (cues included) without stumbling and without recourse to the printed page or to audible sound."[5]

When one has studied a particular score over a period of years; rehearsed and conducted it numerous times, then this process can occur naturally.

It is a source of concern to this writer, when adjudicating junior and senior high band and orchestra contests, to observe a conductor totally enamored with the score during the contest performance. In many cases the group has rehearsed the work on a daily basis for two or three months. (Many of the these conductors are not beginning teachers and some have actually conducted this same work at contests three or four years previously.) By the time a performance such as this has arrived, the score should be simply a blueprint (a reminder) of the conductor's musical intentions and a mere glance here and there should suffice. More attention should be directed to communicating and encouraging the actual essence of the music to the ensemble through expressive gestures and active eye contact. The conductor must be an effective communicator of musical ideas, and when the face and eyes focus on the score, the communication with the musicians basically stops.

Just because a score is memorized does not necessarily mean the conductor will conduct without one. In a recent workshop, Leonard Slatkin, conductor of the National Symphony Orchestra in Washington, D.C., remarked that even if he had memorized a score, whether or not he used a score in performance related directly to how physically and mentally rested he was prior to the performance, which can vary greatly, especially if a group is on tour. He saw no need in putting the entire orchestral performance in jeopardy just to demonstrate he could conduct without a score. Many fine conductors often conduct with the score, especially those whose repertoire includes more than the tried and true literature of the past.

With the discussion above on score study and these comments on memorization, it is fairly evident how one should approach score memorization. For further information on the subject, refer to the Elizabeth Green conducting text, *The Modern Conductor,* Chapter 16, page 242, for a detailed approach to this process.

In conclusion, be reminded that to fully ingest and absorb a musical score it is imperative to spread the study over an extended period of time. That amount of time directly relates to the experience of the conductor and the complexity of the musical composition. There are no short cuts, and trying to cram a fairly complex score with an overnight study session can produce disastrous results.

Instrumental versus Choral Conducting

Instrumental conductors will likely have numerous opportunities to conduct vocalists and choral groups in a variety of situations ranging from church choirs and combined instrumental and choral groups in schools and churches (oratorios, cantatas, requiems) to stage productions involving soloists and vocal groups in a community theatre situation. Fine instrumental conductors should be prepared to work with vocalists and choral groups in all situations.

Some have said, "Conducting is conducting regardless of the medium." While this is partially true, there are certain factors in dealing with vocalists and choral groups that differ from working with a purely instrumental group. Some of the factors that are specifically unique to the choral tradition should be examined.

Factors Unique to Choralists
- Text
- Diction
- Vocalists each have a score in hand
- Score appearance—normally 4 to 6 parts (rarely more than 8-10)
- Visual line of communication (setup)

By its very nature, choral music exists on a continuum of words or text. Much of the early choral tradition was sung a cappella, and because of this, choral conductors have traditionally been drawn into a conducting style that emphasizes the words and a "rhythm of the words" conducting style. More emphasis has been placed on contouring the phrase, guiding the entrance and exits of voice parts, and painting textual and musical images through gestures that do not emphasize beat patterns or icti. Textual pronunciation helps synchronize vocal ensemble precision. Diction is possibly the most distinctive feature of choral music, and without proper enunciation of vowels or precise articulation of consonants the total verbal meaning of the music will be incomprehensible to the listeners. The fact that choralists have a score in their hand means they always know what all other parts are doing; therefore, they have the big picture starting from the first rehearsal. More often than not, choralists will memorize their music and can direct total attention to the conductor in a performance. Vocal scores usually have four to six parts. Although it is rare, there are examples of vocal scores having up to 20 or more lines (parts). The visual line of communication between the choral conductor and the singer tends to be more direct, simply because of the basic setup and the lack of a music stand or a musical instrument to serve as a distraction.

Instrumental Conductors Working with Choral Groups
Remembering the ideal conductor should be comfortable working with any ensemble, the instrumental conductor planning to rehearse a choral group must be able to confront two basic issues:
- attacks and releases, and
- diction (vowels and consonants).

Frederik Prausnitz states in his book, *Score and Podium:* "Attacks and releases must be given to a chorus far more consistently than is necessary with an orchestra. There is a world of difference between the needs of singers in sustaining a long tone and the self-sufficient way in which a well-schooled brass section will manage its long chords. Choruses are far more dependent, but also more immediately responsive to direct manipulation from the podium, than their orchestra counterparts."[6]

It behooves all prospective instrumental conductors to gain experience singing in a choir and to study private voice to acquire a basic understanding of vocal diction. Being familiar with the various types of male and female voice classifications, plus having a basic knowledge of the physical aspect of singing to include typical characteristic warmup exercises for vocal groups, are all part of the total picture for the instrumentalist to be competent in working with a choral ensemble. Diction, the most distinctive feature of vocal music, is indeed the primary subject to be dealt with as a choral conductor. The vowels are the vehicle for the tone (sound), and the consonants are to assist in the meaning or intelligibility of the text. It is important that the sustaining tone of the note be on the vowel sound and the consonant be carefully placed to ascertain clarity. Another aspect to consider is that choirs must sing in more than one language. Familiarization with the International Phonetic Alphabet can be extremely helpful. There are numerous books available dealing with diction, but the best place to learn is in a vocal ensemble under the tutelage of a fine choral conductor. Several of the suggested conducting textbooks listed at the end of this chapter (Green, Demaree, and Prausnitz) also deal with the subject.

Factors Unique to Instrumentalists

- The instrument is external.
- Lack of text or "rhythm of the words"
- Each instrumentalist sees only his part
- Score—full score of 20 to 30 lines (parts)
- Setup inhibits optimum line of communication with conductor
- Many instruments are transposing

The fact that the mode of communication of the instrumentalist is apart from his body presents a different challenge in musical expression. Also, instrumentalists do not have the advantage of seeing a score as they play. Only through rehearsing can they learn what is written in the other parts. The typical band score will have at least 25 separate parts, many requiring a transposition to know the sounding pitch. Instrumentalists in ensembles do not typically memorize their music. The presence of a music stand and an external instrument in their hand serves as a distraction inhibiting a continuous line of communication with the conductor.

Choral Conductors Rehearsing Instrumentalists Must Confront the Following Issues:

- necessity of a clear ictus and a steady takt
- a large score with numerous instruments requiring an understanding of the transposition of basic band and orchestral instruments
- basic understanding of the nature of wind instrument sound production and articulation permitting the conductor to communicate stylistic elements to the ensemble
- using rehearsal letters or measure numbers rather than page numbers (a habit some choral conductors form when working with choirs)
- the use of passive conducting gestures during narration or recitatives so the instrumentalists can count measures of rest and keep up (When working with the piano and a choir everyone has a score, an advantage not afforded the instrumentalist)

• use of a full score during rehearsal and performance so proper attention and cueing can be given to the orchestra. Too often the choral conductor will conduct a combined instrumental-choral performance using only the octavo.

In a sense, "Conducting is conducting," and there are a myriad of factors common to both instrumental and choral groups. The fundamental musical skills required of each conductor are the same: a good ear; an understanding of musical style, tempo, balance, blend, tone, dynamics, intonation, and phrasing; and the ability to plan, organize, and accomplish an effective rehearsal.

Choral and instrumental performers have different traditions, training, personalities, and expectations. It is in the interest of the conductor who wants the widest possible range of conducting experiences to educate himself in the basics of both traditions, even though most conductors tend to have a specialty in one area or the other.

Podium Etiquette and Proper Attire

> **Timothy Stalter**
> **Director of Choral Activities,**
> **University of Iowa**
>
> "Since choral conductors generally have limited time to rehearse an instrumental ensemble for a combined choral/instrumental work, it is of utmost importance that the conductor first know what he or she wants to hear regarding tone, articulation, dynamics, phrasing, etc., **before** stepping onto the podium. Second, the conductor needs to be able to show this internal sound image through clear conducting gestures which balance both the objective and the subjective. If the gestures are not producing the desired result, a conductor should sing it; the instrumentalists will make the technical adjustments necessary to achieve the conductor's image of the piece."

The manner in which a conductor enters the stage in preparation for a concert should be one of confidence, poise, and aplomb. Stand tall and enter the stage at a fairly brisk pace and walk with authority and certainty. Stage entrances and exits should not be as if strolling through a park or walking by the seashore. Always make eye contact with the audience and recognize applause with a friendly nod of the head or a reserved bow. Many groups, especially professional ensembles, stand as the conductor enters the stage, thus sharing, along with the conductor, acceptance of the applause. Mount the podium, complete a brief overview of the ensemble establishing eye contact, then prepare for the downbeat only after the audience has settled into a quiet mode.

Soloists should precede the conductor when making a stage entrance, even if the conductor is a female. Frequently during stage exits a male soloist will step aside just before the stage exit and allow the female conductor to precede him. The same general decorum will apply when there are several soloists exiting the stage.

The conductor can assist the audience in knowing when to applaud through body language and by keeping the hands up between movements. At the end of an especially reflective, tranquil, or serene work, the conductor can control the length of silence before allowing an audience reaction by hiding the release with one hand in the front of the body then slowly lowering the hands to the side, dropping them and relaxing the body as a signal that it is time to applaud. There are also times at the end of a work with a particularily big, loud ending that instantaneous applause is appropriate and the conductor can do a large visible cutoff.

Know ahead of time what ensemble soloists are going to be recognized and practice having the band stand on cue. (A list of soloists on the last page of your score is a good practice.) If a guest composer or arranger is in the audience, have the houselights raised and acknowledge his or her presence. There may be occasion to ask the guest to come to the stage for acknowledgement. After the conductor departs the stage, the ensemble should be seated when the concertmaster (the first clarinet or another designated person in a wind group) sits. If applause continues, return almost immediately and have the ensemble stand to be recognized.

In this day when casual dress is becoming the norm for most public gatherings, it is important for the conductor to be sensitive to what is appropriate for a formal evening concert. Proper concert attire for the male conductor should consist of well-tailored clothes and shined dress shoes. A tuxedo with a black tie and cummerbund, or one with tails, a bib and a white tie are always acceptable for an evening concert. If the ensemble members are wearing suits, ties, and nice dresses, then it is also appropriate for the conductor to wear a dark suit with white shirt and tie. Female conductors must be discreet in selecting proper attire for the podium. Black dresses of midcalf length in a conservative style are most appropriate. Female conductors are best served when not conducting in short skirts (above the knees), backless dresses, formal (prom-style) dresses with frills and lace or tightly fitted apparel. Black or other darkcolored suits are also appropriate. Pops concerts or less formal performances allow for more casual attire but always remain sensitive, diplomatic, and tactful in selecting apparel for the podium, remembering the necessity of not becoming a distraction because of the conductor's high visibility to the audience.

Rehearsal Matters

H. Robert Reynolds, recently retired director of bands at the University of Michigan, says, "For most band conductors, rehearsing means talking; but if you want to increase your rehearsal time, just conduct better and insist that they follow. When you guide their ears, rather than letting them use yours, the band will get better so fast you won't believe it!"[7]

Rehearsing is the process of diagnosis and ascribing. The sound is filtered through the conductor's aural images he or she hears and ascribes (attributes or assigns) it to a particular area or section; then prescribes (give a direction) some advice to correct the problem. Obviously, this definition can apply to all ensemble members, not just the conductor. Everyone should be listening intently and making individual adjustments to correct problems that stand in the way of creating beautiful music. With younger students the responsibility falls more with the conductor, but this whole process of listening must be taught and encouraged from the earliest days of instrumental study. Ideally, much of your correction can be accomplished through conducting gestures.

The scope and length of this chapter does not allow for an in-depth presentation on rehearsal techniques and procedures, but the following helpful hints and suggestions will promote an efficient and productive rehearsal:

• Approach every rehearsal with the proper preparation, a plan, and genuine enthusiasm for the literature to be rehearsed.

• Possess an aural image of the music to be rehearsed and constantly compare that image with what is being heard in the rehearsal; too often critiques are given without proper thought and preparation.

• Insist that the ensemble members know their parts (own the music) so ensemble matters (the big picture; real music making) can be addressed.

• If technical matters are preventing artistic expression on a particular work, then it is likely that the work is too difficult for the group. Making a real musical statement is more important than impressing the neighboring band directors or other music leaders by programming music too advanced for the ensemble.

• Encourage ensemble members to treat every rehearsal as if it were a concert. Warren Benson, composer and long-time faculty member at the Eastman School of Music, said, "There are no rehearsals; only concerts." Progress is faster when students possess this mental attitude.

• Strive to use allotted rehearsal time with great efficiency. There is no need to start at the beginning of a piece every day. Focus on the areas where the problems exist. Constantly monitor the pace of rehearsals.

• Do not conduct a work the same way every time. The director is not polishing a machine, but striving to provide some musical spontaneity that will make the music come alive in a truly artistic manner. Is the ensemble communicating on an artistic level? Is the conductor eliciting an emotional response in the listener as well as the ensemble performers?

• Play more and talk less; this will require improved conducting skills. It will also evoke a positive reaction with the players; they enjoy making music. If the conductor must stop the rehearsal, he or she must make comments succinct and relevant. This is not the time to give a private lesson.

• Offer critique with a loving attitude and do not talk condescendingly to the players. Be firm, direct, and honest, but do not attack personalities.

• Do not be reticent or overly reserved in demonstrating a true love of music. This passion and affection for great God-given art can be contagious.

Masterful and proficient rehearsal techniques are not acquired overnight or even in a year or two. They develop not only as a result of study and self-evaluation, but through frequent observation of seasoned, veteran conductors in the profession. Take advantage of every opportunity to watch guest clinicians of orchestras, bands, and choirs at state and national conventions as they rehearse the various all-state groups. Take notes; try new approaches; videotape rehearsals; invite respected colleagues in to observe a rehearsal, and make every attempt to refine and polish podium skills and rehearsal techniques. It will pay lifelong dividends.

Conclusion

Conducting is, indeed, a silent art, and the more skillful the physical gestures, the greater the probability of developing a masterly vocabulary of nonverbal communication. Conducting is a reflection of overall musicianship, and conducting techniques must be both accurate and effective, as well as musically appropriate. Zubin Mehta, former conductor of the New York Philharmonic, was asked if there was one word that he thought really defined the conductor. Mehta thought for a few seconds and said, "Yes. The conductor is a catalyst." A catalyst precipitates an event or rouses the mind and spirit to action. The conductor must strive to provide the impetus or stimulus to incite significant change in the stylistic interpretation of the music. It is truly a worthy goal and one to which all conductors should aspire.

Suggested Books on Conducting

- *The Art of Conducting,* by Donald Hunsberger and Roy Ernst (New York: Alfred A. Knopf, 1983)
- *Basic Conducting Techniques,* 4th ed., by Joseph A. Labuta (Upper Saddle River, NJ: Prentice-Hall, 2000)
- *The Complete Conductor: A Complete Resource for the Professional Conductor of the Twentieth-Century,* by Robert W. Demaree, Jr. and Don V. Moses (Englewood Cliffs, NJ: Prentice-Hall, 1995)
- *Conducting: A Hands-On Approach,* by Anthony Maiello (Miami, FL: Warner Brothers Publications [Belwin-Mills],1996)
- *Learning to Conduct and Rehearse,* by Daniel L. Kohut and Joe W. Grant (Englewood Cliffs, NJ: Prentice-Hall, 1990)
- *The Modern Conductor,* 6th ed., by Elizabeth A. H. Green (Upper Saddle River, NJ: Prentice-Hall, 1997)
- *Score and Podium: A Complete Guide to Conducting,* by Frederik Prausnitz (New York: W. W. Norton, 1983)

Recommended Reading for Conductors

- *The Composer's Advocate,* by Erich Leinsdorf (New Haven, CT: Yale University Press, 1981)
- *Face to Face with an Orchestra,* by Don V. Moses and Robert W. Demaree, Jr., and Allen F. Ohmes (Princeton, NJ: Prestige, 1987)
- *A Guide to the Understanding and Correction of Intonation Problems,* by Alfred Fabrizio (Fairport, NY: Silver Fox Publishing Co., 1993)
- *The Maestro Myth,* by Norman Lebrecht (New York: Birch Lane Press, 1991)
- *Of Music and Music-Making,* by Bruno Walter, translated by Paul Hamburger (New York: W. W. Norton, 1961)

[1]Willi Apel, *Harvard Dictionary of Music* (Cambridge, MA: The Belknap Press of Harvard University Press, 1977), 197.

[2]Jack Westrup, "Conducting," *The New Grove Dictionary of Music and Musicians* (Washington, D.C.: MacMillan Publishers Limited, 1980), 641-643.

[3]Erich Leinsdorf, *The Composer's Advocate: A Radical Orthodoxy for Musicians* (New Haven, CT and London: Yale University Press, 1981), 4.

[4]Ibid., 3.

[5]Elizabeth A. H. Green, *The Modern Conductor,* 6th Edition (New Jersey: Prentice Hall, 1997), 243.

[6]Frederik Prausnitz, *Score and Podium: A Complete Guide to Conducting* (New York: W. W. Norton, 1983), 499.

[7]John E. Williamson (Kenneth Neidig, editor), *Rehearsing the Band* (Cloudcroft, NM: Neidig Services, 1998), 69-70.

Jim Hansford (B.M.Ed., University of Southern Mississippi; M.M.Ed. and Ph.D., University of North Texas) has been Professor of Music, Director of Bands, and Coordinator of Instrumental Studies at Oklahoma Baptist University in Shawnee since 1990. Hansford, a respected educator-conductor for over 30 years, stays active as a guest conductor, clinician, and adjudicator in public schools and churches. At UNT Hansford studied conducting with Maurice McAdow and Anshel Brusilow. His teaching experience includes seven years in the public schools of Texas and 27 years at the university level, including faculty positions at Southeastern Oklahoma State University and Wayland Baptist University. In addition to conducting numerous high school regional honor bands in Texas and Oklahoma, he has conducted the Kentucky Baptist All-State Orchestra, the Texas Baptist All-State Band on three occasions, and has served as conductor of the Oklahoma Baptist All-State Symphonic Band since 1992, including tours to England and British Columbia. At OBU, Hansford teaches advanced conducting, instrumental music education and applied low brass, in addition to serving as conductor of the Symphonic Band and the OBU-Shawnee Community Orchestra. Jim Hansford has served numerous churches as an interim and supply music minister and is a member of First Baptist Church, Shawnee, where he serves as a deacon, choir member, and instrumental coordinator.

CHAPTER 3

Arranging for Instruments

by Camp Kirkland and Jeff Cranfill

Arranging for instruments, particularly for church instrumental groups, is a daunting task because of the unique nonstandardized instrumentation of these groups. Generally, church ensembles are made up of woodwinds, brass, and a rhythm section, and sometimes strings. Such groups are generally capable of playing a variety of styles of music—from the symphonic to the contemporary.

Existing traditional and contemporary music provides a great wealth of musical material in a variety of styles that praises, honors, and glorifies God. The arranger's task, in this discussion, is most often to take one of these existing hymns or songs and create a musical setting where the message can be successfully communicated by a group of instruments. The following ideas and techniques have proven effective for many arrangers. These principles are also appropriate for writing instrumental accompaniments to vocal/choral arrangements.

Preparation

Arranging is the practice of putting preexisting musical material in a different setting. If God gave the gift of music, then He is the source for wisdom and ideas in arranging. Those who desire to arrange can and should ask God to give a fertile musical mind. It follows that if He is the inspiration, then God gets the glory!

"If any of you lacks wisdom, he should ask God, who gives generously to all without finding fault, and it will be given to him" (Jas. 1:5, NIV).

Twelve chromatic tones exist in western music for melody and harmony, and provide building blocks for most musical ideas. Frankly, new groupings of these sounds are difficult to create. Therefore, is it futile to compose new arrangements of the great hymns and songs available? No. Every arranger is going to add a personal touch to his or her work that becomes discernible to the listener over time. However, it has been said that the definition of "originality" is one's ability to conceal one's sources.

Listen to a wide range of musical styles regularly—in a variety of styles and performance media. Music resourcing builds a "vocabulary" of musical ideas. Arrangers must consistently be listening and studying scores whenever possible—analyzing them to discern how other writers and arrangers achieve sounds and "feels." To a degree, there is nothing new under the sun.

"What has been will be again, what has been done will be done again; there is nothing new under the sun" (Eccl. 1:9, NIV).

Writers' arrangements are a product of the musical material that has been ingested over their lifetimes. Abundant listening helps arrangers to keep fresh ideas coming.

Have the Necessary Tools

- a computer/midi set up with good notation software, or
- good staff paper, soft-lead pencils with eraser
- a piano or keyboard—Some people write at the piano, others will occasionally check chords or melodic lines. Either way, access to a keyboard can be important.
- a metronome for accurate tempo selection
- a stopwatch to time the piece—The performance time of an arrangement is important, especially for music to be used in a worship service.

Ronn Huff, a prolific arranger, stated that arranging is 90 percent craft and 10 percent inspiration. Rather than waiting for great ideas, writers are better served by learning melodic, harmonic, and orchestration tech-
niques from which to draw in
creating and developing musical
themes. Good music involves good
writing skills which can be developed with experience and time.
Also, if no deadline exists, create
one. There is nothing like a deadline to spur on creativity.

Getting Started

Instrumental music is most effective and appropriate in worship when it brings to mind the text of the song, or provides an emotional connection for the listener to meditate on a Scripture passage. Melody, or in the case of a vocal arrangement, lyrics and melody must predominate. Assure that the message or the musical setting enhances the lyrics of the song. Where there is a vocal text to the piece, study the words and develop musical material that supports, illustrates, or magnifies the meaning.

Select the title(s) and instrumentation for the arrangement. Obtain permission from the copyright holder when the song is not in public domain. Set up the score (instrument names, clefs, and order) before beginning to write. If notation software is available, the arranger should save the score layout as a template for future arrangements.

Map out a tentative verse and key structure—keep in mind the length of the piece and where it will be used. Good brass keys are (in order of usefulness) B♭, F, E♭, A♭, C. That is because most wind instruments, which comprise the bulk of the church ensemble, are more comfortable there. G major and D major can be used for orchestral works because they are excellent keys for string players. Young string players can play sharp keys more easily than flat keys. Keys outside this range often pose problems for amateur players and are best avoided when possible. Score the piece at concert pitch, and then transpose the parts for each instrument.

Form

A setting appropriate for a worship service probably should be between two to three and one-half minutes. Obviously a concert piece can be as long as the program, players, and listeners will allow. A church orchestra piece form might look like the following:
- Introduction—sets the mood for the piece
- Verse 1
- Chorus 1
- Transition—change key or mode, tempo, meter, instrumentation, feel, dynamic
- Verse 2
- Transition
- Chorus 2
- Ending

Begin sketching in the melody, counter lines, or accompaniment figures where they achieve the desired sound and feel. Treat the arrangement like a multiple-choice test. Start at the place in the piece where ideas come first. Again, keep the message of the words in mind. When a transition is reached—at the end of a verse or chorus—use melodic fragments or original material (perhaps from the introduction) to lead the piece in a new direction (key, tempo, feel, etc.). The process called motivic development involves using musical material—melodic, harmonic, or rhythmic—throughout a piece. This adds a sense of continuity, order, and flow.

As the melody and accompaniment take shape, countermelodies can be added from time to time to add texture and variety. A countermelody is a line that contrasts with the main melody, usually in a different register featuring a different instrument. Strive for quality rather than quantity—frequently less is more.

Then fill out the orchestration as needed. It is often helpful to fill in the score by families of instruments.

The ending is obviously the last part the listener will hear. The ending should conclude and underscore the message and the musical material. Consider employing material used earlier in the arrangement (motivic development).

Endings can be created:
- in a higher or lower register,
- fast or slow,
- loud or soft,
- major or minor,
- in the existing key or a different key,
- rhythmic (punctuated) or sustained.

Orchestrating an Existing
Piano Accompaniment for Solos or Anthems

When a song is copyrighted, make sure to get permission from the copyright holder before orchestrating it. Lay out the score first, numbering the measures, and putting in all key changes as in the original. Scan the piano/vocal part. Fill out introductions, interludes, modulations, endings, or full-sounding passages. Look for places to double vocal lines, but not compete with the melody.

Add countermelodies where they seem to fit. They may not be in the original, but if they fit the chords and texture, they should work. Also look for places to accompany the vocal parts, using string pad, low brass pad, woodwind pad, etc. Arpeggiated piano parts can be written as sustained chords in the same register. Make sure the instrumental material enhances and supports but does not cover up the vocal parts.

Orchestration

Consider beginning with a brass quartet or quintet, including trumpets, trombones, and possibly French horns or tuba. This is the core of the church orchestra. Write for instruments in family groups: e.g., brass family, string family, and so forth. Consider how the instruments of each family will relate to each other. Also consider how instruments of similar registers (SATB) relate to each other.

An interesting arrangement will usually include a variety of textures. Some different textures include:
- Melody alone, or in octaves,
- Solo/soli with accompaniment and/or countermelody,
- Harmonized melody (more homophonic),
- Tutti (everyone playing),
- Contrapuntal—melody against another melodic line
- Accompaniment alone—to set up melody (introductions and transitions).

Along with changes in texture, it is important to allow wind players places to breathe, and allow some additional places for brass players to rest.

Tessitura refers to the register in which an instrument plays—the higher an instrument plays, the more intense and passionate the sound will be. It will sound brighter and usually louder. The lower an instrument plays, the less intense and warmer the sound will be. The color is darker and usually sounds softer. The dynamic range also affects the intensity of sound: loud equals more intense; soft equals a more gentle sound.

Woodwinds

Woodwinds can be utilized in a multitude of ways. Each woodwind instrument can carry a melody with a warm, distinctive timbre. Woodwinds can also be doubled in unison or octaves. Flutes can double violins in unison or one octave higher. The flute is excellent at performing countermelodies or obbligati. Flutes can double the French horn an octave or two higher for a nice timbre.
- An oboe can carry melody, solo lines, doubling with other woodwinds, or strings. Be careful writing oboe parts of extreme ranges.
- Clarinets have different attributes in different registers. One should avoid

throat register solos. Clarinets work well doubling flutes (in octaves), oboe unison, horns, and violins in the lower register.

• Piccolo—as a solo instrument, it sounds pure, almost whistle-like. On top of the woodwind section, the piccolo adds great strength.

• The woodwind section in octaves can be quite strong, also on trills and scalar runs.

• Two-part flutes, doubled one octave lower by two-part clarinets, with the oboe on a more independent line, produces a sweet sound.

• Trio stacking—flute 1, flute 2, clarinet 1 (oboe), clarinet 2 doubles flute 1 one octave lower—is a beautiful, classy, sometimes emotional sound created to harmonize melody or accompaniment.

• Bassoon—works well doubling cello or trombones. Bassoons are effective on countermelodies (softer) and bass lines.

• Bass Clarinet—the lowest woodwind voice, has a mellow sound. It can double the cello, bassoon, trombone, or bass (watch range).

Brass

Brass instruments provide power, emotional intensity, and a change in texture in the midst of an arrangement. Here are some specific ways that brass instruments may be used in arrangements:

• Trumpets are effective playing melody and fanfares. They provide power and finesse. As a section, trumpets sound good on unison lines, in octaves, harmonized melody, even accompaniment (be careful of range, dynamic). Trumpets are used appropriately to double other melodic instruments.

• Trumpets and trombones sound well together in octaves, on unison lines, or in chordal harmony (thick, strong sound). Fanfares are an important staple for brass arrangements. (See example at top of next page.)

• Trombones sound best with open scoring, as chord pads, as accompaniment instruments, playing unison melodies or countermelodies, and playing in octaves with bass trombone/tuba for great strength.

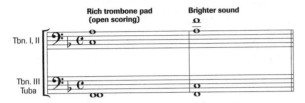

• Tubas can delineate bass lines, possibly an occasional melody. Often tubas play more sustained passages than the string bass or the piano left hand.

• French horns, the noble, versatile hybrid between woodwind and brass, have great range. The horn is a blend of brass and woodwind section. Horns are very effective doubling violins and clarinets in unison. In the lower register, horn lines can be rich and noble. Horns can double with any section. They can provide unison countermelodies. Horns can double with trumpets one octave lower to add strength and depth.

• Doubling with trombones, the horn adds strength. On top of low brass chords, the horn section is rich.

• More advanced horn players sound great on soaring lines, often in the upper register (alone, or with strings and or woodwinds). Horn rips add excitement and emotion.

Percussion

The percussion section is the most varied in the kind of timbre and dynamic range it can provide. Each percussion instrument requires expertise and sensitivity on the part of the arranger to create an effective arrangement.

• Timpani are most exciting playing on endings, pedal points, and outlining the bass line. Timpani rolls with crescendo add intensity and excitement.

• Bells can double melody on occasion or high countermelodies. Keep rhythms uncluttered. They add strength, beauty, or clarity, depending on range, doubling, and dynamic level.

• Chimes can be very festive-sounding. They add nobility to a melody (horn, clarinet, violin). Punctuation by the chimes on the chord root at times is effective, and it is sometimes ominous when used alone.

• Snare drums can be compelling for punctuating rhythmic figures and creating military and triumphant lines. Playing long rolls can add suspense.

• Drum sets can keep time and help to establish the musical style.

• Suspended cymbals can be utilized for rolls with yarn mallets, to add emotion on crescendos, to punctuate endings, and to help and sustain musical texture and intensity.

• Crash cymbals must be used sparingly, and are great for suggesting majesty and strength in a musical score.

• Tambourines can play well on or off the beat in gospel, rock, and other contemporary styles. They can also sound exciting when punctuating orchestra rhythms.

• Wind chimes add a mysterious, ethereal quality, and sometimes add gentleness.

A myriad of percussion instruments are not listed here, all of which have special uses. Congas, bongos, timbales, guiros, cabasas, castanets, and other instruments can provide unique energy and intensity to a musical score. Many of these instruments have Latin roots, and are now used in symphonic and popular music, and can be quite effective in church music.

Strings

The string section has a multitude of uses in church orchestral arrangements. Strings work well in octaves, and on chord pads in softer passages. Excellent string literature, bowing techniques and fine chamber music should be studied by the arranger to develop a clear understanding of the string player's capabilities.

• Violins can double a melody (unison or octaves), or sometimes play countermelodies with woodwinds or horns. Advanced players can inspire the listener with soaring lines in the upper register.

- Violas can double violin 2 or cello, or horn, or can play with violins in octaves.
- Celli can double basses (unison or in octaves), play melodies with violins (unison or octaves), double melodies with French horns, and play countermelodies.
- Viola/cello parts can double trombone 1 and 2 parts.
- Basses can articulate the bass line. The bass line helps determine the style of the piece. Pizzicato basses or electric basses have a limited sustain sound.

Due to the difficulty of finding enough good string players, most church orchestra arrangements are written to function well without strings. Many available orchestra arrangements provide a synthesizer string reduction to aid this. If the church orchestra does have an accomplished string section, the arranger should write challenging and musically interesting lines for the players. Advanced string players appreciate having something to play other than whole notes. One may also develop a simplified part for less experienced string players. Also, the fine arranger will include brass articulations, bowings, and dynamic markings to enable the players to execute his or her musical ideas.

Techniques and Ideas

The arranger must learn from each arrangement. Take chances and experiment. An idea that does not work can always be changed. Seek to grow regarding repertoire of styles, chords, orchestration, forms, and settings. Skillful variety is key in effective church orchestra arrangements. Since the words are not being sung, instrumental music relies on musical devices to provide variety for each verse.

After something is written, the arranger must do one of three things: write the same thing again, write something different, or end the piece.

To add variety in an arrangement	To add emotion or "drama"
• Change key/mode	• Forte piano
• Change dynamic	• Suspended cymbal roll—crescendo
• Change orchestration/texture	• Timpani roll—crescendo
• Change melody instrument	• Tempo changes
• Use chord substitutions	• Dynamic changes
• Change accompaniment type	• Pedal points—sustained pitch,
• Change meter	either high or low, during a
• Change rhythmic feel	melody or chord progression.
• Change style	• Delay, stretching
• Change register/tessitura	• Repetition

When an arranger is staring at the score without a clue as to what to do next, the solution begins with prayer—God is the One who can free the musical imagination.

When the Writer Is Stuck

• Move on to another part of the arrangement.

• Listen to a special favorite piece of music. It often helps to lubricate the creative process.

• Do something noncreative—mow the yard, bake a cake, etc. Such activities are good ways to clear the mind.

• If time does not allow the luxury of diversion, just begin the writing process. Write something. If it does not work, then try something else. An encroaching deadline does wonders for promoting creativity!

Avoiding Problems

• Be careful of instrument ranges, especially for less-experienced players. (See Appendix for Range Chart.)

- Be careful of keys, as mentioned earlier.
- Be sure to give players sufficient rest during a piece.
- Check the score and parts for mistakes—errors in transposition, accidentals, wrong notes, etc.
- Be aware of technical demands on individual instruments—make sure the parts are attainable by the group for which the arrangement is written.
- Be certain that the rest of the orchestration does not obscure parts, especially the melody.

Conclusion

With proper preparation, the right tools, a time commitment, and practice, arranging skills can be well-developed. Seek God for ideas; listen to great music, study scores, and experiment. As mentioned earlier, writing for the church instrumental ensemble is challenging, but well worth the effort. Fine instrumental settings of sacred texts can lead worshipers into God's presence.

Resources

- Coda Music Technology, Finale notation software, 1-800-843-2066
- Judy Green Music—music paper, supplies, books, (213) 466-2491, Hollywood, CA
- *The Technique Of Orchestration,* 6th edition, Kent W. Kennan and Donald Grantham (Upper Saddle River, NJ: Prentice Hall, 2002)
- *Orchestration,* Walter Piston (New York: W. W. Norton, 1955)
- *Instrumentation/Orchestration,* Alfred Blatter (New York: Longman, 1980)
- *Arranging Concepts Complete,* Dick Grove (Van Nuys, CA: Alfred Publishing Co., 1985)
- *The Contemporary Arranger,* Don Sebesky (Van Nuys, CA: Alfred Publishing Co., 1974)
- *Music Arranging and Orchestration,* John Cacavas (Miami, FL: Warner Bros. Music, 1985)
- *The Professional Arranger Composer,* Russell Garcia (New York, NY: Criterion Music Corp., 1954)
- *Sounds and Scores,* Henry Mancini (Miami, FL: CPP Belwin Inc., 1986)
- *Arranged by Nelson Riddle,* Nelson Riddle (Bel Air, CA: Warner Brothers Publishing, 1985)

Camp Kirkland is a composer, arranger, and clinician. He has been a church orchestra director for 17 years, in addition to being a high school band director, and college band director/instructor of low brass/professor of music theory. He has published over 1000 works.

Jeff Cranfill is Associate Minister of Music, First Baptist Church, Snellville, Georgia, and formerly at Red Bank Baptist Church in Chattanooga, Tennessee. Before following God's call into the church orchestra ministry, he served as the band director and music department chairman in Christian schools in Georgia and Mississippi for 12 years. An Atlanta native, he earned Bachelor and Master of Music degrees from Georgia State University. His ministry includes arranging and composing music for church orchestra, choir, band, various ensembles, and full orchestra. Many of his arrangements have been published.

The Instruments of the Orchestra

Woodwinds, Brass, Percussion, Strings

INTRODUCTION

by John G. Gage

Webster defines harmony as "a combination of parts into a pleasing or order-ly whole," and orchestra as "a group of musicians playing together." In order for an orchestra to play in harmony, it is necessary for the conductor to have a basic knowledge of the sonorities and capabilities of the various instru-ments, so they may be combined in the most effective fashion to produce an "orderly whole."

The instrument section is divided into four families: woodwinds, brass, percussion, and strings. In the following pages, each orchestra instrument is described as to basic construction, sound production, effective usage and potential playing difficulties. Basic solutions are suggested for potential into-nation problems, technical stumbling blocks, and poorly written parts. Instrument selection and maintenance is also addressed. One of the most valuable resources in each of the following chapters is the listing of suggest-ed study and resource materials at the end of each section.

Each writer in the instrument section has been carefully chosen as unique-ly qualified in his or her area of expertise on each respective instrument. Although it is beyond the scope of this book to comprehensively cover the idiosyncrasies of every instrument, the information that follows should enable the conductor to have a basic understanding of each instrument and a resource to assist in making helpful suggestions to players.

WOODWINDS

AN INTRODUCTION

by Christopher Bade

The following five chapters contain a considerable amount of information on the woodwind section. Writers address instrument history, basic pedagogy, intonation, specific technical problems, and instrument procurement. Additionally, they address the differences between performing in the professional music world as compared to being a member of the local church orchestra.

In general, fairly proficient woodwind players exist in most areas of the country. Public school music programs have contributed to a greater accessibility of instruments, thus raising the standard of performance. Still, finding professional players in local church orchestra settings is not the norm. Players will be students at various levels of maturity or adults who may not have been playing regularly for some time. Obviously, nonprofessionals will require more rehearsal time and, despite the possible "fear" factor, many will be willing to serve.

Many players will have a background that includes a wind band experience. Woodwinds, particularly clarinets, form the basis of this ensemble. Church orchestrations often double winds and strings. Not every church can field a complete instrumentation, so directors should be aware of "substitutions." It is common for church orchestrations to employ exposed woodwind solos or obbligati to add color, to restate a melody, or to provide a simple counterpoint to the vocal line. Many players have participated in solo and ensemble contests, so they will be aware of these soloistic usages.

Woodwind players are adept at "fitting in." Capitalize on their warm, rich sonorities and light textural capabilities to set the proper mood for transitional reflective moments during the worship experience.

CHAPTER 4

The Flute and Piccolo

by Rebecca Danner Remley

Instrument Design

A Brief History. The flute's recorded history begins with archeological findings in ancient tombs. These flute-like instruments of wood or clay apparently had religious significance since they were found buried with other valued items. The first major improvement was when some unknown person plugged the end of the tube with wood and made a small opening slightly lower than the piece of wood. Then came tone holes. A three-holed Egyptian flute has been found dating back to 200 B.C.

During the Middle Ages and Renaissance, the flute gradually changed from a vertically played instrument to a horizontal instrument, referred to as being "transverse." Around 1650, the transverse flute was in general use. Between 1830 and 1850, Boehm, an inventor who started playing flute because of a lung illness, experimented with changes to the flute. Boehm worked with acoustics and tuning, added covered keys so that the holes could be larger, and made other improvements. This makes Theobald Boehm the true inventor of the modern flute.

How the Flute Makes a Sound. The flute produces a tone by the air vibrating inside the tube. This vibration is caused by the airstream splitting as it strikes the opposite edge of the embouchure hole—part of the air going into the flute and part of it going outside the instrument. The longer the length of tubing, the lower the sound. The flute is also able to produce harmonics on the very fundamental sounds. This is how the flutist produces the second and third octaves of the flute. A more beautiful tone is produced in the upper registers by realizing this concept and practicing harmonics.

> *"Music is language; the flute is one of its mediums of expression, and when I play I try to convey the impression of laughing, of singing, of talking through the medium of my instrument in a manner almost as direct as that expressed by the human voice."[1]*
>
> *—Marcel Moyse*

Parts of the Flute and How to Put Them Together. There are three parts to the flute:
- the headjoint (the section with no keys and an embouchure plate),
- the body (the long part with a lot of keys), and
- the foot joint (the shorter part with keys).

When assembling the flute, be sure that the tenons (ends) are clean. Grease, oil, or silver polish should never be used on the tenons. If they are wiped very clean they should go together with a slight twist. If it is difficult to assemble, the flute should be taken to a repair shop to be checked. When assembling the instrument, avoid grabbing the key mechanism or the embouchure plate that is merely soldered on the headjoint and can come loose. The headjoint should be inserted into the body with a twisting motion and the embouchure hole aligned in direct line with the first key on the front of the body. (Never have the headjoint pushed completely in. The flute is designed to play better "in tune" with the headjoint out 1/8" to 1/4".) The rod on the foot joint should be aligned in the center of the last key on the body. (Small adjustments to the alignment are sometimes necessary because of finger length and tuning, but this is a good place to start.)

Playing Technique

Flute Stance and Hand Position. The flutist should remember to always stay relaxed and comfortable. There should be no tension. (If playing the instrument hurts or is uncomfortable, it is probably wrong.)

- **Feet**–should be shoulder width apart when standing, with the left foot slightly in front of the right.
- **Sitting**–NEVER hook either arm over the chair back. Negotiate with a stand partner so that both players can see the music while keeping a proper position (or, better yet, each player could have his own stand and music). The head should be turned slightly to the left and the flute angled across the body.
- **Head**–should be erect.
- **Left hand**–wrist should be L-shaped.
- **Right hand**–wrist should be straight with fingers curved.
- **Fingers**–should be just above the keys (or slightly touching the keys) in a ready position. Never let fingers fly or left little finger droop.

Embouchure. Start by using just the headjoint when working to achieve a good sound. Center the headjoint on the lower lip, in "The Valley of the Chin." (The closer side of the embouchure hole should be where the color of the lip meets the flesh of the chin.) Say the word "pure" or "pooh," feeling that the bottom lip rolls out as if blowing a kiss or pouting. Keeping the lips in this shape, blow lightly across the hole to the far edge. Remember to be relaxed at all times. A tight embouchure will produce a strident sound and a sharp pitch.

For notes in the first octave of the flute, bring the corners of the mouth back as if saying "ee." To reach the high registers, bring the corners of the mouth forward as if saying "oo." Practice these two sounds—low and high—with just the headjoint and in front of a mirror until you can comfortably change from low to high as well as from high to low.

Tonguing. When tonguing, the flutist should maintain a consistent tone quality at all times through the extremes of register or dynamics. Remember to maintain or increase air support and resist the temptation to allow the embouchure to open.
  • **Single tonguing**—When single tonguing, use the tip of the tongue with a very light stroke. Use either the T or D consonant along with an oh, ooh, or ee vowel sound. (The different vowel sounds increase the range of possible colors.) Remember to keep the air constant and relax the back of the tongue.
  • **Multiple tonguing** (double or triple)—The use of multiple tonguing increases the flutist's technical ability. When double and triple tonguing, use T and K (with various vowel sounds) at slower speeds and move to D and G for faster speeds. Work at strengthening the K or G syllable and use a constant air column in order to produce equal tone on both the front tongue stroke and the back. There are three common patterns for triple tonguing:
    1. TTK TTK,
    2. TKT TKT, and
    3. TKT KTK.
When practicing double and triple tonguing, the following method is recommended.
    Step 1—Single tongue the passage;
    Step 2—Use the K or G syllable throughout;
    Step 3—Double or triple tongue the passage.
  • **Flutter tonguing**—This is not actually an articulation, but a special effect. It first came into use in the symphonic repertoire of Richard Strauss. It is accomplished by rolling the tongue rapidly against the roof of the mouth as in rolling the letter "R" in brrrr. A second way to accomplish a flutter tongue is to use a guttural "R" by vibrating the soft palate in the back of the throat almost like gargling.

Breathing. The ability to breathe correctly and to conserve when exhaling is vital for a flutist because of the lack of resistance when playing the flute. Try these exercises to achieve a proper breathing technique:

Without the flute:
    1. Bend over from the waist with the head relaxed and looking at your knees, and place your hand just below your waist.
    2. Expel all the air with a strong "wooosh" of sound.
    3. Inhale deeply, feeling the expansion of the waist and back area.
    4. Repeat the process at least two more times, and on the last time, hold the breath in the body and gradually move to an upright position, retaining the air inside the body.

5. One will feel relaxed, full of air, and ready to begin playing.

Or standing straight up:

1. Keep head and neck free of tension, with shoulders dropped and relaxed.

2. Exhale first, with the same "wooosh" so that the body is ready to inhale naturally.

3. Inhale, checking with the hand below the waist that the abdominal area is moving in and out correspondingly with exhalation and inhalation.

4. Repeat at least three times.

With flute:

Set the metronome at quarter note = 60 and choose a comfortable, mid-range note. Exhale ("wooosh"), inhale a good breath, and then play that note for four beats. Inhale again and gradually hold the note longer and longer each time. Or:

With metronome at quarter note = 60, and using an eight-beat pattern:

1. Exhale quickly ("wooosh"); Inhale, play the note for four beats, inhale four beats,

2. play for five beats, inhale three,

3. play for six, inhale two,

4. play for seven, inhale one,

5. play for eight full beats, inhale quickly and play for another eight beats.

Vibrato. One of the most expressive tools for phrasing, projection, and tone development is the use of a well-executed vibrato. Vibrato, by definition, is a slight variation in pitch and/or intensity in a sustained note. A vibrato should neither be too slow nor too fast. It is imperative to develop the ability to vary the speed and width of a vibrato. In fast passages a vibrato is not necessary and traditionally a vibrato will speed up in the higher registers.

Common Problems and Solutions

Fingering faults—The most common fingering fault is not raising the left index finger on the second octave D and E♭. A definite tone color change will occur if these notes are fingered incorrectly.

Braces—If a flutist has braces, a lower or higher placement on the lip should be tried. If the braces still cause pain, wax should be applied between the wires and the lower lip.

Small or weak tone—The flute may be turned in too far. Turn out to normal position.

Breathy sound—The air is not centered over the embouchure hole. Practice in front of a mirror until the triangle of condensation caused by the air stream is in line with the hole.

Open or fuzzy tone—The flute may be turned out too much. Turn in to normal position.

> **Sam Levine**
> **Nashville studio musician**
> **and Christian recording artist**
>
> "On my good days, I approach practicing as an act of praise and playing as an act of worship. This is my Father's world and music, even in the most elemental form of scales or long tones, is an expression of His love."

Loud and rough tone–The player may be blowing too hard and forcing the sound. Practice breathing exercises and long, controlled tones.

Notes drop to a lower pitch while trying to play a higher one–The air stream direction is not correct. Practice with the closed headjoint to achieve the low pitch (corners back) and the high pitch (corners forward).

Weak sound–Check for leaks in the instrument.

Tight, thin sound with no flexibility–The embouchure plate is placed too high on the lip.

Very sharp–The corners of the mouth are pursed too tight.

Intonation

Follow these pointers to learn how to play "in tune":

• Warm up the instrument before working on intonation because pitch is highly affected by the air temperature.

• If there are extended rests in a piece of music, or if the instrument will not be played for a long time, it is imperative to blow warm air through the instrument before playing again.

• Check the placement of the headjoint cork. (See instructions in the section on Regular Maintenance.)

• Tune a recommended pitch to set the length of the instrument. If this note is sharp, pull the headjoint out to increase the total length of the instrument. If it is flat, push the headjoint in to shorten the instrument. Then, continually tune because each note has its own pitch tendencies.

• If the note sounds "out of tune," there are two recommended ways to approach it: (a) cover the embouchure hole, or direct more of the air into the instrument which lowers the pitch; and (b) uncover the embouchure hole or blow more air across and out of the instrument which raises the pitch. There are many methods used to explain to students how to accomplish this, including "raising or lowering the head," "directing the air to the floor or wall," "moving the lower jaw forward and backward to change the direction of the airstream," and the most common "rolling the flute in and out," which often can result in poor hand position.

• Become aware of notes that present pitch problems and learn how to correct them.

• Practice matching pitches with a partner.

• Remember that air pressure and dynamics affect intonation, so be prepared to adjust at the ends of phrases and when breath is in low supply.

• NEVER STOP LISTENING!

The Five Most Common Misuses of a Flute

1. A flute in the low register is usually very quiet. Double this with a trumpet in a comfortable range and the flutist might as well not play.

2. Do not overuse glissandi and difficult trills in sacred arrangements.

3. Do not overuse the practice of writing notes an octave lower and having the flutes read 8va instead.

4. Not writing a separate flute part for a descant and expecting the flutist

to "read off of the score" when everyone should know that it takes two hands to play a flute.

5. Not writing a second flute part and expecting a vast number of flutes to be able to play above the staff in tune.

Basic Care and Maintenance

Daily Flute Care. After playing the flute, clean it before putting it away. Moisture left inside the flute can cause faster pad deterioration. Cleaning the inside can be done by threading a pre-washed soft cloth through the slot on the cleaning rod (wrap the cloth around the rod) and running the rod through the inside of the flute. The outside of the flute may be wiped with a plain damp cloth to remove finger marks. Stay clear of the pads while wiping the outside of the flute. If dust collects between the keys or springs, a Q-tip™ or a small paintbrush can be used. Never use commercial silver polish on a flute.

When not in use, keep the flute closed in its case to help protect the finish from unnecessary exposure to impurities in the air, especially in geographic areas affected by salt or sulfur content. Also, keeping the instrument in its case helps prevent the possibility of damage by dropping it accidentally. Do not store the instrument in areas of extreme temperature changes such as in the car, next to radiators, or in front of windows where direct sunlight can cause extreme heat.

Regular Maintenance.

Sticky pads—Take a lens paper and place it under the sticky key. Then, depress the key and gently pull the paper out.

Cork placement—The cork placement of the headjoint should be checked frequently. To check placement, place the snub end of the tuning rod into the headjoint. The line around the rod should be directly in the middle of the embouchure hole. Unscrew the crown slightly. If the line is in too far, use the tuning rod to push it out slightly. (Sometimes, merely tightening the crown will accomplish this.) If the line is too far out, push the crown to adjust it. This greatly affects the flute's tuning with itself.

Oil keys at proper pivot points—Oil the key mechanism occasionally and sparingly. Once every month should be sufficient and oil should be applied with a special key oiler to prevent excessive application. Carefully wipe off any excessive oil.

Repairs

Springs—Occasionally the springs on the flute will slip to the wrong side of the pin, causing improper keys to open or close. Look at someone's flute to see where a spring belongs and use a spring hook (or in a bind, a small crochet hook) to move it to the proper side.

Because of the intricacies of a flute, use a professional in a repair shop for most repairs, especially for any suspected bent keys or rods or for pad replacement. A general overhaul should be done by a competent repairperson every few years. It is well worth the money.

Tips on Purchasing a New or Used Flute

Ask a professional flutist, an experienced band director, or a flute teacher for their recommendations. Always realize the importance of a new or creditable instrument. Check thoroughly any used instrument and if you don't feel comfortable doing this, ask someone who plays regularly to check it and play it. Be sure to figure the price of repair into the selling price of a used instrument. Even if a used instrument is in seemingly good repair, a professional repairperson should at least adjust and oil the mechanisms.

Other Members of the Flute Family

The flute family is comprised of several instruments in varying sizes. These include, in the order they are most common, the piccolo, the alto flute, the bass flute, and the E♭ soprano flute.

Piccolo. The modern piccolo is available in a choice of materials—wood, silver, and plastic, or some combination of these. The wood version is the oldest model and is fitted with a silver mechanism. It is preferable for orchestral playing because it is less shrill than the metal instrument and has a darker tone color. The metal piccolo is most suitable for the marching field and other outdoor performances where moisture and temperature are apt to damage the instrument. A good warm-up for the piccolo is to warm up on the 2nd and 3rd octaves of the C concert flute since that simulates the embouchure position used on the piccolo. When this warm-up is finished, switch to the piccolo.
A common mistake in composition is not allowing enough rest time for the flutist to switch to the piccolo and back. They should have enough rest time to not only switch instruments, but to get the second instrument warm.

If a flutist wants to learn the piccolo, a suggested book is: *A Piccolo Practice Book,* by Trevor Wye and Patricia Morris (London: Novello & Co., 1998). This text describes the differences in playing the piccolo from the flute, suggests alternate fingerings, has techniques for playing softly, and numerous other excerpts and tips on playing the piccolo. There is also a list of the common piccolo auditions and literature written for the piccolo.

The Alto Flute. This "harmony flute" is pitched in G. It comes with either a straight or curved head joint. A player must have long enough fingers and arms to play the straight version. Some alto flutes come with two headjoints so that the player can choose. The alto flute has a mysterious, picturesque effect and is best used in its lower two octaves. The alto flute is a regular in the flute ensemble and recording studios.

The Bass Flute. Pitched in C, the bass flute sounds exactly an octave beneath the regular C flute. Professor Abelardo Albisi of Milan, first flutist at La Scala, designed the instrument to be held vertically to make the tone holes accessible to the fingers. The embouchure itself was a short horizontal tube, blown transversely as on a regular flute. The modern bass flute has a transverse head, but the tube is bent so the player can reach, by key extensions, all of the tone holes. The bass flute is frequently used in the flute ensemble. The best known examples in the orchestral literature are in Stravinsky's *Rite of Spring,* Ravel's *Daphnis and Chloe,* and Bollings' *Suite for Flute and Jazz Piano.*

Resources
Fingering Charts
• Flute manufacturers will usually have free flute fingering and trill charts.
• Most method books contain fingering charts.
• See Web site resources.

Books
• *The Flute and Flute Playing: In Acoustical, Technical, and Artistic Aspects,* Theobald Boehm (New York: Dover Press, 1964)
• *Kincaidiana: A Flute Player's Notebook,* John C. Krell (Santa Clarita, CA: National Flute Association, 1973). Based on notes taken by John Krell while studying with William Kincaid.
• *A Handbook of Literature for the Flute,* James J. Pellerite (Bloomington, IN: Frangipani Press, 1978). An annotated compilation of graded method materials, solos, and ensemble music for flutes.
• *The Flute Manual,* Thomas E. Rainey, Jr. (New Wilminghton, PA: Son-Rise Publications & Distribution Co., 1988). A comprehensive text and resource book for both the teacher and the student.

Method and Technique Books
• *Flute Etudes Book: 51 Flute Etudes in All Keys,* Mary Karen Clardy (Valley Forge, PA: European American Music Corporation, 1995)
• *Flute Fundamentals: The Building Blocks of Technique,* Mary Karen Clardy, (Valley Forge, PA: European American Music Corporation, 1993)
• *The Advanced Flutist: A Guide to Multiple Tonguing, Vibrato, and Sensitive Fingering,* William Kincaid, (Bryn Mawr, PA: Elkan-Vogel, Inc., 1975, 1982). Two volumes. Advanced techniques.
• *The Art and Practice of Modern Flute Technique,* William Kincaid (New York: MCA Music Publishing). Three volumes. A progressive study.
• *Mel Bay's Flute Handbook,* Mizzy McCaskill and Dona Gilliam (Pacific, MO: Mel Bay Publishing Co., 1994). An inexpensive book with valuable exercises.
• *Practice Books for the Flute,* Trevor Wye (London: Novello Publishing, 1999). In five books covering tone, technique, articulation, intonation and vibrato, and breathing and scales, or an omnibus edition which includes all five books.

Periodicals
• *Flutists' Quarterly,* the publication of the National Flute Association. Comes free with membership.

- *Flute Talk,* a division of the Instrumentalist. Write to Flute Talk, 200 Northfield Road, Northfield, Illinois 60093. One year—$15.00.
- *Flutewise,* a magazine of Theodore Presser. Check their Web page.

Web sites
- *National Flute Association,* http://nfaonline.org
- *Flute World,* http://www.fluteworld.com
- *Gemeinhardt Flute Manufacturers,* http://www.gemeinhardt.com (has fingering charts and other resources)
- *Kristin Ohlin Flute Page,* http://kristin.newdream.net/flute (includes links to other flute pages).
- *Larry Krantz Flute Page,* http://users.uniserve.com/~lwk/welcome.htm

[1]Marcel Moyse (1889-1984), a legendary French flutist and teacher who had a profound influence on flute and woodwind playing in the 20th century.

Rebecca Danner Remley is Assistant Professor of Music at Samford University, teaching flute, theory, composition, and music technology, and is a freelance composer/arranger.

CHAPTER 5

The Oboe
and English Horn

by Jon S. Remley

Basic History and Design

Double-reed instruments were the first types of reed-blown instruments created by man. Museums in Egypt contain examples of double-reed instruments dating back thousands of years. There is evidence to support the idea that the "flutes" spoken of in the English translations of the Old Testament were actually double-reed instruments, as a double-reed instrument called the *halil* was known to have been used in the worship of the early Hebrew people. The name for this instrument comes from the same root as the word "hallelujah."

The basic design of an oboe is very simple—two reeds vibrating against each other with the resultant sound being enhanced by a conical resonating chamber. The construction of the reed, the construction of the instrument, and the manner of playing all yield to the distinctive sound of the oboe. As with all woodwind instruments, basic pitch is controlled by the length of the instrument along with the position of the tone holes of the instrument.

Tone Production

Embouchure. The embouchure of the oboe is most simply described as "point and pucker." To form the embouchure, drop the jaw and place the reed on the center of the lower lip. The tip of the reed should extend beyond the lower lip just enough for the tongue to reach the tip of the lower blade. Both lips then close around the reed. A proper embouchure thus accomplished should show the chin pointed and both lips puckered. Although, for control of tone color and dynamic, some influence over the reed will need to be exerted by the lips; any pressure on the reed should be initiated from the sides of the reed, not the top and bottom. Since the sound resonates in the oral cavity before it resonates in the instrument, the inside of the mouth should remain as open as possible without altering the embouchure. This can be accomplished by thinking of directing the airstream toward the bridge of the nose while remembering to point the chin and pucker the lips.

The Reed

A good reed is essential for a good tone. It should be made of reed cane, not of artificial material. Reeds made of artificial materials do not need to be soaked and always respond, but they will never give the oboe a professional sound. Obtain a reed with a long or "American scrape." The short or "French scrape" will produce a sound that is too bright for most ensemble playing. Most oboe players in church orchestras are not going to make their own reeds, so either the director, the oboist, or both must know a good supplier for reeds. The best solution is to know a good reed maker. A list of several reed suppliers in different areas of the United States is given at the end of this chapter. Reeds from a private supplier will usually be more expensive than those available at the music store, but the extra expense is nearly always worth it.

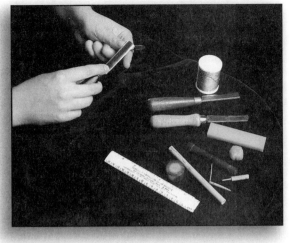

Before playing the instrument, the reed must first be soaked. Soaking the reed can be done in the mouth but will be more quickly and successfully done in water. A 35 mm film canister or similarly sized container is ideal for this purpose. Best results will be obtained if the water is room temperature or slightly warmer. There is no need to soak more than the part of the cane that shows beyond the string winding.

Tonguing

The tongue should rest naturally in the mouth, as relaxed as possible. The reed should be tongued on the tip of the bottom blade of the reed by whatever part of the tongue naturally contacts it by using the appropriate tonguing syllable. Notes in the lower ranges should be tongued with the syllable "dah" or "tah" while notes in the higher ranges should be tongued with the syllables "dee" or "tee."

Common Pitfalls

Even if the instrument is in good playing order and the player has a workable reed, the player may still have problems in tone production.

• Taking too much reed into the mouth causes a harsh, bright, unrefined tone.

• Inadequate control over the vibrating surface of the reed causes a harsh tone. It will also likely cause the player to play sharp to the pitch. There should be enough pressure from the sides of the reed to allow the player to control the tone color produced by the instrument.

• "Biting" the reed causes a sharp, pinched tone due to excessive pressure from the player's lower jaw. This is perhaps the most common tone production pitfall of all, as it is much more natural for one to hold the reed by jaw movement than by inward movement of the corners of the mouth.

• Along with causing pitch problems, biting will cause the tone to sound bright and pinched.

• If the player is playing the tuning note in tune and is biting, it is likely that it is to compensate either for inadequate air stream support, a hard reed, or both. This problem will manifest itself not only in tone problems, but also in pitch problems throughout the range of the instrument.

• Lack of adequate air support causes a weak, muffled tone and occasional pitch problems.

• Inadequate air support is the root of several problems.

• If the embouchure is otherwise correct, it will cause the tone to be weak and lacking in resonance.

• Pitch will be a problem throughout the instrument.

• Notes employing octave keys will be flat to pitch and may not produce in the octave desired.

• In order to compensate for these problems, the player will probably resort either to taking in too much reed, "biting" the reed, or both.

• Taking too little reed in the mouth causes a small, flat, muffled sound. This usually results from an over-correction of having taken in too much reed.

• If the tip of the reed is not allowed to vibrate inside the mouth but is instead vibrating against the lips, a small, stuffy, nonresonant sound will be produced that may be flat in pitch. Players with this problem frequently complain about difficulty with instrument response.

Technique

Hand position. All fingers (but not thumbs) should be curved. The most common error is the straightening out of the left-hand ring finger. A straight left-hand ring finger will cause the adjacent little finger to straighten and the adjacent middle finger to become angular instead of curved. This will hamper the fluidity of the technique by slowing the fingers. This problem can also occur in the right hand, though it is not nearly as common. The fingers of both hands will and should angle slightly upward toward the reed, with the left-hand fingers angling slightly more than those of the right hand.

Breathing. Breath should be taken in primarily through the mouth, although some air will come in through the nose. Though the oboe does not need a large volume of air for proper tone production, it does need strong and constant support of the air column. The support mechanism and procedure for good playing is the same as that for good singing. Always think of breathing from the bottom of the lungs, filling to the top, and support down and out.

Range Expectations. The wise conductor will be sensitive to the level of experience and expertise of his or her players. The oboe is most difficult to play in its extremities. Any note below second-line G should be considered a low note; as the notes get progressively lower, they become progressively more difficult to play well. Successful performance of low notes becomes compounded by any leakage of air in the upper joint (a common occurrence). The easiest range of the oboe is that from second-line G to C above the staff. Any player who has even moderate expertise should be able to perform well in this range. A moderately good player will probably be familiar with fingerings up to F, an octave above the treble staff, although he or she may not be comfortable with notes above D above the treble staff. A good player should be comfortable with all notes from low B♭ to high F. The notes above high F are best left to professional and other expert players.

Technique Tips. There are a number of "tricks" that make oboe technique easier but which the player may not have learned. The conductor can assist the player by keeping these in mind and suggesting them when appropriate. Listed below are a few of the most common helpful tips.

• An E♭ key is available for the little fingers of each hand. They operate the same tone hole and can be used interchangeably.

• Many instruments have an F key available for the left hand little finger. It may be used interchangeably with the F key operated by the right-hand ring finger, as these keys operate the same tone hole.

• When playing between middle C or D♭ and E♭, use left-hand E♭.

• Avoid sliding the right-hand ring finger from the D key to the F key. When going between these two notes or F and others employing the right-hand ring finger, use left-hand F or "forked" F instead.

• When sliding from one little finger key to another (e.g. low B♭ to low B or low C to low C♯), wipe the little finger across the forehead or on the side of the nose to collect facial oil. The finger will be able to slide much more quickly.

Tuning and Vibrato

Tuning. The reed must be in tune before the instrument can be played in tune. The optimum pitch of the reed, played at the "throat" (where the string begins) is C. Ideally, when first blown softly, then with increasing wind pressure, the reed should sound only octave Cs—no other pitches. If the reed varies greatly from this standard, it should be adjusted or not used. A reed that causes the player to be sharp may be pulled out slightly (no more than 1/8"). A reed that causes the player to be flat will likely cause the player either to put more reed in the mouth or to resort to biting—neither of which is desirable. Avoid reeds that are too hard to be played comfortably or too soft to be able to support the pitch in all registers without undue embouchure manipulation.

With a reed that is in tune and a good, open embouchure, the oboe should play most pitches in tune with itself. A tuning standard of A=440 or A=439 is suggested because a pitch standard much higher than A=440 will create response problems on the lowest notes of the instrument. As with any instrument, tuning is a matter of constant vigilance that is done with that wondrous gift of God, the ear. Remember, however, that pitch problems can be caused by the reed, the instrument, or the player.

Vibrato. Vibrato is a two-edged sword. Done well, it can enhance the tone, move the musical line, and cover slight pitch problems. Done poorly, it can destroy the tone, obliterate the musical line, and cause pitch problems. Vibrato should be a part of every oboist's playing and should be utilized on most notes of discernable duration. For most oboists, it should be generated by a periodic pulsation of the air stream. In order to overcome the airstream resistance caused by the construction of the reed, it requires more muscle energy to produce than that required by any other wind instrument. Although studies suggest that the oboe vibrato is primarily a variation of pitch, the listener should not be aware of pitch change and should instead perceive only a movement within the tone being played.

Five Good Uses for the Oboe

• **Color**—The oboe is perfect for adding color to the orchestra. It can be used to express a variety of emotions.

• **Solos and ensembles**—Choral anthems or church orchestras often include an oboe solo of some kind. The oboe lends itself beautifully not only to solos within church orchestra music, but to solos and small ensembles for preludes and offertories. A number of excellent arrangements are available for oboe and other instruments (piano, organ, flute, etc.) that are designed for use in the church.

• **Countermelody**—The oboe is useful for countermelodies as it is for melodies and solos. Since it is an alto instrument, it works best when playing a countermelody against the voice or against the melody of a soprano instrument such as flute or violin. It is not as suitable for playing countermelodies with brass instruments.

- **Substitution instrument**–Because of its versatility of color, the oboe substitutes well for a variety of instruments, particularly flute, violin, viola, and clarinet. In Baroque or baroque-style music, it can successfully substitute for trumpet.
- **As a harmonic instrument in melodic rhythm**–The oboe blends beautifully with soprano, alto, or tenor voices, either vocal or instrumental. When combined with another instrumental voice, it can easily switch from the secondary to the principal voice for a change of color.

Five Common Misuses of the Oboe

- **Range and color**–As the oboe ascends in its range, the natural color becomes brighter. Care should be taken to avoid asking for a dark color in higher notes or a bright color in lower notes.
- **Range and dynamics**–Nearly any dynamic can be asked for in the most facile range of the oboe (G4-C6), although the lower pitches are naturally softer and the higher pitches are naturally louder. Below G4 and above C6, the tendency of the oboe is to play more loudly as one plays further into the extremities. Care should be taken to adjust dynamic expectations accordingly.
- **Range and balance**–Refer to "Range and dynamics" (above) and to the range and dynamics tendencies for other instruments in this book, and always remember the natural tone colors and dynamic tendencies of each instrument. For example, it is not a good idea to ask oboes and brasses to play in unison at the same dynamic level, nor to ask both the flute and the oboe to play *pp* on low C.
- **Writing flute/oboe parts** (as one part)–Although they sound well when played together, the flute and the oboe are very different instruments. Unless one is designing a composition or arrangement to accommodate a variety of possible ensemble instrumentations, care should be taken to write the flute and the oboe as separate parts.
- **Trills and runs**–The color of an oboe trill and the excitement created by a scalar run on the instrument are very effective tools in a composition or arrangement, though often overused. Arrangers should always treat trills and runs judiciously and with considerable forethought.

Care and Maintenance

Assembly/Disassembly. The oboe, clarinet, and bassoon all have "bridge keys" that allow one part of the instrument to operate a key on another part of the instrument. These keys should be carefully aligned. On the oboe, two of these keys, one on each side of the instrument, bridge the top joint to the middle joint; one such key bridges between the middle joint and the bell. In all cases, there is a top key and a bottom key. All bridge keys on the oboe are fragile and will bend if they hit against other keys. The careful player will experiment to discover which places on the oboe cause the upper of each bridge key to lift. Careful assembly and disassembly will help to ensure that the bridge keys do not bend, thus causing a misalignment of the instrument.

Lubrication. All friction points on the oboe must be periodically lubricated. The corks on the end of the joints at the point where the joints come together are most commonly lubricated with cork grease or petroleum jelly. Because it is the most permanent lubricant, new corks will likely need cork grease. However, after the cork is "broken in," cork grease can become caked and messy. In that case, petroleum jelly is a good substitute. It will have to be applied more frequently than will cork grease, but it tends to be a cleaner substance to work with.

Grease corks as needed. If the instrument is difficult to put together, grease the corks. If the corks are well lubricated and the instrument is still difficult to put together, the corks may have to be slightly reduced in circumference. A professional does this best. Obviously, do not lubricate the corks to the extent that the instrument does not hold together well.

The other friction points requiring lubrication are those in the keys. The most obvious friction points are at those places where the shafts containing the rods on which the keys are placed connect with the pivot posts that are screwed into the body of the instrument. However, careful observation of the mechanism of the instrument will reveal many places in the middle of the shafts where the shaft is cut to allow movement of the key. Special "key oil" is made for this purpose, but one may also use a lightweight oil such as sewing machine oil or gun oil. This writer prefers clock oil. Many music stores and oboe accessory dealers carry clock oil as well as key oil. Oil the instrument at least once every six months. The less often the instrument is used, the more often it should be oiled.

Water in Tone Holes. Every oboist at some point will have to deal with the problem of getting water in the tone holes, which may cause a gurgling in the sound, pitch problems, or nonresponse of the note or the octave. Following are common solutions to this problem.

• Always hold the oboe so that gravity takes water down the back of the instrument where there is less of a chance of it wandering into a tone hole.

• Blow down through the tone hole.

• Place lens paper between the key and the tone hole and press down on the key.

• Disassemble the offending part of the instrument and swab with either a swab or feather.

The most serious water problem to face is that of water in the octave keys. If this should happen, the above solutions will probably not work, although they should be the line of first resort. If they do not work, try one of the following:

• With a screwdriver, disassemble the octave mechanism and remove the key from the offending tone hole. Blow down through the tone hole and reassemble.

• Remove the top joint from the instrument. Cover all tone holes and the opening at the end of the joint. Blow into the receiver (the hole where the reed goes) so that great pressure into the instrument is achieved. While maintaining the pressure, press the key of the offending tone hole.

• As before, remove the top joint and close all places where air may escape. Create a vacuum by sucking air out of the top joint. While maintaining the vacuum, press the key of the offending tone hole. If the tone hole is the thumb octave, the key may not open, in which case the player may have to switch hands and operate the thumb octave manually.

• If none of the above solves the problem, use another instrument. The octave key may have to be removed with a special tool made for this purpose, cleaned out, and reseated in the instrument.

The Bore Oil Controversy. Most oboes are made either of Mpengo (African Blackwood) or a synthetic substance. Both are extremely dense materials that will not absorb bore oil. Therefore, as a lubricating substance for the purpose of prolonging the life of the instrument, bore oil has little use. Over the past few years many players have begun to use a spray bore oil, not to preserve the instrument, but to lubricate the bore so that water inside the bore runs more quickly and freely out of the instrument. This has helped many players who were plagued with frequent occurrences of water getting in the tone holes, since the less time that the water stays in the instrument, the less chance it has of getting in a tone hole.

Swab or feather. A swab or a feather is widely used to deal with excess water in the instrument. A swab is a piece of material, usually silk, rayon, or sometimes cotton, connected to a string that has a weight at the end of the string. The purpose of the swab is to remove moisture from the instrument.

The major advantages of the swab are:

• The swab is more quickly used if it is of sufficient length so that the instrument does not have to be disassembled to use it.

• The swab lasts longer than a feather, is less messy, and easily fits in a case.

The major disadvantages are:

• It leaves the bore drier, which many players feel hampers the response of the instrument.

• Many technicians claim that swab users have a greater problem with water in the tone holes than do feather users, as each time the swab passes the undercutting of the tone holes, tiny amounts of fabric residue can be removed from the swab. Over time, this residue can attract water to the tone holes. If the player chooses to use a swab, it is recommended that only a pull-through swab be used. Swabs that are not easily pulled all the way through the instrument can become impacted in the upper joint of the instrument, causing considerable aggravation and requiring professional removal.

Feathers are turkey feathers that have been treated to remove the natural silica from the feather (important to keep from scratching the bore of the instrument). The purpose of the feather is not so much to remove moisture from the instrument as to spread it around, as a moist bore responds more readily than a dry bore. The major advantages of the feather are:

• More moisture is retained in the bore, which may enhance tonal response.

• Use of the feather may reduce the chance of residue building up in the tone holes and may reduce the amount of water getting into the tone holes.

Periodically replace the old feather with a new one. The player will know when the feather has outlived its usefulness. Regardless of whether one chooses the swab or the feather, the instrument should have excess moisture removed from the bore after playing and before putting the instrument into the case.

Temperature/Humidity Situations. Cracking is most commonly caused by expansion and contraction over a period of time, but may be triggered by excess expansion and contraction. This expansion and contraction comes primarily from changes in temperature and/or humidity. Both can be controlled to a certain extent if the player is careful to follow the following guidelines:

• Avoid playing a wooden oboe in any area in which there are temperature or humidity extremes.

• Avoid carrying the oboe between areas of considerable temperature or humidity change when it is out of the case.

• Once the case is opened in a warmer area, allow the oboe to adjust to room temperature before playing.

• If the case is opened in a considerably colder area, warm the upper joint by holding it between the arm and the chest before playing.

• Keep moisture inside the case through the use of humidifiers (available from music stores and/or oboe accessory dealers), orange peels, or the like. This is more for the benefit of the pads than the wood, but it is still important.

Minor Repairs

In order to survive, an oboist has to be able to make quick, minor adjustments from time to time. Entire books on instrument adjustment are available, but most players will be better off to stick to the easier adjustments. Here are a few that anyone can use:

• Sticking pads—put a dollar bill between the offending pad and the tone hole. Close the key and pull the bill back and forth a few times. The bill is not made of paper and is slightly abrasive.

• Springs—keep a spring hook handy for those times when a spring comes unhooked. Outside of rehearsal or performance, practice unhooking and hooking the springs so that no panic ensues if a spring does jump off.

• Adjustment screws (the little screws on the instrument)—The oboe has numerous adjustment screws. An inexperienced person should avoid working with the adjustment screws on the upper joint. However, some of the keys on the middle joint are accessible to nearly anyone. Every oboist should learn to adjust the following:

1. The adjustment screw at the top of the middle joint that prevents the G♯/A♭ key from opening when the F♯/G♭ key, the key played by the first finger of the right hand, is closed. Overadjustment will prevent the F♯/G♭ key from closing completely.

2. The adjustment screw on the key covering the D♯/E♭ tone hole. Careful balancing of this adjustment ensures the ability to press left-hand D♯/E♭ while right-hand C♯/D♭ is being played without the D♯/E♭ tone hole becoming uncovered. This is a very important adjustment, especially in keys of four or more flats and four or more sharps.

3. The adjustment screw on the key covering the C♯/D♭ tone hole. Proper adjustment of this screw allows the oboist to play back and forth between low B or B♭ and C♯/D♭ without sliding the right-hand little finger back and forth between the low C key and the C♯/D♭ key. Although not as often used, this makes the technique involved in this operation much faster and easier.

Purchasing an Instrument

Before buying an oboe, check with a local professional for suggestions on make and model. Although the best oboes are made from wood, there are some very respectable synthetic oboes available, and in many cases, especially if the church is going to own the instrument, a synthetic instrument is the best choice.

An instrument purchased from an individual or a business should be test-played. If the purchaser is not confident of his or her level of discernment between instruments, ask or hire a local professional for help. Following are key issues in an oboe purchase:

- Physical condition of the instrument
- Evenness of scale
- Quality of tone (darkness/brightness)
- Focus of tone
- Evenness of tone throughout the scale
- Response
- Key placement and "feel"

To save time and have peace of mind, purchase an instrument from a reliable dealer whenever possible. There are many reliable dealers around the country. See a listing in the resources section of this chapter.

The English Horn

The oboe family is comprised of several instruments, including the musette, the oboe, the oboe d'amore, the English horn, the baritone or bass oboe, and the heckelphone. Although the use of the oboe d'amore is not uncommon in Baroque music, by far the two most commonly encountered instruments in this family are the oboe and the English horn.

The English horn, or *cor anglais,* is the tenor instrument of the oboe family. It is pitched in the key of F and sounds a perfect fifth lower than the written note. It uses the same basic fingering system as the oboe, though a few fingerings, particularly above C6, are different. Fingering charts that address the differences in fingerings are easily available both in print and through Internet resources.

Tone production on the English horn is accomplished by using a slightly larger air stream than on the oboe, but with slightly less air pressure. Control of tone on the lower notes is easier than on oboe, while control of tone on the upper register is more difficult. The range of available dynamics and of tone color is more limited than that of the oboe. The tone is more mellow than that of the oboe and will not project as readily. The embouchure is somewhat more relaxed, and more reed will be taken into the mouth than is done with the oboe.

Because the English horn is played less often than the oboe, workable reeds are more difficult to find. As with the oboe, if one does not make one's own reeds, a reliable supplier, usually a private party who sells oboes and/or oboe equipment, is the best option. The reed is larger, thicker, and more open than the oboe reed. Usually, wire will be used in the manufacture of the reed to control the tip opening.

Resources
Major Repairs
Both the oboist and the music director should become as confident at instrument adjustments as possible. However, for complex repair jobs, the following sources are recommended:
- Paul Covey - Covey Oboes, Atlanta, GA
  (404) 367-9000 or (888) 440-OBOE, www.oboes.com
- Pat McFarland - McFarland Double Reed Shop
  Atlanta, GA, (404) 321-5356, www.mcfarlanddoublereed.com
- Alvin Swiney - Affordable Music Co.
  Virginia Beach, VA, (757) 412-2160, www.corkpad.com
- John Symer - John Symer Woodwinds
  Collingwood, NJ, (856) 858-0605, www.oboes.com
- David Webber (bore adjustments only) - Webber Reeds, Chandler, AZ
  (480) 726-6800 or toll-free (877) 932-7332, www.webreeds.com
- Carlos Coelho - Carlos E. Coelho Woodwinds
  6709 Meadowgreen Drive, Indianapolis, IN 46236
  Phone/Fax: (317) 826-0087, http://members.aol.com/CarlosOboe/index.htm

Dealers
- **Carlos Coelho** - Carlos E. Coelho Woodwinds
  Indianapolis, IN, (317) 826-0087 http://members.aol.com/CarlosOboe
- **Paul Covey** - Covey Oboes, Atlanta, GA
  (404) 367-9000 or toll-free (888) 440-OBOE www.oboes.com
- **Mike Aamoth** - Midwest Musical Imports
  Minneapolis, MN, (800) 926-5587 www.mmimports.com
- **David Weber** - Weber Reeds, Chandler, AZ
  (480) 726-6800 or toll-free (877) 932-7332 www.webreeds.com

Professional Organization
- *International Double Reed Society*, www.idrs.org

Reed Suppliers Available on the Web
- **Paul Covey** - Covey Oboes, Atlanta, GA
  (404) 367-9000 or toll-free (888) 440-OBOE, www.oboes.com
- **Stephen Hiramoto** - North Texas Oboe Reeds and Supplies
  Dallas, TX, http://homes.aol.com/oboereeds/ntreeds.htm

CHAPTER 5 The Oboe and English Horn

- **Pat McFarland** - McFarland Double Reed Shop
  Atlanta, GA, (404) 321-5356, www.mcfarlanddoublereed.com
- **Marsha Taylor** - Kestrel Reeds, Eugene, OR, www.oboe.org
- **Singin' Dog Double Reed Supplies** - Sugar Land, TX 77496-7286
  (281) 265-OBOE (265-6263), www.singindog.com
- **David Weber** - Weber Reeds, Chandler, AZ
  (480) 726-6800 or (toll-free) (877) 932-7332, www.webreeds.com

Fingering Chart Website
- www.wfg.sneezy.org

Technique and Method Books

If an oboe player could own only one book, it should be the Barret Oboe Method, more commonly known as "The Barret Book."
- *A Complete Method for the Oboe,* A. M. R. Barret (New York: Boosey & Hawkes, Public Domain)

Aside from Barret, a few of the more widely used books at the elementary, intermediate, and advanced levels are listed below:

Elementary
- *Elementary Method for Oboe,* N. Hovey (Chicago: Rubank, Inc.)
- *Oboe Method,* Vol. 1, K. Gekeler (San Antonio, TX: Southern Music Co.)
- *Oboe Student,* Vol. 1, F. Weber and B. Edlefsen (San Antonio, TX: Southern Music Co.)

Intermediate
- *Intermediate Method for Oboe,* J. Skornicka and M. Koebner (Chicago: Rubank, Inc.)
- *Method for Oboe,* T. Niemann/B. Labater (San Antonio: Southern Music Co.)
- *Practical and Progressive Oboe Method,* A. Andraudr (San Antonio: Southern Music Co.)

Advanced
- *48 Famous Studies for Oboe,* W. Ferlingr (San Antonio: Southern Music Co.)
- *Studies for the Advanced Teaching of the Oboe,* G. Gillet (Paris: Alphose Leduc.)
- *Vade-Mecum of the Oboist,* A. Andraudr (San Antonio: Southern Music Co.)

Reference Books
- *The Oboe,* P. Bate (London: Benn, 1956)
- *The Oboist's Adjustment Guide,* P. McFarland (Atlanta: McFarland Double Reed Shop, 1981)
- *Oboe Technique,* E. Rothwell (London: Oxford University Press, 1985)
- *The Oboist's Companion* (London: Oxford University Press, 1977)
- *The Art of Oboe Playing,* R. Sprenkle and D. Ledet (Evanston, IL: Summy-Birchard, 1961)
- *The Reed Maker's Manual*—Book and Video, D. Weber and F. Capps (Phoenix, AZ: Weber Double Reeds, 1990)

Jon S. Remley is Director of Instrumental Studies at Samford University in Birmingham, Alabama, and orchestra conductor at Dawson Memorial Baptist Church in Homewood, Alabama.

CHAPTER 6

The Clarinet
and Bass Clarinet

by Robert F. Wall and Christopher Bade

The Clarinet

The clarinet as we know it today developed over a period of about 300 years. An instrument named the chalumeau, which had a range of an octave, was the direct ancestor of the clarinet. Johann Denner, a Nuremberg instrument maker, added a register key to the chalumeau around 1690 which allowed it to produce notes a 12th higher. Although it is unclear when the name clarinet was actually attributed to this improved chalumeau instrument, it is certain that the earliest clarinets served as a substitute in the orchestra for the clarion trumpet, a rather shrill, high-pitched trumpet, because it seemed to blend better. By the end of the Classical period, clarinets in pairs were fairly standard fixtures in the orchestra. Keys were added to the instrument gradually which allowed it to play in a variety of keys. Around 1810 an instrument with 13 keys, produced by the French virtuoso Ivan Mueller, seemed to solve the problem for awhile. The fingering system used today was developed and promoted all around Europe by the French clarinetist Hyacinthe Klose, and is based on the fingering system developed by Theobald Boehm during the mid-1800s for the modern flute. An assistant to Klose, August Buffet, developed the needle spring, and invented several other mechanical necessities to make this system possible. The Klose method for clarinet is still widely used around the world.

Today, the clarinet family consists of seven different-sized instruments in three different keys. The typical church orchestra leader or Christian school band director will primarily encounter the B♭ soprano and the bass clarinet. Instruments included in the clarinet family are as follows.

Most Common Clarinets

• **B♭ Soprano**—the most popular beginning instrument. It is regularly used in bands, orchestras, and chamber ensembles of all types. It sounds a major second lower than written.

- **B♭ Bass**—used in bands, orchestras, and a variety of chamber ensembles. It sounds a major ninth lower than written.

Other Popular Clarinets
- **E♭ Soprano**—the smallest member of the family and in the key of E♭, it sounds a minor third higher than written.
- **A Soprano**—most often used in classical symphony orchestras (not church orchestras). It sounds a minor third lower than written.
- **E♭ Alto**—most often found in band. The alto clarinet sounds a major sixth lower than written and can play alto saxophone parts. This clarinet has more than its share of intonation and tone quality problems.
- **E♭ Contra-alto**—most often found in band, this instrument is now the most common of the contra clarinets. It sounds an octave and a sixth lower than written and can play baritone saxophone parts. It can add a good bass sound to the church orchestra.
- **B♭ Contra-bass**—the lowest-sounding member of the clarinet family, this instrument sounds two octaves and a major second lower than written. It can play the regular bass clarinet part, which will sound an octave lower. Although this instrument is somewhat outmoded, it is still used in chamber ensembles, wind orchestras, wind ensembles, and large university bands. Its cost alone makes it prohibitive for most groups.

There are other clarinets that the instrumental director may encounter, but they are obsolete and seldom found in the United States. They include the C clarinet (nontransposing) and the basset horn, pitched in F and similar to the alto clarinet but with a narrower bore. Mozart was particularly fond of this instrument for use in some opera orchestras and in various chamber works.

General Characteristics
All clarinets function alike and play in treble clef. Fingerings are the same, although some alternate fingerings may be used to correct tuning on different instruments. The embouchure is basically the same for all clarinets with minor allowances made for the different-sized mouthpieces. (See bass clarinet information beginning on page 97 of this chapter.)

Clarinets are single-reed instruments utilizing the vibration of the reed against the mouthpiece to produce the tone. Basically, the clarinet is a long tube with various sized tone holes placed at strategic locations on the larger tube. The tone holes are opened and closed with the fingers and/or pads to produce the various pitches. This is an oversimplification of the playing process, however, this basic principle holds true for all clarinets.

The major considerations for the instrumental director in working with the clarinet section are the embouchure, breath support (airstream speed), hand position, and equipment. Intonation on clarinet is influenced by all of these factors and will be discussed later in the chapter. The following information regarding fundamentals is for B♭ soprano clarinet but will, with only minor variations, apply to the entire clarinet family.

Embouchure

Clarinet embouchure formation is a critical factor in successful clarinet performance. The embouchure is used to direct the airstream through the mouthpiece and to control the vibration of the reed producing a warm, characteristic clarinet sound. For these vibrations to occur, the embouchure must neither be too constrictive nor too loose. One method that will assist in forming a correct clarinet embouchure is as follows:

• Let the mouth relax. The slight space between the upper and lower teeth is just enough for most B♭ clarinet embouchures. This space will necessarily be larger for the larger mouthpieces.

• Anchor the mouthpiece under the upper teeth with approximately one-half inch of the tip of the mouthpiece inside the mouth. Do not initially place the mouthpiece on the lower lip. This concept of first positioning the mouthpiece on the upper teeth is paramount!

• Bring the lower lip up to touch the reed. No undue pressure is needed.

• Form a tight "ee" syllable with the lips to create the correct chin formation. The chin should be stretched taut.

• While keeping the chin in this correct formation, form a tight "u" or "cue" syllable with the lips focusing around the mouthpiece for a tight seal. Pronouncing the German syllable ü makes a great seal around the mouthpiece.

It is primarily the embouchure, in conjunction with the air stream, that controls tone production. One extremely important point to make is that the embouchure must be a constant. It does not change for the various registers of the clarinet. (See the explanation of "registers" later in this chapter.) Many players tend to use more embouchure pressure to play higher tones causing the clarinet to be sharp, edgy, and bright sounding.

Breath Support (Airstream Speed)

Breath support is a crucial factor that will affect both tone production and intonation on the clarinet. In general, the clarinetist should always blow a fast cold airstream all the way through the instrument. Think of pushing the air an arm's length from the body. This is the length the air must travel through the B♭ clarinet. The airstream must be lengthened for the larger instruments in proportion to their size. To create a characteristic clarinet sound the throat must be in a relaxed, open position (think "ah" or "oh"). This is true for all registers. (See explanation of "registers" later in the chapter.) The tongue should be arched in the back of the mouth so that the sides of the tongue touch or almost touch the top, upper back teeth (think the word "whee"). This will create a valley in the tongue. The idea is to create a venturi (point where a smaller pipe intersects a larger pipe) with the tongue in the back of the mouth, which will produce a fast airstream through the mouth and into the mouthpiece. The airstream should produce a "hissing" sound. Be careful to always keep the throat open and relaxed; only the tongue arch is used to create the fast, hissing airstream. Proper embouchure and breath support go together to create that characteristic warm, beautiful clarinet sound.

Hand Position

Proper hand position is essential to good technique on clarinet. Fingers should be relaxed and naturally curved with pressure light enough that no tone hole impressions are left on the fingertips after playing. Some clues that indicate too much finger pressure include "white" fingernails while playing and "broken down" knuckles, not naturally curved. The fingers should be kept close to the instrument and not excessively raised over the keys. One-half to two-thirds of an inch is about right for the best technique and pitch. Following is an explanation of each hand position.

Left-Hand Position—extremely critical to good technique in the throat tone register. Start with the left hand held straight up. Point the fingers so that no curve is detected and no space is between the hand and thumb. Point the tip of the thumb out so that a check mark is created. Keeping the thumb in that position, relax the fingers so that they curve normally. Place the clarinet into the hand so that the thumb covers the back tone hole ring while allowing the tip to lightly touch the register key. The thumb should be at 1:00 with the register key at the 12:00 position. The fingers should fall on the correct tone holes with the naturally curved finger position. The index finger should wrap around the A♭ and A keys, slightly touching them.

Right-Hand Position—The right-hand finger position is easier to form. Place the right thumb under the thumb rest so that the rest sets between the tip of the thumb and the first knuckle. The cuticle of the thumb should be about the middle of the rest. Never let the player place the thumb rest past the knuckle since this is laying groundwork for future technique problems. Let the finger pads cover the tone holes, keeping them naturally curved. Try not to touch the bottom side key of the upper joint with the index finger of the right hand.

Equipment

When addressing the area of equipment one is broaching a very large and extremely subjective topic. Two basic truths do apply to all clarinets:

1. Wooden instruments almost always sound and play better than resonite (plastic) instruments. An exception is that the larger clarinets, bass and contra, frequently work well in resonite.

2. A good quality mouthpiece and reed are essential to good tone production and intonation. There are no shortcuts in this area.

The following discussion will focus on four critical areas: mouthpieces, ligatures, reeds, and instruments. Each of these areas is very subjective and the

opinions stated are the result of the author's 45 years of playing experience.

Mouthpieces. The mouthpiece is the most crucial factor in clarinet tone production and intonation. There are numerous styles, sizes, and types of mouthpieces, each with a myriad of different facings (the area on which the reed fits) and bore configurations. The subject is too broad and extensive to broach here, but the best recommendation is to stay with a medium-faced mouthpiece with medium reeds. Hand-faced mouthpieces are usually better for tone production and intonation than machine-faced mouthpieces, regardless of brand. It is advantageous to blend and balance if the clarinet section in school bands can have matching mouthpieces. Many directors require beginning students to purchase identical mouthpieces. Intermediate and advanced players should consult a professional clarinet teacher for advice on specific mouthpieces. Consult the "Resources" section at the end of this chapter for additional information on this subject.

Reeds. Much like mouthpieces, reeds come in many brands and sizes and one look at the reed section in a catalog can be overwhelming. Most reeds will work fine as long as the reed "fits" the mouthpiece. Reeds come in different sizes ranging from "1," the softest, to "5," the hardest, with half-size designations in between. It is critical that the reed size be fitted to the mouthpiece facing. Generally, the lower-strength reeds (1 to 2-1/2) are used for open to very open facings. The medium reeds (3 to 4) are used on medium to medium open facings and the harder reeds (4-1/2 to 5) should be used on the close-faced mouthpieces. Reeds that are too soft for the mouthpiece facing tend to produce a flat, unfocused sound. Reeds that are too hard for the mouthpiece facing produce a stuffy, fuzzy sound and display a lack of response.

In recent years the fibercane reed has gained some popularity among players; however, the use of these reeds is still controversial among many professional performers. While some band directors allow them to be used in their marching band because they are very durable, others are not willing to permit it since they feel it produces a harsh, strident tone. Some accomplished performers on the lower (bass) clarinets support their use saying the tone is quite acceptable on these larger bore, larger mouthpiece instruments, although many admit the reed tends to be less sensitive to subtle nuance and, in some cases, it is less responsive to the softer dynamics. Let it suffice to say the final decision on fibercane reeds must be left to the director or the more advanced performer.

Ligatures. The ligature is a clamp-like device that holds the reed on the mouthpiece and it can also greatly influence tone production, intonation, and response on the clarinet. Ligatures range from the basic metal style that comes with the student line instrument to the rather expensive specially designed models made from a variety of different materials. Different plating on metal ligatures even creates different tone colors and responses.

Intonation and Tuning

Although all of the factors discussed above are paramount as one seeks to attain the high goal of good intonation, the most critical factors include mouthpiece, breath support, embouchure, and tone conceptualization, with an emphasis on mouthpiece. Knowing that, following are some additional ideas and suggestions about tuning the clarinet.

Clarinets are made by the manufacturers to play slightly sharp if all the joints are completely closed. However, if the clarinetist plays with correct embouchure and the instrument is adjusted to the right length, a good quality clarinet with a good, hand-faced mouthpiece and reed combination—referred to in clarinet circles as the "setup"—will usually play well in time. The clarinet is tuned by adjusting the various joints to the correct length. This is done by "pulling out" or "pushing in" the barrel, bell, and middle joint of the clarinet as needed. In general, lengthen (pull out) to lower the pitch and shorten (push in) to raise the pitch.

Start with two tuning notes: open "G" (concert F) and third space "C" (concert B♭). Tune the "G" first by adjusting the barrel to match the given pitch. Next, tune the "C" by adjusting the middle joint and bell. Check the clarinet on its upper written G, F, E, D, and C and if there is a consistent deviation they can be adjusted at the middle joint. The third space "C" and the "B" just below can be further adjusted at the bell joint. With these notes tuned, check the upper A, B, and C. They should be fairly well in tune but if not (frequently sharp), then the problem lies with either improper embouchure pressure or bad mouthpiece tuning. If flat, the problem is likely too soft a reed. Try to work with embouchure pressure and reeds first. If still out of tune, a mouthpiece change may be needed. The throat tones, especially "G," "G♯," and "A," are often sharp and it may be necessary to cover the second and/or the third tone holes of the left hand and all the tone holes of the right hand or various combinations of these options to lower the pitch. Of course, this is possible only if the tempo and speed of the notes make it practical. There are some "resonance" fingerings that will help intonation and tone quality of the throat tones. These are illustrated in the Tom Ridenour book listed in the "Resource" section of this chapter.

Registers

There are four "registers" on the clarinet. They are the chalumeau (lower), throat, clarion (middle), and altissimo (upper).

Special Problems

The Break. What is commonly known as "the break" on clarinet occurs between the third line B♭ throat tone and the B♮ in the clarion register. It is at this point that the tone produced ceases being a fundamental pitch and becomes the third harmonic. The notes fingered begin duplicating those pitches a 12th lower. For example, once the register key is depressed with the left thumb, the fingering for low "E" chalumeau will produce the third line "B♮"; the fingering for low "F" will produce third space "C," etc. These fingering duplications will continue through the top note in the **clarion register** (high "C"). In a scale passage, the technical challenge for the beginning or inexperienced student is to quickly move from the relatively simple fingering of throat tone "A" or "B♭" to a fingering using all fingers and the left thumb (B♮) in one smooth and continuous motion. The challenge is to get all the tone holes covered properly in one synchronized motion.

Students should begin to produce notes in the **chalumeau register** with a full, resonant sound indicating that the concept of proper air support, a firm embouchure, and a secure hand and finger position are developing at an acceptable pace. The process of crossing from the chalumeau register to the clarion can be accomplished easily (if good embouchure, hand position, and airstream are present) by playing a chalumeau note and slurring up to the corresponding clarion pitch after depressing the register key with the left thumb. After notes in the clarion register have developed some security, it is time to develop the technique of moving from the throat register to the clarion register, a more slowly developing procedure because it requires so much finger movement. Since all the notes of the **throat register** can be played with the right hand down (even though it is not the regular fingering), using this right hand down concept will assist the beginning clarinetist in negotiating the break when moving from this register. This "right hand down" technique will set the stage for more advanced fingering options as the student matures.

When a player has a problem with the "break," it is invariably caused by stopping the airstream in the throat. To correct the problem, have the player play the upper note first and slur down to the throat-tone pitch. This usually works well because the air direction is to the bottom of the horn for the upper note. Have the player reverse the procedure keeping the airstream the same, without restriction. Once the player feels the airstream "carrying" the sound to the clarion register, the problem can be solved. This concept of a continuous and fully supported airstream cannot be overly emphasized.

Altissimo Register. Playing in the altissimo register, those notes above high "C," offers a real challenge for some players. This is often the result of a player trying to adjust the embouchure to make the high notes respond. The only thing that changes registers on the clarinet is fingerings. Remember that the embouchure should be a constant! The thumb opens the register key on the back of the clarinet to produce the clarion register and higher. The index finger of the left hand is raised to go from the middle to the high register, with correct fingerings. Done correctly, this requires no embouchure change. The only thing the embouchure will be required to do is adjust slightly for intonation, if needed. Some teachers advocate a technique for smoother slurs by using a first finger half-hole (rolling the index finger down; not sliding) when slurring from the clarion register to the altissimo. This technique, along with adjusting the breath support, will assist in preventing the altissimo notes from "popping" out at a louder dynamic. Additionally, there are several ways to "finger" each of the notes in the altissimo register.

Best Uses for the Clarinet
- Great solo instrument
- Very agile instrument; effective performing trills and rapid passages
- Blends well with French horns, especially in lower register
- Good harmony instrument when used with flutes, oboes, or strings

Common Misuses of the Clarinet
- Ineffective as a fanfare instrument, like trumpets
- Double tonguing is not a standard technique for the clarinet.
- Writing above the top of the practical range is not a good idea.
- Rapid passages across the "break" are not advisable for young players.

Basic Care and Maintenance
- The clarinet should be "swabbed" out after each use to remove excess moisture from the bore of the instrument.
- Oil the clarinet by placing several drops of "bore oil" on the swab and pulling it through the bore of the clarinet several times. NEVER squirt oil into the instrument. Use oil as recommended by the instrument manufacturer.
- The clarinet key mechanism should also be oiled one to two times a year depending on climate. Care must be taken when oiling the keys. The best way to oil the keys is to place one drop of key oil on a small piece of aluminum foil. Use a needle or pin to dip into the drop of oil. Get a small drop of oil on the tip of the needle then touch the needle to the key where the rod and post join. The small drop of oil should go into the rod and lubricate the screw inside. Do this for all the rods and posts. Be careful not to get the oil on the pads. One drop of oil from the bottle should be enough to oil the entire clarinet mechanism with some left over.
- The corks on the mouthpiece and individual joints of the clarinet need an application of cork grease from time to time. Do not use too much—only enough so the joint fits easily. Wipe off any excess.

Other than swabbing, greasing the corks, wiping moisture from the keys, cleaning the mouthpiece, and oiling the bore and keys when needed, there is little additional maintenance for the clarinet.

Repair

Unless the instrumental director has knowledge of instrumental repair, all pad replacement, cork replacement, and key straightening should be left to the professional repairperson. These repairs require specific tools and special skills in adjusting and fitting. A "Valentine Emergency Pad Repair Kit" can be used if a trip to the repair shop must wait. However, these pads and cork replacements are for emergency, not permanent repair.

Quick Fixes for Emergencies

• Use a paper match to heat the glue in a pad cup to reseat a pad that has fallen out but is still in good condition. Do not overheat the pad cup—heat it just enough to melt the shellac.

• Use a rubber band to secure keys with a broken spring. Be careful not to cover other keys that do not need the help.

• Use plumber's Teflon™ tape (the type used to seal water pipe joints) to help tighten old, loose cork joints. Just make a few wraps around the cork to make it fit—no need for cork grease.

Tips on Buying a Clarinet

All major instrument manufacturers produce quality instruments. Preference depends primarily on the player and, to a degree, the instrumental director. Buffet, LeBlanc, Selmer, Yamaha, and other reputable instrument manufacturers, make clarinets in a variety of models and price ranges that are used in many bands and orchestras throughout the world. At the time of this writing, one should expect to pay $2000 or more for a new, professional clarinet and as little as $325 for a new, resonite, student-line clarinet. Intonation may vary slightly from brand to brand, but intonation is affected more with mouthpieces and reed combinations than with instrument brand. A wooden clarinet is usually a step-up instrument. Beginning and intermediate clarinetists should always be on the lookout for a better quality instrument. It is advisable for the beginning player to enlist the assistance of a local professional clarinetist or an experienced band director to help in the selection process.

New Clarinets

When buying a new clarinet, stay with one of the major instrument makers as mentioned earlier. Check with local music stores and some national instrument mail order companies to see which offers the best price. Remember that buying from a local merchant usually means faster service if repairs or adjustments need to be made. Buy the best instrument your budget will allow. Quality student-line instruments for beginners are acceptable as long as you realize that in two or three years a better quality instrument will be desired. The professional line instruments are made for professional players; therefore, they are made to higher standards and will perform better and last longer. Always get the best mouthpiece available when buying a new clarinet. The mouthpieces that come with the instruments are not always the best choice. Here again, a professional clarinet teacher or an experienced band director can offer advice.

Used Clarinets

When buying a used clarinet, have the instrument checked by a good repairperson or an experienced professional or band director, if possible. If you must check the instrument yourself, look at the pads to see if any have broken skin coverings. Also, check the color of the pads. Dark-colored pads usually mean that the pads are getting old and might soon need to be replaced. Pads should be white or yellow, depending on the brand of the pad. Check to see if the keys move easily and if the long rods are straight. Bent rods mean problems. Look into the bore to see if there are any "checks" (small cracks). Also, examine, the outer body for cracks—some small cracks can easily be fixed, but those that go into a tone hole are more difficult to remedy. The best advice is to have an advanced player play the instrument and see if it is truly responsive and in good working order. Finally, do not forget to evaluate the condition of the case. It may be necessary to replace the case since it serves as protection for the instrument.

Resources

Clarinet Mouthpieces

The following are some examples of good hand-faced mouthpiece makers. Each offers several different facings.

- James Pyne, Pyne/Clarion, Inc., 1672 Rushing Way, Columbus, OH 43235, (614) 766-7878
- Rick Sayer, Sayer Woodwinds, Box 164, Clarendon Hills, Il 60514
- Charles Bay, Bay-Gale Woodwind Products, P.O. Box 3935-C, Westlake Village, CA 91359, (805) 497-8161

Reeds

The following are a few of the many brands of reeds that are available for clarinet. Final choice of a reed is at the discretion of the player. The reed brands listed here are the choice of the author and are listed in order of preference.

- Zonda (from Argentina)
- Vandoren (from France—traditional and V-12)
- Marca (from France)
- Olivieri (from Spain)

Ligatures

This list is far from exhaustive, but it will give the conductor a place to start. They are listed in order of preference of the author. Remember: ligatures should be tried out just like the instrument or mouthpiece since each will play a little differently, even within the same brand and model.

- Rovner (several models)
- Harrison (different platings, gold preferred)
- Charles Bay
- James Pyne (hand-woven material)

General Reference Books
- *The Clarinet Doctor,* by Howard Klug (Bloomington, IN: Woodwindiana, Inc., 1997)
- *The Clarinet Master Class: A Guide to Scale Studies,* by Rosario Mazzeo (Elkhart, IN: H. & A. Selmer, Inc., 1969)
- *The Clarinet and Clarinet Playing,* by David Pino (New York: Charles Scribners, 1989)
- *Clarinet Fingerings: A Guide for the Performer and Educator,* by Tom Ridenour (Duncanville, TX: Ridenour Clarinet Products [611 N. Royal Oak Drive], 1985)
- *The Educator's Guide to the Clarinet* (Duncanville, TX: Ridenour Clarinet Products, 2000). Email: rclarinet@aol.com
- *Guide to Teaching Woodwinds,* 5th edition, by Frederick W. Westphal (Dubuque, IA: Wm. C. Brown Publishers, 1990)

Reed Working Books
- *The Reed Guide: A Handbook for Modern Reed Working for All Single Reed Woodwind Instruments,* by George T. Krick (Decatur, Il: Reed-Mate, Co., 1989)
- *Handbook for Making and Adjusting Single Reeds,* by Kalmen Opperman (New York: Chapell & Co., 1956)

Technique Books
- *The Clarinet Instructor,* by Norman Heim (Delevan, NY: Kendor Music, Inc., 1968)
- *Melodious and Progressive Studies for Clarinet,* Volumes I and II, by David Hite (San Antonio: Southern Music Co., 1971)
- *Artistic Studies for Clarinet,* Book One (from Italian school); Book Two (from German school) (San Antonio: Southern Music)

Altissimo Register
- *The Development of the Altissimo Register for Clarinet,* by Norman Heim (Delevan, NY: Kendor Music, Inc.)

Robert F. Wall is Principal Clarinet and Associate Conductor of the Clear Lake Symphony, Houston, Texas. He is also Orchestra Director at University Baptist Church in Clear Lake, Texas.

Mr. Wall has Bachelor's and Master's degrees in clarinet performance. He has studied clarinet with Santy Runyon, Houyt Fischer, David Seiler, Larry Mentzer (Principal Clarinet, San Antonio Symphony), and Thomas D. Thompson (Associate Principal Clarinet, Pittsburg Symphony).

Mr. Wall is a retired Texas public school band director, having retired after 26 years of service. He now teaches private lessons and does master classes in clarinet performance at several local Houston high schools.

The Bass Clarinet

by Christopher Bade

The bass clarinet in B♭ is common to most school ensembles and is increasingly more common in church orchestras. Although there are contra-alto and contra-bass clarinets that sound lower, it is generally accepted that the bass clarinet in B♭ is the bass voice of the clarinet family.

Successful players can be musicians who actually began on the bass clarinet (rare) or those who were "converted" to it from the soprano B♭ clarinet or other woodwind instrument. Virtually all of the fingerings are exactly the same as on the B♭ clarinet (see below for one exception), but the fingers are spread slightly wider and the breath capacity required is larger. Since the vast majority of bass clarinetists are converted B♭ clarinet players, the following descriptions and suggestions are offered from that perspective.

Most performing groups have only one or two bass clarinetists because their written parts often double the bassoon, cello, or string bass. (This can be an asset if the group is missing these bass voices.)

Bass clarinets are usually much more difficult to keep in proper repair due to its size, cost, and its relative complexity. (Few individuals own bass clarinets, so they seldom invest in maintenance themselves.)

Differences

In comparison to the B♭ soprano clarinet, the following differences are cited:

Equipment

- A neck strap is necessary to alleviate the burden on the right thumb.

- A larger mouthpiece is required, which necessitates a larger embouchure setting. It is best to use a fairly open mouthpiece such as a Selmer.

- An extended neck (like that on a saxophone) which is primarily horizontal to the player's embouchure. Many bass clarinet players may appreciate an after-market neck that is more vertically similar to the angle of a B♭ clarinet. (An excellent model is made by Charles Bay of California.)

- Reeds are obviously larger and yet must vibrate freely. Generally, reed quality is not so crucial as on the B♭ soprano. Usually reeds of 2-1/2 or 3 strength are sufficient.

• A longer tube (larger and longer upper joint and lower joint) means having a larger breath capacity to produce enough air to actually play the bass clarinet.

• The metal bell (similar to saxophone) should have a soldered peg assembly on it. Proper alignment of the extended bell is important.

• A floor peg is necessary to alleviate the vertical weight of the instrument.

Embouchure

A slightly larger and rounder grip on the mouthpiece is required. It is crucial that it be slightly more relaxed; not too tight and not too loose. Having a flat chin is desirable but not so vital as on the B♭ clarinet. Less pressure/grip on the mouthpiece but a very relaxed throat, fast airflow, and proper tongue placement ("hee") is essential for good tone production. Certainly one must determine if he is comfortable with the angle (or "horizontalness") of the neck. Most instruments, particularly older ones, are fitted with the horizontal style neck (similar to saxophone). Some new instruments come equipped with a more vertical neck. A slightly more generous portion of the lower lip over the bottom teeth produces a more characteristic tone quality. (Not having enough bottom lip produces a dull sound.)

Fingering

With only one important exception, fingerings on all clarinets are the same. On the bass clarinet and the other large clarinets, the use of the "open" first finger in the high register is essentially different. Instead of opening the entire pad of the first finger on bass clarinet, the cup and pad have a small vent hole that is covered during normal use. For the upper register, the index finger is moved to the attached plate allowing only the vent hole to be opened. This important difference is frequently overlooked and can cause response problems.

Posture

With the instrument positioned between the legs, lean the top of the instrument away so that the player will lean into the instrument. The bell should be slightly closer to the player's body than the top. Of course, the exact angle will be determined by the required angle for the correct embouchure.

Helpful Tips

The bass clarinet is really just a BIG clarinet! All of the proper playing techniques learned on the soprano B♭ clarinet (posture, hand position, breathing, articulation, oral cavity placement, etc.) are used. In addition:

1. Sit upright and far forward in the chair. Lean the instrument away so that the player leans into the bass clarinet.

2. Use a neckstrap and peg with a nonskid surface at its base (or a cello "donut").

3. Maintain arched fingers for proper technique. Since the bass clarinet has buttons, larger keys, and longer reaches, one is tempted to develop "flat fingers" and this should be avoided.

4. Most bass clarinets go to low E♭, which means having an extra key for the right-hand little finger. (If the instrument goes down to low C then there will also be keys for the right-hand thumb to play.)

5. It is sometimes difficult to get the pitches F2, F♯2, and G2 if the tongue placement is too low. Higher notes can also be problematic.

6. Tuning problems include: B1, C2, and C♯2 (sometimes D2) which are often very sharp; low E♭, E, F which can be flat. It is best to tune to open G or C1.

7. Lethargic articulation is problematic due to a wider reed, larger mouthpiece, and longer tube which requires more breath. Be certain that the air speed is fast, diaphragmatic support is steady, the tongue is centered on the reed during articulation, and the tip of the tongue is touching at or near the tip of the reed.

8. Use the lower register to assist/teach the upper register(s). The majority of the parts played will utilize the low register. Getting a round full tone in this register more easily "translates" to a vibrant tone quality in the higher registers.

The bass clarinet, along with the other low-pitched clarinets, share similar problems and differences, but with a general knowledge and understanding of these basic variances, the seasoned player can make a fairly rapid and smooth transition to these instruments.

Resource

• There is a clarinet discussion board at the following Selmer Web site which includes a specific section on the bass clarinet and the other large clarinets. It is highly recommended. http://www.selmer.com/clarinet/discus/index.html

Christopher Bade is Associate Professor of Music at Oklahoma Baptist University where he teaches clarinet, saxophone, music theory, and music history. He regularly performs with the Tulsa Philharmonic on clarinet and bass clarinet. Bade earned his doctor of musical arts in clarinet performance at the University of Illinois, where he studied with Howard Klug.

CHAPTER 7

The Bassoon

by Ruth Shelly Unger

The bassoon is a member of the double-reed family—the same family of instruments as the oboe, English horn, and contrabassoon. It functions as the bass voice of the woodwind choir. While its lowest note is a B♭, like its soprano counterpart the oboe, the bassoon is pitched in C. The bassoon reads bass and tenor clefs, as do the trombones and cellos. It sounds in the octave written.

The Reed

The double reed consists of two pieces of bamboo cane *(arundo donax)* wired together and scraped to vibrate freely. As the reed vibrates, the air is set in motion, creating a sound.[1] The reed is a critical element because, to a large degree, the reed determines the response, pitch, and quality of sound. Simply put, a $30,000+ bassoon does the player no good in the absence of a working reed. In general, a good reed vibrates freely, is symmetrical, golden in color, without cracks or chips on its blades or any hint of mold and/or other debris on its interior or exterior. The reed fits onto a skinny metal tube called a crook or bocal, which is attached to the wing (also called the tenor) joint. These, along with the bass joint, boot, and bell, comprise the modern-day bassoon.

Stand vs. Sitting

When seated, a strap is used to hold the bassoon in place. When standing, the player uses a neck strap or any of a variety of harnesses that distribute the weight of the bassoon across the back. Balance is the key: whether sitting or standing the player must keep the weight of the instrument from resting on the left hand. Too much weight on the left hand affects the ability to play rapid technical passages and can cause pain and distress to the muscles in the hand and forearm.

Intonation

The bassoon has tremendous pitch flexibility. This explains why it is possible for a beginner to finger the correct note and produce something other than the desired pitch. A nice sound and good intonation are inextricably linked to proper air support and a good embouchure (position of the mouth in relationship to the reed). Players are accustomed to modifying fingerings and embouchure, as well as space in the throat and mouth, to achieve acceptable results. The overall pitch of some instruments may be improved by switching to a longer or shorter bocal (i.e., adjusting the overall reed length may also yield positive results). Adjustments in intonation should NOT be made by pushing in or pulling out the bocal.

Pitch Tendencies

The open note on the bassoon is F below middle C. Its tendency is to be sharp, particularly if the reed is not well balanced or amply wet and the player is not sufficiently warmed up. It is customary for bassoons to tune to A in the orchestra and B♭ in the band. Either will work in the church orchestra setting. In the lowest fifth of the range, the bassoon tends to be built sharp to improve the overall pitch in the highest register. Depending on the make of the bassoon, the pitches just above middle C (D, E♭, E, and F) often tend to be flat. An electronic tuner to develop the player's ear and a fine teacher to develop the player's technique are the best insurance against poor intonation.

Writing for the Bassoon

The bassoon provides excellent sonority when paired with any of the other woodwinds. Bassoon and French horn are also a fine combination. The bassoon may be employed for its lyrical quality and lush color. It excels in providing richness as the bass voice of the woodwind choir. It does equally well used melodically in its upper and middle registers. Since the bassoon projects less well in these registers however, care must be taken to reduce the numbers and dynamics of the accompanying instruments. When doubling with the cellos and string bass, the bassoon adds color and volume. Composers and arrangers alike are encouraged to exercise their imagination and to explore the full range of what the bassoon has to offer, rather than reducing the bassoon to a comedic role, endless walking bass lines, and/or doubling of the low brass or cello part. Since most players in the church orchestra setting will probably be amateurs, a comfortable range from B♭ to A or B♭ above middle C is recommended. Although the bassoon can play more than a perfect fifth higher (as demanded by some of the 20th-century solo and orchestral literature), the response in this extreme register is unpredictable and the fingerings are complicated and unwieldy. The A below the bass staff is encountered in the generic C bass hymnals, but the pitch does not exist on the bassoon.

Playing Difficulties

Some musical devices work well for the bassoon; others do not. Bassoonists are no exception here: No one likes to practice a needlessly difficult part for a musical section where their presence appears to have no effect one way or the other. The following is an attempt to arm the reader with an understanding of and respect for what works well with little effort as opposed to what is tricky for the bassoonist.

• Trills sound great on bassoon and only those in the lowest octave should be avoided.

• Upward slurs, even between the extreme registers, can be played with ease and great rapidity.

• The bassoon projects well and can play loudly in the lowest register with relative ease.

• It is extremely challenging to play the lowest fifth of the instrument in tune with good control at a pianissimo dynamic.

• Downward slurs of a perfect fourth and descending intervals wider than an octave can be very challenging for the player.

• Rapid tonguing is more difficult in the extreme low register. For example: the outcome of writing multiple bars of tongued, moving 16th notes at an allegro tempo in the lowest fifth of the range is uncertain. If clarity of articulation and pulling behind the tempo surface, the part may need to be simplified. Often in wind ensemble music the "real" part is shown with a simplified version (e.g. fewer notes, altered octave, etc.) appearing in cue-sized smaller print.

All of this is categorically NOT to say one should eliminate downward slurs, low and soft, or low and rapidly tongued passages: just recognize the challenge it presents for the player.

Modifying Existing Parts

In existing arrangements, the bassoonist is often asked to play a generic cello/bassoon part. Most of these parts need to be modified to be bassoon user-friendly. When supplying the bassoonist with a cello part, several relatively simple adjustments are needed.

• Remove the tremolos (they are not idiomatic for the instrument and in general do not sound well) and any double-stops.

• Evaluate how the bassoon will sound when playing glissandi and groupings of more than eight notes in a single beat and adjust the part by deleting, simplifying, or leaving the part unchanged.

• Replace *pizzicato* markings with *staccato* or *secco staccato* and remove the word *arco*.

• Recognize that constant playing is needlessly fatiguing for a double-reed player and often of no significant value to the musical whole. When doubling the bass line, insert a few measures rest occasionally.

Selecting an Instrument

A medium range, new student-model wood bassoon ranges from approximately $4,000 to $8,800 as of this writing. Fox, Shreiber, Puchner, Yamaha, Moosemann, Amati, and Kroener share this market. (Heckel is world-renowned for its professional bassoons, which, even used, command prices in the mid-$20,000s and higher.)

Regular Maintenance

Regular maintenance includes swabbing out the boot and wing joints after each rehearsal or performance. This significantly reduces the chances of wood rot in the boot joint. The bocal also needs to be cleaned regularly with a bocal brush or bocal swab. In addition, the instrument should be routinely examined by a competent repairperson to quiet the key mechanism, make sure all corks and felts are in place, and ensure that the instrument is sealing properly.[2] Caring for a bassoon is similar to caring for an automobile. A combination of preventive maintenance and "repair or replace anything that doesn't operate properly" yields optimal results. Proper care extends the life of the bassoon and preserves what is a fairly substantial investment on the part of the owner. A competent repairperson should be engaged for major repairs such as repadding, overhauling, and voicing a bassoon.

For Individual Study

Every bassoonist should be acquainted with the *Weissenborn Method for Bassoon with 50 Advanced Studies* (published by Carl Fischer and/or Cundy-Bettoney). It is a standard text that carries the bassoonist from the simplest whole-note exercises through demanding etudes that explore the whole range of idiomatic writing for the instrument. Rubank (published by Hal Leonard) also has a series of method books for bassoon. As a player becomes more proficient, the *25 Scale Studies* and the *Concert Studies, Volumes 1 and 2,* all by Milde (published by International), will provide additional challenges. Numerous Baroque sonatas and concertos, including those by Vivaldi, Telemann, and Boismortier, in addition to the Mozart and Weber concertos for bassoon and more contemporary solo literature, will complement work on scales and etudes.

Suppliers of Double-Reed Products and Music

- Forrests Music, 1849 University Avenue, Berkeley, CA 94702, (800) 322-6263, www.forrestmusic.com, Email: forresdr@ix.netcom.com, sales@forrestsmusic.com
- Jones Double Reeds, Box 3888, Spokane, WA 99220-3888, (509) 747-1224, (509) 838-5153 (fax)
- Vidger's Bassoon Supplies, 11746 Goshen Ave., #3, Los Angeles, CA 90049, (310) 231-0220

[1]It is best if the player is proficient in making his or her own reeds. When this is not the case, the player's teacher or the professional in a nearby symphony may prove to be viable sources of quality reeds. Failing this, handmade or partially handmade reeds may be obtained from a handful of individuals and double-reed suppliers throughout the United States. A sampling of these is listed above.

[2]Contact the bassoonists in the nearest professional symphony and ask whom they would recommend for instrument care.

Ruth Shelly Unger is bassoonist with the Pandean Players, one of the most active and enduring chamber ensembles in the United States. She is also second bassoonist with the Augusta Symphony and a founding member of the Georgia Sinfonia. With degrees from Rice University's Shepherd School of Music and Indiana University, Ms. Unger serves on the music faculty of Georgia State University, Clayton College and State University (prep school), Agnes Scott College, and Morris Brown College. She also maintains an active private studio.

CHAPTER 8

The Saxophone

by Edson Dickinson

The saxophone has become an extremely popular choice for beginning instrumentalists. Its use in popular music has given the instrument more exposure to the public than ever before. Often frowned upon by orchestral purists, the inclusion of the saxophone in the church orchestra is more often out of necessity than out of preference. But the saxophone can make a valid contribution, can fill musical needs in several sections, and gives countless players the opportunity to use their God-given abilities in His service.

History

When Adolphe Sax invented the saxophone in 1841, he was attempting to create an instrument that combined tone qualities found in the woodwind, brass, and string families. The first saxophone that he built was a bass saxophone in C, and it was this saxophone that Hector Berlioz heard the inventor play during a visit to his Paris workshop. Berlioz wrote this critique of the saxophone: "an instrument whose tone color is between that of the brass and the woodwinds. But it even reminds one, though more remotely, of the sound of the strings. I think its main advantage is the greatly varied beauty in its different possibilities of expression. At one time deeply quiet, at another full of emotion; dreamy, melancholic, sometimes with the hush of an echo."[1]

Although the saxophone is not considered a standard member of the symphony orchestra, many great composers have used it in their works. Richard Strauss, Massenet, Hindemith, Honegger, Milhaud, and Prokofiev have all scored for the saxophone, to name a few. The saxophone very quickly found a home in military bands of the late 1800s, and is to this day is a respected member of the modern wind ensemble. In the early 20th century the saxophone began to be used in the dance bands of the day, much to the dismay of those who sought the instrument's legitimate acceptance. The mouthpiece was retooled to produce a sound that could compete with the noisy environment of the dance hall, and the "edgy" tone quality that was produced has become the standard saxophone sound. Indeed the saxophone has thrived in the realm of popular music, becoming a standard member of jazz ensembles, and a preferred solo instrument in much of today's "pop" music.

The Saxophone Family

The saxophone family includes four standard members, ranging in size from smallest to largest:
- soprano in B♭,
- alto in E♭,
- tenor in B♭, and
- baritone in E♭.

Through the years there have been many variations in size and pitch. Some of these unusual instruments include the mezzo soprano saxophone, bass, F baritone, C soprano, and sopranino to name a few. The lowest-pitched saxophone is the contrabass, which stands seven feet tall! Of course, most of these oddities are obsolete or used only rarely, but there is the occasional player that will show up with an old C melody saxophone. This instrument, which has an interesting history of its own, is also obsolete, and should not be used. It is best to steer these players to one of the standard four.

Although the fingering system is the same for all saxophones, the alto saxophone is the preferred instrument for beginning students. Its relatively small size and ease of accessibility to a young person's fingers make it a much better learning instrument than the tenor or baritone saxophone. The soprano saxophone is usually considered only as a secondary instrument since it is mainly thought of as a solo instrument, and also because it is considered the most difficult saxophone to play.

The Parts of the Saxophone

The saxophone consists of two basic parts: the neck and the body (except in the case of the soprano, which is all one piece). The neck attaches to the top of the body of the saxophone, and the whole is a conical metal tube that has been folded over, forming what is called the bow of the saxophone. A hard rubber or metal mouthpiece slides on the end of the neck, which is covered there by a piece of cork. Like the clarinet, the saxophone relies on the vibration of a single reed attached to the mouthpiece to produce the sound. It should be noted that the saxophone is a complicated instrument, and because of the size of the keys and key cups it is more susceptible to damage than some other woodwind instruments. Care should always be taken when handling the saxophone, and one bent key cup could cause the whole instrument not to play.

The type of mouthpiece used is vital in producing the proper saxophone tone. Adolphe Sax himself described the mouthpiece as having a large round interior, or what is known as an "open chamber." Most modern mouthpieces have parallel sidewalls inside that create the "edgy" strident sound so often heard in popular music. Actually, the ideal situation would be for saxophonists to use two different mouthpieces: a hard-rubber open-chamber variety that would be used for orchestral work, and another more narrow chambered one for jazz.

The reed is attached to the table (bottom) of the mouthpiece by a ligature. The reed is made of bamboo cane, and since the best cane is grown in France, look for French-imported reeds. The reeds are identified by how thinly the tip has been shaved, and as a player gains experience, he or she will move from soft reeds to harder reeds. Plastic reeds are also available, but they usually produce a very "edgy" tone.

Producing a Sound: The Embouchure

The saxophone embouchure that should be used in orchestral settings is a nonchanging embouchure. In other words, the embouchure should not change when the player moves from a low note to a high note, and the player's head and neck should also remain in the same position. Using only the mouthpiece and neck, place the upper front teeth on the top of the mouthpiece as far as the fulcrum (the place where the reed begins to separate from the mouthpiece table). Most of the bottom lip is placed over the bottom teeth, and then the lips are wrapped around the mouthpiece forming an exaggerated "OOO" syllable. The lower jaw should be pulled back and down slightly, as in a slight overbite position. The inside of the mouth and throat should remain as open as possible, as if the player is yawning. It is important that proper firmness is achieved by bringing the sides and corners of the mouth into the center as far as possible. When air is released into the mouthpiece and neck, a proper embouchure should produce a pitch right around an A♭. If the note produced is below an A♭, the bottom lip should be firmed up. If the note produced is above an A♭, the bottom jaw should be relaxed into more of an "AW" position. Once the proper embouchure is achieved, blowing a large, steady stream of air into the mouthpiece will produce the sound. The muscles of the diaphragm and abdomen should be firm and the shoulders relaxed.

Playing in Tune

Intonation on the saxophone is controlled by the mouthpiece's position on the instrument's neck. When tuning the instrument, the player should attempt to match a B♭ concert pitch. If the saxophone is flat, the mouthpiece should be pushed in farther on the cork of the neck. Conversely, if the instrument plays sharp, the mouthpiece should be pulled out until the pitch is matched. Another good pitch to check is fourth line D, a note that is frequently sharp on the saxophone. The mouthpiece can be pulled only to the point where it does not cause flatness on the notes below it. After that, the D must be manipulated with the oral cavity, the embouchure (drop the jaw, open the throat), or with an alternate fingering (an added right-hand little finger). The most difficult note to tune and to play with a mature tone on the saxophone is the third-space C♯, played with no keys depressed. Early on, young players must learn to deal with this problem by putting the right-hand down and/or adjusting the embouchure as mentioned previously. In certain instances an appropriate alternate fingering may be possible, depending on the musical line. It should be remembered that each saxophone would have its own unique tuning problems. Saxophonists must discover these inconsistencies and learn to adjust the firmness of their jaw to compensate. Relaxing the jaw will lower pitch; tightening the jaw will raise the pitch of the saxophone.

Often a saxophonist will play every note in tune on their instrument except one. If this is the case, usually the saxophone is out of adjustment. The height of the pads over the tone holes affects intonation. The saxophone note E♭ is often played below pitch on poorly regulated saxophones. Occasionally the saxophone's middle C will sound above pitch. If all the other notes are relatively in tune, then these are probably adjustment problems. The upper range (above high G) of many saxophones will often be played sharp. This is usually an embouchure problem, and the player should be encouraged to relax their jaw slightly on these higher notes.

Purchasing a Saxophone

There are many different brands of saxophones on the market today, and the decision to buy a new or a used saxophone often complicates the process of buying an instrument. The best resource for finding the saxophone that is right for a player is still a local music instrument dealer. Most local stores carry both new and used instruments for sale.

The most reliable brand names are Yamaha, Selmer, Keilwerth, and Yanagisawa. These companies produce student-line instruments as well as professional models that range in price from less than $1000 for student instruments to over $5000 for a top-of-the-line saxophone, at the time of this writing.

If purchasing a saxophone for a beginner, one will discover a used saxophone would be a cost-effective choice. Bundy, Yamaha, Vito, King, and Cleveland are companies that continue to produce good student-line saxophones. One should be able to find a used student saxophone in good condition for less than $500. Newspaper ads are another great source for finding used instruments.

Whether one is buying for a beginner or a more experienced player, the instrument should be in perfect working order. The pads should be a consistent light brown color with no tears or worn spots. The pads must cover the tone holes completely or the saxophone will not play properly. The springs on the saxophone tend to become weak over time, and may cause the keys or the key cups to respond sluggishly. Although there are those who disagree, the outside finish of the saxophone has nothing to do with how well the instrument plays, but may be an indication of how the instrument has been treated. If the instrument or case has a disagreeable odor, it could be a sign of the presence of a fungus on the saxophone that will eat away the finish. The best course of action when buying a used instrument is to have an experienced player test it before a purchase is made.

There are also some very valuable "vintage saxophones" that one might encounter in searching for a used instrument. Some of these older saxophones are more than just collector's items; they are well-made and great-sounding relics that continue to be used by some of the best professional saxophonists. The Buescher "Aristocrat," the Conn "M" series, Martin, and the Selmer Mark VI series are a few of these vintage instruments that would be a valuable prize if one were to locate one in good condition. The Internet has become a great resource for finding instruments of this type.

Mouthpieces

The selection of a mouthpiece depends greatly on the style of music being performed. An open chamber mouthpiece such as a Caravan would be a good choice for producing a classical sound and is the type of mouthpiece that Adolphe Sax originally designed.

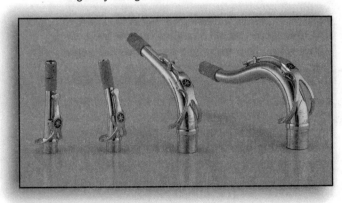

For more commercial or jazz-oriented music where more "edge" is desired in the tone quality, a mouthpiece with a more restrictive tone chamber is desired. Most of the mouthpieces being produced today fall into this category.

These mouthpieces are usually numbered

according to the size of the opening between the reed and the tip of the mouthpiece. Examples of good mouthpieces for beginning alto players are a Bundy #4 or Selmer C* mouthpieces. Selmer E or Meyer 6 mouthpieces have wider openings at the tip and therefore produce a bigger sound. Most professional jazz players use a mouthpiece with wider tip paired with a softer reed, such as a 2-1/2 or 3.

Reeds

Reeds are machine-filed pieces of bamboo that attach to the bottom of the saxophone mouthpiece by way of a ligature. It is the vibration of the reed as air is blown into the mouthpiece that produces sound from a saxophone, just as the vibration of the strings on a violin produce its sound. The vibration of the reed and the timbre of the sound produced is mainly determined by the thickness and quality of the reed. This makes the reed the single most important part of the instrument, and the selection of good reeds becomes a priority for any serious saxophonist.

Reeds are usually numbered according to the thickness of the tip from 2 through 5 including half sizes, with 2 being the thinnest. Most beginning players start with a 2 or 2-1/2 thickness. As players mature and are expected to produce a sound with more volume and flexibility, a thicker reed is preferred.

There are many different brands of reeds available, and some reeds are engineered to produce a specific tone quality. When selecting reeds, one should look for a golden yellow color of cane, an even distribution of the fibers running to the tip, and a discernable "heart" in the middle of the reed. In order to make reeds last longer, they should be rotated and stored in a reed guard to prevent them from warping.

Posture

Posture is an important part of playing the saxophone correctly. The saxophone can be played in a seated or standing position. In either position the saxophone, as it rests on the end of the neck strap, must be able to be brought to the player's mouth while the player's head and neck remain in a natural, relaxed position. The player should never have to stretch or tilt the neck or shoulders to reach the mouthpiece. When seated, the saxophone should hang down to the outside of the player's right thigh. It is permissible to hold the alto saxophone between the player's legs as long as there is no stretching or tilting of the neck.

Another important part of posture is finger position, especially the position of the left hand. The tips of the fingers must be directly on the keys ("pearls") with the joints of the fingers curved slightly. When the player presses down and lifts up the fingers, care should be taken to keep the fingers very close to the saxophone, not letting the fingers lift off the keys. It should be as if the fingers were glued to the keys themselves.

The right-hand position is not quite as critical, and is used in a little more relaxed manner. It is still very important to keep the fingers of the right hand close to the keys while playing, but it is actually better to let the fingers overlap the keys a little, and the fingers need not be as curved at the joints as the left hand.

The Role of the Saxophone in the Church Orchestra

The saxophone has been used almost exclusively as a substitution instrument in the church orchestra, doubling a variety of other instrumental parts. The alto saxophone is usually used as a double for French horn, and most published orchestrations provide alto saxophone parts that are transposed from French horn parts. If alto saxophone parts are not included in the orchestration, but there are French horn parts on the score, most church orchestra directors write out alto parts by transposing the horn part up a whole step, and then adding two sharps to the horn key signature to find the alto saxophone's key signature. The range of most French horn parts is very accessible on the alto, and usually falls well within the saxophone's written range of treble clef B♭ below the staff, to high F on the third ledger line above the staff. In the case of transcribing an alto saxophone part from concert pitch, the transposition is achieved by writing the alto part a major 6th above the concert pitch and adding three sharps to the key signature. The reader can also remember that the key signature transposes the same interval as the part.

Encountering an accidental while transcribing can sometimes cause problems. When transposing an accidental involving the concert pitches B♭, E♭, or A♭, the flat symbol will transpose as a natural symbol on the alto part. When transposing an accidental involving concert B♮, E♮, or A♮, a sharp symbol will be added to the transposed alto sax note.

Tenor Saxophone

The tenor saxophone has traditionally been used as a substitution for trombone in the church orchestra. Although most orchestrations that are published today include this substitution part, there are occasions when a tenor saxophone part will need to be written. The transposition of a trombone part to tenor saxophone is achieved by lowering the trombone part by a 5th, adding two sharps to the key signature, and changing to treble clef. As with the alto saxophone, there are some problems that occur with accidentals. When transposing an accidental involving B♭ or E♭, the flat symbol will transpose as a natural symbol on the tenor part. When transposing an accidental involving the trombone's notes B♮ or E♮, the transposed notes will be preceded by a sharp symbol for the tenor.

Scotty Willbanks
Saxophone, Newsong

Q: How did you learn to use your instrument as an instrument of worship?
A: "I didn't think the saxophone would ever be used in church. When I played for the first time, I bought an accompaniment track to "Holy Ground" and played for the congregation. People were moved to worship. It was an eye-opening experience for me. I realized God can use my instrument like a voice or a pastor's message to minister encouragement to people and draw them into God's presence."

Baritone Saxophone

The baritone saxophone is usually used as a substitute for bass trombone or tuba, although if the player is advanced it is possible to use the baritone saxophone as a substitute for cello. In any of these likely substitutions, it is not necessary to transcribe a part, because the saxophone player can read directly from the original trombone, tuba, or cello parts. As long as the original part stays in bass clef, all the baritone saxophone player has to do is add three sharps to the key signature, and read the notes on the page as if they were treble clef notes. Since the alto and baritone saxophone are both pitched in E♭, the same problems with accidentals that affect the alto will also affect the baritone saxophone. As players read the music, they must be prepared to change the accidentals when encountering the concert pitches B♭, E♭, or A♭ (or the sharp or flat versions of these notes).

[1]Sigurd M. Rascher, "Once More—The Saxophone," *The Etude,* February 1942.

Resources

* *The Art of Saxophone,* by Larry Teal (Summy-Birchard, 1963), distributed by Warner Brothers
* *Guide to Teaching Woodwinds,* 5th edition, by Frederick W. Westpal (Dubuque, IA: Wm. C. Brown Publishers, 1990)
* *The Saxophonist's Manual,* by Larry Teal (Ann Arbor, MI: University Music Press, 1978)
* *The Saxophonist Workbook,* by Larry Teal (Ann Arbor, MI: Encore Publications,1988)
* *Teaching Woodwinds,* William Dietz, editor (New York: Schirmer Books, 1998)

Edson Dickinson is Instrumental Director, First Baptist Church, Jacksonville, Florida, and an arranger.

BRASS

AN INTRODUCTION

by John G. Gage

The brass section of a church orchestra provides many varied colors and textures to enhance the worship experience. Rich low brass chords, exciting trumpet fanfares, and soulful French horn melodies can create both drama and beauty and provide a confident foundation for ensemble and congregational singing.

The accurate tuning of the section in preparation for playing is one of the most important elements needed to ensure a solid performance. Brass instruments tune to the lowest voice heard, so an in-tune tuba is a must. In order to avoid a natural tendency to tune sharp, the tuba should be tuned to the piano at the beginning of each rehearsal and service. Other members of the brass section are then tuned to the tuba. If a tuba player is not available, tuning should be to the piano or the lowest voice in the group. Other instruments such as the bari sax, bass clarinet, electric bass, and even left-hand piano may substitute in the absence of a tuba.

The endurance and experience of the brass section must be considered when programming the literature using this section. Church orchestrations often have the brass players involved with greater frequency than symphonic pieces. Young brass players will lack the endurance to play extended periods without a rest, and will not be able to play as high as experienced players. Well-structured practice, using the correct techniques, can be very beneficial to players wanting to maximize their abilities and endurance.

Occasionally, parts may need to be revoiced downward so as to be playable, or may need to be omitted altogether in order not to overpower choir or solo voices. Often, effective revoicing can be accomplished by simply taking the first trumpet down an octave. Trombone harmonies played in too low a range tend to be muddy, so revoicing may not be the best option for them. French horn players must develop a good ear so as to hear the note before articulating it. This will help them avoid missed pitches.

The use of sound baffles or other volume reduction techniques may be necessary to make the brass section balance with other instruments used, especially when combining with the choir and congregation. Players may need to be positioned facing inward to additionally refocus the direction and volume of brass instruments. Each brass player should be encouraged to assume personal responsibility for balance by playing with musicality and sensitivity.

By utilizing trained brass players in worship, the worship experience is heightened. The players can use their gifts, training, and investment to bring glory to God.

CHAPTER 9

The French Horn

by Jeffrey H. Girdler

The horn (commonly referred to as the "French horn") is considered to be one of the oldest musical instruments. Its origins can be traced to the animal horn used by ancient humans as a signaling device. Our ancestors quickly discovered that by buzzing the lips together against the narrow end of a hollowed-out animal horn, a loud and penetrating sound was produced—traveling over distances far greater than the human voice ever could. The shofar, or ram's horn, is fully documented and described in the Bible. From Joshua and the army of Israel as the walls of Jericho fell before them, to inspiring composers of both sacred and secular music, the horn has progressed steadily over the centuries. Its music gives birth to feelings ranging from carefree joy and jubilation to the most impassioned depths of soul-searching anguish.

Fundamentals

The horn, as with all brass instruments, is simply a hollow length of metal tubing. Larger at one end than the other, it is coiled in such a way as to enable the player to hold the instrument comfortably and efficiently. While many players begin to learn on either single Bb or single F instruments, the standard of the performance industry is the double horn, a hybrid Bb/F combination that affords the player the best characteristics of both instruments.

A mouthpiece is fitted into the very small opening at the narrowest end of the horn. Usually funnel-shaped, the mouthpiece has a very thin edge or "rim"—the area that comes in contact with the lips. Nearly 17 feet of coiled tubing gradually flares through all the many pretzel-like coils to a medium-sized bell. Normally, the edge of the bell is planted firmly on the player's right thigh and supported by the left hand that manipulates the four valves. The right hand is placed strategically in the bell (addressed later in more detail). The player propelling air through gently closed lips, exciting the air stream through the instrument by vibrating or "buzzing" the lips together, produces sound. From that point of "buzz," the body of the instrument acts as a large amplifier, projecting the sound out to the listener.

Different pitches or notes are achieved by altering lip tension (this is called "embouchure"), thus varying the pressure or speed of the air moved through the instrument.

Proper formation and development of the horn embouchure is the single most important aspect of horn playing. With the mouth held in a semipuckered position (a smiling whistle, also called the puckered smile), the upper and lower teeth must be held slightly apart, and the inside of the lips must touch the teeth. The lips should be gently closed (as in saying the word "hum"). The mouthpiece should be placed in the center of a semipuckered embouchure position, with two-thirds of the mouthpiece on the top lip and one-third on the bottom lip. By blowing a fast stream of air through the embouchure, and by tightening the lip tension, upper register notes will be produced. Lower register notes are played by slowing down the air speed and relaxing the lip tension. Middle register notes are formed from a common balance of lip tension and air column speed. Essentially, as the player loosens or tightens the lips, accurate lip tension controls the pressure of the air column, forcing the pitch higher or lower.

The Attack

To begin a note (the attack), proper lip tension and air speed must be combined with precise action of the tongue. Before the attack, the tongue is held behind the two front teeth and should touch them slightly (the tongue should never go beyond the lips, between the teeth). After a breath, the action of gently "spitting" a tiny object such as an eyelash or a spit ball off the tip of the tongue, combined with saying the syllable TOO, will start the tone. Much practice is required to coordinate and synchronize lip tension, air speed, and tongue action to produce a neat, clean attack.

Hand-in-Bell Technique

The hand-in-bell technique is unique to the horn. It contributes to its characteristically mellow sound, and is essential for control of pitch (intonation). A correct and convertible hand position can be achieved by:

1. hanging the right arm loosely at the right side;

2. closing the fingers gently with the thumb touching the index finger, forming a natural "cup," as if dipping water from a stream;

3. raising the right forearm as if shaking somebody's hand, and then inserting the cupped hand into the horn bell. The back of the fingers (knuckle side) should touch the inside of the horn bell on the side away from the body; with the thumb knuckle against the inside top of the bell.

The hand acts like a door on a hinge. By "closing the door" over the bell opening, the sound will be muffled and the pitch will be drastically lowered. The hand-in-bell technique is one of the horn player's most expressive tools, and unfortunately one of the techniques most often abused (e.g., hand stuffed too far in the bell, hand lazily lying on the thigh outside the bell, hand nowhere near the bell, etc.). It is very important to observe proper right-hand position in the bell!

Intonation

The horn can be an intonation nightmare because of its huge range, size of tubing—the longest of all the brass family—and general design flaws. However, the horn has built-in remedies for these potential hazards. On the standard double instrument, there are 9 to 12 individual tuning slides to pull or push. Lip tension can also raise or lower the pitch into proper tuning (known as lipping a note). Additionally, opening and closing the hand in the bell, along with alternative fingering combinations, can all help to ensure that the quest for perfection is not hopeless!

If there is no electronic tuning device available, or the player is relatively inexperienced, the tuning slides can be pulled and measured with a ruler to put the instrument in tune with itself (if the hand-in-bell position is correct). Once in tune with itself, it is much easier to match intonation with keyboards or ensemble. (Most horn manufacturers are able to provide tuning slide charts with exact information for the student.)

There are, of course, more sophisticated methods of tuning that are reasonably efficient. If a player is grossly out of tune, the slides should not be pushed or pulled right away as a "quick fix." The horn does not react like a trumpet when adjusting slides. Intonation problems are usually due to inexperience, lack of practice, out-of-shape lip muscles, lazy air support, or faulty hand-in-bell placement. Before pulling slides randomly to tune specific pitches, these other issues should be investigated.

Tubing Used in Tuning the Horn

• **Water Slide**—This slide should be left all the way in. It is used as a convenience in cleaning the instrument. It is *not* used for tuning, although it is part of the F horn tubing and will affect only the tuning of the F horn.

- *Main Tuning Slide*—Tunes both B♭ and F horn open tones. No separate B♭ tuning slide is required.
- *F Horn Tuning Slide*—Tunes F horn open tones.

Valve Tone Tuning Procedure for Double Horns

Follow these steps to get B♭ and F horns in tune with each other:

1. **Always tune the B♭ horn first.** Tuning the F horn first will throw it out of pitch when the main tuning slide is moved to tune the B♭ side of the horn later. The main tuning slide affects both horns simultaneously.

2. Push tuning slides all the way in.

3. Using the **main tuning slide,** throw the horn into B♭ and tune the open tones of the B♭ horn. You may need to pull the main tuning slide from 1/4" to 1/2" to bring the B♭ horn down to pitch. (The entire horn is purposely built sharp when the main tuning slide is pushed all the way in. So when you pull the main tuning slide and bring the horn down to pitch, the F horn will still be sharp, though the B♭ horn is on pitch.)

4. From the point on, do not touch the main tuning slide.

5. Release the change valve and the horn goes back to F.

6. Pulling the **F tuning slide,** tune the open tones of the F horn. At this point, both the B♭ horn and F horn open tones are in tune.

7. Draw the valve slides **first on the B♭ horn, then on the F horn.** This brings all valve tones into tune.

Denise Root
University of Connecticut
Instructor of Horn

"Through wonderful teaching and dedicated practice, I have attained a level of excellence that enables me to worship with the horn. I am thankful for the opportunity to express my gratitude to Christ and give Him honor through my instrument."

Idiosyncrasies

The horn usually fills out the mid-range texture in most harmonic schemes. The most common challenge of playing the horn is locating the correct pitch, and then staying with it. There is no quick fix for finding correct partials. Practice and experience build the ear and the confidence simultaneously. Duet playing of the soprano and alto lines right out of the hymnal can be of tremendous value in helping to train the ear. A more experienced player on trumpet, flute, or clarinet can be combined in a duo with a less experienced horn player for good effect. Do not forget to transpose—the horn is pitched in F. If reading from a hymnal, one must read the written notes up a fifth (or down a fourth, if ranges are inappropriate), in order to sound concert (hymnal) pitch.

A good bit of training can come from practicing just the open F horn tones on the staff and getting a "feel" for them in the lip. The ear will begin to recognize their connection. Small-group playing is the key to developing good pitch relationship. It is well worth the extra effort of transposing parts (again, hymns work very well) to develop that essential ear and lip coordination.

Endurance can also be a challenge, even for the experienced player. In some cases, horn mouthpiece rims are not much thicker than the edge of a dime.

Constant pressure applied against the teeth to the very sensitive small lip muscles can render the player "noteless" in a relatively short time. Be careful how hard and how long the horn player rehearses the night before a performance. Grace and benevolence on the part of the conductor during rehearsal can greatly increase the chance of a successful onstage performance by the player.

Use and Abuse of the Horn

The horn is at its best when used in the middle of its range (on the staff). The mellow beauty of its tone not only blends with and gives depth to the middle of the ensemble, but also soars in glissando from the bottom to the top of the staff. This technique is often used in church orchestrations. The horn usually finds its place with saxophones, trombones, low clarinets, violas, and celli, and sounds terrific reinforcing the tenor vocal parts. For solo lines, keep the horn primarily in the staff and utilize the two octaves from G (two ledger lines below the treble staff) to the high G (the top space on the treble staff).

Using the horn as the alto or tenor line in a brass quartet is fine. Don't forget that the horn part must be transposed, as it is written for an instrument pitched in F. A simple comparison: when the ensemble plays third line B♭ concert, the horn plays first space F. An amateur player should not be expected to transpose a piece of music by sight. To avoid potential disasters, the part must be transposed and written out.

Care and Maintenance of the Horn

For all its tubing and its unique shape, the horn does not take a lot of maintenance to keep it running correctly.

• Valves should be oiled monthly under the valve caps and then the horn should be turned over and the inner bearing oiled (between the two rubber stoppers or corks).

• The slides should be greased using commercial slide grease, or regular automotive wheel bearing grease.

• A cleaning "snake," specifically made for the trumpet and the horn, should be run through the leadpipe at least once a week.

• Fingerprints should be wiped off the metal with a soft cloth.

• The horn should never be set down on a chair or on the floor, and should always be placed in its case when it is not being held by the player.

Restringing a broken valve string can be very tricky. An easy way to figure this out is to simply look at how the other valves are strung. All horn teachers and most band directors can assist with this process. Stringing starts at the top of the valve lever. One end of the string is knotted and then passed through the hole (use forty pound test braided fishing line, not monofilament). The string is drawn down and passed around the rotor spindle, looped around the small screw at the end of the stop arm, and then passed around the other side of the spindle. The string-end is inserted through the hole at the bottom of the valve lever and wound once around the tightening screw. Before the string set screw is tightened, all the slack should be taken out of the string. However, valve action will be hindered if the string is too tight. A broken string is nothing to be feared. It cannot hurt anything vital.

Purchasing New and Used Instruments

If purchasing a new horn, U.S. made instruments—for example, Conn, King, Holton, Bach, and Yamaha—are preferable. Both the student and professional models have proven themselves to be sturdy, durable, and reliable. They will return the investment many times over if even minimally maintained.

Local newspapers, the Internet, etc., are good sources for locating a used horn. A standard Bb/F double horn is preferable. Patient searching will unearth good deals. Perhaps someone purchased an instrument for his/her child to play in school and now it sits unused in an attic or basement. It is important, however, to inspect the horn closely.

Care must be taken to ensure that the valves are not "frozen" (i.e., will not move up or down), thus incurring an expense from $50 to $150. Horns with major dents (i.e., bell crushed, leadpipe crooked, etc.) should be avoided.

As of this writing, used double horns are available from as low as $400 to $500 with new instruments ranging from $1200 to $1500 and up. The average cost of a new horn as of this writing is about $2000.

Resources

- *An Illustrated Method for French Horn,* by William Robinson (Wind Music, Inc.). The recommended method for beginning players; profusely illustrated with photographs and accompanying texts.
- *Methods for French Horn* (Elementary, Intermediate, Advanced I and II), by Skornika Rubank (Belwin). The famous "Rubank" books progress logically from one level to the next, offering a great variety of scale exercises, etudes, and some very nice duets. Can be used as complete methods or as supplements.
- *Practical Studies for Horn* (Vols. I and II), by Robert Getchell (Belwin Mills). Two books of progressive etudes that explore a variety of keys, rhythms, intervals, and dynamics with pleasant and well-written musical material.
- *Sixty Selected Studies* (Vols. I and II), by C. Kopprasch (Carl Fischer). These etudes, known by many as the primary pedagogical source for horn playing, emphasize both high and low playing and are arranged in a progressive manner. A must for the serious player!
- *The Art of French Horn Playing,* by Philip Farkas (Summy-Birchard). This is the definitive American text on horn playing and is a must on the desk of every music director and serious player. It is well written and carefully conceived, easy to read, and considered by many to be the outstanding resource/reference text for horn playing.

Jeffrey H. Girdler was a member of the United States Navy Band in Washington, D. C. for 30 years. He served as a member of the faculty at The University of Maryland School of Music where he taught French horn and conducted the horn ensemble.

CHAPTER 10

The Trumpet

by Douglas Smith

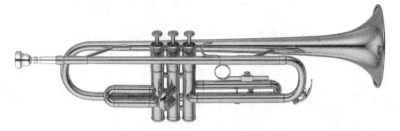

The first record of the trumpet in the Bible is found in the book of Numbers, Chapter 10, where God instructs Moses to make two trumpets for ceremonial use: "And the Lord spake unto Moses, saying, Make thee two trumpets of silver; of a whole piece shalt thou make them: that thou mayest use them for the calling of the assembly, and for the journeying of the camps."

Short History

Early trumpets of the Renaissance, Baroque, and Classical periods were much like the silver tubes of Moses. The closest instrument we have now to those tubes is the valveless bugle on which boy scouts play "Reveille" in the morning and "Taps" at night.

The baroque trumpet, or "clarino," had one distinct melodic advantage over the bugle: the tube was essentially twice as long—bent or wrapped on itself so as to be handled conveniently. Whereas the bugle, in the hands of a capable player, could get 6-8 tones, the natural baroque trumpet could get perhaps twice that number.

Because of the predominance of string instruments in that era, many movements of baroque masterpieces—e.g., Handel's *Messiah*—appear in keys that favor strings. D Major is the favorite key for strings, and so D Major is by far the most common key found in baroque works.

Because of that fact, most of the natural (valveless) trumpets made in the baroque era were built in the key of D Major. If the music called for another key, say C Major, the trumpet player would have to insert a bit of extra tubing, called a "crook," to access the new key.

It was not until the early 19th century that the valve was invented. The two most often given credit for the valve were Saxon Heinrich Stolzel, a horn player in the Berlin Royal Opera Orchestra, and Silesian Friedrich Bluhmel, a relatively undistinguished musician who played in a recreational mine company band. These two took out a 10-year patent for valves in Berlin in 1818. They felt that diverting the sound through extra tubing would certainly compromise such a heroic tone. Beethoven never wrote for chromatic trumpet; neither did Brahms. When Berlioz wrote his *Fantastic Symphony* he had parts for two chromatic cornets, but the trumpets were still natural.

Happily, valves were finally incorporated into trumpet design. Subtle improvements have been made in recent history, but trumpets of the future will probably not differ significantly from those of today.

Making the Sound

To make a sound on a brass instrument—any brass instrument—the player must place the circular, cupped mouthpiece on the lips and buzz through it. It is a very simple process that closely parallels that of speaking or singing. When one uses his or her voice, there are "lips" inside the body known as the vocal folds. When the vocal folds do not come together, the person can still form the words, and the breath coming from the lungs causes a whisper. When the vocal folds come together there is produced a vibration, and consequently a voice.

It is entirely possible to "whisper" through a brass instrument by blowing through the mouthpiece with lips apart. Once the lips are allowed to touch each other inside the mouthpiece, the wind from the lungs sets them in motion producing a vibration, or buzz, and consequently a musical tone.

The mouthpiece of a trumpeter ideally resides on the middle of his or her mouth with roughly half the mouthpiece covering the upper lip and half covering the lower lip. Some players have an irregularity of the teeth which causes the mouthpiece to be slightly off center.

Also, the angle of the trumpet should be maybe 15 to 30 degrees downward from the mouth. The size of the jaw and the angle of the teeth contribute to the vertical angle.

Slight physical deviations from these norms are not a matter of great concern, unless difficulties are encountered making a desirable sound.

There is one condition which may affect trumpet players: the "widow's point." When the mouth is closed, the lips should form a line which is almost completely straight from corner to corner. A person whose upper lip drops down into a point at the middle is best counseled to play an instrument other than trumpet.

Changing the Pitch

In all brass instruments there are two ways of changing the pitch:

1. modify the airstream by muscles of the face and mouth—the embouchure, and

2. change the length of the tubing.

A bugler, or a player of a baroque natural trumpet, cannot change the length of the tubing, so all pitch changes must be made by modifying the airstream. It has long been assumed that such modification is the result of tightening the lips for the high notes and relaxing them for the low.

Research has shown that isometric contraction of the lips does indeed help change the pitch, but there are two other contributors: to ascend in pitch, brass players—without exception—arch their tongues as if whistling a high note. Also, in most instances—and here, there are some exceptions—the bell of the trumpet dips for the high notes and ascends for the low, a technique referred to by Donald S. Reinhardt as the "pivot."

As for changing the length of the tubing, one needs to compare the trumpet with the trombone. When a trombone pulls the slide all the way in, called "first position," the player uses the shortest length of tubing possible; when a trumpet is played "open," the player uses the shortest length of tubing possible.

If a trombone needs to play a half step lower, the player merely pushes his slide out to "second position," and the pitch becomes one-half step lower; when a trumpet needs to play a half step lower, the player presses his second valve, which diverts the air through his shortest slide, and the pitch becomes one-half step lower.

The trombonist's third position is paralleled by the trumpet's first valve slide for a full step; the trombonist's fourth position is paralleled by the trumpet's third slide (or first and second combined), etc., for one and a half steps.

The playing of a chromatic scale results in combining lip control (modifying the airstream) with valve combinations (adjusting the length of the tubing). The mere practicing of a chromatic scale is one of a trumpet player's most valuable exercises.

Intonation

Playing with good intonation is vital for all musical performers, whether they sing or play. With a trumpeter, there is one rule of thumb: "You can't tune a bad tone." If the tone is not clear and characteristic—if the trumpet doesn't sound like a trumpet—it will not be possible to achieve good intonation.

There are two contributing ingredients to intonation: the equipment and the player.

The instrument should be of the highest quality available for an accessible price. Most band and orchestra directors know brand quality. Sometimes they specify brands for their own groups. A professional trumpet teacher would be quick to share ideas of desirable brands, and should be sought as a consultant.

Once the instrument has been secured, maintenance must begin.

The **mouthpiece** is the greatest determiner of tone quality and intonation. It should always be clean. When looking through the mouthpiece backwards—from the shank end—it should be spotless and glistening. If not, a mouthpiece brush, or even a pipe cleaner, should be used to clean it.

One other problem affects a mouthpiece—denting—flattening of the shank end. If it is dropped, and the end slightly flattened, it must be brought back to true round. Most hardware stores have small, inexpensive rounded metal punches that may be inserted ever-so-gently into the end of the mouthpiece and maneuvered to renew the original roundness. Care must be maintained so that the pressure is not so great as to split the metal.

The instrument must be kept clean inside by rinsing out frequently, and scouring by means of a "snake brush." The leadpipe—that stretch of tubing to which the mouthpiece is attached—is the most critical part of a trumpet proper. If only one part can be cleaned, it should be the leader pipe.

Dents in the instrument also affect intonation, and again, the closer the dent is to the mouthpiece, the greater its chance of affecting the tone/intonation. A dent in the bell section has little if any affect on tuning, but a dent in the leader pipe can be quite detrimental.

Temperature of the instrument also affects intonation. "You can't tune a bad tone" can now be joined by another axiom: "You can't tune a cold trumpet."

Ideally the inside of the trumpet should have air at 98.6 degrees before the tuning note is given. If an instrument is tuned at 72 degrees Farenheit—room temperature—the air inside will be warmed by 98.6-degree breath coming from the body of the player. When this happens, the pitch goes sharp—sometimes extremely sharp. So, to avoid a change toward sharpness during a performance, it is necessary to warm the inside air prior to the tuning note.

Most Frequently Used Trumpets

B♭ Trumpet. By far the most common trumpet in use today is that in B♭. Unless a high school player goes to an arts magnet school, or studies with an orchestral player, he will undoubtedly have a B♭ trumpet for a majority of his playing. Even if he does obtain professional guidance, he will still have a B♭ trumpet, along with others below. Nearly 100 percent of parts written for American church use are B♭ trumpet parts.

C Trumpet. The second most common key for a trumpet is C. Most symphonic players use a C trumpet more than any other, because many orchestral parts are in C, and to transpose D, F, E, E♭, etc., parts is more easily done from a C Trumpet than from a B♭.

L–R: Piccolo Trumpet, Fluegelhorn, B♭ Trumpet

A player who brings a C trumpet to church can read directly from the hymnal, or another nontransposed score, and can cover for oboe—usually muted—directly from the part.

D Trumpet. Trumpets in D are used almost exclusively to perform baroque works written in D. Most professionals prefer to use the A Piccolo trumpet below.

E♭ Trumpet. Most often a player will choose an E♭ trumpet to play one of two classical concertos, one by Franz Joseph Haydn, and one by Johann Nepomuk Hummel. Unless one of those two works is scheduled, it would be rare indeed to encounter an E♭ trumpet in church.

Piccolo Trumpet (in B♭ or A). When a person secures a Piccolo trumpet, it most often comes equipped with two leader pipes, a shorter one for B♭ and a longer one for A. Anyone advanced enough to have such an instrument should be advanced enough to know how to use it.

American church orchestra parts sometimes are written in a very high range, and trumpeters often feel that the B♭ Piccolo trumpet helps them reach and control the extremely high range with more confidence than if playing the regular B♭ trumpet. Here the player does not have to change the key, but merely the octave.

The baroque works written in a high tessitura, most often in sharp keys, lend themselves well to the A Piccolo trumpet. For instance, a piece such as "Hallelujah" from Handel's *Messiah,* has a rather high range, key of D Major, and so the player of an A Piccolo trumpet performs it in the rather comfortable key of F Major.

Trumpet Alternates

B♭ Cornet. The silhouette of a B♭ cornet looks as though it is shorter than a trumpet, but the tubing is exactly the same length. If it were not, it could not be a B♭ cornet. The sound—because of a greater proportion of conical tubing—should be slightly less brilliant than that of a trumpet.

For church use, a cornet provides no problems for the minister of music. Hand the cornet player a trumpet part, and think no more about it.

B♭ Fluegelhorn. Anybody who brings a fluegelhorn to rehearsal probably also has a trumpet or cornet. It is also in the key of B♭, and can read any part that a B♭ trumpet or a B♭ cornet can read.

The difference is the sound—a smooth, plaintiff sound which resembles that of a French horn more than a B♭ trumpet. A fluegelhorn may be used as an ensemble instrument, but is used more frequently for solos.

Roles

Aside from the rather obvious use in brass ensembles, bands, or orchestras, there are ways in which one trumpet can contribute to a church service:

Prelude. There are worship leaders who want to begin in a spirit of joy. A trumpet is capable of producing "Reveille" arrangements of familiar hymns or not-so-familiar classics which embody the desired spirit. Others prefer to begin reverently and focus the attention of the people on prayer, Scripture, testimony, or baptism.

Offertory/Meditation. Here the "Taps" personality is usually preferred. Quiet melodies work well, sometimes played on cornet or fluegelhorn, sometimes muted, but always oriented toward encouraging the thoughts and prayers of the people toward God.

Anthem Accompaniment. Many anthems are written with a single trumpet part to interact with, or highlight, the singing of the choir. Some anthems have parts for two or more brass instruments, but can be performed with one trumpeter and an additional keyboard to carry the remaining part(s).

Postlude. Although trumpeters often share an organist's consternation at playing when people's attention is dissipated, the postlude nevertheless provides an opportunity for the "Reveille" style to ring freely with complete abandon.

Congregational Singing. Even though listed last, this is the involvement of greatest importance for a trumpet player. As a pastor from Texas said after a trumpet-infused song service, "Now that I know what a trumpet can do for congregational singing, I will never again be satisfied without one."

With creative instrumentation, the trumpet can inspire and ignite the heart of the worshiper. A trumpet descant can, and the collective expression from the pews is one of sheer ecstasy.

Enhancing the Effectiveness

Let us establish an axiom whereby a trumpeter can be expected to succeed in his church performances:

The administrator, minister of music, or worship leader must provide **music** and a **situation** which makes the trumpeter feel good and sound good.

The **music** should have a conservative range, accessible entry notes, and ample resting spots. It should complement the voices, whether choral obbligatos or congregational descants. It should never compete with important vocal lines.

Fletch Wiley
Visual Muse Productions,
Concert Trumpet Artist

Q: How did you learn to use your instrument as an instrument of worship?

A: "I didn't grow up in the church, so my earliest musical leanings were of self-discovery and personal growth in music. I began playing piano when I was five, and took up the trumpet when I was 10. I loved both jazz and classical music for the trumpet, which led to a very balanced approach to music. It wasn't until I was out of college that I became a Christian, and that caused me to think about not only what I was doing, but for whom I was doing it. Becoming a Christian caused a major attitudinal shift for me, focusing away from myself and onto the lordship of Christ. I think using your gifts to worship is a lifelong discovery process: skill and humility need to walk side by side. We must never shy away from using our gifts, even our virtuosity, to extol the praises of Him who set us free."

The **situation** has several component parts. A trumpeter will need to:
1. see the music well in advance of the service.
2. know specifics of rehearsal, and indicate whether he will be there.
3. have a marked order of service elements.
4. have a comfortable place to sit.
5. have a music stand that works.
6. have a chance prior to the service to tune. (No tuning as the choir rises!)
7. have hymns to play during the service which keeps him warmed up for exposed performances.

The different voices of the trumpet can all be made welcome in our diverse modes of worship. Now to those who play, those who compose, and those who minister through music comes the challenge of making the trumpet one truly effective, worthy voice.

Resources*

International Trumpet Guild, www.trumpetguild.com
A nonprofit organization, founded in 1974, to promote communications among trumpet players around the world and to improve the artistic level of performance, teaching, and literature associated with the trumpet.

Method Books
- *Complete Conservatory Method for Trumpet,* Jean Baptiste Arban, Edited by Edwin Franko Goldman and Walter Smith, Annotated by Claude Gordon (New York: Carl Fischer, Inc., 1982). The Trumpet player's "Bible."
- *Technical Studies for the Cornet,* Herbert L. Clarke (New York: Carl Fischer, Inc., 1984). A standard for all trumpet players. Studies based on scale and chord patterns in all keys.
- *Advanced Lip Flexibilities,* Charles Colin (New York: Charles Colin Publications; 1980). Studies for developing flexibility and range.
- *The Piccolo Trumpet,* David Hickman (Denver: Tromba Publications, 1973). Etudes, duets and orchestral excerpts for piccolo trumpet, with some text explaining the basics.
- *Trumpet Lessons with David Hickman* (Denver: Tromba Publications, 1989). Text and exercises dealing with different aspects of trumpet playing.
  Vol. I, Tone Production
  Vol. II, Embouchure Formation and Warming Up
  Vol. III, Embouchure Development: Power, Endurance, Upper Register
  Vol. IV, Technique: Articulation and Finger Dexterity
  Vol. V, Psychology of Performance
- *The Art of Jazz Trumpet,* John McNeil (Brooklyn, NY: Gerard and Sarzin Publishing Co., 2000). Part one of this book is a history of jazz and its important trumpet players. Different styles are explained. Part two contains jazz exercises. A CD of examples is included.
- *Brass Tactics; Strategies for Modern Trumpet Playing* (1997), and *The Brass Tactics Companion: More Advice from the Real World* (1999), Chase Sanborn (Toronto, Ontario, Canada: Chase Sanborn). Practical infor-

mation about equipment (trumpet, flugelhorn and piccolo) and about how to practice. Lots of practical drills and information about setting up your regular practice routine. www.brasstactics.net

- *Playing Techniques and Performance Studies,* Arturo Sandoval (Milwaukee, WI: Hal Leonard Corp., 1994/5). Three books containing exercises with explanations that cover everything from fundamental trumpet techniques to advanced techniques in classical and jazz trumpet. Each book includes a CD containing examples played by Sandoval.
  Vol. 1, Basic Techniques and Concepts for Developing a Solid Foundation
  Vol. 2, An Extension of Basic Techniques and Playing Concepts
  Vol. 3, Advanced Techniques and Concepts for Trumpet Mastery
- *Daily Drills and Technical Studies for Trumpet,* Max Schlossberg (New York: M. Baron Co., 1965). A standard for all trumpet players. Contains exercises for all aspects of the trumpet.
- *Take the Lead: A Basic Manual for the Lead Trumpet in the Jazz Ensemble,* Dominic Spera (Lebanon, IN: Houston Publishing, Inc.; 1992). Practical information about the responsibilities, duties, and demands of being a lead trumpet player. Includes information about different jazz techniques (falls, etc.) and about different styles.

Publications for Trumpet by Douglas Smith
- *Thine Is the Glory* (Lorenz). Ten solos of medium difficulty with organ (piano) accompaniment taken from a broad spectrum of hymnic literature.
- *Classics for Trumpet and Keyboard* (Lorenz). Thirteen solos in accessible keys with organ (piano) accompaniment from such composers as Bach, Handel, Mouret, Marcello, and Purcell. Each work has a 2nd part for optional duet.
- *61 Trumpet Hymns and Descants,* Volumes 1, 2, and 3 (Hope). A prime resource for the trumpeter involved with congregational singing, including hymn tunes as well as descants, based on harmonies of hymnals in common use.
- *Trumpet Hymns and Fanfares* (Lorenz). Forty-four freely-composed fanfares and hymn embellishments for one, two, or three trumpets, based on harmonies of hymnals in common use.
- *Duets for Trumpet Based on Hymnbook Harmony* (David E. Smith). Twenty-five duets designed to be accompanied by keyboardist playing from hymnals in common use.
- *Hymns and Spirituals: Virtuosic Duets for Trumpet* (Lorenz). Thirteen challenging duets, unaccompanied, based on hymn and spiritual tunes.

Douglas Smith has served as Professor of Instrumental Music at Southern Baptist Theological Seminary since 1975. He holds degrees from Carson-Newman College (B.S.), The University of North Texas (M.M.E.), and the University of Michigan (D.M.A). He has performed with the Knoxville (TN) Symphony, the Waco (TX) Symphony, the Louisville (KY) Symphony, and the American Wind Symphony in Pennsylvania. He served as principal Trumpet with the Fort Worth Symphony from 1969-73. Most of his published music is designed for use in worship.

*Michael Kiefer provided a partial listing of resources for this chapter. Michael holds a B.M. in Instrumental Music Education and a M.M. in Trumpet Performance. He is a freelance arranger, and plays trumpet with the Casas Adobes Baptist Church Orchestra in Tucson, Arizona.

CHAPTER 11

The Trombone

by Douglas Yeo

In his *Treatise on Orchestration,* Hector Berlioz described the trombone in a most colorful and accurate way:

"In my opinion the trombone is the true head of that family of wind instruments that I have named the epic one. It possesses nobility and grandeur to the highest degree; it has all the serious and powerful tones of sublime musical poetry, from religious, calm and imposing accents to savage outbursts. Directed by the will of a master, the trombones can chant like a choir of priests, threaten, utter gloomy sighs, a mournful lament or a bright hymn of glory, they can break forth into awe-inspiring cries and awaken the dead or doom the living with their fearful voices."[1]

Among all brass instruments, it is the trombone alone that has survived a nearly 500-year evolutionary process intact in its original form—an elongated "S" shape. To be sure, refinements to the trombone have been made over the years, but the basic shape and mechanics remain the simplest of all wind instruments: a mouthpiece which accepts air and the vibrations of the lips, a hand slide which lengthens and shortens the column of air inside the instrument, and a bell section which amplifies the sound. Nothing could be simpler.

The Instrument

The basic configuration of the trombone is known as a "straight" trombone—that is, an approximately 12-foot long uninterrupted tube of cylindrical bore brass. While it usually reads bass clef at concert pitch, the trombone, as we most commonly know it today, is frequently referred to as the Bb trombone. The tenor trombone comes in a variety of bore sizes—the bore being the inner diameter of the slide tubing and a common method of gauging a brass instrument's size. A trombone with a .547" bore is the largest tenor trombone made, favored by many professional symphony and band players. The slightly smaller .525" instrument is favored by many jazz and commercial players, while the still smaller bored .500" instrument is the one with which most beginners (and some jazz artists) utilize. Valve trombones were greatly in favor in Europe in the 1800s and they enjoyed a brief period of success in America. However, apart from some jazz players and those who switch to trombone from other valved instruments, the valve trombone is rarely seen in the hands of players today.

To the "straight" trombone can be added a valve to the bell section, operated by the left thumb, which has the effect of adding enough additional tubing to the instrument to lower its pitch by a fourth to F (often referred to as an "F attachment" or "trigger" trombone). Bass trombones, which have a bore of .563", always have one such F valve and often come configured with a second valve, further lowering the pitch to Eb or D.

Trombone mouthpieces come in myriad sizes but with two distinct shank sizes. A large shank mouthpiece (typically for large bore tenor and bass trombones) cannot fit in a trombone slide designed for a small shank mouthpiece. However, a small shank mouthpiece may be put into a larger trombone slide by way of a small sleeve adaptor.

Mechanics of Sound Production

The trombone employs the same basic principle of all brass wind instruments in determining pitch—that is a column of air is lengthened and shortened (in the case of the trombone, by the hand slide), combined with varying tension of the embouchure (mouth and lip muscles). There are seven basic slide positions on the trombone beginning with a fundamental of Bb in first position. The overtone series caused by movement of the lip creates upwards of eight distinct pitches in each position, thereby giving the trombone an extensive range. (See slide position chart below.) When the F or Eb/D attachments are added to a tenor or bass trombone, activation of additional tubing with the left hand by way of a rotary valve creates more pitch options. When

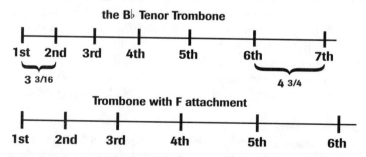

Notice that the positions get slightly longer as the slide expands.
Also, notice that a position is lost once the F-trigger is depressed.

utilizing the F attachment valve, the trombone has only six positions, and with two valves, only five positions are possible. It must be kept in mind, however, that the positions of the trombone, which are unmarked on the slide (like the finger board of a violin, rather than the frets of a guitar), are a mere guideline since, depending on a note's position in the overtone series, a note in a given position may need to be sharped or flatted a bit to play it perfectly in tune. The human ear is the best slide chart.

Embouchure

The word "embouchure" is used to refer to both the muscles of the lips and mouth which form to produce the "buzz" required to make a sound in the trombone, and to refer to the actual placement of the mouthpiece on the lips.

As regards mouthpiece placement, most players quickly find a spot where the mouthpiece fits comfortably and a good tone can be produced. Players are about equally divided as to whether the upper and lower lip are equally on the mouthpiece—those who have more upper than lower, and those who have more lower than upper lip on the mouthpiece. There is no "correct" way, as successful players have all three mouthpiece placements. It is important, however, to be sure that the mouthpiece is not placed either so high or low on the lips that the rim actually rests squarely on the edge of the pink of the lip and the beginning of the skin; such a placement is simply too high or low to allow good tone production.

Many factors combine to lead a player to choose a particular mouthpiece placement, the most significant being dental structure. Players with an overbite, or with protruding teeth may exhibit an unusual mouthpiece placement (as may also be the case with players having braces), but it is most important that the player simply place the mouthpiece where it feels most comfortable. Many misguided teachers, under the impression that there is a "correct" mouthpiece placement, have attempted to change the embouchure of a player who, despite a somewhat unconventional mouthpiece placement, is able to play quite well. An embouchure change is a radical event and should only be undertaken with the guidance of a professional teacher who is able to work with the student on a long-term basis to help him through the change.

When playing, the muscles of the embouchure should be both firm and relaxed, with the corners of the lips taking on a firm feeling as if one is making a facial expression showing disgust. Firm corners, but supple and relaxed pink of the lip in the mouthpiece, will help the tone to be steady and the quality of sound to be good.

Tonguing

To the uninitiated, the thought of playing in a legato style on the trombone would seem to be an oxymoron: how can an instrument with a moving slide connect notes smoothly without having glissando or "smearing" between the notes?

The key, of course, is good tongue/slide coordination. In this, the trombonist is no different than a valved brass player who needs good tongue/valve coordination, except the consequence of not getting it quite right on the trombone is usually a glissando; whereas on a valve instrument, the note will not sound on time but will "break."

To execute successful legato on trombone, attention must first be paid to the slide arm motion. Players should understand that articulation on the trombone is done with the tongue and air, not with the slide. Hence, a hard, jerky slide motion accomplishes nothing other than encouraging body tension. A swift, fluid slide motion in all kinds of playing—whether legato or detached—will help the player keep this important concept in mind.

With the relaxed slide arm motion comes the delivery of the air, which must be thought of as being constant and uninterrupted. In contrast to detached playing, when the tongue syllable "tah" (or, to encourage a more relaxed tongue and more open sound, a "toh" syllable) may be employed to separate the notes, in legato playing, the tongue should not be thought of as something which actually stops the air but, rather, gently touches the airstream in order to allow time to move the slide to the next note. A tonguing syllable such as "dah" or "doh," whereby the tongue does not pull back quickly from the teeth but instead gently falls from the roof of the mouth, will give the desired connected effect. A player can first learn this tonguing concept while playing a string of slow quarter notes of a single pitch in one position, say middle F. Understanding the concept of keeping the air continuous while delivering a soft tonguing syllable—and avoiding any hint of bulging, "football shaped" notes—is the first step toward execution of a successful legato.

Once having understood this concept, it leaves to the player only to quickly and smoothly move the slide from one note to another, exactly coordinating the touch of the tongue in the production of "dah" or "doh" with the movement of the slide. Beginning with playing two notes a half step apart and gradually increasing the interval, the player can employ these techniques and create a smooth legato. Players should always keep in mind that in legato (indeed, in ALL) playing, it is the phrase which is to be shaped, not individual notes.

Advanced players will know that there are many ways to play smoothly between notes. Not only can the tongue produce a smooth legato, but depending on the pitches involved, "natural" slurs (that is, moving between notes which are in different partials of the harmonic series), valve slurs, and even attacks made without tongue at all (so called "air attacks") can all be part of the legato articulative palate.

Hand Position

The greatest impediment which keeps instrumentalists from achieving a good sound and successful technique is body tension. Clearly, tension in one part of the body can manifest itself as a problem in another, as muscles are interdependent. In holding the trombone, each hand/arm has unique tension issues which should be understood so a player can approach the instrument in a natural and comfortable way.

The left hand supports the weight of the trombone and does so with a hand position not unlike that of a person simulating with his hand a track meet official holding the starting gun. The thumb goes around the bell brace (or rests on the F attachment valve paddle) while the index finger rests against the mouthpiece. Having said this, care should be taken not to squeeze the trombone between the thumb and index finger; rather, the set screw which holds the bell and slide section together should rest comfortably on the butt of the left hand and a minimum of force should be used to keep the horn from slipping out of the hand.

The remaining three fingers customarily curl around the hand slide brace; however, players may discover that this results in a tense and unnatural "crunch" for those fingers. This "crunch" results in three fingers being jammed in a very small space which can often lead to a painful pinch of the flesh of the hand when the slide is moved quickly into first position. A solution to this is to have the third and fourth fingers straddle the hand slide brace, having only two fingers on the lower side. This hand position has the effect of loosening the tension on the hand and giving more overall relaxation to the grip.

The right hand should grasp the slide in a relaxed manner, as well. As has been mentioned in the discussion of tonguing, slide motion has nothing to do with articulation. A smooth right arm/hand motion in all styles of playing is essential. It must also be kept in mind that there are many body "hinges" which relate to the slide movement–the shoulder, the elbow, the wrist, the hand, and the fingers. A smooth slide motion is predicated upon using the fewest hinges necessary, beginning with those closest to the slide itself. Therefore, when moving the slide one or two positions, movement of the fingertips or wrist is usually enough, whereas longer movement between positions will utilize the elbow and perhaps shoulder, as well. The player should hold the slide in a comfortable and natural way. This natural position can be found by letting the right arm hang at one's side, and then simply bending the elbow until the forearm is parallel to the floor. One will see that his hand and wrist is neither perfectly horizontal nor per-

Traditional "strained" left-hand grip

"Relaxed" left-hand grip

pendicular to the ground. The hand has a natural curl to it and can then be brought to the slide. Holding the slide with the bottom slide tube coming between the third and fourth fingers (which act like a scissor) and the thumb and second and third fingers gently holding the hand brace will allow for the fingertips and wrist to move the slide in a very relaxed manner. Again, tension in the way a player holds the slide will always get in the way of an easy and relaxed slide technique and sound, so care should be given to avoid tension at all times.

Problems and Solutions

An understanding of the trombone requires a discussion of some handicaps the instrument brings to the player so the teacher or conductor can assist in developing creative solutions and strategies.

1. Size. As mentioned earlier, the B♭ trombone, regardless of bore size, is essentially a 12-foot long tube of brass which doubles back on itself twice. (In fact, the French word for "paper clip" is "trombone"—an apt description if there ever was one.) The hand slide has seven basic positions that can be related to the seven different combinations of open and closed valves on other three-valved brasses (trumpet, cornet, horn, baritone, euphonium, and tuba). While the valved brasses do not require the player to move anything but his fingers, the trombonist, in order to reach seventh position, must move the slide nearly three feet. To many young players, this is simply not possible. The immediate frustration of attempting to play an instrument on which one cannot play a full chromatic scale because the outer slide positions cannot be reached cannot be overstated.

Solution: Young players may experience frustration when they cannot reach the outer slide positions (5th, 6th and 7th positions). It may be advised to wait until a player has reached the middle school years and he can accurately and quickly reach all seven positions before seating him in an orchestra which requires reading music with the full chromatic range. A slide "extension" is marketed which can attach to the outer slide brace and thereby give a player some extra reach to the outer positions. Some teachers start students on an F attachment tenor trombone, which allows the playing of the notes in outer positions on inner positions.

2. Mechanical Issues. In order to function properly, the trombone slide must be able to move freely, a process helped by the application of a small amount of slide creme to the bottom of the inner tubes (known as the "stocking") while water is sprayed on the slide, causing the water to interact with the creme, forming a well-lubricated surface. Various applications are available including those made by all instrument companies, as well as Slide-O-Mix, Trombontine, and SuperSlick, all of which are a variation of simple facial creme or silicone and soap. Problems arise, however, when a dent occurs in the slide along the outer tube. Dents of even a small size can cause the slide to "stick" and not move smoothly; the more serious or numerous the dents, the more difficult moving the slide becomes. Since the trombone is the only wind instrument that takes up a large amount of varying space when it is played, accidents happen frequently as the slide bangs into chairs, stands, and the bodies of fellow players who have the misfortune to sit in front of the impish trombonist.

Solution: Various companies make slide protectors consisting of a tube of clear, lightweight plastic that may cover the outer slide tubes of the trombone. These protectors add negligible weight to the slide, but can bear the brunt of contact with a chair or stand that otherwise would create a slide-damaging dent. There is, however, no substitute for a player being careful with his

instrument. A player should never leave the instrument unattended on a chair or on a trombone stand. It is also helpful if, when configuring an orchestra set-up plan, consideration were given to the trombonists' slide in the same way one would give string players a little extra room so they can bow freely.

3. Clef. The trombone was conceived as a nontransposing instrument. In its early years, trombones read music corresponding to the type of instrument—the alto trombone reading alto clef, the tenor trombone reading tenor clef, and the bass trombone reading bass clef. Today, in orchestra and wind band music, bass clef is used primarily in trombone parts, although it is still necessary for the advanced player to master the alto and tenor clefs for repertoire that calls for them.

Solution: The flexibility of a trombone player being able to read tenor and treble clef (including the B♭ treble clef transposition) cannot be overstated. While most church orchestra music will be written in bass clef, a trombonist who reads other clefs can "pinch hit" for a cello or trumpet if he or she reads other clefs.

Care and Maintenance of the Trombone

Whether new or used, a trombone needs particular care, and the player should understand that with some regular maintenance, the instrument would serve him well for many years.

The trombone slide should be removed from the case first, always ensuring that the slide "lock" is securely fastened first. The mouthpiece may then be inserted into the slide and the bell section fastened to the slide receiver and the securing nut fastened tightly. It is recommended that the young trombonist secure the bottom of the slide on the floor before attaching the bell.

There are only two moving parts on the straight tenor trombone—the hand slide and the tuning slide. Each is lubricated in different ways.

As previously mentioned, the hand slide should be lubricated with any of a number of slide cream products. All slide cream products use as their base a substance not unlike unscented facial creme which produces a light coating on the slide onto which water is sprayed from a small hand-spray bottle which causes the water to bead up on the creme and create a smooth interaction between the inner and outer slides.

After taking the outer slide off and wiping off the inner slide with a clean, dry cloth, use only a tiny bit of slide creme, less than half of the smallest fingernail, for both inner slide tubes. Rub the creme evenly onto the whole length of the stocking and then spray water on the entire inner slide. Replace the outer slide and spray water again and regularly as needed. This procedure will keep the slide running smoothly for a few days after which the inner slide should be wiped down and the process repeated.

Many trombones come equipped with oil for use on the slide—this is NOT recommended as a lubricant. Oil is messy and less effective than slide creme and water.

The tuning slide should be lubricated with a thick grease; some players recommend using a lanolin-based product, but as it is not heat stable and tends to break down quickly, many players use a silicone-based grease, available from local scientific supply houses. Grease designed for high vacuum situations is colorless, odorless, heat and cold stable, and does not wear down easily; it is ideally suited for trombone tuning slides.

For bass trombones and tenor trombones equipped with an F attachment, the rotary valves in the bell section should be lubricated with valve oil every few days. Remove the bell section tuning slides and pour some oil into the valves while vigorously moving the valve triggers. A few drops of oil on the valve spindle and on the rotor under the valve cap are also recommended. The linkage between the valve and the trigger mechanism can sometimes be noisy, and since there are so many kinds of linkages, general care guidelines cannot be given. Most have some kind of "ball and socket" mechanism that can be silenced by sensitive adjustment of the various set and retaining screws and nuts, or by putting some valve oil or slightly heavier woodwind key oil in the ball joints. However, NEVER put key oil or silicone lubricant on the valve itself!

It should go without saying that a player should never play his trombone without first cleaning his teeth. Every few weeks the entire trombone should be cleaned thoroughly. The mouthpiece may be washed with water and dish detergent, and scrubbed with a mouthpiece cleaning brush, available at any local music shop.

To clean the bell and slide, run some warm (not hot) water in the bathtub with common liquid dish detergent and put the inner slide, outer slide and bell section into the tub (one at a time); allow them to soak for a few minutes. Purchase a trombone cleaning "snake" (a four- to six-foot long flexible piece of metal which is sheathed in plastic with a small brush on either end) at a music shop. Run the snake through the tubing several times and then thoroughly rinse and dry the instrument with a clean cloth. After drying, lubricate the tuning and hand slides and the valves.

There should never be a need to polish the instrument except to periodically rub off any water spots that may accumulate. Most brass instruments are lacquered and, as such, do not need polishing; in fact, using a brass polish on a lacquered instrument could strip the lacquer and mar the finish. Silver-plated instruments should require no more than a periodic rubdown with a silver polishing cloth.

Writing for the Trombone

Composers and arrangers would do well to keep in mind the following when scoring for the trombone:

1. The trombone often is scored to play the tenor line in hymn-like compositions. However, extended playing above middle C can be very tiring. Provide periods of rest for trombone players when they are scored above the bass clef staff, or allow them periodic passages into the lower register to provide some rest.

2. The glissando is an effect that can be uniquely executed by trombonists among brass instruments. However, a true glissando can only be played between two notes on the same "partial" of the harmonic series. Writing a glissando that requires a "break" in the harmonic series usually leads to head scratching on the part of the player. Any advanced player with a thorough knowledge of alternate positions can provide advice as to what glissandi are appropriate.

3. Most trombonists are comfortable using a straight and cup mute. A trombone section will give best results if all of the mutes are matched (that is, all mutes be made of metal, or fiberglass, or cardboard). Bucket mutes for trombones are heavy, expensive, and unwieldy. "Waa-waa" mutes can deliver colorful effects, but care must be taken not to write notes for trombone which require use of the F attachment (operated by the left hand) at the same time a player is required to hold and operate a "waa-waa" mute (also held by the left hand).

4. Competent players do not have difficulty executing rapid technical passages in 16th notes up to quarter note = 90. For faster tempi, double tonguing may be required of the player with a corresponding diminution in clarity among players who do not keep up their skills with practice every day. Rapid changes in the direction the slide moves can be awkward and should be avoided if possible.

5. There is a difference between writing a "3rd Trombone" and a "Bass Trombone" part. If the orchestra has a bass trombone player, give him parts that utilize the low range of his instrument (down to pedal B♭). A bored bass trombonist may begin taking his part down an octave that will disturb the orchestration and balance; this "freelancing" on the part of the player can be short-circuited with an interesting part that includes judicious writing in the low register.

6. While often relegated to harmonic functions in the orchestra, the trombone can be an effective solo instrument as its range closely mirrors that of the human voice. Berlioz was not alone in recognizing that the trombone was unique among brass instruments in its ability to express a wide range of emotions. Trombones blend well with horns and tuba and the bass trombone can double the bass line or play with the celli or bassoons.

Recommended Instruments

When asked which trombone is "best," the only proper answer is that the best instrument for any given player is the one that suits him. There are many fine manufacturers of trombones including Yamaha, Bach, Conn, King, Benge and others. At the time of this writing, new beginner instruments (small bore straight tenor trombone) can be purchased from around $400

while professional large bore tenor trombones
can go for upwards of $2000 and bass trom-
bones up to $3000. Custom trombone makers
like Edwards and Shires make instruments that
can cost even more. A used instrument can
often be found for sale at a considerable discount off the price for a new instrument and
assuming it is in good working order, can be
quite serviceable. When selecting an instrument,
consider the quality of craftsmanship (Does the
slide work smoothly? Do the valves work easily?
Does the horn have a comfortable "feel" in the
hands? Are the braces solid and secure? Do the
tuning slides move easily?), the response when
playing (articulated playing, slurs, loud playing,
soft playing), and whether it is from a reputable
company which will stand by its work. In recent
years, the instrument market has been flooded
with poor quality instruments that bear tricky brand names which are
designed to make consumers think they are buying an established name
brand instrument. Avoid them!

Resources for Trombone

The following materials are among the most standard study and performance materials for both tenor and bass trombonists. A sensible practice reg-
imen should include warm-up studies (including long tones, flexibility, and
articulation exercises), lyrical studies, technical studies, and solo playing. For
occasional players who may not have time to practice an hour or more each
day, it cannot be emphasized enough that even a few minutes a day spent
playing an instrument will reap great benefits.

There are many group method books for beginning players, all of which
stress the fundamentals of reading music and basic slide position literacy.
Study of piano is always a valuable tool to the instrumental musician, and a
rudimentary knowledge of music theory is also helpful. This list is by no
means comprehensive, but is intended to give a starting point for materials
for players of all abilities.

Method Books
- *Warm Up Exercises,* Emory Remington/ed., Donald Hunsberger (Accura
  Music). Sensible warm-up studies by the legendary teacher at the
  Eastman School of Music.
- *Mastering the Trombone,* Edward Kleinhammer and Douglas Yeo (EMKO
  Publications–www.yeodoug.com). A systematic discussion of all aspects of
  trombone playing with text and exercises.
- *Intermediate Method,* Brian Kay (www.apollobrass.com). One of the best
  progressive methods for the intermediate player.

- *Method for Bass Trombone and F Attachment Tenor Trombone,* Alan Ostrander (Carl Fischer). An excellent introduction to the use of the F attachment for tenor and bass trombone players.

Etudes and Studies
- *Melodious Etudes for Trombone, Volumes 1, 2, 3,* Joannes Rochut/Marco Bordogni (Carl Fischer)
- *Studies for Trombone, Volumes 1, 2,* Kopprasch (International Music)
- *40 Progressive Studies,* H. W. Tyrrell (Boosey & Hawkes)
- *24 Studies for Bass Trombone or Trombone with F Attachment,* Boris Grigoriev/ed., Alan Ostrander (International Music)
- *Advanced Studies for B♭ Bass (or Bass Trombone),* H. W. Tyrrell (Boosey & Hawkes)
- *36 Studies for Trombone with F Attachment,* O. Blume/ed. Reginald Fink (Carl Fischer)

Solo Collections
- *First Solos for the Trombone Player,* Henry Charles Smith (G. Schirmer)
- *Solos for the Trombone Player,* Henry Charles Smith (G. Schirmer)
- *Trombone Essentials,* Douglas Yeo (G. Schirmer)

Trombone Related Internet Resources
- Douglas Yeo Trombone Web Site, http://www.yeodoug.com
  (250 pages of articles, FAQ, resources, Christian testimony, etc.)
- The OnLine Trombone Journal, http://www.trombone.org
  (The premiere web-based trombone magazine with articles, interviews, reviews, used instrument classifieds, etc.)

[1]Berlioz, Hector (enlarged and revised by Richard Strauss), English translation by Theodore Front, *Treatise on Instrumentation* (Edwin F. Kalmus, 1948), 302.

Douglas Yeo is Bass Trombonist of the Boston Symphony Orchestra and Music Director of the New England Brass Band. He maintains an award winning web site at www.yeodoug.com; his critically acclaimed solo recordings include *Cornerstone, Proclamation,* and *Take 1.*

CHAPTER 12

The Euphonium and Baritone Horn

by Gerald P. Armstrong

The euphonium and its cousin, the baritone horn, are perhaps the most versatile of the brass instruments. There are important similarities and differences between the instruments, factors that will impact the information provided under "Responsibilities of the Church Instrumental Director." An examination of these similarities and differences introduces the considerations of this chapter.

Characteristics Common to Both Instruments

• Both sound in the same octave as the trombone, one octave below the trumpet, and one octave above the tuba.

• Like the trombone and B♭ trumpet, both are considered to be B♭ instruments, which simply means when the euphonium or baritone horn sounds without any valve being depressed, the overtone series of B♭ is produced. There are those who consider it a C instrument since it sounds concert pitch.

• They produce sound when the lips buzz while the instrumentalist blows a focused air column into the mouthpiece of the instrument.
• A practical range for both instruments when played by capable amateurs is from E (first line below the bass clef) to G (third line above the bass clef), but competent performers will play B♭ (fourth line above the bass clef) and higher.
• Both can have either three or four valves, but it is more common for baritone horns to have three valves and euphoniums to have four valves. When the fourth valve is added, the range is extended down a fourth and, in essence, the B♭ instrument becomes an F instrument.
• A unique quality of these instruments is that they are both transposing and nontransposing, capable of playing either treble clef or bass clef scores.

Differences Between Euphoniums and Baritone Horns
• The defining difference is that a euphonium has a larger bore (tubing size) than a baritone horn and, in general, a higher percentage of conical tubing (bore).
• Although most contemporary baritone horns have three valves played with the right hand, there are "three plus one" instruments that have an additional piston valve played with the index finger of the left hand. Some euphoniums have four piston valves, played with the right hand, but these are exceptions.
• Mouthpieces for the two instruments vary principally by bore size, with the euphonium using a larger mouthpiece.

Responsibilities of the Church Instrumental Director to the Euphonium Player
As regards many of the problems relating to instruments and instrumentalists, the church instrumental director should seek (or have the instrumentalist seek) the advice of a teaching professional. Public and private school directors, college instructors, and private lesson teachers are available for counsel in most communities. There are, however, emergency problems that can be solved easily. Many potential problems can be avoided with knowledgeable care. In addition to being an easy-to-follow conductor, the church instrumental director can enhance the ministry of the euphonium (baritone horn) player by understanding and performing certain other responsibilities.

Music (parts) assignment will affect the sound of the church instrumental ensemble (orchestra) and the attitude of the euphonium player. Most euphonium players learned to play in school bands where the instrument frequently plays melody or interesting countermelody, with limited duty playing rhythmic and harmonic "fill" parts. Many of the current church orchestra arrangements utilize euphonium to double Trombone II parts, which consist principally of "fill" with few opportunities to play melody. The director may need motivational skills to help former band players accept the Christian servant role of playing low profile parts.

When playing from a treble clef part, the euphonium/baritone horn is a transposing instrument, with fingering of a three-valve instrument being the same as B♭ trumpet. The written notes are transposed a major ninth higher than the desired "concert pitch" (e.g. the pitch of B♭ is written as C on the treble clef part).

When assigning treble clef parts, there is the temptation for the uninitiated director to simply "give the baritone player something to play to keep him happy" if a treble clef baritone part is not provided.

• The treble clef player may be willing, even eager, to play a B♭ trumpet part, but the director must anticipate the sound of that trumpet part being doubled one octave lower. The sound produced might actually invert chords by requiring the baritone to play lower than the tuba.

• Most church orchestra arrangements provide a tenor sax/baritone part because both are treble clef instruments in B♭ sounding in the same range. It is important to note that "doubles Trombone II" is frequently written on the part.

• The treble clef part provided for B♭ bass clarinet is also playable by baritone horn and there may be occasions when the baritone might substitute most capably for bass clarinet, particularly if a strong melody is required, but the baritone sound may not blend into a woodwind passage in either quality or quantity, and the range may extend below that of the baritone.

The bass clef player is playing a non-transposed part (B♭ is written B♭) and has the option of playing parts for euphonium/baritone, trombone, bassoon, cello, and, with limitations, tuba or even French horn (when the part is transposed). The same guidelines given for utilizing B♭ bass clarinet parts on euphonium also apply to the bassoon of the woodwind family and to the cello of the string family. Most church ensembles have few, if any, celli, and a euphonium can usually perform cello solo passages, depending upon the range and articulation required. The fullness of tone makes the euphonium a good performer of Trombone III parts, but a strong player will probably resent playing only in the lower register of the instrument. When played in the upper registers by a capable player, the euphonium has a timbre not unlike the French horn, and the instruments blend well. A lower French horn part (in F, treble clef) could be transcribed for euphonium playing in the upper register.

When a euphonium player is asked to play the tuba part, it is an assignment for which the instrument is inadequate, even if the player is willing. The lower register of the euphonium is the most difficult to project, and it still sounds an octave higher than the arranger desired when the part was conceived for tuba. An exception would be a part indicating "Baritone/Tuba," written in octaves. In theory, the fourth valve permits the euphonium to descend chromatically from the lowest E on down to the pedal note B♭, which would permit upper tuba notes to be played on a euphonium at the desired pitch. In fact, this will not occur with acceptable tone quality or intonation, unless a quality player is performing on a more expensive instrument possessing a "compensating" system.

The euphonium or baritone horn has a darker and more mellow tone than the tenor trombone because of the larger bore of its tubing, which is more akin to the bore size of the bass trombone. Even so, the blend of euphonium and trombone playing together is quite comfortable. Because it has less air column resistance than the trombone, marcato attacks are more difficult on the euphonium. The director will need to give special rehearsal attention to accented passages to ensure precise articulation. On the other hand, music passages requiring speed and agility are more easily articulated on instruments having valves.

The seating placement of the euphonium/baritone horn in the ensemble will affect the balance of sound, especially if some instruments are being amplified. Careful attention should be given to the direction the sound emanates from the bell. Also, to be discussed under "Care and Maintenance" is the ever-present potential for damaging instruments in a crowded performance area.

Inexperienced players will need more attention from the director than "veterans." A fingering chart for B♭ trumpet (for treble clef baritone horn) and a euphonium-fingering chart showing four-valve fingering in bass clef should be available when assistance is needed. The director should listen for air escaping from faulty water keys, sticky or noisy valves, and faulty intonation—things that might not be significant to inexperienced players.

The director must continually encourage good tone production. Insist upon good posture. Remind euphonium players to breathe deeply, support the air column with abdominal and back muscles, feel an open throat, avoid excessive pressure of the mouthpiece against the lips ("pressing" is often the result of too-long rehearsal or too-high parts), keep the facial muscles firm without tensing (avoid puffy cheeks), use a sufficiently long and quick stroke of the tongue saying "tee," "tah," or "tu" for accents and a less energized "dee," "dah," or "du" for legato playing. And, above all, listen and emulate good tone. A damaged or badly worn mouthpiece and dented tubing are deterrents to good tone and intonation.

Tuning the Instruments

The instrument must be warmed to body temperature before tuning. The instrument should not be kept in any environment that will overheat or overcool it prior to playing.

The player's embouchure must be warmed up prior to tuning. This includes breath support that must be exercised through warm-up playing, using correct playing posture.

Basic tuning of the euphonium or baritone horn is to B♭, called "B♭ concert," second line of the bass clef (C, first line below the treble clef), using the primary tuning slide of the instrument. B♭ concert, one octave higher, should also be used in basic tuning. The use of electronic tuners is valid, but a tuning device should be used only to help develop the player's listening skills. Some players purchase their own tuners, which fit easily into the instrument case. Like B♭ concert, F (fourth line of the bass clef) is fingered open (no valves depressed) and makes a good secondary pitch to check while tuning.

The F attachment of the euphonium (or baritone horn), fourth valve tubing, must also be tuned. There is a moveable slide on this attachment for this purpose. Tune on F, first space below the bass clef, while depressing only the fourth valve. On most euphoniums, a secondary tuning check may be made by playing F, fourth line of the bass clef, in open valve position and then while depressing only the fourth valve. Although the timbre will change, the pitch should remain constant.

Problem notes on three-valve instrument, for the most part, involve the third valve, with these fingerings being sharp in pitch. The worst culprits are C concert (second space in bass clef or first line below treble clef) fingered 1-2-3, F concert (first space below the bass clef or third space below the treble clef) fingered 1-3, and E concert (just below) fingered 1-2-3. Pulling out the slide on the third valve will lower the pitch on these problem pitches, but, because they vary in "sharpness," it is not a panacea.

Using the fourth valve greatly alleviates third-valve pitch problems. Depressing only the fourth valve is an immediate substitute for the valves 1-3 combination. The problem of sharpness involving valves 1-2-3 is virtually solved by using the valves 2-4 combination. Be sure to pull the fourth-valve tuning slide to the best-compromised setting for both notes.

"Lipping up or down," adjusting the embouchure (mainly the lips and jaw while blowing a focused air column), is essential to good intonation on a valve instrument, no matter the pitch being played. Be prepared to "favor" pitches for best intonation.

Mouthpieces

Mouthpieces vary in design, and the design affects the tone and response of the instrument. The bore size of the mouthpiece stem must properly match the insert (lead) tube of the instrument. The rim or lip cushion should be comfortable to the player's teeth and lips. The cup depth will greatly determine the richness of the tone produced, and a deeper cup is preferred for euphonium or baritone. The cup shape recommended is concave rather than "vee." A quality new instrument will be provided with a good mouthpiece, but an experienced player may wish to "customize" to his/her embouchure and playing needs. It should be noted that an excessively deep cup increases the difficulty of articulating rapidly, of playing accents, and of playing in the upper register.

The mouthpiece plating will wear off in time and mouthpieces nick easily when dropped. A worn place or even a tiny indentation on the rim can make the embouchure uncomfortable.

Obtaining Instruments

High school euphonium players are usually supplied an instrument, resulting in a ready supply of players for church ensembles who don't own instruments.

The church music director can appeal to the congregation for instruments stored in closets and attics. An instrument repairperson can give an estimate on the cost of restoring discovered treasures to varying degrees of condition. Get written estimates.

Local music stores that cater to school bands and orchestras are a source of instruments with the obvious advantages of purchasing locally. The disadvantage is that few local dealers can match the discounted prices offered by businesses that deal nationwide. National franchises offer discount prices in local stores in major cities.

"Mail order" discount stores usually offer the most competitive prices. See the resources section at the end of this chapter for suggested dealers. The listing is not intended to be exclusive, only representative.

Care of the Instrument

Piston valves become noisy when pads, corks (if applicable), or valve springs need replacing. Take sample parts to the instrument shop when purchasing replacements.

Piston valves responding sluggishly need valve oil or possible new valve springs.

Rotary valves need oil and occasional replacement of valve cords (strings).

Replacement of water (saliva) release valve springs and corks (commonly called "spit keys") is an infrequent necessity. Noticeable air loss or water-oil spots on clothing will indicate that this maintenance is past due.

Cleaning a euphonium involves putting a large instrument in harm's way. Careful preparation of the cleaning area is critical to avoid damage to or loss of parts.

The most fragile parts of the instrument are the valves, which should be removed for a complete cleansing. Avoid the unthinkable: dropping a valve on a hard surface. A carpet, throw rug or even a large towel can prevent this calamity. As each valve is removed, take apart the valve, setting aside the pads and corks, if applicable, on a clean, dry surface or in a container. The valves can be set aside for washing.

Fill a bathtub with enough water to partially cover the instrument. A rubber mat or a large towel should be placed under the instrument to avoid damage to the instrument or to the porcelain finish of the tub. Add 1/8 cup or more of dishwashing detergent to the water and stir. Do not use abrasives. Remove the slides and carefully place the horn, the slides, and then the valves in the mixture to soak.

A trombone cleaning brush, available in instrument stores, is a good cleaning device to scrub the tube interiors. An old toothbrush effectively cleans valves. A soft cloth will clean the exterior.

Rinse and carefully dry all metal parts, placing them on a soft surface. Shake water out of valve cavities.

Lightly coat all slides with cork grease, Vaseline, or a similar lubricant before reinserting into the horn.

Reassemble the valves, replacing pads and corks or cords as needed. Each valve will have a valve number stamped on top to ensure reinsertion into the corresponding tube on the instrument. Oil thoroughly, but not excessively, with valve oil before reinserting valves into the horn.

Check the corks and springs of water release keys.

Play the instrument as a final check.

A crowded orchestra pit is the normal environment for church ensembles, providing ample opportunity for instrument collisions. The euphonium, because of its sturdy construction, usually gets the better of accidents under these circumstances, raising the responsibility of the euphonium player to avoid bumping other instruments. However, the tubing of a euphonium will also dent, resulting in altered tone and intonation. A good steward will want to maintain the beauty of his or her instrument's appearance.

Resources
Practice Method Books

The director should help the treble clef player realize that his or her options for parts to play are broadened when the player also reads bass clef. Most treble clef players could teach themselves to play bass clef using an elementary bass clef method that provides euphonium fingerings. Any euphonium player, youth or adult, who aspires to musical improvement should be encouraged to study with a private lesson instructor who will recommend study methods appropriate to the player/student.

Treble clef players can play from method books for B♭ trumpet or baritone horn treble clef. Space limitations prohibit detailed descriptions of method books, but the following are designed for ensemble or individual instruction:

- *Essential Technique* (Baritone TC), Rhodes/arr. Bierschenk/Lautzen (Hal Leonard Corporation)
- *Master Method, Books 1, 2, 3* (Baritone TC), Peters (Neil A. Kjos Music Company)
- *Medalist Band Method Books 1, 2, 3* (Baritone TC), Ployhar (Warner Brothers Music Publishers)
- *Technique Through Performance* (Baritone TC), Erickson (Alfred Publishing Co., Inc.)
- *Tone and Technique* (Baritone TC), Ployhar/arr. Zepp (Warner Brothers Music Publishers)
- *Visual Band Method 1* (Baritone TC), Niehaus/arr. Liedig (Alfred Publishing Co., Inc.)

The methods for B♭ trumpet listed below have proven successful in developing professional teachers and players, some for over 50 years.
- *Arban's Complete Method for Trumpet,* J. B. Arban (Carl Fischer, Inc.)
- *Brand Method for Trumpet or Cornet,* Saint-Jacome (Carl Fischer, Inc.)
- *Vizzutti Trumpet Method Books 1, 2, 3,* Allen Vizzutti (Alfred Publishing Co.)

Bass clef players play from method books designated for Baritone/Euphonium (bass clef), Trombone/Baritone, Trombone/Euphonium or Euphonium/Tuba. There are many excellent method books available, of which these are representative.
- *Essential Technique* (Baritone BC), Rhodes/arr. Bierschenk/Lautzen (Hal Leonard Corporation)
- *Master Method 1, 2, 3* (Baritone BC), Peters (Neil A. Kjos Music Company)
- *Medalist Band Method 1, 2, 3* (Baritone BC), Ployhar (Warner Brothers Music Publishers)

- *Rubank Advanced Method for Trombone/Baritone, Vol. 1, Vol. 2,* Himie Voxman and William Glower (Rubank, Inc.)
- *Rubank Intermediate Method for Trombone/Baritone,* J. E. Skornicka and E. G. Boltz (Rubank, Inc.)
- *Tone and Technique-Baritone BC,* Ployhar/arr. Zepp (Warner Brothers Music Publishers)
- *Tuba Resource Book,* edited by R. Winston Morris (Indiana University Press, 1996). A comprehensive source of euphonium/tuba music and methods books.

Dealers
- Wichita Band Instrument Company – Wichita, KS (800) 835-3006 www.wichitaband.com
- The Woodwind and the Brasswind – South Bend, IN (800) 348-5003 www.wwandbw.com
- Taylor Music – Aberdeen, SD (800) 843-1938 www.taylormusic.com

Web Sites
- J .W. Pepper Music, Atlanta, GA, www.jwpepper.com
- Robert King Music, Boston, MA, www.rkingmusic.com

The late Gerald P. Armstrong retired after 23 years as the Senior Consultant, Instrumental Music, Baptist Sunday School Board, Church Music Department (now LifeWay Christian Resources, Music Publishing and Recording), Nashville, Tennessee. Earlier, he served as a high school band director, and played in the U. S. Army Band, 1st and 7th Divisions. Armstrong co-edited three instrumental books and wrote three handbell method books. Gerald P. Armstrong died on May 21, 2000.

CHAPTER 13

The Tuba

by Charles A. Krause and Jim Hansford

What Is a Tuba?

The tuba, the largest of the brass instruments, is the most recent addition to the modern orchestra. The serpent, bass horn, Russian bassoon, and ophicleide were precursors to the modern tuba. They employed cup-shaped mouthpieces, conical tubing, had usable fundamentals, and all played the same bass part in the orchestras of their day. The instrument was created to replace the old wooden serpent whose tone was not a match for those of the other brass instruments. The tuba, the helicon, the valve trombone, and the euphonium emerged in Europe during the mid to late 19th century. Berlioz and Wagner were some of the first major composers to utilize the tuba in their compositions. The sousaphone, suggested by John Philip Sousa and later named after the famous march king, was developed around 1895. This instrument's round shape allowed it to be carried across the player's shoulder which provided an ideal alternative for tuba players in parade bands. Modern tubas have an oblong shape, a conical bore, a bell pointing upward (sometimes outward), and a large cupped mouthpiece. There are three types of tubas which are built in four different keys:

- **Double-bass,** BB♭ or CC
- **Bass Tuba,** E♭ or F
- **Tenor Tuba,** B♭

The most common of the three is the BB♭ tuba, a nontransposing instrument that always plays in the bass clef. Unlike the string bass, which sounds an octave lower than written, this tuba sounds the actual written pitch. Tuba music is written for the B♭ tuba and in order to change from a tuba in one key to a tuba in another key, one must learn a new fingering system. This is a challenging and lengthy process and usually only attempted by the most serious tuba performers.

Tubas come in various sizes from 3/4 to 6/4, and there is no standardization between manufacturers. The 4/4, or full size instrument, works best for most players, but a 3/4 size tuba is better suited for young students and small groups such as a church ensemble. **BB♭ tubas** usually come equipped with four or five or occasionally even six valves (both rotary and piston type). The additional valves extend the range downward, but, more importantly, they provide the player more fingering combinations which will permit more tuning options in the lower register. Since orchestral music is frequently written in sharp keys, the **CC tuba** is often the instrument of choice for many professional orchestral tubists. With the CC instrument, fingering combinations and general facility tends to be more "friendly" in the sharp keys. Additionally, the CC tuba, produces a slightly brighter tone quality which is advantageous to projection and balance for the single tuba player in the orchestra. On the other hand, most wind band tubists usually prefer the B♭ tuba because of its rich, dark tone quality. There was a time when the **E♭ tuba** was recommended for the young beginning tuba player because of its size, but, because of the popularity and refinement of the 3/4 size instrument, the use of the E♭ instrument has diminished considerably. The B♭ tenor tuba is actually a euphonium.

Basic Fundamentals
Embouchure

Although other brass instruments support a two-thirds upper or lower lip mouthpiece placement position, the generally recommended placement for the tuba is a one-half upper and lower lip position and centered left to right. Because of the large mouthpiece, this position seems to provide for optimum lip vibration and flexibility. The entire circumference of the mouthpiece must touch the skin of the lips to properly produce the tone. In order to produce the proper vibration to create a sound, it is important that the lips be held together. As the air is blown through the closed lips, a vibration will occur if the proper muscle tension is present. The pitch of the note is determined by the

length of the tube, which can vary depending on the valve combination and the tension of the player's embouchure. The greater the tension, the higher the pitch. Although most teachers encourage a moist lip embouchure to provide a lubricant for embouchure flexibility, there is a small percentage of instructors who support a dry lip approach. It is strictly a matter of individual preference. A relaxed embouchure, regardless of the dynamic range being played, is essential, and no excess pressure should be used in pressing the mouthpiece into the face. The mouthpiece pressure should be only enough to provide a complete seal to ensure there is no air leakage around the mouthpiece. Excessive mouthpiece pressure inhibits blood circulation in the lips and promotes rapid fatigue. Initial establishment of proper embouchure is, indeed, a critical issue.

Playing Position

One of the biggest problems that a player has with the tuba is finding a comfortable position for playing the instrument. Since the tuba should rest on the chair between the player's legs, the choice of a proper chair is extremely important. A cloth-covered chair is recommended to provide more stability to the instrument. Plastic or metal chairs tend to allow the instrument to slide around and cause problems with posture and embouchure placement. Some young tubists place a small pillow or foam rubber pad between the legs to provide the necessary stability. The correct height of the tuba in relation to the player's mouth is extremely important. It is critical that the height of the mouthpiece meet the player's lips without any straining, stretching, or crunching of the neck. Often, a beginning player who is too short to reach the mouthpiece may sit on a book or pillow to correct the problem. More mature performers rest the instrument in their laps or hold it between their legs as they sit on the edge of the chair. Tuba stands are available for purchase and may be appropriate in certain situations, but are not recommended by this writer since they work contrary to the musical goal of having the instrument be an extension of the body. When holding the tuba, the player's body should be either vertical or leaning slightly forward in a commanding pose. Do not allow the left hand to grasp the leadpipe or mouthpiece, but extend the arm around the instrument and grasp some secure tubing on the front side of the tuba as if cradling the instrument. Because one needs the maximum amount of air to play the tuba correctly, proper posture and instrument position are essential.

Tonguing

The tongue plays a very important role as an articulating device. For initial sounds the tongue acts as a valve allowing the air to flow through the lips producing the vibration. When playing a long series of notes in rapid succession the tongue briefly interrupts the air column and initiates the next note. For notes in the middle register the tongue should strike the roof of the mouth near where the gum meets the upper teeth. In the high register the tongue may move further back on the roof of the mouth. In the low register the tongue will move further down near the tip of the teeth, and on extremely low pitches it may strike between the teeth, but it should never interfere with the embouchure. The muscular action of the tongue can improve with exercise, moving quickly and cleanly with precision. Except for timing, the tongue should operate independently of the embouchure. The tongue arches naturally, and should quickly return to the rest position near the floor of the mouth where it will not hinder airflow. Except for special effects or certain types of jazz articulation, the tongue should not be used to stop long notes or final notes in a phrase because of the undesirable sound produced ("UT") upon conclusion. Tones are ended by simply discontinuing the breath supply in a controlled manner. When performing rapidly articulated passages, the tongue actually interrupts the continuous airstream and, for a split second, stops the sound, but each time the tongue retracts, a new sound is initiated. Multiple tonguing on tuba is a formidable and arduous technique and should be undertaken by the serious advanced student only after single tonguing has been mastered.

Breathing

The tuba, like the flute, is a high air-flow-rate instrument, so the tuba player has to be able to inhale large, deep breaths. Considering the length, large bore, and the general size of the tuba, it becomes evident early on that a tuba player needs to have a considerably large capacity for air intake and be able to produce a strong, consistent airflow. More than the other brass instruments, tuba players are often required to rapidly produce copious amounts of air. Since hyperventilation is a common problem among young tuba players, it is highly recommended that these students pursue a rigid program of exercise including swimming and running. A player should practice inhaling through his or her mouth and nose simultaneously. To increase the capacity of intake it is recommended that the player actually drop his jaw, while keeping his upper lip set on the mouthpiece, to inhale quickly and quietly. As in proper vocal production, the resonating cavities of the body—the frontal sinuses, the skull bones—maximize resonance and efficient tone production. Anything that hinders the resonance of the body will affect the quality of vibrations flowing through the instrument. Arnold Jacobs, former tubist with the

> **Ernie Collins**
> **recording musician since 1974**
>
> "Come, let us consider now the tuba! The tuba, compared to the rest of the orchestra, seems unimportant.
> It's not the melody.
> It's not inspiring.
> It's not flashy.
> It's not the solo trumpet part!
> But, it's your part, your job, your gift to add to the ensemble.
> It's important to you."
>
> *"Whatever you do, work at it with all your heart, as working for the Lord, not for men" (Col. 3:23, NIV).*

Chicago Symphony for over 40 years and world-renowned pedagogue, covers this subject in great detail in the book *Song and Wind.*

Quality of Sound, Range, and Intonation

The note range of a tuba will depend on the expertise of the player, but is generally around two to three octaves beginning with F, three octaves below middle C. The inexperienced player will often find it more difficult to play in the upper register, but the low register is challenging and will be ineffective without considerable breath support. The middle register on the tuba (first E below the staff to fourth line F) will likely be the easiest to learn. The teeth are slightly open with a normal overbite and the lips are pursed and relaxed just enough so they may be blown ever so slightly into the cup of the mouthpiece as the sound is produced. In the low register (those notes below the E) the lips are even more relaxed and the jaw is projected and lowered. In this low register many teachers allow some slight controlled puffing of the cheeks to permit the lips to vibrate fully (a concept that is frowned on by teachers of the higher brass). The upper register (those notes above fourth line F) still requires that the teeth be slightly apart, but the lower lip (and the upper lip to a slightly lesser degree) begins to roll inward and the air stream becomes directed more downward as if blowing fuzz off the chin. With the lower registers, the air stream is directed straight down the leadpipe. As the pitch ascends in the upper register, the air is directed gradually downward. It is imperative that the student guard against applying too much pressure of the mouthpiece against the lips, a habit along with squeezing the lips together, that can develop especially as one begins to develop the upper register. A beautiful and resonate warm tone in all registers should be the goal of every tuba player.

Most tubas have three or four piston or rotary valves. The valves alter the pitch by increasing or decreasing the tube length through which the air must pass, allowing the player to produce all the tones of the chromatic scale. The fourth valve is used to extend the range of the instrument down a fourth but, more importantly, it provides alternate fingerings for improving out-of-tune valve combinations. The younger tubist may often sharpen notes in the lower register because of an unrelaxed embouchure. The most effective use of the fourth valve is the 2-4 combination in place of the 1-2-3 combination for the very sharp low B♮. The fourth valve can also be used to replace 1-3 for low C. On both of these combination fingerings, the fourth valve slide needs to be pulled to a compromised position that will allow the best possible tuning. Some players actually develop the technique of manipulating various tuning slides while playing. One of the best ways to improve intonation awareness is to work regularly with a tuning device and learn the pitch tendencies of each note on the instrument.

Tuning is a concept that must begin in the early stages of beginning instruction. Two ways to approach basic tuning are as follows:

1. The main tuning slide can be placed in the correct position for general tuning, and the embouchure can be used to further correct the tuning of specific problem pitches.

2. The main tuning slide is also set, but the player can utilize the valve slides for careful tuning of individual notes rather than depending on the embouchure to favor so many pitch discrepancies.

Some teachers feel that "lipping" the pitch up or down has an adverse effect on tone quality. Most instructors will utilize a combination of several tuning methods depending on the particular situation, but this writer feels that it is quite important to properly adjust the main tuning slide and all valve slides to the best setting so that slight embouchure adjustments will favor pitches to the proper tuning. Obviously, the best tuning mechanism is the ear. The temperature of the room can greatly affect the overall pitch of an instrument, especially one as large as the tuba. As the temperature rises, the pitch of wind instruments go sharp.

Writing for the Tuba

The tuba adds depth and warmth to the overall sound of any instrumental ensemble, but to the wind band it is truly an essential instrument. The tuba can double the string bass part, although it must be remembered that tuba players need to breathe frequently, and the part will require some editing to provide for such opportunity. Also, if the tuba is playing a string bass part it should be read down one octave. (The double bass or string bass sounds an octave lower than written, thus the parts are written up one octave.) For inexperienced players these edited parts will need to be written out, but a mature player can usually make these editing adjustments on the spot unless the music is particularly complex. On occasion the tubist may be asked to play a timpani part or double a third trombone, but in the final analysis the conductor must consider the musical appropriateness of such substitutions, especially with the timpani. Wide interval skips in the tuba line are especially challenging and should be used with care, especially with less-experienced players. As with all brass instruments, a variety of tonguing options are available on the tuba including double and triple tonguing and even flutter tonguing, but it must be remembered that because of the size of the instrument and the resulting air column, these techniques should be limited to the highly accomplished performer.

Mouthpieces

In general, new instruments purchased from reputable companies will come equipped with a standard mouthpiece that is quite acceptable. If the mouthpiece wobbles in the leadpipe or does not fit the shank properly (going in too far or not far enough) it can adversely affect pitch. A properly fitting mouthpiece should go in the leadpipe approximately one inch and should fit snugly. It is a good policy to encourage (or require) young tubists who have studied for a year or two to purchase their own mouthpiece for use with the school instrument. Since relatively few school tuba players will actually own an instrument, the investment in a mouthpiece gives them some ownership in their musical endeavor. This writer has seen many young tuba players become very protective and proud of their mouthpiece. Additionally, it is recommended that the student purchase a mouthpiece pouch in which to keep it when not in use. This protective covering will prevent the mouthpiece rim from becoming chipped, scratched, or marred in any way that will cause discomfort when placed against the lips. Also, it will help prevent the shank from becoming bent or dented. There are a variety of acceptable mouthpiece pouches on the market from which to choose. Considering the price of tuba mouthpieces, the relatively low cost of a plastic pouch will be well worth its price.

Mutes

Tuba mutes are used only on rare occasions in contemporary band and orchestral literature or unique solo works. Stonelined mutes are the least expensive. At the time of this writing mutes ranged in price from around $80 to $200, depending on the quality, size, and kind of mute. A better choice when considering overall tonal response and tuning consistencies will be a name brand metal mute. Most mutes do affect the intonation of the tuba to some degree, usually by sharpening the pitch. Pulling the main tuning slide will correct this, or some performers have success shaving off some of the cork or adding to the cork on the sides of the mute. A great deal of attention needs to be paid to the sound and pitch of the instrument when using a mute. If you find a mute that does not alter the pitch, treat it with extreme care.

Purchasing

Because of the expense of tubas, younger students usually do not own their own instruments. Most schools and many churches generally provide these instruments for their students or members. Obviously the more serious players or college music majors will own their own instrument. There are many places to purchase either used or new tubas. (See resource list.) Never buy a used tuba without checking it out firsthand or having an instrument repairperson check it over. At the time of this writing, the cost of a new tuba can vary from $2000 to $10,000 or more. When purchasing a used instrument, remember to consider the repair cost that might be necessary to bring it up to playing condition. In most cases a top-quality, used professional instrument will be a better choice than a new student line instrument. Consult your local band director or an area professional tuba player for advice in selecting a quality brand instrument to meet your needs.

Care and Maintenance

Dent Repair. Even though tubas are big, they are somewhat fragile and vulnerable to dents. Large dents can affect intonation and small dents, especially in the leadpipe, can restrict airflow. Dent removal should be left to the professional instrument repairperson.

Valves. Piston type. Partially remove the piston and place oil directly on it. **Rotary type.** Put oil in the slide that leads to the valve. The rotor will need oil in two other places: (1) On the bushing under the valve cap (just a drop), and (2) on the front side of the bushing where the rotor mechanism attaches. Oil the rotary valves every day the tuba is used to prevent excessive wear and to promote long life. Valves or valve slides that become stuck should be removed by an instrument repairperson or an experienced band director.

Outside cleaning. Instruments can be wiped off with a damp cloth; washed in lukewarm water (not immersed), or cleaned with commercially available cleaning cloths which can be purchased at most music stores. Do not use Brasso, or any other unapproved metal polishing cloths on a lacquered instrument. The finish will likely be destroyed.

Inside cleaning. This process should be completed about once a year. Since much of the buildup of sediment will occur in the leadpipe near the mouthpiece, that is where the attention should be directed. Remove all slides and flush the instrument well with lukewarm water. Do not allow the entire tuba to completely fill up with water—it can be quite unmanageable. Pull all valve slides and clean well with a commercial "cleaning snake." Piston valves should be removed and cleaned thoroughly, removing all oily residue. It is not recommended that an inexperienced person remove the rotary valves. After the final rinse and a thorough drying, ascertaining that all water has been removed from the instrument, the slides and valves should be relubricated before reassembling. For school instruments it is recommended that they be cleaned on an annual or biannual basis in an acid bath by a professional instrument repair technician.

Slides and Pads. Lubricate slides with slide grease and check valve pads or rotary valve bumpers for deterioration. Other options for tuning slide lubrication include Vaseline, anhydrous lanolin (available at a pharmacy), and STP.

Conclusion

The tuba can play many different styles of music, from Dixieland to classical. The tuba is an enjoyable instrument to play, but is challenging to master. The size of the instrument and the airflow required should be critical considerations before a player begins to study tuba. Just as any piece of music would not be complete without a bass line, a band or orchestra is not complete without the warm, intense, resonate tone of the tuba. A Christmas tradition that occurs in many large cities is the Tuba Christmas, where players from all walks of life and with all sizes and shapes of tubas gather to play Christmas carols as a giant ensemble. It is truly a unique experience to participate in or just observe one of these joyous occasions.

Resources
Instructional Methods

Beginner
- *Foundation to Tuba and Sousaphone Playing,* William Bell (Carl Fischer)
- *John Gage Warm Ups*
- *Tuba Warm-ups/Daily Routine for the Tuba,* William Bell (Charles Colin)

Intermediate
- *Advanced Studies for B♭ Bass,* Tyrrell (Boosey and Hawkes)
- *Herbert L. Clarke Technical Studies* (Carl Fischer)
- *Intermediate Method,* Skornicka and Boltz (Rubank)
- *Arban Method* (Carl Fischer)

Advanced
- *70 Studies for Bb Tuba,* Blazhevich (Robert King)
- *60 Selected Studies for Tuba,* Kopprasch (Carl Fischer)
- *Progressive Technique,* Knaub (MCA)
- *Studies in Bach,* Bixby-Bobo (Robert King)

Research References
Books
- *Brass Players' Guide,* Robert King (Music Sales Inc., 140 Main St. North Easton, MA 02356)
- *Arnold Jacobs: Song and Wind,* Brian Frederiksen (Wind Song Press Limited, 1996), info@windsongpress.com
- *The Tuba Source Book,* R. Winston Morris and Edward Goldstein, editors (Indiana University Press, 1995)
- *Tuba Music Study Guide,* Frank Woodruff (Southern Music Company)

Web Sites
- TUBA–www.tubaonline.org
- TubaNet–www.chisham.com
- Tuba Exchange–www.warrior.w1.com
- www.ChurchOrchestra.com

Charles A. Krause is Minister of Instrumental Music and Choral Music at First Baptist Church, Roanoke, Virginia, and the Principal Tubist with the Roanoke Symphony Orchestra.

Jim Hansford is Professor of Music and Director of Bands, Oklahoma Baptist University, Shawnee, Oklahoma.

PERCUSSION

AN INTRODUCTION

by Steve Kirby

Percussionists have the wonderful opportunity of adding color and "effects" to the music of the church orchestra. Whether they play a timpani roll for suspense or a mark tree for ethereal effects, percussionists have a definitive and important role in the church orchestra.

The church percussionist, like a classical symphony percussionist, must be versatile in reading treble clef and bass clef. For example: all timpani parts are written in bass clef, and keyboard mallet instruments are written in treble and bass clef. Percussionists need to know how to play all the different percussion instruments and, on occasion, play several at the same time! This includes the traditional percussion battery, as well as ethnic instruments (African, Latin, etc.).

A typical church orchestra percussion part is written for two to three players. This more closely resembles a symphonic percussion part than it does an institutional wind ensemble part. And like the symphonic counterpart, church percussionists will occasionally need to call in a few extra "hands" to cover auxiliary parts. Church orchestras very seldom use a side drum and a bass drum as the main rhythm components. Church orchestras are rhythm-section based, and utilize a drum set as opposed to the typical side drum(s) and bass drum(s) seen in most institutional ensembles.

What skill level is required to play the percussion parts written for the church orchestra? The parts written require a good reader. One must be able to play with accuracy and feeling. Very seldom will parts be improvised. If improvisation is required, a basic knowledge of contemporary music styles can be helpful. Percussion experience in a high school or college band, orchestra, or wind ensemble greatly improves the success of playing a church orchestra part properly. If one compares church orchestra percussion parts to symphonic percussion parts, one will find the church parts (in general) less difficult but with more notes written. Compared to a wind ensemble, one will find the church percussion parts about the same level of difficulty, but playing less frequently.

Writers and arrangers for church instrumentalists are becoming increasingly aware of the text or lyric of a piece. Basing their arrangements on the lyric gives the music the proper texture for that situation. Percussion parts then become the "icing on the cake," often setting the tone for the entire arrangement.

Steve Kirby is Minister Through Instrumental Music, Idlewild Baptist Church, Tampa, Florida. In addition to his ministry there, Steve has published numerous arrangements and appears often as a guest conductor and clinician.

CHAPTER 14

Percussion

by Michael Katterjohn

Instrumental directors are often afraid to discuss percussion instruments. Purchasing instruments is often perplexing, especially selecting sizes and brands. The list of percussion instruments continues to grow. Percussion instruments proliferate, and changes come along almost yearly. Even experienced conductors have questions about percussion instruments and playing techniques. There are some basics about percussion technique, however, that will remain constant. This chapter will simply introduce basic percussion techniques.

Snare Drum

The most basic percussion instrument is the snare drum. This is the instrument on which most beginners will start and where they will learn the basic techniques of all percussion instruments.

Instrument Design

The snare drum is composed of several different properties that will determine the sound of a drum:
- Shell
- Heads
- Tension Rods
- Snares
- Size

The shell of the drum can be metal or wood. The metal shells can be aluminum, steel, copper, brass, smooth or hammered. The wood shells can be maple, birch, beech, or mahogany. The metal shell will have a higher, thinner sound while the wood shell will have a deeper, thicker sound.

Each drum will have two heads, a batter head on top and a snare head on the bottom. The batter heads will come coated, clear, with a dot, smooth white, pin stripped, black, fiber, skin, or in several combinations. Each difference will change the sound of the drum and/or limit the uses of various styles to be played. For instance, wire brushes can only be used on the coated heads. The "swish" sound that is characteristic of the brushes will not be heard on a smooth head. The snare head will be too thin to allow the best response of the snares, which vibrate against it.

The tension rods of the snare drum determine the tension consistency of the drum. Each drum will have 6 to 10 lugs (tension rods) that will be determined by the size and expense.

The snares will be wire snares on concert snare drums and gut snares on marching drums. If the part calls for "field drum," a marching snare with gut snares should be used.

There are three common sizes to look for in concert snare drums (depth x diameter): 3" x 13", 5" x 14", and 6-1/2" x 14". These sizes may vary from 1/2" to 1" in size, with the 5" x 14" being the most common. Generally, the smaller the drum, the higher the pitch will sound.

Playing Techniques

The basic technique of the snare drum is divided into six categories:
- Grip
- Stick Size
- Wrists
- Sticking
- Stick Height
- Rolls

The **matched grip** is the accepted concert grip. Both hands are held in the same manner, with the thumb and first finger creating a fulcrum about 5" from the back of the stick, wrapping the remaining fingers around the stick. This grip has the palms of the hand facing the floor and the thumbs facing each other. The **traditional grip** is used for marching and will make the percussionist learn both grips, as the other percussion instruments use the matched grip. See the suggested resources to find specifics on the traditional grip.

The size of the stick should be determined by the size of the players' hand and the volume to be played. Generally, 7A, 7B, 5A, 5B, 2B, Vic Firth General, and Bolero sticks, along with other brands, will serve most purposes.

The wrist is the most important part of playing percussion. The wrist will improve speed and rhythmic accuracy. A percussionist should constantly strive to improve wrist motion, strength, and accuracy. Some pedagogues do not advocate using the arms when playing the snare drum, because using the arms will produce an undesirable volume.

There are two basic forms of sticking: hand-to-hand and right-hand-lead. For the serious percussionist, the hand-to-hand, or alternating, sticking will allow the player to develop both wrists equally. This method will cause the left stick to always follow the right stick, no matter what the rhythm. Right-hand-lead will usually produce accents on notes that have no accents written every time the right hand is used. In a series of two sixteenth notes and one eighth note, the sticking would be RLR RLR RLR, etc.

Stick height is directly related to volume. If a player raises the stick 8" off the drumhead to play a passage, that passage will be louder than if the player only raises the stick 2" off the drumhead.

Two basic styles of drum rolls will provide the sounds needed for most church music. The buzz, or crushed roll, provides a smooth, connected roll that should be used for all the symphonic style pieces. The open roll can be used on the march or military style music to give that open or outdoor feeling. As a side note, make sure the percussionist has the drum set up at belt height and that the snare bed is perpendicular to the body. This will allow all rolls to have a good snare sound and all dynamic changes to be consistent.

Tuning the Snare Drum

Tuning the snare drum is not difficult if one understands the purpose. A fine-tuned drum will have a crisp snare sound, a good stick response, and a rather high pitch. When tuning the drum, the snare head (bottom) should give a little when applying pressure to the center of the head with one's finger. This is to allow the head to vibrate freely with the wire snares. The batter head (top) should be tighter to give the stick plenty of bounce. To tune the heads, use a cross-tuning method. Choosing any tension rod, rotate the rod 1/2 turn to the right with a drum key. Go directly across the drum to the corresponding rod and repeat the procedure. Moving to the right of the rod just adjusted, give this rod a 1/2 turn to the right and go directly across to that corresponding rod, which should put you on the rod to the left of the one you have started on. Continue this crisscross procedure until all of the rods have been tightened. If the head needs to be tighter, then go through the entire procedure with 1/4 turns. This procedure will allow equal tension on the head and will allow the head to keep from warping.

The snare tension adjustment knob adjusts the tension of the snares against the bottom head. It should be adjusted so that there is a crisp snare sound at loud and soft volumes, loud and soft rolls. Turn the adjustment knob right to tighten the drumhead, left to loosen it.

If the snare drum comes with a tone control knob, turn this knob to the left until the felt muffler on the inside of the drum disengages the drumhead. This will allow the drumsticks to have the proper response off the drumhead. If, after tuning the heads, there is still too much ring from the drum, there are several dampening devices that will not change the stick response. Consult a local music store.

Musical Ideas

The snare drum can be used to enhance the music, and not just as a rhythm machine. To create more tension in a passage, a snare drum roll can be written in. If the music has a march type feel and the drummer is musical, allow the player to improvise the part. Some composer/arrangers write simplified parts to portray a general idea. Rim shots can be used to accent certain passages, such as rhythmic brass punches. On slow arrangements that do not have a heavy eighth-note feel, brushes could be used in a circular motion on the snare, with quarter notes on a suspended cymbal with the right hand.

Common Problems

When dealing with drummers, there are two common mistakes in the basic playing technique: playing too loud and not using the wrist. Here is a suggestion to help in controlling the percussionists' volume.

If a 14" drum is divided into three equal sections from the outside rim to the center, Section 1 being closest to the rim and Section 3 being closest to the center, each area will have corresponding dynamics and stick heights. Use this chart to help:

If a percussionist is having trouble using his wrists, this warm-up can help:

With a firm matched grip, using only the wrist and playing on the knee while seated, have the percussionist play single strokes, with the right hand only, for 2 minutes. The stick height should be 8". Then, change to the left hand and repeat the procedure. After a 15-second break, the percussionist should continue with a series of

Section 1	pp	1"
	p	2"
Section 2	mp	3"
	mf	4"
Section 3	f	6"
	ff	8"

singles: RLRLRLRL, etc.,
doubles: RRLLRRLLRRLL, etc.,
triples: RRRLLLRRRLLL, etc., and
quads: RRRRLLLLRRRRLLLL, etc.

At the end of this exercise the percussionist should be sore but ready to play. If he diligently uses this warm-up every day, everyone should see improvements within a few weeks.

Care and Maintenance

Wiping off fingerprints to slow down corrosion, turning the snares off with the snare release lever to release tension on the snares, and covering the drum to prevent dust from getting on the batter head, will extend the life of the drum.

Simple repairs can be done to keep the drum in good playing condition. If a drumhead breaks, a local music store can order replacement heads. Loosening all of the tension rods and removing the counterhoop can remove old heads. Replace the old head with the new one, replace the counterhoop and tension rods and, after finger tightening the rods, use the tuning procedure mentioned earlier in this chapter. To replace the bottom head, you will need to remove the snares by following the procedure in the next paragraph.

If the string or plastic that holds the snares in place breaks, order snare string to replace it. Loosen the screws that held the string or plastic, and rethread the new string through the two holes in the end of the snares and through the mechanism with the screws. After pulling the strings tight, tighten the screws. Some adjustment of the snare tension adjustment knob will be needed.

To remove those ugly black marks from the batter head, use any kitchen cleaner. Spray the cleaner directly on the head and scrub off with a paper towel. Remember to wipe off any extra cleaner that may have gotten on the hoop or on the shell of the drum. If the cleaner chosen does not work, try another.

Purchasing Snare Drums

When purchasing a new drum, stay with the well-known brand names. At the time of this writing, new drums will retail from $150 to $970 for a 5" or 6-1/2" x 14" drum. There are many music stores and mail-order catalogues that will discount at least 20 percent. Some music stores sell used trade-ins for very reasonable prices. Again, stay with major brand names. If there are still questions about the choice, ask a local band director or a professional percussionist for suggestions.

Timpani

The most important aspect of the timpanist is how well the player can match pitch. Percussionists must have "a good ear" to play timpani. They can be trained by using singing exercises, interval studies, or by playing scales on the timpani (timpani is the plural of timpano).

Instrument Design

The timpani is composed of several properties that will determine the quality of the drum:
- Bowl
- Head
- Tuning Rods
- Foot Pedals
- Tension Adjustment Knob
- Tuning Gauges
- Size

The bowl of a timpani is made of either copper or fiberglass, with the better copper bowls being suspended. The copper bowls will have a fuller resonance than the fiberglass, which tend to sound muffled.

The heads can be white, clear, or calfskin and can have a regular or an extended collar. The collar of the timpani head is the part of the head that extends from the edge of the bowl to the metal hoop surrounding the head. The extended collar can only be used on timpani that are made for the extended collar. Calfskin heads are very hard to maintain and are not recommended for church orchestras.

The tuning rods are used to give the head its pitch. The procedure is the same as tuning the snare drum, but is a more exacting science. The pitch at each tuning rod must be the same and is important to avoid hearing multiple pitches each time the drum is struck.

The foot pedals come in three styles: accelerator type, ratchet type, and friction type. The accelerator type is the most common and the easiest to use. This type of pedal works likes the accelerator pedal in a car. Push down with the toe and the pitch gets higher. Push down with the heel and the pitch gets lower.

The tension adjustment knob is used to keep the foot pedal from slipping from the position it is set. After checking the lowest pitch of the drum (see next paragraph), turn the knob to the left if the pedal pops up from its lowest position, and to the right if the pedal pops down from the highest position. It may take a few turns to make the adjustment properly. Avoid overadjustments, which will cause the other position to need readjustment or may even break the spring.

Timpani tuning gauges are an option that can be ordered with the timpani or put on at a later time. These gauges are used to help the timpanist find pitches quickly. Although helpful, these gauges can be used as a crutch instead of developing the ear and can be inaccurate.

There are four common sizes in a set of timpani: 23", 26", 29" and 32". Each instrument has a fundamental pitch, which is with the pedal in the lowest position, and a practical range of a fifth. The 32" should be tuned to D below the bass clef staff, and has a practical range from D-A. The 29" should be tuned to F below the staff, and has a practical range from F-C. The 26" should be tuned to B♭, second line of the staff, and has a practical range from B♭-F. The 23" should be tuned to D, third line of the staff, and has a range from D-A. If the budget is tight, buy the 26" and 29". The third instrument to purchase would be the 23" and then the 32".

Playing Technique

The basic technique of playing the timpani is divided into six categories:

- Grips
- Mallets
- Sticking Styles
- Set-Up
- Playing Areas
- Rolls

There are two grips used to play timpani. The German grip is the same as the matched snare drum grip. The French grip is different in that the thumbs are on top of the mallet shaft with the palms of the hand facing each other. More professional timpanists use the French grip.

Each timpanist should have four types of mallets: soft, medium, hard, and wood. There are a variety of descriptions and names for these four types of mallets, as well as different types and styles of handles. The timpanists should determine their own preferences.

The manner in which a timpanist strikes the timpani has various techniques. In most cases, the timpanist will need to have a concept of drawing the sound out of the drum. This is accomplished by bringing the mallet to a position one

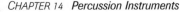

foot above the head after striking the head. This should be done in a quick or slow, fluid motion, determined by the style of the music. The timpanist should decide whether to use a cross-sticking technique to get from drum to drum, or to use the diddle approach. The diddle approach allows the timpanist to get to another drum by putting a double right or a double left at the end of a series of notes to avoid a cross-over. Basically, if there is a series of straight sixteenth notes that change drums every beat, in 4/4 time, for two measures, the timpanist would use the hand-to-hand method, which would create cross-sticking every other beat, or the use of paradiddles (RLRRLRLL) which would eliminate the cross-sticking.

The timpani should be set up so that the pedals are facing the center of the players' body. When the player is leaning against a 30" stool, the feet must have easy access to all pedals. The same is true if there are two or four timpani. The most common set up is with the largest timpani to the left of the player.

There is one primary playing area, two to four inches from the rim, close to the player. This is the area in which the timpanist will produce the fullest sound. Other spots can be used for special effects. The composer/arranger will specify those other areas in the music.

Rolls on the timpani have two specifics. All rolls on the timpani are SINGLE STROKE ROLLS! Do not allow the timpanist to bounce his mallets when doing a roll. This will only muffle the sound. The pitch determines the speed of the roll. The higher the note, the faster the head will vibrate; the lower the note, the slower the head vibrates. The timpanist should find the speed that produces the most consistent tone without interfering with the natural vibration of the head.

Tuning Timpani

One facet of tuning the timpani comes with the initial tuning of each drum. When each instrument is at its lowest pitch, a process called clearing or balancing the head is done. This is accomplished when the tension around the perimeter of the head is equal, resulting in a clear tone. The timpanist should make sure the pitch is the same at each tuning rod.

The other facet involves changing pitches at the beginning of, or during, a piece of music. The timpanist will need to know how to match and transpose pitches at the octaves. A pitch pipe, the bells, or a tuning fork can be used to create the desired pitch. The player must then transfer the pitch to the octave that corresponds with the desired pitch. A good timpanist will have a repertoire of songs that can be used to help find intervals between drums. The most common intervals, the fourth and fifth, can be determined by singing "Here Comes the Bride" and "Twinkle, Twinkle." Tuning gauges can be purchased for some timpani, but are sometimes unreliable if the pitches are not checked before each performance. The timpanist's best tool is the ear.

There are three methods used to produce a pitch for tuning purposes. The **flipping method** is executed by placing the middle finger on the timpani head and "flicking" the head. The **tapping method** is executed by tapping the head softly with the tip of the middle finger. The **humming method** is executed by humming the desired pitch 2" to 3" above the timpani head. When the pitch is correct, the head and bowl of the timpani will resonate that pitch. After using one of these methods, the timpanist must adjust the pedal to the desired pitch.

One of the most exciting techniques used on the timpani is the "$f\,p$ crescendo roll." The timpanist should hit the head at a forte volume, allow the sound to decay for 1 to 2 seconds, then start a roll at a soft volume and crescendo by increasing the stick height, not the speed.

A common problem for most timpanists is the technique of dampening. Dampening is effectively executed by placing as much surface area of the hand on the timpani head as is possible. This is done on rests and loud passages that have long notes resonating into other pitches. This technique should be practiced to allow for maximum effectiveness.

Another problem that always affects the determination of a good timpanist is the sound produced at loud volumes. Some timpanists will attempt to play the timpani at a volume that it is not capable of producing. Just as there is a line that should not be crossed for wind players, the timpanist should always produce the best tone possible. Again, "drawing" the sound out of the drum, not beating it into the drum, is the best way to produce the best tone.

Care and Maintenance

The timpani need very little maintenance. Manufacturers provide drop covers to cover the drums when they are not being used. The timpani rims should be wiped off after every use. If the timpani heads need changing, the rim of the bowl should be wiped off and a very thin layer of a lubricant can be applied to the rim. This will allow the pitches to be changed without the "creaking" sound that sometimes occurs when the head rubs against a dry bowl rim. Do not use wax or soap as the lubricant. Cork grease, adhesive Teflon™ tape, slide grease, or silicone spray can be used. A thin film is best, as a thick film will reduce the resonance of the drum. Timpani heads need to be replaced every one to three years depending on use and condition of the heads. The tension adjustment rods should be lubricated each time the heads are changed.

Purchasing Timpani

When in the market for a set of timpani, call local music stores to find the availability of a used set. Sometimes there are great deals on used timpani. When buying used or new, make sure the timpani have copper bowls. Most of the church orchestra music can be played on three timpani. The 23", 26", and 29" timpani would be sufficient sizes. Ludwig has a set of three Standard Series, polished copper kettles that list for $7,800. The same three with fiberglass bowls list for about $6,000. The Professional Series, copper bowls, lists for $9,000. Yamaha has a set of Symphonic Series timpani for $9,100 as of this writing. For the best prices, shop around.

Sticks and mallets used by percussionists come in hundreds of styles and variations.

Keyboard Mallet Instruments

Keyboard mallet instruments are very important in church music today. These instruments are melodic in nature and add a strong timbre to the ensemble. From the bold majestic sound of the chimes to the soft ethereal quality of the bells, these instruments bring a variety of moods to a piece of music. The xylophone can give a brilliant, staccato quality to a flute part and the vibes can add a rich, mellow quality to a low clarinet line.

The three most commonly used keyboard mallet instruments in the church orchestra are xylophone, chimes, and orchestra bells. These are the melodic instruments of the church orchestra percussion section.

Xylophone

The most common range of the xylophone is 3-1/2 octaves. This will sufficiently cover the needs for this instrument. The xylophone sounds an octave higher than written to avoid excessive ledger lines. The bars of the xylophone are made of either rosewood or a synthetic material such as Kelon. The synthetic material is more durable and very rarely needs retuning and, therefore, is the better choice.

The type of mallets used will depend on the passage. A pair of hard rubber, polyball, acrylic, or plastic mallets will provide the timbre and the style needed for most passages in church orchestra music. The shafts of these mallets will be rattan, birch, or fiberglass/plastic. The type will depend on the player's preference.

Orchestra Bells

The most common range of the bells is 2-1/2 octaves. The orchestra bells sound two octaves higher than written to avoid excessive ledger lines. The bars of the bells should be made of a steel alloy and not aluminum. The steel alloy will provide a clear resonate sound that is characteristic of a fine set of bells. Placing two or three fingers on each bar that has been played can dampen the bells. Brass, plastic or acrylic mallets will provide the best results for most of the music written for church orchestra. The shafts of the mallets will be the same as the xylophones.

Chimes

The most common range of the chimes is 1-1/2 octaves, which starts at middle C and stops at the

G at the top of the staff. The tubes of the chimes and the striking caps at the top of each tube should be made of brass. The 1-1/2" diameter tubes are recommended for a "church bell" sounding chime and for the most projection possible. Most chimes come with a foot-dampening pedal that works like a sustain pedal on a piano. For clarity, each chime can be hand dampened after being struck.

The best mallet for the chimes is a plastic carpenter's hammer. These mallets produce a hard attack and a full tone. The other acceptable mallet is the wound rawhide mallet. The rawhide from this mallet tends to spread and produces a nonarticulated sound when it is used regularly. The chimes are to be struck only on the cap at the top of each chime.

Playing Technique

The grip for all the keyboard mallet instruments is the matched grip, which is the same as the snare drum grip that was recommended. The mallets are held with the thumb and first finger about six inches from the end of the handle. The rest of the fingers are wrapped around the handle. The first finger should not be extended, which would place the mallet at the second joint of the finger. The playing position of the mallets should be at a 90° angle to each other. For the **chimes,** the mallet should be, approximately, at a 90° angle to the chime. A draw stroke should be used when striking any bar or chime. This will allow the sound to be drawn out of the instrument in much the same way the timpani are played. The **xylophone bars** are to be struck in the center of the "white" keys and at the end of the "black" keys during fast passages to facilitate quickness. The **bells** should be struck in the center of all bars to provide consistent tone quality and full resonance. Rolls will be seen for the **xylophone** primarily. Some composers will write rolls for the bells, but not for the chimes. All written rolls should be played as a rapid single-stroke roll.

The player should stand in the middle of the range being played. If movement is needed, the player should use a side-step approach rather than crossing his feet to get from one octave to another. A cross-step will cause the player's body to turn with the step. These instruments need to be addressed in a parallel manner.

The keyboard mallet instruments will use a hand-to-hand sticking, unless a passage calls for a double sticking. If this double sticking is used, it should only be used between intervals of a third or less.

Purchasing

A set of orchestra bells will cost from $850-$1250, list. A xylophone will cost from $2,500-$4,000, list. A set of chimes will cost from $4,000-$6,200, list as of this writing. As always, shop around for the best price.

Percussion Accessories

There are many percussion accessories used and written for in today's church orchestra arrangements. The most common accessories will be discussed in this segment.

Suspended Cymbal

The cymbal itself should be a medium- or thin-weight cymbal, 16"-18" in diameter, and should have a quick, smooth response on rolls. The suspended cymbal can be mounted on a drum set cymbal stand. This pole-type stand should have adequate felt washers and rubber post insulators to prevent the cymbal from touching any metal parts. For all rolls, the percussionist should use a pair of medium yarn marimba mallets. Sometimes composers will ask the player to use timpani mallets. *Please do not use them!* The timpani mallet is

made for the timpani, not the suspended cymbal. Other mallets, such as snare sticks, triangle beaters or wire brushes, may be used if they are required. All single hits on the suspended cymbal should be done with a glancing blow, with one or two snare sticks or marimba mallets. All rolls should be done near the edge, at a three o'clock and nine o'clock position on the cymbal. Grabbing the cymbal with either hand can dampen the cymbal. L.V. (or a curved line after a single note) is the symbol for letting the cymbal ring after being played. If these symbols are not used, the player should dampen the cymbal on the following rest.

Suspended cymbals will list from $300 to $380. A cymbal stand will list from $80 to $120.

Crash Cymbals

The crash cymbals can be used as an explosive climax to the music or played delicately as a soft punctuation. The better crash cymbals should have an easy and even response, should have a complete sounding range from a low fundamental through the high overtones, and have a slow decay with even duration. They should be 18 to 20 inches in diameter. Top-of-the-line brand names, such as Zildjian or Sabian, will assure a good quality cymbal and a desirable sound. There are three main categories for these cymbals: "French," "Viennese," and "Germanic." The "French" cymbal has a light tone and fast response. The "Viennese" cymbal is a general-purpose crash cymbal. The "Germanic" has a thick dark sound. Personal preference will determine the sound quality used, either that of the conductor or the players. The writer of this article recommends the "French" style.

The straps used for the crash cymbals should be made of leather. Avoid using the leather pads because they will tend to absorb the sustaining quality of the cymbals. These straps should be checked regularly to avoid a loose knot. Many percussion books will have diagrammed instruction on how to tie a knot in case it comes loose. Holding the strap with the thumb and first finger, close to the cymbal itself, will give the percussionist the best control. The rest of the strap can be positioned in the palm of the hand. Do not insert the hand inside the strap. This will cause the same results as the pads. The cymbal player should hold both cymbals at different angles, striking them together in a "flam" effect, hitting the tops of the cymbals together first, and then the bottoms. This technique will avoid an "air pocket" which can destroy a great climax.

A cymbal rack or table should be purchased to provide a place of rest when crash cymbals are not being used. It should be padded with a soft material to avoid metal against metal contact when placing the cymbals in the rack or on the table.

Crash cymbals will range from $250 to $350 a pair.

Triangle

The triangle can be played on either the middle of the bottom side (orchestra side) or the top of the closed side (band side). Both areas will have a distinct timbre. The player can determine the side used, which should be the one best suited for the music. The most popular sizes are 6" and 8" triangles. The triangle should never have a harsh sound. The rolls should be played in either of the two closed corners and should never use all three sides. A basic spring style clamp with string attached is needed to hang the triangle when it is not being used. The clamp is also used to hold the triangle when it is being played. The percussionist must be able to see the conductor, the triangle, and the music at the same time.

Triangle beaters come in various weights. The beater should be selected based on the music being played. There should also be at least one pair of triangle beaters of equal weight for the more technical passages.

Quality triangles will list from $40 to $60, as of this writing. Clips will run from $5 to $15. A set of beaters can range from $5 to $45, depending on the variety, number, and brand name of each set.

Tambourine

The tambourine that will best suffice for most concert situations is a 10", wood shell, skin head with a double row of silver jingles. For the pop songs, the plastic or metal shell with no head and a double row of silver jingles will always produce a contemporary sound. The shape is not important.

Most of the tambourine parts written for church orchestra can be played with the tambourine at eye level, slightly tilted, and struck with three fingers near the rim.

The tambourine should be held with the thumb on the head and the other fingers wrapped around the other side of the shell. The shake roll should be done with a rapid rotary motion of the wrist, like turning a doorknob. Each shake roll should start and end with a single stroke. To produce a thumb roll, rub the thumb along the edge of the tambourine with an exact amount of pressure so that the friction will produce a vibration and sound the jingles.

Quality tambourines will list from $50 to $125, as of this writing. There are less expensive tambourines that can be purchased for about $25.

Bell Trees and Mark Trees

Bell trees and mark trees (wind chimes) are used extensively in church orchestra music. The bell tree is a percussion instrument that consists of graduated brass bells placed on a single rod with the larger bells at the top. They are played with brass mallets in a gliding motion from top to bottom. The mark tree or wind chimes are generally made of individually suspended tubes which are hung from a piece of wood. These tubes can be solid or hollow, definitely pitched, or pitched generally from high to low. The tubes can be made of aluminum, copper, glass, or ceramic. Most often, dragging the index finger along the tubes will create the ethereal effect desired in the music. The writer of this chapter likes the Spectrasound brand because each tube is pitched differently from high to low.

As a general rule, the bell tree should be used on all passages that have the markings for two beats or less. The mark tree should be used on all passages that have the markings for one measure or more. Sometimes the markings and the instrument do not make musical sense. First, try what is written. If that does not make sense for that passage, then change either the length of the marking or the instrument.

Bell trees will list around $140, and wind chimes will list around $100, as of this writing.

Latin Percussion Instruments

Latin percussion instruments can add a great deal to any Latin style piece of music. In most cases, a conga drum (ad lib) part will be included in the percussion and

conductor's score. If there are enough players, the addition of other Latin percussion instruments will greatly enhance the feel of the music. Bongos, claves, maracas, guiro, cowbells, cabasa, timbales, shakers and vibra-slap can be added to give the music an authentic Latin sound. Techniques and notations for these instruments can be found in many percussion books and in videos.

Conclusion

Percussion instruments can be great fun. There is so much variety in the sounds that can be produced, as well as variety among the instruments in the percussion family itself. Do not hesitate to experiment with sounds and mallets. Adapt percussion parts that do not make musical sense. Most of all, the conductor should not hesitate to tell the percussionist what is needed for the best musical effect.

Resources

- *Percussion Manual,* F. Michael Combs (Wadsworth Publishing Company, 1995—out of print) [textbook with etudes]
- *Teaching Percussion,* Gary D. Cook (Gale Group, 1988) [extensive textbook]

SNARE DRUM
Beginning
- *Vic Firth Snare Drum Method, Book I, Elementary,* Vic Firth (Carl Fischer, 1967)
- *Beginning Snare Drum Method* with play-along cassette, Al Payson (Park Ridge, IL: Payson Percussion Products, 1972)
- *Fundamental Studies for Snare Drum,* Garwood Whaley (Joel Rothman Pub., 1973)

Intermediate
- *Portraits in Rhythm,* Anthony J. Cirone (Warner Brothers, 1997)
- *Vic Firth Snare Drum Method, Book II, Intermediate,* Vic Firth (Carl Fischer, 1967)
- *Intermediate Snare Drum Studies,* Mitchell Peters (Mitchell Peters, 1976)
- *Musical Studies for the Intermediate Snare Drummer,* Garwood Whaley (Joel Rothman Publications, 1971)

Advanced
- *The Solo Snare Drummer-Advanced Etudes and Duets,* Vic Firth (Carl Fischer, 1978)
- *The Snare Drum in the Concert Hall,* Al Payson (Meredith Music Pub., 1970)
- *Advanced Snare Drum Studies,* Mitchell Peters (Mitchell Peters, 1971)

TIMPANI
Beginning
- *Simple Steps to Timpani,* Anthony Cirone (Belwin Mills, 1991)
- *Basic Timpani Technique,* Thomas McMillan (Warner Brothers, 1985)
- *Fundamental Studies for Timpani,*Garwood Whaley (Joel Rothman Pub., 1973)

Intermediate
- *Timpani Tuning Exercises,* Bob Tilles (GIA Publishing, 1971)
- *Musical Studies for the Intermediate Timpanist,* Garwood Whaley (Joel Rothman Publications, 1971, 1972)

Advanced
- *Modern Method for Timpani,* by Saul Goodman (Belwin-Mills, 1948)

- *Technique for the Virtuoso Timpanist,* Fred D. Hinger (Jerona Music Corp., 1975)
- *Thirty-Two Solos for Timpani,* Alexander Lepak (Windsor Music Pub., 1975)

KEYBOARD MALLETS
Beginning
- *Simple Steps to Keyboard Percussion,* Anthony Cirone (CPP Belwin, 1991)
- *Elementary Marimba and Xylophone Method,* Al Payson (Payson Percussion Products, 1973)
- *Fundamental Method for Mallets,* Mitchell Peters (Alfred Publishing Co., 1995)
- *Fundamental Studies for Mallets,* Garwood Whaley (Joel Rothman Pub., 1974)
Intermediate
- *Mallet Technique,* Vic Firth (Carl Fischer, Inc., 1965)
- *Fundamental Method for Mallets,* Mitchell Peters (Alfred Publishing Co., 1995)
- *Musical Studies for the Intermediate Mallet Player,* Garwood Whaley (Meredith Music Publications, 1980)
Advanced
- *Modern School for Xylophone, Marimba and Vibraphone,* Morris Goldenberg (Hal Leonard Corp., 1981)
- *George Hamilton Green's Instruction Course for Xylophone,* George Hamilton Green (Meredith Music Publications, 1984)
- *Stout Etudes for Marimba, Book II and Book III,* Gordon Stout (Studio 4/Alfred Publishing Co., 1982

Percussion Resources (Manufacturers and Distributors)
- Steve Weiss Music, P. O. Box 20885, Philadelphia, PA 19141, (215) 3291637
- Vic Firth, Inc., 323 Whiting Ave. Unit B, Dedham, MA 02030, (617) 326-3455
- Latin Percussion, 160 Belmont Avenue, Garfield, NJ 07026, (201) 947-8067
- Brazilian Imports of Santa Cruz, P. O. Box 1454, Santa Cruz, CA 95061, (408) 423-6751
- Ludwig Industries, 1728 N. Damen Avenue, Chicago, IL 60525 (312) 276-3360
- Paiste AG, CH-6207, Nottwel, Switzerland, 045-541333
- A. Zildjian Company, Longwater, Drive, Norwell, MA 02061

Textbooks on Percussion
- *Contemporary Percussion,* Reginald Smith Brindle (London: Oxford University Press, 1973)
- *Timpani Technique for the Virtuoso Timpanist,* Fred Hinger (Levonia, NJ: Hinger, 1975)
- The Development of Drum Rudiments, William F. Ludwig (Chicago: Ludwig Drum Company, n.d.)
- *Teaching Percussion,* Gary D. Cook (New York: Schirmer Books, 1995)

Michael Katterjohn is Director of Bands at Davidson Fine Arts School and Percussion Instructor at Augusta State University in Augusta, Georgia, since 1994. He is a freelance percussionist in the area and has performed with the Augusta Symphony, Augusta Choral Society, and the Augusta Opera. He is drummer for the contemporary praise and worship music at Grace Baptist Church in Evans, Georgia. Michael has also written and published several church orchestra arrangements.

STRINGS

AN INTRODUCTION

by Terry C. Terry

In the next five chapters one will find basic information on the members of the string section. In some cases there are notes about the differences between what one might encounter in the world of professional players and those found in a local church.

If the director is blessed to be in an area with a good string program in the school system, he may find himself with a number of players. Since professional musicians in local church settings are not the norm, players will be students, or adults who may not have been playing regularly for some time. In either case, there may be a real "fear" factor to overcome.

In symphonic music, strings form the foundation of the orchestra. In contemporary church music, strings still play most of the time, but often string parts can be omitted, played by a synthesizer, or may be doubled at strategic points. The director ought to spend time assessing the responsibilities of the string section in every score, since this varies greatly depending on publisher, series, or intent of the music. Church orchestra music may feature solos for violins, but less frequently for other strings.

Commercial recordings often reveal violins written in unison, with occasional divisi parts, and some passage work which is technically difficult and may be written too high. Often a simplified violin part will be included in the orchestration. Occasionally there will be a simplified viola or cello part. Directors should keep in mind that amateur string players will have less endurance than professionals, though still asked to play most of the time.

Professionals are accustomed to making notations in their parts (fingerings, bowings, tempo changes, etc.); younger players need to learn this skill. Generally, professionals play perfectly after one reading. Students and amateurs require much more rehearsal. Appoint a "leader," the most experienced violinist perhaps, to help mentor or coach less-experienced players with fingerings, bowings, when to "tacet," who plays the solo, etc. Having a section leader mark bowings in advance will also save rehearsal time. Also, having a flow sheet for every service will significantly cut down on wasted talking time in rehearsals.

String sections take up more space within the orchestra. String players must hear themselves well to play in tune; therefore, their acoustic environment should be carefully considered.

CHAPTER 15

The Violin

by Celeste Myall

Few instruments evoke the strength or depth of emotional response in listeners as that called forth by a beautifully played violin. Its richness of tone and purity of expression have led many to compare it to the human voice. In an orchestra its presence is pervasive as it serves the functions of both worker and queen bee, providing sustained and continuous accompaniment for all of the other instruments even as it establishes thematic context and basks in the spotlight in the climaxes.

It is small wonder, then, that during the liturgical seasons of celebration, especially Christmas and Easter, music directors in churches of all sizes throughout the country find themselves scrambling to put together an instrumental ensemble which will feature at least a few violins. The presence of a full orchestra invigorates the choir, the visual stimulus of the added musicians creates a more celebratory atmosphere, and the warmth and richness of sound inspires the congregation with a heightened sense of worshipful reverence and awe.

After only a few such experiences, however, most church music ministers will confirm that the emphasis in this chapter's first sentence is key. Poorly played violins may well evoke emotions, but they are not the kind which one normally expects to find in worship. Yet most church music ministers, with the exception of those who serve well-financed churches in major metropolitan areas, find themselves dealing with just that as they stand in front of an orchestra whose violin section is composed largely of amateur or young student players of widely varied talent and development.

What follows is a brief, bare-bones primer designed to help the church music minister and music educator survive these joyous occasions. Armed with a rudimentary understanding of acoustical design, position playing, idiomatic uses, and common hazards should help church musicians, regardless of their own musical backgrounds, as they help their violinists realize their fullest potential as they contribute to an enriched, inspiring worship experience.

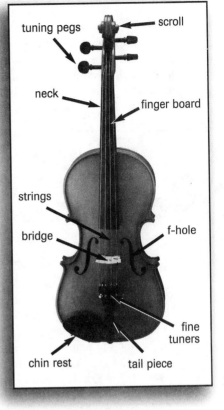

Instrument Design

Sound is produced on the violin by a vibrating string which is set in motion either by drawing the bow across the string or by plucking the string with the fingers. The vibrations of the string are carried by the bridge to the top of the instrument, through the sound post, to the back of the instrument. The vibrating air, thus amplified, is released to the open air through the f-holes on either side of the top.

Changing the length of the string alters the pitch of each string. For the purpose of tuning, this is accomplished with the tuning pegs on the scroll and/or tuners on the tail piece. There are four strings tuned in fifths with the bottom tuned to G below middle C. To alter the pitch while playing, the fingers press the string to change its vibrating length.

Tone and volume are a product of many elements working together. These include how the left hand fingers touch the string, the vibrato employed, and, very importantly, the placement, speed, angle, and pressure of the moving bow.

Fundamentals of Playing Technique: The Left Hand

Positions and Shifting

The most troublesome issue for violinists of all ages and levels of advancement is that of intonation. Unschooled listeners might never notice how far off pitch a singer might stray, nor complain about an out-of-tune piano, but will inevitably become critics when confronted with out-of-tune violin playing. There is, after all, a reason why everyone, whatever their musical understanding, loved Jack Benny's tortuous routines with his violin. With its high pitch and purity of tone, intonation problems on the violin are impossible to ignore.

A whole host of elements contribute to the difficulties violinists face on this front. Beyond the obvious absence of keys or frets to visually and tactilely place the pitch, other contributing obstacles include: the very small distances between the pitches, the shrinking distances as the pitch rises, the increasing lack of comfort for the hand and arm as the pitch rises and the fingers move up the fingerboard, and the influence on each pitch which is exerted by that which has come before.

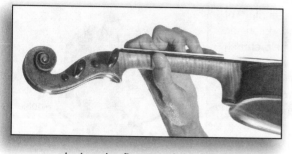

Positions

In order to understand the challenges in pitch production that face developing violinists, one must have a basic grasp of position playing. The fingers of the left hand are numbered one through four beginning with the index finger. As noted earlier, placing the fingers of the left hand on the string to change its length alters pitch. In most instances, violinists will use a different finger for each note (A, B, C, etc.), but on the same note, B and Bb for example, will usually use the same finger for sharps or flats.

When the first finger of the left hand plays the note above the open string (E on the D string, for example), the hand is in first position. Beginning players stay in first position for at least one year, usually much longer, and first position is always "home" to any violinist. When the entire hand moves up toward the bridge one note (for example, first finger plays F on the D string), the hand is in second position; one more note up (G on the D string), is third position, etc. Violinists usually learn third position after first, then fifth, and then back to second. Thus, intermediate level players are not as comfortable in the even positions as in the odd.

Violinists change positions (shift) for many reasons, the most obvious being to reach higher notes. The highest note in first position without extending the fourth finger is B, although even young players can extend to C. To play higher pitches, the violinist must move the left hand up the neck to various higher positions. (Intermediate level violinists should be comfortable with notes as high as D two ninths above middle C; advanced high school students with F or F♯).

Violinists also choose to shift in order to affect changes in color and tone. The same note played on different strings has a different timbre—the lower the string, the more mellow the sound. Finally, shifting often creates greater technical ease in fast passage playing. In such instances it is better not to go back and forth between strings repeatedly, and that can usually be avoided by shifting to another position.

While all of these reasons make shifting an essential tool in playing, it remains the largest single cause of intonation problems. If the hand does not reach or overreaches the correct place on the fingerboard, not only will the first note be out of tune, all notes following in that same position will be difficult to control, as well. For that reason, shifting causes substantial anxiety, especially in younger, less experienced players, who often respond by shifting prematurely. Shifting is most successful when the hand moves quickly. When players give in to the tendency to shift prematurely, the hand, while moving too soon, will actually move more slowly. To counter this tendency, string players should be taught to hold the note before the shift—in practice even to  an exaggerated length—a practice which will train them to keep from cheating that note while taking too much time on the shift itself.

Another common tendency, which leads to shifting-related intonation problems, is the tendency to shift with the wrong finger. If a young violinist is shifting from the first finger in one position to a note played with the second finger in another position, he will often try to go directly to the new finger. The appropriate and far more reliable technique is to shift to the same finger, referred to as the auxiliary note or, in Suzuki terminology, the ghost note, and then to play the new finger above it. A good practice technique is to first practice shifting to the "ghost" or auxiliary note, and then to practice shifting to the written note. This has the effect of grounding the new position in relationship to the old, and makes for a much more accurate gauging of the exact distance to be moved between positions.

The effects of shift anxiety are not, however, limited to intonation problems. Less-experienced players also tend to respond to tension by losing independence between right and left hands, leaning into the bow with the right hand at the same time as they shift with the left. This causes heavy slides and also interferes with the left hand's ability to move quickly and lightly. Many of the shifting problems that produce unattractive sounds can be corrected by the consistent application of three maxims:

1. hold the note before the shift,

2. shift to the same finger in the new position, and

3. maintain independence between the left and right hand at the shift, resisting the temptation to lean into the shift with the bow.

Non-Shift Related Left-Hand Challenges

A few other basic concepts can aid in producing cleaner intonation, even while playing within a single position. Most importantly, fingers should be left down until it becomes necessary to pick them up, a very basic rule of violin playing that is often overlooked by younger players. Beyond the improved physical efficiency gained from elimination of wasted motion, there are substantial additional advantages to this practice. If a note is in tune, it is a good idea to hold onto it in case you have to play it again. Since notes are judged against each other, keeping the finger down gives a base for placing the next finger; lifting the fingers unnecessarily also can cause coordination problems.

There is, however, a Murphy's Law of finger pitch "memory." A finger that has played "low" (for example, C♮ on the A string in first position) will tend to remember that place through many notes played with the other fingers of the left hand, and will consequently play a subsequent higher note (for example, F♯ sharp on the D string) too low.

Another common pitfall for younger players is the tendency to split the difference between half steps and whole steps. Because notes with the same name are usually played with the same finger, (C, C♭, C♯), some adjacent fingers will play half steps and others whole steps. Many younger players tend to hedge these intervals with whole steps that are too small and half steps that are too large. Many Suzuki teachers refer to fingers playing half-steps as "friends," and the higher the position the better friends they become. This always holds true when playing adjacent fingers. When the same finger plays a half step, however, the player must usually feel a somewhat larger distance than intuition would suggest.

Because the design of the instrument forces the left hand to be strongly turned up and out with the elbow held underneath, perfect fifths cannot be played so that they feel directly across from each other in first position, but, rather, must be felt, though only very slightly, successively higher on each lower string. For this reason, many young players are often under the pitch on the G string. As the hand moves up the violin, this changes, and by fourth position, the intervals are more directly across. In fifth position and higher, fifths are higher on the higher strings.

Here again, three fairly simple guidelines can lead to greater accuracy. Players should:

• **leave the fingers down** once they have played until they are required to move,

• **be careful** to give half steps and whole steps the appropriate distance, and

• **be constantly aware** of the effect which the shape and position of the hand have upon the placement of fingers from string to string.

Fundamentals of Playing: The Right Hand

Just as nervous tension and anxiety lead to counterproductive actions in the left hand, so can they lead to difficulties in the right hand—most commonly, unattractive tone and lack of rhythmic control. While it is essential that the fingers and wrist of the right hand be firm but relaxed while moving the

bow, many young players tend to grab hold of the bow, gripping it in an effort to feel more secure. While such a response may indeed help the player to feel better, it causes the sound to become thin and tense. It also inhibits the flexibility needed to play rhythmically and accurately.

Pulling the bow straight across the string is often difficult for younger players. While it is acceptable, and perhaps even

tension screw   tip

frog   hair

preferable, to pull the bow "in" (toward the bridge) just a little, pulling away from the bridge causes the sound to lose focus and makes it more difficult for notes to "speak." String supply companies even offer several products that attach to the violin during practice which trap the bow and force the player to pull the bow in a straight line.

One reason younger players have trouble pulling a straight bow relates to the part of the arm used. The upper two-thirds of the bow (from the tip to below the middle) is played with the forearm only. In the lower third of the bow (near the frog), however, the player should use the whole arm, from the upper arm. Often players who end up with a bent wrist at the frog have not followed through with the upper arm in the lower half. It is extremely important, however, that the whole arm not continue past the lower middle, or the bow will go in a circular direction, rather than straight. As noted above, this will create an unfocused sound.

Players purposefully adjust the way the bow travels on the string to affect changes in volume and quality of sound. In louder passages, the bow moves a little more slowly, with more pressure, closer to the bridge. In softer passages, the bow should move a little more quickly, with less pressure, toward the fingerboard. In general, the bow should lean a little away from the bridge, although in louder passages, the bow hair should be flat, and in quiet passages, tilted back more.

Less-experienced players often bow too close to the fingerboard. The bow should not be placed over the fingerboard unless this is indicated in the music (*sul tasto*). While the placement of the bow varies according to the volume of the music as noted above, in general, the normal placement for the bow is about halfway between the fingerboard and the bridge.

A few other things to remember relating to bowing:

• Strong beats are usually played with a down bow, while pickups usually start up.

• When the bow moves slowly (in very long phrases), the violinist should "save" the bow at the beginning of the stroke, rather than running out of bow and trying to save at the end.

• If the down bow and up bow are not the same rhythmic duration (for example, two beats on the down bow and one on the up) and the volume is to remain the same, the player must lighten the pressure on the up bow to avoid a crescendo on the shorter note.

• Fast running notes on separate bows that have the down bow on the beat (this is usually the case) should be played in the middle of the bow—they speak much more easily there. Fast running notes on separate bows that are "backward" (with the strong beat coming on an up bow) are usually played closer to the tip.

• Passages marked *marcato* or *staccato* are almost always played in the upper half of the bow (toward the tip) with a very firm attack at both the beginning and the end of the note.

Independence of the Hands

One of the main problems facing violinists is the difference in motion between the two hands. While the left hand fingers are striking the fingerboard in a vertical motion, the right hand is usually drawing the bow in a horizontal motion. Younger players often try to "help" with the bow by jabbing each note, even in a slurred passage. Conversely, the motion of the left hand should be strong and quick even in very legato sections.

This is especially true in light *spiccato* passages where less-experienced players often throw the bow at the string rather than having a horizontal approach in the arm. Notes speak much more quickly and can therefore be much shorter if the bow is moving in a horizontal fashion, even if it only connects with the string for a short time.

Other Things to Watch Out For in Younger Players

The most common and potentially most damaging "bad habit" in younger players is collapsing the wrist of the left hand up against the neck of the violin. This is referred to as "squeezing." In addition to keeping the fingers from dropping naturally and cramping the hand, this position can cause serious physical problems in even very young players.

The violin should not be held completely off to the side of the body but more in front.

Harmonics

Harmonics are another area of violin performance which cause great anxiety for both players and conductors. There are two main kinds of harmonics—natural and artificial.

Natural harmonics are played with one finger and sound the note indicated at the octave indicated. These harmonics are notated by a circle above the pitch. All notes in the harmonic series for each string will ring as natural harmonics (above the open string: one octave, one octave plus a perfect fifth, two octaves, etc.).

The most commonly used natural harmonic is one octave above the open string. Although when played as a normal note, this is played by the fourth finger in fourth position, the harmonic is played by extending the fourth finger and opening the hand in third position.

Almost all moderately advanced violinists understand natural harmonics and how to play them. Many younger players, however, make the mistake of moving the left hand up as well as opening the hand, causing the finger to be too high and the note not to ring.

Artificial harmonics are more complicated and cause many more problems than natural harmonics. They are usually notated by writing the bottom note and indicating the touched note with a diamond. (See example.) They are played by putting one finger down in the normal fashion and touching a note either a minor third, a major third, a perfect fourth or a perfect fifth above the bottom note.

By far the most commonly used artificial harmonic is played by touching a perfect fourth above the bottom note. This sounds a note that is two octaves above the bottom note.

This is a very convenient way to ring (or even play) a very high note that is surrounded by lower notes and is used frequently in both solo and orchestral music. Other less common artificial harmonics are played:

• by touching a minor third above the bottom finger, which rings two octaves plus a perfect fifth above the bottom note.

• by touching a major third above the bottom finger, which rings two octaves plus a major third above the bottom note (two octaves above the top note).

• by touching a perfect fifth above the bottom finger, which rings one octave plus a perfect fifth above the bottom note (one octave above the top note).

These harmonics also ring off an open string, which means the player has to touch only one finger.

These are much easier to play than harmonics that require two fingers. Unfortunately, sometimes these harmonics are sometimes indicated differently, and often the sounding pitch is also shown, which can confuse younger (or even older) players.

For artificial harmonics to ring, both fingers need to be in the right place. Because the fourth finger is extended for natural harmonics, and because natural harmonics are learned first by all violinists, the tendency in younger, less-experienced players is to overextend the note above the first finger, causing the note not to ring. Have the player push down the third or fourth finger, depending on which harmonic is played, to check the pitch.

By far the most useful trick for conductors to know is that all harmonics, especially artificial ones, ring much more easily if the bow is near the bridge. Even when the player's fingers are not exactly right, if the bow is near (not on) the bridge, they will ring, and often if the fingers are right but the bow is too close to the fingerboard, they will not.

Best Uses of Violins

- Long, sustained melodic lines
- Fast-running notes (not too high and not slurred) supported by long tones in woodwinds and brass
  - Doubling of choral lines (like *Messiah*)
  - Ethereal or "spooky" effects (accomplished by high notes or tremolo)

Most Common Misuses of Violins

- Too many flats in the key signature. In general, violins play much better, and much better in tune, in sharp keys.
- Too many fast scales—when used sparingly this can be very effective, but overuse ruins the effectiveness of this technique. In general, too many very fast, very high, slurred scales, played during loud sections of the music tend to encourage "faking" in younger and intermediate players, a habit which can carry over to other, more exposed and more essential sections of the music.
- Very high first violin parts without the support of doubling at the octave by the second violins or the violas. In general, too high for too long is not too good.
- Too many half-step modulations causing very problematic keys for all but the most advanced players.
- Extended passages of very high, very fast separate notes are difficult for all but the most advanced players.

Purchasing a Violin

Violins and violin outfits (complete with bow and case) come in all price ranges. Because a good quality violin is a major financial investment, many companies offer a "rent to own" policy, usually with 80 percent of rent applied toward purchase. Unlike many instruments, good violins hold their value. Always check the dealer's policy on trade-ins. Many will offer a fair trade if the violinist later decides to buy a more expensive instrument.

Some violins are completely factory-machine produced, some are a combination of factory produced and hand-finished, and some are made entirely by hand. For a beginning player, the price of an instrument that is completely hand made can be prohibitive. Those instruments that are finished and "set-up" by hand, however, will respond much better and there is usually not much difference in price.

Lower-priced, entry-level instruments are often fitted with all steel strings. These stay in tune much better than soft-core strings (where a soft substance, such as gut is wrapped in aluminum, silver, or steel), and they can be tuned with a fine tuner (see violin illustration). Steel strings do, however, produce a more tense, occasionally shrill, sound. When players have advanced to an intermediate level, most switch to some kind of soft-core string (with the exception of the E which is often steel) for a warmer sound. Because the length of soft-core strings must be changed more to change the pitch, these are almost always tuned entirely by the pegs.

Most violin bows are made from wood, but many bows of good quality are now made from fiberglass or other synthetic materials. For a younger player, these can produce very good results and offer substantially greater durability. Unlike wood bows, fiberglass bows do not warp, and they are much harder to break. Even many professional players are now purchasing back-up bows made from substances other than wood because of their relative affordability, quality, and indestructibility.

Lauren McMinn
Violin Instructor and Orchestra Director, Parkway Hills Baptist Church, Plano, TX

"The greatest joy and fulfillment I have found musically is when I play for the Lord. Why? Because in worship, my instrument is my voice—the expression of my heart's praise to Him. This is such a good thing because my violin can sing far better than my voice ever will. Stringed instruments can be used so many ways in worship, but regardless of their setting, I know the Lord is pleased when I use the fullest extent of my training and the honest expressions of my heart to shower Him with glory."

Care and Maintenance

Violins are delicate instruments and highly susceptible to changes in temperature and humidity. Never leave a violin in an extremely hot or cold climate—especially in a car or trunk.

In dry climates, humidifiers are necessary for the instruments to respond properly and to keep them from cracking. There are two or three types of humidifiers that fit in the f-hole of the violin; there are also humidifiers that can be put in the violin case.

Since the bridge carries the vibration, controls the height of the strings from the fingerboard, and establishes string spacing, it is extremely important that an expert fit it. A poorly fitted bridge can create a host of problems. If, for example, the bridge is too thick, the tone will also be thick. If it is too high or too low, the strings will be too high or too low off the fingerboard, making them difficult to play and possibly even resulting in player injury.

The hair on the bow should be loosened completely whenever the violin is not being used. This not only helps to keep the bow hair from stretching, it, more importantly, reduces the pressure on the bow stick.

Rosin, which is rubbed on the bow hair to help it stick to the string, should not be overused. It should be wiped off the instrument and strings after playing, to protect the violin finish.

Bowing Techniques

This list works for all string family instruments.

- **Col legno**—literally, with wood; a kind of glassy sound produced by playing with the stick, rather than the hair of the bow. It is a purely orchestral effect.

- **Détaché**—detached bowing, notes not connected to each other

- **Jeté, ricochet, saltando**—down bow that is "thrown" to bounce, generally two to six notes

- **Legato**—smooth connected bows, the most usual bowing

- **Louré**—usually used in very expressive passages, where two or more notes of the same pitch are played in one bow with a slight separation between them

- **Marcato**—pauses between bows, but the bow remains on the string

- **Martellé**—quick, hammerlike bowings, short detached with good separation between notes

- **Pizzicato**—trick, not a bowing at all, plucking the string with the finger

- **Spiccato**—bouncing bow, short notes

- **Staccato**—In true staccato form, a series of short notes played up-bow. Often taken to be short notes bowed separately.

- **Sul ponticello**—a nasal, brittle sound produced by playing closer to the bridge

- **Sul tasto**—playing over the fingerboard, a flute-like effect

- **Tremolo**—comes in two types, unmeasured, when the bow is moved as quickly as possible in short bows at the tip, and measured, when the desired effect is even 8ths, 16ths, or 32nds.

Bows should be rehaired and strings changed on a regular basis. The length between each is determined by the amount of time the violin is played. In general, once a year is adequate for intermediate and high school players, but those who practice and perform regularly and for long periods of time will need to do this more frequently.

There are many reasons for a violin to have an unwanted "buzz." Some—a button on the player's shirt, a loose screw on a fine tuner—are easy to fix. Others are more serious. One of the most common is an open seam. This is not a serious problem; in fact, violins are designed to respond to humidity and temperature changes by coming apart at the glued seams rather than allowing the wood itself to crack. A professional violin repairperson must glue open seams.

Conclusion

While these few concepts can by no means lead to a complete under-standing of the violinist's art, they can help the church musician or music educator identify and isolate the more common causes of problems in the violin section. This rudimentary understanding, coupled with the help of at least one experienced professional hired to lead the section (undoubtedly the most important insurance for a good performance), will certainly help. If, however, you would like to gain a more in-depth understanding, the follow-ing is a listing of excellent resources.

Resources

Method and Technique Materials
Beginner
- *Suzuki Violin School* (Summy-Birchard, Inc., 1980, 1981)—designed for individual instruction and practice
- *Essential Elements for Strings* (Hal Leonard, 1994)
- *Strictly Strings* (Alfred Pub. Co., 1996)
- *Fiddlers Philharmonic* (Alfred Pub. Co., 1996)

Intermediate
All of these are designed for individual instruction and practice and avail-able in different editions from various publishers.
- *Etudes,* Mazas
- *42 Etudes,* Kreutzer
- *Introducing the Positions,* Whistler

Advanced
These are also designed for individual instruction and practice.
- *Schradieck School of Violin Technics* (especially *Book I*)
- *Caprices,* Rode
- *Caprices,* Dont
- *Violin Hymns and Obbligatos, Vol. I and II,* Doug Smith (Lorenz, #30/1755L)

Suggested Readings
- *How to Design and Teach a Successful School String and Orchestra Program,* by Jacquelyn A. Dillon and Casimer B. Kriechbaum, Jr. (San Diego, CA: Kjos West, 1978)
- *Teaching Stringed Instruments in Classes,* by Elizabeth A. H. Green (Tichenor Publishing, for the American String Teachers Association with National School Orchestra Association, 1987)
- *Orchestral Bowing and Routines,* by Elizabeth A. H. Green (American String Teachers Association, 1990)
- *Guide to Teaching Strings,* by Norman Lamb (McGraw Hill Higher Education, 2002)

- *Face to Face with an Orchestra,* by Don V. Moses, Robert W. Demaree, Jr. and Allen F. Ohmes (Princeton, NJ: Prestige Publications, 1987)
- *The String Play,* by Phyllis Young (Austin, TX: University of Texas Press, 1986)

String Websites
- www.maestronet.com
- www.thestrad.com
- www.hweisshaar.com
- www.violink.com
- www.stringsmagazine.com

String Suppliers (Repair, Products and Tools)
- Shar Music Products, P. O. Box 1411, Ann Arbor, Mi. 48106-1411, 1-800-438-4538
- International Violin Company, 1421 Clarkview Road, Suite 118, Baltimore, Maryland 21209, 1-800-542-3538
- Hans Weisshaar, Inc., 627 N. Larchmont Blvd., Los Angeles, California 900004, (323) 466-6293
- Metropolitan Music, P. O. Box 1415, Stowe, Vermont 05762, 1-802-253-4812
- Meisel Music, 32 Commerce Street, Springfield, New Jersey 07081, 1-201-379-5000
- Ideal Music, 53 West 23rd Street, New York, New York 10010, 1-212-675-5050
- Southwest Strings, 1050 South Park Avenue, Tucson, Arizona 85719, 1-800-528-3430

String Texts
- *The Art and Science of String Performance,* Samuel Appelbaum (Sherman Oaks, CA: Alfred Publishing, 1986)
- *Violin Playing As I Teach It,* Second Edition, Leopold Auer (New York: Dover Publications, Second Edition, 1980)
- *Principles of Violin Playing and Teaching,* Ivan Galamian (Englewood Cliffs, NJ: Prentice-Hall, Inc., 1962)

Celeste Myall served on the faculty of Hardin-Simmons University School of Music from 1978 to 2001, teaching violin, coaching chamber music, and conducting the Abilene Collegiate Orchestra, an orchestra comprised of students from both HSU and Abilene Christian University. A graduate of the Manhattan School of Music, where she earned her masters under the tutelage of renowned violin pedagogue Raphael Bronstein, she has performed widely both as a soloist and a chamber musician, in addition to serving for many years as the concert master for the Abilene Philharmonic. Having recently moved to Nashville, she now teaches violin and chamber music at Belmont University, performs throughout Middle Tennessee as a chamber and orchestral musician, and is a frequent guest clinician for school, church, and regional orchestras.

CHAPTER 16

The Viola

by Terry C. Terry

Fundamentals of Instrument Design

The viola is the alto member of the string family. While violins and violas are very similar in shape and design, violas vary in size from 14 to 17-1/2 inches. The instrument is wider, and ranges from 1 to 3-1/2 inches longer than violins. The sounding length of the strings is a little more than 2 inches longer than the violin. Because the viola is heavier than the violin, it is more difficult to hold. The space between half steps is further. Viola strings are heavier and more difficult to press to the fingerboard, and more arm weight is needed to produce the sound. The sound of the viola is distinctive, much darker and mellower than that of the violin.

As with all string instruments, the length of the string, along with its diameter, determines the pitch. The strings are pitched in fifths, starting with C below middle C, then G, D, and A. As the string vibrates, the vibrations are transferred through the bridge to the top of the instrument, and by way of the sound post, all the air inside vibrates, in turn vibrating the top and back of the instrument and projecting the sound through the f-holes. As the fingers stop the string, the vibrating length is shortened, thus raising the pitch.

The viola is one of the few instruments that plays in the alto clef. The clef sign marks the middle line as middle C. The alto clef comfortably accommodates pitches in the first position, with only a couple of ledger lines. For extended play in the upper ranges, violists read treble clef.

Fundamentals of Playing Technique

Observe beginning players, and even high school students, to ensure that the left elbow is pulled under the viola. This posture will help to maintain a better

wrist position. The wrist should also be straight to avoid muscle tension. Bluegrass fiddle players often play with the instrument resting on the wrist. The fingers are more flexible and able to move more quickly if the wrist position is correct. Younger players tire easily and the wrist is likely to become the support for holding the instrument.

Playing Position

The hand should be fluid to permit all fingers to reach the notes with ease. The center of balance is near the second and third fingers. The knuckle line is at a 30 or 40 degree angle to the viola neck, varying with the length of the little finger. The hand is higher when on the C string, and lower on the A string. In violin, the left-hand thumb is opposite the index finger, or behind the index finger. On viola, the thumb can be brought up closer to middle finger—finger two—so that fingers three and four can be reached more easily. The thumb is often the source of tension in the hand of young players. Fingers should drop vertically on the string with a movement from the base knuckles impelled by the larger arm muscles. Fingers must be independent of each other at the base joint, and should not touch each other except at the fingertip while playing half steps. The wrist must never collapse, and young players tend to struggle in this area. The elbow position must be flexible, varying with the string in play (to the left for higher strings, to the right for lower strings). Younger players may need to be reminded not to grip the viola too tightly with the chin. Chin tension can lead to grinding of teeth and can tense the neck and upper back muscles.

The position of the right hand on the bow is also critical. The right-hand position is the same as for the violin, the cello and the French-bowed bass. (See the violin chapter.)

Generally, the hair of the bow should be flat on the string. Younger players may need to be reminded that the bow hair does not tip away from the face.

Conductors should consider bow distribution in interpreting a musical score. Any tension in the hand or arm other than a natural relaxation of the bow onto the string will hinder tone production greatly. One should control the angle of the bow to the string through the rise and fall of the wrist and the inward pull of the ring finger. Legato bowing is achieved by a relaxed right hand, in particular, a right index finger. Consult the resource list at the end of the chapter for more information on bowing.

Intonation Problems

Out-of-tune playing is generally attributed to faulty technique or a poor ear. Improving the playing position and reducing muscular tension often clear up many intonation difficulties. A lack of pitch perception may be a more serious matter. The basis for playing in tune on a string instrument is being able to play any fingered note in tune with the open string of the same name, so that the instrument resonates. Excess speed, an uncomfortable left-hand position, and poor orientation of the fingers to pitch locations on the fingerboard all can cause poor intonation. A conductor can encourage the young player to set the hand position to conform to the contour of the viola neck and fingerboard. Molding the hand to fit the perfect fourth interval, developing a "feel" for finger patterns, and training cross-string fingerings as well as ascending-descending fingerings can greatly aid intonation. Great time and care should be taken to see that open strings are in tune. Players must listen to the pitch, and actually hear it before playing. Hearing and vocalizing the pitch also improves the ear of the player. When playing in any position, it is critical that a player keeps that position "anchored," by keeping one finger down. This is particularly important in positions beyond first.

Shifting is more difficult for the violist than the violinist because the distances are greater on the larger instrument. Shifting is an action of the arm with a follow-through of the hand and finger. A slight closing of the arm from the elbow joint results in an amazingly long and effortless trip for the finger in playing position. Concentration on the elbow movement takes the strain from shifting the finger from one position to another. In preparing to shift, the contact points, base of the first finger, thumb, and finger in play, must be loosened to reduce friction while the jaw and collar bone maintain a firm hold.

Vibrato is a facet of string playing that is as much related to temperament and taste as it is to technical development. Vibrato production for the violist is produced in the same way as vibrato production for the violinist. However, the viola vibrato will often be wider. It is possible to develop a vibrato that will be largely centered in the fingers, the hand, or the arm. A combination of three movements offers the player greater contrast in musical shading and more individuality in the sound.

Idiosyncrasies

Because holding a viola is an awkward venture, in addition to a chin rest many violists may want a shoulder rest. A shoulder rest for beginners can be a piece of foam with a sturdy rubber band. Older players may also use a piece of foam, but may prefer something more substantial for ease in holding the viola. A variety of shoulder rests are available from string accessory manufacturers.

As with all string instruments, violas are very susceptible to temperature and humidity fluctuations. Keep the instrument at room temperature whenever possible. Hotter temperatures cause the wood to expand, dry out, and crack. While extreme heat can even cause glue to fail, cold temperatures can cause the wood to contract and crack. A certain degree of humidity is important to keep the instrument from drying out. Humidifiers to be placed inside the instrument or case are available for purchase.

The viola is most effective when playing the "alto" or "tenor" line in the string family. It can provide depth when doubling the violin melody line down an octave, or doubling the cello at the octave above. Strong lyric counter-melodies are also effective when played by a sensitive violist.

Whenever possible, it is recommended that church music arrangers avoid writing viola parts higher than A above the treble staff, or playing in keys with more than four flats (a preference for all string players). Double stops should be avoided as well. Viola parts should not be relegated to half and whole notes for long periods of time. It is also best not to switch back and forth between alto and treble clef. Violists are comfortable reading ledger lines up to the A above the treble staff, but if a passage lies in that upper octave for an extended period, treble clef is appropriate. Avoid changing clefs for three or four notes, particularly in quick passages. Players prefer to read a few ledger lines rather than shift their thinking from one clef to another too often.

Basic Care and Maintenance

The bow should have rosin applied before every lengthy practice session or performance. Rosin allows the bow hairs to grab the string so that it can vibrate properly.

After each rehearsal or performance, rosin should be removed from the strings and the body of the viola with a soft cloth. Rosin left on the strings will affect the tone by preventing the bow from "grabbing" the string properly, and rosin left on the body of the viola eats into the varnish. Rosin should also be wiped off the stick of the bow when it collects there.

The hair of the bow should be loosened before the bow is put away. This removes the tension from the bow and prevents warping of the stick. A bow should be rehaired once a year—more often if it is used several hours a day.

Common Simple Repairs

Replacing strings—String should be secured on the fine tuner, pulled across the bridge at the proper groove, and wrapped around the peg. It may take some experimentation to perfect string replacement. Do a bit of winding on the peg and realign the other end on the bridge. Also note that after some time (a year or more) strings may become "false." One can identify a false string by plucking an open string and finding that the pitch of the tone wavers greatly. When pitch variation occurs, it is time to replace that string. One should never play on a frayed metal string.

Bridge adjustment—Sometimes it is necessary to adjust the bridge. Adjustments should be done with great care, by holding the viola between the knees and holding the bridge with both hands. It should tilt very slightly away from the fingerboard, from the perpendicular to the top of the instrument. On occasion, the sound post falls down and must be reset. That needs to be done by someone with the proper tools. It is critical to loosen all strings immediately, should the sound post fall. Failure to do so could cause the top to collapse from the pressure of the bridge carrying all four strings.

> **Laura Apperson Violist in the Amabile String Quartet, teacher at Arizona School for the Arts**
>
> "Pray while you play is my motto. I constantly am running a dialogue with God. He listens to the quiet prayers we whisper while we are using His musical gifts. I have found He can bring a new joy to your playing, calm your nerves, and make music a worship experience every time you play. Just talk to Him. He's listening."

Tips on Purchasing

Shar Music in Ann Arbor, Michigan (phone 1-800-248-7427) is an excellent resource. Web purchases can be ordered at www.sharmusic.com. A local string teacher will be knowledgeable about locating instruments and accessories.

As with all instruments, used instruments may be less expensive. A professional should check out potential purchases for a student, church, or school. Unlike most other instruments, fine strong instruments appreciate in value—older can be better!

Resources
Beginning
- *Foundation Studies, Books 1 & 2,* Wohlfahrt/Isaac
- *Strictly Strings* - Highlans/Etling

Intermediate
- *Forty Two Studies,* Kreutzer/Pagels (Hal Leonard, 1986)
- *Scale System,* Flesch/Karman (Carl Fischer, 1942)

Advanced
- *Twenty Four Caprices,* Rode/Pagels
- *Sixteen Fantasy Etudes,* Fuchs (Ricordi, 1961)

Additional Resources
Refer to the listing on pages 183-184 for additional string family resources.

Terry C. Terry (B. Mus., Ph.D, University of North Texas) is Editor-in-Chief, Music Publishing and Recording, LifeWay Church Resources, a division of LifeWay Christian Resources of the Southern Baptist Convention, Nashville, Tennessee. Terry has played with the Waco (TX) Symphony, the Fayetteville (NC) Symphony, and numerous community orchestras in the past 30 years.

CHAPTER 17

The Cello

by Timothy H. Cierpke

When addressing the subject of the cello, its construction, and its method of performance, one should keep in mind that the cello is a vital member of a family, i.e., the violin family. The surviving members of the violin family, which had its origins in the 15th and 16th centuries, are the violin, viola, and cello. The string bass, which is often mistaken as the largest member of the violin family, is in actuality the lone surviving member of the Renaissance viol family. Referred to as the bass viol, it is part of what is commonly called the string family.

The cello and string family pose two basic problems for the church instrumental director. One, how to act and feel competent as a director when working under the withering gaze of the hired symphony player, the consummate professional who tends to simply "tolerate" the church director. The second challenge, the one we will address, is to become comfortable working with string players of varying abilities, who currently participate in our thriving/struggling church instrumental ensemble or who potentially may contribute in the future.

The primary way to be conversant with an instrument is to become familiar with its components and the technique required to perform on that instrument. The fundamental shape and design of the cello and the bow used to play the instrument have survived relatively unchanged since the 16th century. Traditionally, the woods used in making the cello are generally maple and spruce, although some school instruments are made of plywood. The key components of the cello are the four strings, the wooden bridge that supports the strings, the tuning pegs and fine tuners that are used to raise and lower the pitch of the strings, and the end pin, with which the player supports the instrument on the floor.

Tuning

The strings are tuned in fifths in descending order beginning with the A just below middle C. The resultant pitches A, D, G, and C can be adjusted up and down by carefully turning the tuning pegs or fine tuners which many string instruments have mounted near the bridge. Warning: do not attempt to tune a cello or other string instrument without securing the proper tuning methodology from a competent, experienced player. The bridge supporting the strings should be checked periodically for warping or leaning from its normal vertical position—the bridge is free-standing. The end pin is of telescope construction and can be extended to suit the player.

Bow

The bow, of French origin, has two chief components—the stick and hair. The stick can be made from pernambuco wood, rosewood, brazilwood, or fiberglass. The hair can come from the mane or tail of horses or can be synthetically produced. The hair is tightened to a suitable tension to play the instrument and loosened for storage by means of an adjustable screw. The rosin is an important external component that must be applied in an adequate amount onto the hair to create the proper "stickiness" to produce a tone.

Tone Production and Posture

The process of producing a tone is by means of drawing the bow across the string of choice with sufficient pressure and at the correct proportional speed or by plucking the string with the right index or middle finger. The player should sit with comfortably erect back posture and both feet positioned flat on the floor. The cello should be positioned in a three-point stance, i.e., contact within both legs and just below the chest-bone. The end pin, when properly extended, should allow the player to maintain a comfortable playing position. The most common problem with incorrect positioning can be traced to the end pin being extended too much or not enough. Both arms should be relaxed and away from the sides of the player. The distance of the arms from the sides will vary proportionately, depending on the string being played. Wrists in both arms should generally be level and fluid in movement, while the fingers of both hands should display rounded, flexible joints.

Intonation

Playing "in tune," or with good intonation, is the most difficult aspect of playing the cello or any string instrument. Provided the right hand bow technique is satisfactory, the development of the accuracy of pulling the strings by the left hand down onto the fingerboard (located on the "neck" below the strings) at the proper location to play the desired pitch is a long-term development. There are no frets or markings to identify the locations of pitches. The player learns the locations of pitches by experiencing the feel of arm position and hearing the pitch generated. Younger or less-experienced players can be expected to struggle to produce good intonation. The best advice for the director in dealing with inexperienced players is to display abundant patience and encourage the players to constantly listen to the tones they are producing. Players can adjust the pitch by slightly shifting the position of their fingers to produce the accurate pitch. If the player has developed a working vibrato, the player can "shade" the vibrato higher to raise the pitch and lower for the opposite effect.

Selecting a Quality Instrument

Sadly, the majority of the problems associated with playing the cello and any string instrument well and with good intonation lie within the quality of the instrument itself. If one is fortunate enough to have a professional or quality amateur musician as a member of the church instrumental ensemble, the instrument used by that player is normally of high quality and the player is comfortable with its performance. Often, the junior high, high school, or college-age player is saddled with a school-issued instrument or sub-par hand-me-down which is difficult to play due to poor construction, old and brittle strings, and depleted, worn-out bow hair. The poor quality of string instruments available to young players is the primary source of frustration for the players and in many cases, causes the players eventually to abandon the instrument.

Local symphony or professional players are an excellent resource for the church instrumental ensemble director in locating potential instrument purchases for young players looking to invest in their first personal instrument or upgrading their current instrument. String players are notorious for their ability to network for their needs and the instrumental ensemble director would be wise to "befriend" a local professional.

As a general rule, a professional player should be consulted when negotiating an instrument purchase with an individual. Some fantastic bargains can be had, but just as easily the purchaser can be "gouged" by a vastly inflated price. The purchaser should always seek an appraisal issued by a reputable instrument repairperson. When purchasing from an instrument dealer, secure a professional musician's assessment of the instrument through inspection and demonstration.

Care and Maintenance

The church instrumental director can contribute to improvement in the condition of the school-issued or poor quality instrument by offering to assist financially in the replacement of old strings and worn-out bow hair. A set of inexpensive steel cello strings can cost as little as $35.00-$40.00. Upgrades can certainly be made as a wide variety of types of strings with different cores and wrappings are available, ranging in cost up to $135.00. A professional cellist should be consulted for recommendations since the veteran player would be familiar with the strengths and weaknesses of the various brands and compositions of strings available.

The rehairing of a wooden cello bow with real horse hair or artificial hair, by a competent instrument technician, usually will cost $25.00-$35.00. If the bow that needs rehairing is fiberglass, most technicians recommend the purchase of a new bow as the cost is comparable to rehairing the old bow. Fiberglass bows are commonly paired with school-issued instruments. Replacement of strings and bow rehairing should be a yearly goal.

Other remedies available to improve the instrument are the replacement of a sagging or warped bridge and the adjustment of the "sound post" (critical dowel positioned inside the instrument below the bridge). These remedies are relatively inexpensive but must be performed by a competent professional instrument technician. The technician can also execute a "once-over" inspection to check for open seams and cracks on the instrument that rob it of its ability to give peak performance.

The player can preserve the condition of the instrument by exercising care in its daily maintenance. After each use, the player should wipe the rosin dust off the strings and surface of the cello. Rosin that is allowed to accumulate can, over time, harm the finish on the instrument and adversely affect the tone. In addition, the cello should never be left in a hot or cold car or near heaters/air conditioners during the day prior to a rehearsal/performance. It may be a nuisance to carry an instrument into a restaurant, but the preservation of the instrument is more important than a little inconvenience.

Performance Applications

Assuming the instrument is in good working condition and is ready to contribute to the ensemble effort, what are the best ways to utilize the cello? The primary function of the cello in a diverse ensemble is to provide a stable bass

Valorie McDonald
member Hyde Park Baptist Celebration Orchestra, studio teacher, Austin, Texas

"As with other aspects of life, my faith gives music added dimension and perspective. While faith affects my music and how I experience it, music enhances and expresses my personal relationship with Christ. Music teaches me, leads me in worship, and acts as the ideal manner in which to share my faith.

line along with the string bass, trombone, baritone, tuba, baritone sax, or bassoon. The cello, however, can also be a marvelous solo or melody instrument and can double with, or take over, a theme-line from any treble instrument by means of its mellow tone. The use of *pizzicato* (plucking the string) creates a unique effect and enhances the sense of tempo. The cello, as is the case with all the string instruments, is very flexible and can execute all types of technical maneuvers: fast passages, long sustained tones, trills, tremolos, and chords. Other features the cello, and the strings, offers is its enormous range of dynamic possibilities and wide range of pitches (highs and lows).

A primary challenge of the cellist is to play with good intonation. The instrumental director must know the ability and limitations of the players in the ensemble and should avoid having a player who plays with faulty intonation play an "exposed" solo passage. Because of its ability to blend well with other instruments, the cello can be used in a supporting role if the player is still in a state of development and lacks the confidence and ability to function in a solo capacity.

The configuration of the instrumental ensemble within the playing area is an important consideration. Obviously, the placement of each instrument is dependent upon available space and quantity of instruments. High priority should be placed upon the grouping of the string instruments together to aid in the maintenance of bowing synchronization, good tuning, and accumulation of a unified string timbre. If there is a balanced minimum of 10 string players and space allows, the players can be arranged in traditional fashion, i.e. I violins, II violins, violas, celli, and basses left to right in a semicircle around the director. If the ensemble is smaller or space is limited, the strings can be grouped on either side of the director with violins in front of the violas, celli and basses.

The director, to help create a safe and functional environment for the cello performers, can follow some simple guidelines:

1. Keep plenty of space between players. Cello players need bowing room to allow them to play freely without the fear of poking their neighbor.

2. Always begin each rehearsal/performance with the opportunity to tune the instruments. Allow each family to tune separately with the following suggested sequence: woodwinds, brass, and strings.

3. Designate a "leader" among the string players, usually the best and most experienced violin player, to suggest proper bow patterns and fingering patterns for the string players to observe.

4. To avoid catastrophes and consternation, do not allow cellists to lay their instruments on their chairs or to set their instruments on the floor during a rehearsal break or prior to a rehearsal/performance. Players tend to weave in and out of the chair scheme in a rehearsal/performance area and do not seem to see potential disasters waiting to happen.

5. Do not allow anyone to pick up and play on an unattended instrument.

6. Encourage female cellists to wear pants or full, floor-length skirts when performing.

7. Provide a special area that is out of the normal traffic flow for the storing of cases during rehearsals/performances. Sharing of space within a choir

room rarely proves to be a satisfactory arrangement. Do not allow cases in the performance area.

Instrumental directors who are informed in all aspects of string performance are apt to be more successful in both recruiting and retaining string players for their church ensembles. String players become instantly aware whether the director is knowledgeable about string performance and tend to gravitate toward directors who have sought to learn all they can about the art. Some players will be willing to help "educate" their string-challenged director; however, such players are the exception rather than the rule. The church instrumental director should aspire to be the best musician possible, and the best musician is an informed musician.

Resources

Suggested Reading

- *The Cello,* by Elizabeth Cowling (Totowa, NJ: Scribner, 1983)
- *The Strings: Performance and Instructional Techniques,* by Wolfgang Kuhn (Boston: Allyn and Bacon, 1967)
- *Cello Technique: Principles and Forms of Movement,* by Gerhard Mantel (Bloomington, Ind.: Indiana University Press, 1995)
- *The Art of Cello Playing: A Complete Textbook Method for Private or Class Instruction,* by Louis Alexander Potter (Evanston, IL.: Summy-Birchard Co., 1964, 1980)
- *The Complete String Guide: Standards, Programs, Purchase, and Maintenance* (MENC–Music Educators National Conference, 1988)

Additional Resources

Refer to the listing on pages 183-184 for additional string family resources.

Timothy H. Cierpke, B.A., M.M., D.M.A., is a Professor of Music at Trevecca Nazarene University, Nashville, Tennessee, Minister of Music at Forest Hills United Methodist Church, Brentwood, Tennessee, and a professional cellist. A graduate of Pt. Loma Nazarene University, Samford University, and The Southern Baptist Theological Seminary, the author specializes in instrumental and choral conducting, aural theory, orchestration, cello and string instruction/pedagogy, and has invested over 30 years in cello performance and church music leadership.

CHAPTER 18

The Double Bass

by Lloyd Mims

The Double Bass, sometimes called contrabass, bass viol, or simply bass, is the largest and lowest member of the string choir in the orchestra. It normally provides the harmonic and rhythmic foundation for that family's beautiful resonant sound.

The double bass is actually the oldest member of the string family, having also been a member of the viol family that preceded modern string instruments. Its shape is somewhat different from the other modern instruments, but due to its size, that difference is seldom noticed. The telling factor is that the modern string instruments (violin, viola, and violoncello) all tune in fifths; the double bass tunes, like the viols, in fourths.

The instrument provides the harmonic underpinning for the string choir much as the 16' and 32' stops do on a pipe organ. The presence of the sound is felt more than heard; yet without it, there is something noticeably missing.

The bass is a transposing instrument, but remains a "C" instrument since its transposition is at the octave. The notes written on the page are heard an octave lower. Consequently, the bass, like the longest pipe organ stops, is usually used for doubling the bass line an octave lower than written. In fact, until the 19th century, the bass rarely played parts other than those that doubled the cello line. As the age of virtuosi bass players arrived, composers asked more and more for intricate parts and innovative scorings.

The Bow

The double bass is played with a bow much like the other members of the family. More than other members of the family, however, the bass employs the technique of *pizzicato* (plucking the string). Its size and resonance allow it to be a good rhythmic underpinning while still providing a sound harmonic foundation. Often the bass will play extended passages of *pizzicato,* during which the player will actually lay down the bow on the music stand. Because the strings of the instrument are so thick, it takes more friction to cause them to vibrate. Consequently, there is more horsehair on a bass bow than the other instruments, and the rosin used on the hair is much coarser and stickier.

Bass players have learned to use either the French bow or the German bow; although experienced players can use either, they have a preference when playing passages that are more difficult. Usually a player will use one kind of bow and never switch. The German bow has a larger opening on the frog, and is held like a cross-cut saw. The hand literally pulls the bow across the string by closing the whole hand around the frog. The French bow looks like a larger version of the bows used on all the other string instruments. The thumb and the fingers hold the outer part of the frog, and more agility is found in the wrist than the arm. Players tend to be equally successful with either bow—usually the one they first used to learn the instrument. Though no studies have proven such a hypothesis, some players think that carpal tunnel syndrome affects players who use the French bow more than those who use the German bow.

Tuning and Intonation

As has been mentioned, the bass has four strings tuned at the interval of the fourth. The pitches of the open strings (from lowest to highest) are E-A-D-G. The written symbol for these pitches will cause the instrument to sound one octave lower. The low sound of the strings makes tuning considerably difficult. Upper string players depend heavily on the "pulsating vibrations" they hear while playing two strings simultaneously. The sound of those "perfect fifths" allows them to tune the strings appropriately. However, the bass' open string pitches are so low that the pulsating of even "perfect fourths" is not usually distinguishable to the human ear, especially when other players are tuning instruments simultaneously. Bass players normally employ harmonics to tune the instrument. By lightly placing the first finger on a string in the third position and the fourth finger on the next highest adjacent string, the player can tune the two strings at the "perfect unison" several octaves higher than the open strings. This sound is more easily heard in the midst of a group of musicians trying to tune. One must ensure, however, that the strings are not so old as to give false harmonics.

Bass players learn to play in tune by listening carefully to the pitches they play in conjunction with the rest of the sound emanating from the orchestra. Frequently one will notice a bass player leaning his or her ear closer to the instrument in an attempt to fine tune a passage. Under normal circumstances, the close proximity of the ear to the fingerboard will allow adequate listening ability. Bass players who have not adequately learned to play in tune must spend time in a practice room with the assistance of someone at the piano matching their pitches.

Best Key Signatures

Like the other members of the string family, the bass likes to play best in keys that are designed around the open strings. The absolute best keys for a bass player are G and D and their parallel minors. The increasing number of flats in a key signature means that a player will be unable to use any open strings to check whether he or she is still solidly centering the pitch. (Whereas upper string players are taught to avoid open strings, the low sounds of the open bass strings do not call attention to themselves.) However, music is written without regard to what the best keys for instruments are. Consequently, bass players, like all string players, must learn to play in all keys. The practice room approach with piano assistance is the best help to a player who does not have the ear of a private teacher on a weekly basis.

Playing Position

Due to the fact that successive pitches on low strings require greater stretching of the hand, the bass player will run out of string more quickly than players on upper string instruments. Consequently, bass players must shift hand positions much quicker than the other string players in order to achieve the same number of notes; only two to three half steps are available to the player in one position. Normally, players will push down the first finger (index finger—thumbs don't count until one gets really high) on a string in first position to affect a whole tone above the open string. By pressing the fourth finger (the "pinkie") at the appropriate stretch above the first finger, the player will affect one more whole step. In first position, for example, on the A string, the player can play (open) A—(1st finger) B—(all 4 fingers down) C♯, and then change strings to play the (open) D as the scale moves diatonically upward. On the D string, the player then moves to (1st finger) E, (all 4 fingers down) F♯, but before moving to the G string the hand must shift back into half position to get the G♯ with the first finger and then the A by adding the 2nd finger. Due to its weakness, the third finger (the "ring finger") is never used by itself in lower positions on the double bass; but it always goes down when the fourth finger does. Each spot where one places the hand on the neck of the instrument is called a "position." Beyond fifth position, the thumb must come from out behind the neck and serve as a finger all its own. These upper passages are best avoided in writing if at all possible.

Range

As a general rule, the double bass sounds better when not kept too low. It has more clarity and incisiveness in the medium and upper registers where the pitch is more definite. Fortunately, notes below the low E below the bass staff do not occur very often. In Europe, the five-string bass is fairly popular, allowing the range to be extended down to low C below the bass staff. In the United States, a mechanical device is used to extend the fingerboard of the four-string bass. This mechanical device fits onto the scroll to allow the lowest string to be methodically and accurately lowered; "buttons," when pushed, automatically lower the open string by one half-step. The normal device has four buttons allowing the instrument to reach a lowest note of low C below the bass staff. These devices can be installed on most every model of instrument.

Making Good Tone

Although the double bass is seldom a solo instrument, the sound of the instrument must not be disregarded. Bass players can learn to play legato and beautifully, just like the upper instruments of the string family. If the tone of the bass is "fuzzy," it is usually because the player isn't making good contact with the finger of the left hand in order for the string to touch the fingerboard solidly. Too much tension is dangerous to the player, but too little tension causes sound problems. The most common problem with the sound of the instrument is that the player is not using the bow correctly. Watch especially that the bow is touching only one string at a time. Bass players must learn all the bowing techniques of their upper counterparts: e.g., *staccato, spiccato,* "off the string," "on the string," "hooked," and so forth. Bass players who do not bow correctly, will cause the rhythmic structure of the music to suffer. Encourage the bass players to take their cues from the cellists as well as the concertmaster.

Teaching the Basics of the Instrument

Left hand versus right hand—which is more important? The left hand is the hand that causes the pitches to be changed and affects whether they are in tune or out of tune. The right hand causes the bow to create beauty and acceptable sound. The two hands must work together. Pitches fingered perfectly in tune are worthless if the bow doesn't allow them to become sound.

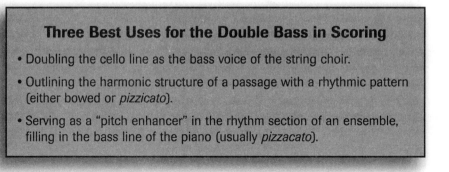

Three Best Uses for the Double Bass in Scoring

- Doubling the cello line as the bass voice of the string choir.

- Outlining the harmonic structure of a passage with a rhythmic pattern (either bowed or *pizzicato*).

- Serving as a "pitch enhancer" in the rhythm section of an ensemble, filling in the bass line of the piano (usually *pizzacato*).

A bow making pleasant and rhythmic tones is no good if those tones are not correctly pitched. Teaching the basics of the instrument is a constant struggle of assessing where the problem lies. The simple fact is that both hands must work in tandem to achieve the goal of acceptable sound. Several aspects have already been mentioned in this regard. Here are a few more things to observe:

1. The bow should be played perpendicular to the strings. If it crosses the strings at an angle, it will usually not produce the best sound. Normally the bow should cross the strings about one-third of the way down between the end of the fingerboard and the bridge.

2. The left hand needs to stand up on the fingerboard with rounded fingers; if it collapses (meaning the palm of the hand is gripping the neck), it will be difficult to make last-second adjustments to the pitch, and shifting positions will be slow and inaccurate. In first through fourth positions, the thumb should be behind the neck opposite the point the second finger would be placed. Vibrato is a viable technique for bass players; it helps immensely with intonation. A collapsed hand cannot perform vibrato.

3. The larger the sound desired, the closer one moves the bow to the bridge; the softer the sound, the farther away the bow should be from the bridge.

4. Rhythmic passages are sluggish when too much bow is used. The problem can usually be fixed by using less bow with more pressure "into" the string from the wrist and arm.

5. When rhythmic passages begin sluggishly, be sure the player has the bow already on the string, ready to go.

Holding the Instrument

Many double bass players stand to play their instruments; in fact younger students are encouraged to do so. Standing helps the player get the "feel" of the instrument and assists in the careful holding of it. When properly positioned, the end pin of the bass is extended to the point where the player's hand—in first position—is touching his or her cheek. The left hand is not a support for the instrument; it must remain relaxed in order to shift and finger the desired pitches; the left leg can be positioned behind the bass for balance. The thumb must remain in the center of the back of the neck of the instrument. The bass player must never hold the ribs of the bass flat against his or her stomach. More experienced players often sit on a stool to play. It is important that an adjustable stool be available to assist with proper body placement and instrument balance.

Placement of the Instrument(s)

All string instruments take up more playing space than woodwinds and most brasses. The space needed for bowing a full bow to the left of the instrument and a full bow to the right of the instrument is considerable. Conductors must be aware that the amount of space given to string players has a direct relationship on their ability to play in tune and with beauty. Double bass players need the most space of all. Like the cello, the double bass has an adjustable end pin that holds the instrument off the floor. This end pin is designed to get a firm grip on the floor. If the floor of the playing area can be easily marred or torn, it is important to supply bass players with a "rock-stop" (foam cup) that holds the end pin securely in place. Bass players can share music—two to a stand, but it sometimes requires more playing room for them to get the proper angle than if they each had their own stand. Sharing music, however, allows one person to continue playing while the other turns the page.

Owning an Instrument

The largest instruments of the orchestra are usually the most expensive. Many players learned to play the double bass because the school they attended owned one. When they left the school, they no longer had access to the instrument. If churches owned an instrument (or two) those players could resurrect their skills and play in a church orchestra as well. Usually double basses are not sitting around in someone's attic like the smaller instruments might be. There are a number of reputable string dealers that sell to schools and churches, many which offer wholesale prices on excellent instruments. Ask a professional string player or teacher in your area. A good plywood bass costs approximately $3,000 while the least expensive hand-carved instruments start around $10,000. The accessories of the bass are more important than the quality of the bass. A good set of strings (about $100) is very important. The bow may ultimately be the most important investment, as it determines so much of the instrument's sound. Be sure a bow made of pernambuco wood is purchased. If one does buy used instruments, check to see if the front of the instrument has become buckled. This damage is caused when the sound post (inside the instrument) falls down while tension remains on the strings; a clear indication is if one hears the sound post rolling around inside the instrument. When buying a used instrument, it is always best to get expert advice from a professional string player. A used instrument in excellent condition with a new bridge and new strings will last a lifetime. Bows need rehairing with some frequency; a bass bow cared for appropriately may need to be rehaired every two years or so. When one is unsure whether to buy a German bow or a French bow, it may be best to buy a French bow. Most players who switch from upper string instruments to the bass will probably play the French bow. Bows should be properly cared for. It is imperative that the hair be loosened after every playing; if not, the stick will become warped and worthless.

Sizes of Instruments

Surprisingly enough, most bass players do not play "full-size" basses. In fact, the virtuosi frequently play a 5/8ths-sized instrument. Professional orchestral players play 3/4-size or 7/8-size instruments. The larger the instrument, the fuller the tone—but the player will find intricate passages more awkward to execute. If one buys an instrument, this author recommends a 3/4-size instrument.

Recruiting Bass Players

Many bass players started out their "string life" as a violinist. If you have access to an instrument but don't have a player, begin scouting for a recruit. A large child who plays violin adequately, but not like a virtuoso, may be a perfect recruit for playing a double bass. On the violin he or she may feel under-

stimulated; however, on the bass, the child feels important and challenged. Talk with the student and his or her parents. They may readily agree. Be sure they know, however, that a large vehicle is needed to transport a bass. When recruiting a bass player in this fashion, offer to pay for two or three private lessons with a good teacher to help the student avoid bad habits from the beginning. Pianists make good recruits for the bass, as well.

Needing a Bass in Your Group?

If the string quartet has been such a popular group for composers through the ages and most music is merely four parts, why use a double bass when a cello is available? The same question might be asked of organs. Why add 16' and 32' stops to a pipe organ? The pedals only double the bass line. The answer lies in why people turn up the bass equalizer on their home or car stereo system. The bass is the underpinning of all musical writing. To add a bass player to an ensemble is to give the group a mature sound. Many choirs perform Handel's *Messiah* every year with a string quartet and organ; the addition of one double bass turns the performance into a truly professional sound. The audience of today has grown accustomed to wanting a full-bodied bass sound.

Rhythmic Parts—Combo Function (electric bass)

The electric bass can be used in a combo-like rhythm section. It is essentially a bass guitar; however, it plays only one note at a time and in a *pizzica-*

to manner. The advantage of the electric bass over the acoustic bass in a combo is that the electric bass utilizes an amplifier and can produce more volume. Most acoustic bass players can quickly learn to play electric bass; the opposite, however, is not true.

Resources
Suggested Reading
- *The Art of Double Bass Playing,* by Warren Benfield and James S. Dean, Jr. (Warner Bros. Publications, 1973)
- *Beginning String Class Method,* by Arthur Edwards (Dubuque, Iowa: Wm. C. Brown Co. Publishers, 1985)
- *Guide to Teaching Strings,* by Lamb and Cook (McGraw-Hill Higher Education, 1993)
- *Playing and Teaching Stringed Instruments,* by Ralph Matesky (Englewood Cliffs, NJ: Prentice-Hall, Inc., 1963)
- *String Method for Class or Individual Instruction,* by Meuller and Rusch (Park Ridge, IL: Neil A. Kjos Music Co., 1961)

Additional Resources
Refer to the listing on pages 183-184 for additional string family resources.

Lloyd Mims, B.M.E., M.M., D.M.A., is Dean of Fine Arts, Palm Beach Atlantic College, Palm Beach, Florida, and formerly Dean of the School of Church Music and Worship of The Southern Baptist Theological Seminary in Louisville, Kentucky. A graduate of the University of Southern Mississippi and The Southern Baptist Theological Seminary, he did postdoctoral study at the Juilliard School and the America-Italy Society. He is also an ordained minister having served churches in Florida, Mississippi, and Kentucky.

CHAPTER 19

The Harp

by Carol McClure

The Instrument

The harp is thought to have evolved from a hunter's bow. The shape of today's harp, with soundbox, curved neck and vertical support column originated in the second millenium B.C. Harps are divided into two categories of classification: those with pedals and those without pedals.

The pedals on a pedal harp provide the ability for the harp to become a chromatic instrument, by enabling the harpist to alter the pitches of all octaves of one string at the same time. The pedals are arranged D C B E F G A, left to right. D, C and B are pedaled with the left foot, while E, F, G and A are pedaled with the right foot. The pedals can be moved two at a time, one with each foot. There are three positions for each pedal: upper (flat), middle (natural), and lower (sharp).

Pedal harps generally come in three sizes. The full-size, grand concert harp, stands above six feet tall, has 47 strings and an extended soundboard for maximum resonance. The concert harp stands approximately six feet tall, has 46 strings and an extended soundboard not quite as wide as that of the grand concert harp. The student model pedal harp has 46 or fewer strings (depending on the manufacturer), stands under six feet in height, and has a straight soundboard.

Non-pedal (also called Celtic or Irish) harps are seen in various shapes and sizes, from two-octave lap harps to elegant 38-string floor harps. The non-pedal harp is a diatonic instrument, although the pitch of an individual string can be altered by one half step through the mechanism of a sharping lever. Sharping levers are standard on almost all non-pedal harps of four or more octaves, but are not standard on all strings of smaller non-pedal harps.

The concert pitch for both non-pedal and pedal harps is C. The instrument sounds at the pitch read in either treble or bass clef. The pedal harp is capable of being played in any key. The non-pedal harp is tuned to a fixed key, usually E♭, F, or C.

Technique

Good harp technique has as its goals a solid, clear tone, no finger noises, and the capability of rapid fluid finger motion, with a possibility of a wide dynamic range. Good harp technique begins with the position in which the harpist is seated at the harp: back straight; shoulders relaxed; harp resting lightly against the harpist's knees and on the right shoulder, while the harpist is seated on the front half of the bench.

The harpist's hands and arms should be relaxed, but positioned in a manner that enables the harpist to play each note evenly and with a full sound. The harpist's elbows are held away from the body, with the forearms parallel to the floor. The wrists are relaxed, and kept tucked in slightly in order that the fingers and thumb might form a "spiral c" position. The finger joints are all rounded, and the thumb is extended "up," away from the fingers. The fingers all follow the motion of the index finger, which is positioned roughly at a 45-degree angle to the strings.

The harp strings should always be played at, or slightly below, their midpoints. The harpist should play a string with the fingertip, closing the finger completely to the palm of the hand, and then should relax the hand immediately as the hand "floats" slightly toward the column in order to reapproach the string from the same position each time a note is played. When the string is played again, the harpist must be careful not to "land" on the vibrating string before plucking it.

Chords, scales, arpeggios, and passages of successions of individual notes all require the same routine technique: thumbs up; fingers down (always allowing a four-finger space between the thumb and the index finger, while the second, third and fourth fingers play approximately on the same plane); firm closure of fingers to the palms of the hands, followed by immediate relaxation. Chords may be played with two, three, or four fingers of each hand. They may be played as block chords or as broken chords. Ascending scales are always executed with 4-3-2-1-4-3-2-1 fingering, while descending scales are fingered 1-2-3-4-1-2-3-4. Arpeggios are performed with the same fingering as scales.

Two well-known techniques that add color to ·harp literature are the glissando and the harmonic. An ascending glissando is played with the index finger as it rapidly presses into the strings from the lowest to highest ranges of the harp. A descending glissando is played as the thumb rapidly presses into the harp strings from highest to lowest ranges. The harmonic is made by plucking a string with the thumb, while simultaneously "halving" the string with the fingers of the same hand, resulting in a tone exactly one octave higher than the pitch of the string being played. Due to the position of the left hand, a harpist is capable of playing double harmonics with that hand, but not with the right hand. It is important to remember that in standard harp literature, harmonics are written where they are executed, and they sound an octave above the pitch of the note indicated in the score. Other techniques that add interest to performance on a harp are fingernail technique (indicated in a score by a half-moon symbol above the designated line) and "près de la table," playing near the soundboard (indicated by the letters "p.d.l.t.").

Both of these techniques produce a sonorous, guitar-like sound from the harp.

The six most common playing problems demonstrated by an amateur harpist all have specific remedies.

1. The most common problem is the "buzzing" sound associated with the harpist's touching a vibrating string before it is plucked. The solution is for the harpist to carefully practice the approach to the string, making sure that the string is not touched before the actual act of plucking the string occurs.

2. Both a muffled overall sound and a muffled glissando sound come from the harpist's rubbing the fingers across the strings before plucking them. If the harpist will firmly close the fingers and thumb to the palm in one decisive action, the player's sound will not be muffled.

3. In the case of the glissando, the harpist should be pressing into the strings as the hand ascends or descends, not merely lightly rubbing across the strings.

4. Uneven ascending scales are another problem for some amateur harpists. If the harpist will keep the forearm parallel to the floor, the thumb up, and the fingers substantially lower than the thumb, particularly at the point of the 1-to-4 cross-over, the thumb and fourth finger will both have room to play correctly, resulting in an even scale.

5. A generally weak sound is a result of the harpist's not closing the fingers and thumb completely at the point of plucking the string. Hand closure with immediate relaxation usually cures this problem.

6. A piercing, "edgy" sound is usually caused by the harpist's playing on the sides of the fingers or thumbs, as opposed to the fleshy pads of the fingers. Since each harpist's fingers are unique, the individual harpist must work to find the optimum spot on each finger that produces the warmest, most pleasing tone possible.

Tuning

A significant aspect of harp playing is the tuning of the instrument. Each string of the harp is individually tuned in the key of C. Even in this day of electronic tuners, this is a formidable task for the neophyte harpist. However, the more the harp is tuned, the more consistently it will stay in tune. Also, the more the harpist tunes the harp, the more proficient the harpist becomes at the art of tuning.

There are several circumstances that can exacerbate the tuning problems of the harp. First, the harp may have regulation inconsistencies. When the harp is not properly regulated, it can be tuned in the key of C, but will sound out of tune as soon as it is played in a different key. The discs (the mechanisms on the pedal harp that actually shorten the strings) may be moving too much or too little; thus, the sharps may be too sharp or the flats may be too flat. The only remedy for this tuning problem is an annual regulation by an experienced harp technician.

Other tuning problems may result from changes in temperature or humidity in the harp's environment. The more consistent the humidity and temperature are kept, the more easily the harp will be kept in tune. The harpist may choose to tune the harp to an electronic tuner, to a strobe, to the organ or piano, or by ear. The strobe is the most exact of these options, while the harpist's auditory tuning will improve the more it is practiced. The typical electronic tuner does not have the exactness that most harpists need. When the harp is performing a work with organ, piano, or handbells, it is advisable to tune carefully to the accompanying instrument.

Unique Qualities and Characteristics

The harp has a few idiosyncracies that govern the way the instrument is played.

First, only four fingers of each hand are used to play the instrument, not five; consequently, a harp part written at the piano may be much more difficult for the harpist to perform than an arranger thinks. Second, due to the diatonic arrangement of the harp strings, rapid chromatic passages are impossible to execute well on the harp.

Similarly, it should be remembered that the harpist has only two feet; therefore, only two pedals can be changed at the same time (one on each side!). Finally, it should be noted that the harp is not the loudest of symphonic instruments. When the harpist is playing a fortissimo passage along with the full orchestra, the harp will not be heard.

The best uses of the harp include arpeggiated chords of three to four notes, extended ascending and descending 16th-note arpeggios, accompaniment figure, eighth-note passages, harmonics (fifth octave A through third octave C) and soft, occasional glissandi. The most common misuses of the harp begin with glissandi: too many and too loud (they will mutilate the harpist's fingers if done repeatedly); too often (they have the same effect as overused timpani rolls or cymbal crashes); too close together in the same piece of music (the pedal changes can not be executed rapidly enough).

Unrealistic expectations of what the harp can do are also very frustrating for both the harpist and the music director. The typical amateur harpist cannot be expected to sight-read an unpedaled harp part in rehearsal. It is always a good idea to give the harpist a harp part in advance. Also, it is not a good idea to say to the harpist, "There's no harp part, so just play the piano part." The harp is NOT a vertical piano, so this approach is generally not a workable solution. It is always best to solicit input from the harpist if you are creating a harp part from a piano part.

Care and Maintenance

The harp has a short list of care and maintenance needs, but they are absolutely essential. Storage for the harp should be provided in a safe, dry, temperature-regulated environment. The importance of this cannot be stressed enough. Many tuning and maintenance problems can be avoided by following this one guideline. Moving the harp safely is an easy procedure. The harp should be covered and strapped to a dolly made specifically for the harp.

Every harp needs an annual regulation, which serves as the harp's annual physical examination. This is extremely important, since the harp may develop structural problems that are not apparent to the amateur harpist. Annual replacement of all of the harp's gut and nylon strings is the primary way of ensuring maximum tone quality from the harp. Bass wire strings should be changed every two years.

Changing a harp string is an easy procedure. Each new string comes in an envelope marked with note name and octave, so that there is no problem matching a new string with its correct place on the harp. The new gut or nylon string is inserted into the empty stringhole from the top of the soundboard and is passed through the soundbox until it hangs through a soundhole in the back of the harp. A knot is tied in the end of the harp string. The string is then pulled upward through the stringhole and the unknotted end of the string is inserted into the eye in the corresponding tuning pin, and is pulled taut. The string is then brought up to pitch by turning the tuning peg with the tuning key. Several tunings will be required to get the new string to maintain the desired pitch. A new bass wire string is always inserted through the soundboard from the back of the harp. It is necessary to give the new wire string as much slack as possible as the tuning process is begun so that the wire string will not break in the process of tuning.

Emergency harp repairs need not strike fear in the heart of the amateur harpist. Two wonderful books, *Affairs of the Harp,* by Samuel O. Pratt, and *Harp Maintenance and Repair,* by Carl Swanson, provide instructions for dealing with most day-to-day harp repairs.

When purchasing a harp for a church, there is a list of questions that can help one arrive at a conclusion about the right harp for a particular situation. Who will be playing the harp—professional harpists, experienced amateurs, or inexperienced students? Will the harp be moved often? Will the harp be used as only a performance instrument, or will it be used as a practice or teaching instrument? How many hours of playing time will the harp get each week? What kind of commitment of time and financial resources will one be willing to render to proper harp maintenance? How much money is one willing to spend on the initial cost of purchasing a harp or harps?

Once the above list of questions is answered, evaluation of what size and condition of harp to buy is discernable. Currently, the price range for new pedal harps (student or no-frills concert size) begins at $10,000 to $12,000, and extends to $35,000 or more for grand concert harps with gold leaf and/or specialty woods. A gold harp or one covered in an expensive wood veneer is truly beautiful; however, it is not a practical expenditure for a church. It will tend to be treated as a lovely piece of furniture, and may not sound any better than a harp costing under $20,000. Every harp is an individual creation and sounds different from every other harp. The sound of the harp "grows" as the harp ages and is played. Currently, new pedal harp brands sold in the United States include Venus (W & W Harp Co.), Swanson, Salvi, Morley, Lyon & Healy, Camac, and Aoyama. No one brand of harp is "the" harp a church or individual harpist should aspire to own. Prices vary widely; a more expensive harp from one company is not necessarily better than a less expensive version of the same size harp from another company.

A word of caution should be offered at this point. Beware of an offer to purchase a brand new harp at a discounted rate that just happens to be sitting at the factory or showroom and is available for immediate purchase. There is a waiting list for new pedal harps of virtually every description. It is probable that a professional harpist or teacher rejected that harp before it was offered for purchase. The harp probably has some flaw that is not visible to the non-harpist (uneven string spacing in the upper register, uneven tone quality, an unusual and annoying sympathetic vibration in the harp). Have any harp checked out thoroughly by a professional harpist before committing to a purchase. This is sound advice whether one is buying a new or used harp.

A gently used, well-maintained pedal harp is a practical and advisable solution for the first harp purchased by a church. Today, a wonderful used concert or grand concert harp can be purchased for $10,000 to $15,000. Used harp brokers who check out their harps thoroughly, and who deal regularly with teachers and professionals, are good resources. Never buy a harp from an estate sale. An older harp is not a wise investment for a church.

> **Patricia Harris**
> **Recording Artist and**
> **Principal Harpist,**
> **Tucson Symphony**
>
> "Sometimes I find it hard to express my love for Christ in words that are adequate. My passion for God is more greatly reflected in the music that I play. I see God's touch of love on the lives of my listeners, and I see His joy in their faces."

Harps and Harpists in the Church

As you evaluate your particular church's needs concerning a harp, please keep in mind the opportunity for training young harpists to use their gifts in worship. An investment of $1500 will provide the following "lever," student model harps: four two-octave harps, two three-octave harps, or one four-octave harp for teaching one's own church members to play the harp. If one is going to invest in the concert instrument, it is advisable to foster the discipling of multiple harpists who will put the harp to use for the glory of God. A method for teaching the harp in the context of the church is now available, along with affordable, quality beginner instruments. Hymn arrangements for harpists of all proficiency levels are widely available, also.

The best way to incorporate the harp into the overall music ministry of the church is to be aware that even a beginning level harpist can really be ministered to and make a contribution to the music program. A beginning harpist is best put to use playing a solo hymn arrangement, or playing a simple accompaniment (chords only) in C, G, or D to a children's choir anthem. The harpist should be given the music and a tape of the anthem far in advance of performance. The intermediate harpist is capable of playing solos, playing in chamber ensembles, playing with handbells or organ, accompanying a soloist or a children's choir. The part can have moving eighth notes and chords, and possibly a few extended arpeggios. The tempo should be moderate, the harp part still basically diatonic, and the harpist should be given the harp part far in advance of the first rehearsal. Under no circumstance should the beginning or intermediate harpist be expected to sight-read in public. The intermediate harpist is capable of playing easy orchestra parts, but they should be pedaled correctly, and rapid pedal changes should not be expected. The advanced harpist makes a wonderful contribution as orchestral player, chamber musician, accompanist, duet partner, and soloist. It is still advisable to give the harpist the harp parts in advance, so that the harpist has time to pedal the part properly.

A professional harpist can be expected to perform as any other professional musician; however, the harpist still needs a few minutes to pedal harp parts in advance. The anthems of John Rutter, "Sanctus" from Gabriel Faure's *Requiem, Ceremony of Carols* by Benjamin Britten, and Robert Shaw's *The Many Moods of Christmas* offer harp parts that professional harpists love to play. Brilliant sight-reading and improvising are rare commodities even among professional harpists today.

Be sure to provide the harpist with ample time to tune. If the harp is going to be placed under hot lights or in a cold draft during a performance, the harp will go out of tune and there is nothing the harpist can do about it.

Wonderful technical studies and repertoire are available for all levels of harpists who wish to participate in a church music program.

Resources
Beginning Harp Technique and Repertoire
(All resources may be ordered from www.lyonandhealy.com.)
- *Method for Harp,* Grossi. Comprehensive technical studies for beginning harpists
- *The Angel's Harp,* McClure. Written specifically for teaching the harp in the context of church; each piece is written as both a technical study and performance piece; very specific technical instructions.

- *The Angel's Harp: 50 Hymn Arrangements for Beginning Harpists,* McClure. Written specifically for beginning harpists to use in church; each piece serves as both a technical study and performance piece.

Intermediate Harp Technique and Repertoire (Pedal)

- *Intermediate Method for Harp,* Pozzoli. Comprehensive technical studies for intermediate harpists
- *The Angel's Harp: Solos for Sunday Morning,* Vols. I-X, McClure. Intermediate-level hymn arrangements covering the entire church year, suitable for preludes, offertories, and postludes, which also serve as comprehensive, intermediate-level technical studies
- *Conditioning Exercises,* Salzedo. Warm-up, technical excerpts for harpists of all levels

Advanced Harp Technique and Repertoire (Pedal)

- *Twelve Etudes,* Bach/Grandjany. Beautiful performance pieces/technical studies for harp based on the violin partitas and sonatas of J. S. Bach, written by the late Marcel Grandjany, professor of harp at the Julliard School
- *Classiques de La Harpe,* Vols. I-XII, Renie. The best of transcriptions of Baroque, Classical and Romantic keyboard pieces for harp, organized as technical studies
- *Orchestral Studies,* Vol. I-III, ed. Zingel. Comprehensive resource for studying orchestral literature

Other

- *Christmas Carols for Lever or Pedal Harp, and One or Two Treble Instruments,* Daniel Burton (La Mesa, CA: Jubal Press, 1999)
- *Twenty Carols with a Friend* (Accompanying the melody, string quartet and harp part included), Patricia Jaeger (Seattle, WA: Herald Music, 1994)
- *25 Easy studies for Pedal and Nonpedal Harp,* Alfred Kastner, Revised and edited by Kathy Bundock Moore (Ellensburg, WA: F. C. Publishing Co., 1993)
- *Thumbs Up!: Beginning Harp for the Adult and College-Level Student,* Second Edition, Kathy Bundock Moore (South Berwick, ME: F. C. Publishing Co., 1999)
- *A Harpist's Survival Guide to Glisses,* Kathy Bundock. Moore (South Berwick, ME: F. C. Publishing Co., 1991)
- *Celtic Christmas: 21 Arrangements for Celtic Harp,* Kim Robertson (Milwaukee, WI: Hal Leonard Corporation, 1999)
- *Mel Bay Presents Christmas Eve: 16 Solos for Celtic Harp,* Sunita Staneslow (Pacific, MO: Mel Bay Publications, 1997)
- *Hymns and Wedding Music for All Harps,* Sylvia Woods (Montrose, CA: Woods Music and Books Publishing, 1987)

Carol McClure is a harpist and concert/recording artist, a respected and widely published composer and arranger, as well as a nationally recognized teacher. She is sought after as a harp pedagogue and draws harp and chamber music students from 10 states. She is also author of a curriculum for young children—*The Angel's Harp*™. Carol holds a B.M. from the University of Louisville, and a M.C.M. from The Southern Baptist Theological Seminary, Louisville, Kentucky.

The Instrumental Music Minister

Developing and Administrating a Church Music Program

Recruitment and Development of Volunteer Instrumentalists

by Bob Williamson and Julie Barrier

Recruitment of volunteer instrumentalists for the church orchestra requires prayer, creativity, and determination. If the instrumental director or music minister wants to create an instrumental ensemble, it is imperative that the church, the pastor, and the accompanists understand the commitment of time and resources needed for such an endeavor. Music is a powerful, emotional language that transcends verbal communication. Players who connect deeply on an emotional level with instrumental music can be reached for Christ through an instrumental music program. The musical language and manifest presence of God in worship can draw men and women to a church orchestra. A church orchestra can be a warm, caring community of believers. Attracting nonbelievers by genuine loving relationships is Christ's principal strategy for evangelism in John 17. Foundational to recruitment of players is the understanding that each potential ensemble member needs a personal relationship with Jesus Christ.

The vision for instrumental ministry should be clearly communicated to the congregation and staff. A guest instrumental soloist or a visiting instrumental ensemble can be a great resource for demonstrating the potential value of an instrumental program. If a visiting player can also share a personal testimony of the impact Christ has had in his or her life, the congregation can see the spiritual potential for ministry, as well. The cost of such a ministry investment would include music, equipment, personnel, and program expenses. When plans are presented and approved, the director can move forward with much freedom in enlisting potential instrumentalists for the ensemble. A critical goal for initiating an instrumental ministry is evangelism and discipleship through worship. The following strategies for recruitment are just a few of the ways that a music minister could locate and develop instrumentalists in his or her community.

The principal prospects for recruitment should be the church members. A churchwide survey is an excellent way to discover potential talent and interests in an instrumental program. Often those who are participating in other areas

of music ministry have instrumental expertise as well as vocal experience. Many fine musicians often sing *and* play an instrument. If prime prospects for a church orchestra are coming from the choir, it may be advisable to first design and schedule a program where participation in both organizations is possible. For example, a worship minister could schedule an instrumental prelude and a choral offertory. Recruiting adults to participate in an orchestra ministry at the outset will prevent scheduling conflicts that student players have with local school band and orchestra programs.

Church members who are instrument owners are a second target group. Worshipers in the congregation often had band or orchestra experience as school children. Former band and orchestra students who have grown up and moved away may leave unused instruments behind with their parents. The parents may be willing to donate an instrument to an eager young musician. Former church players who are unable to continue in an instrumental ensemble may also be instrument donors. Frequently, church members have played in the past but are reluctant to try playing after a long hiatus. Encouragement, persistence, and a noncompetitive playing environment are essential factors in approaching instrumentalists who have not played in a while. The director can encourage a player to attend and rehearse without performing publicly until the person is confident and comfortable.

Another way to recruit players is to offer an available instrument that has been donated to the church music program. Occasionally, the director may assist with scholarships for "refresher" lessons for a player who wishes to further develop his or her instrumental technique. Retired adults are often very interested in resuming musical study after a busy professional career. Many new orchestra members find that being more involved in church music ministry has deepened their own spiritual walk, and also encouraged greater church participation by their family members.

Professional players require special care in recruitment. Three things attract professional players.

1. Authentic, caring personal relationships are critical to drawing in a professional musician.

2. A well-organized program and a high level of musicianship are also powerful drawing cards.

3. Careful consideration for the personal needs of the players is also very important to the professional musician.

The director must be sure to pace rehearsals so that players do not become overly fatigued. Refreshments, follow-up calls, and intercessory prayer teams provide a supportive atmosphere for the volunteer player. Challenging pops and symphonic literature and concert tours can be very gratifying for professional players. If the conductor is a professional musician, his or her participation in university, community, or symphony groups will establish rapport with professional musicians. If the conductor is an accompanist, many relationships can be built through accompanying soloists. Many Christian professional musicians would love the opportunity to teach private students through a church music conservatory. A wise conductor will welcome input and utilize leadership skills and expertise of the Christian professional musician. It is important, however, for the director to maintain spiritual integrity and vision concerning the values and direction of his or her ministry.

Recent graduates are prime candidates for recruitment. High school and college band and orchestra students who have graduated often miss the camaraderie and enjoyment of playing in an ensemble. Web sites of schools and colleges will often have directories of alumni who have been playing in a band or orchestra. High school or college yearbooks are also good places to locate former band or orchestra musicians. Senior adult community band and orchestra members are also excellent recruits. Retired persons often have the time and resources to be valuable leaders in a church orchestra.

A community-wide instrumental workshop is a creative way to identify and motivate local church musicians. A Friday evening and Saturday can be devoted to rehearsals, fellowships, and individual instrument clinics. A few selections of about grade 2 or 3 are chosen, and the group is thoroughly rehearsed to play for a service. Fingerings, scales, balance, and tuning are all addressed during the workshop. The purpose of a workshop is to minimize the shock for the returning player and to make a transition to an ongoing church instrumental program as smooth as possible. The beginning ensemble should have several weeks to rehearse and rejuvenate embouchures and fingers before playing publicly again. University music professors and high school band directors can be invited to assist in the instrumental clinic. Local teachers who participate may encourage their students to be involved in the church workshop. The church instrumental director should develop strong relationships with local high school and college band directors. If the church instrumentalist works in tandem with high school and college music teachers, they may assist the church in its musical endeavors.

An alert instrumental director can discover many prospects. It is essential to get the name, address, and telephone number of any instrumentalist the director meets. However, the primary reason for contacting musicians is to reach them for Christ, not recruit them for an orchestra. The next page contains a director's testimony. Bob Williamson relates a powerful story of a family brought to Christ when the director went in search of a French horn. Never overlook anything "instrumental" in reaching an instrumentalist for Christ.

Bob Williamson is currently serving as the Minister of Music at Tower Grove Baptist Church in St. Louis, Missouri. A native of Missouri, and a former Missouri band director, he holds a B.M.E. from SEMO State University and a Master's in Organ and Music Theory from the University of Hawaii. Bob served LifeWay Christian Resources for three years as Instrumental, Handbell, and Electronic Keyboard Consultant. Prior to that position, Bob served Whitesburg Baptist Church in Huntsville, Alabama, as Associate Minister of Music/Instrumental Director and Organist. He has written for various publications and was one of the orchestrators for *The Baptist Hymnal*, 1991.

Julie Barrier is Associate Minister of Worship at Casas Adobes Baptist Church in Tucson, Arizona.

A Director's Testimony

by Bob Williamson

"I needed a French horn player to serve in my church orchestra. As I awaited God's answer to my request, I noted a classified advertisement selling a Holton French horn for $500. I quickly telephoned the number listed in the advertisement and made an appointment to inspect the instrument. The price was so low, I expected the horn to be damaged or dented. To my surprise, the horn was in excellent condition. The person who met me at the door explained that the instrument belonged to his daughter who was currently studying to be a nurse. The daughter needed the money from the sale of her instrument to buy textbooks.

"I assured the student's father that the price was low, but if he was serious, I would purchase the instrument. As I wrote out the check, the daughter entered the room. The sale of the horn was a surprise to her. She was sad about parting with the instrument. I seized the opportunity to invite her to play in our church orchestra for six weeks. I asked her father to hold the check until she finished the six weeks of service playing.

"One Wednesday evening, I had just explained the meaning of a particularly moving text that the choir was singing that Sunday. The young French horn player raised her hand in orchestra practice and asked if she was able to invite Jesus into her life on a day other than Sunday. At that moment, the rehearsal ended abruptly as the young lady received Christ as her Savior and her orchestra family supported her in prayer and rejoiced in her decision.

"Later that evening, I received a call from her parents, asking my wife and me to come visit the young lady's home. When we arrived, the whole family was in tears. The young nursing student shared that her mother and father prayed to receive Christ. She wanted to be sure she had explained the plan of salvation successfully. The father asked if he could make a "confession" to us. He said that he was a trombone major in college and his wife had a master's degree in flute performance. I noticed there was some whimpering in the background. I heard the sobs of the younger brother who had also prayed to receive Christ in the hallway. I recognized him as the principal trombonist of the city's youth symphony. God had gloriously brought this musical family to Himself to play for His glory. I baptized the whole family on Sunday, and they now serve God faithfully in our orchestra family."

CHAPTER 21

Auditioning and Evaluating Players

by Brad R. Matheson

One of the most difficult and controversial areas of instrumental program management is auditioning or evaluating new members for the program. Many directors welcome the term evaluation over audition to downplay the formality of the process. While an audition refers to a briefer demonstration of ability, an evaluation allows an extended time to ascertain total ability and worth to the organization of a potential prospect. Whatever term one elects to use, the end goal is to disciple and develop Christian worshipers and assimilate these new members into the instrumental ministry. This chapter will cover such items as ministerial philosophy and how it relates to the evaluation process, preparing for the evaluation/audition, and applying the actual process.

The First Step—Ministerial Philosophy

A clear ministerial philosophy will be the primary guiding influence in the assimilation of new members into the instrumental program. Two philosophies emerge as the most widely used. **The Process Philosophy,** primarily an "open door" philosophy, is one that allows any individual who plays an instrument to become a member of the orchestra. While groups such as these fulfill a positive Christian value to include those who desire to worship with an instrument, it can be challenging to maintain the overall musical quality of the group. **The Product Philosophy,** or "invitation only" philosophy, allows the director discretion over who becomes a member of the orchestra. There are some advantages to this philosophy. Through an audition or evaluation process, the director is able to develop the ensemble that conforms to his or her goals in areas such as musicality, commitment, and attitude. Another advantage to this philosophy is the ability to build high musical quality into the ensemble through the gaining and retaining of only the most capable of instrumentalists, as well as balancing the ensemble, both within a section and within the entire orchestra. Whatever philosophy one adopts, whether it is the Process, Product, or a combination of the two, the most important factor is consistency. Develop a sound and fair philosophy based on factors such as overall church ministerial philosophy, one's music philosophy, and even one's personal preference. Once a philosophy is adopted, the director is ready to gain new members into the church instrumental program. Remember, secular managers manage by getting things done through people. Godly managers emulate Christ's example by modeling caring servanthood.

Preparing for the Audition/Evaluation Process

Within any ensemble lies the need for an established method at which new members and/or prospects are assimilated into the group. This process is key in not only educating a potential new member as to the requirements of the program, but also as a way for current members to feel some ownership of the group. With this in mind, a structure should be established utilizing current leadership in key areas of responsibility. In addition to establishing areas of responsibilities, there are tools such as prospect cards, evaluation sheets, and even philosophical guidelines/structure in the form of a brochure that should be utilized. A brief description of these key leadership positions and helpful tools is described below:

• New Prospect Greeter

This person's primary responsibility is as a host/hostess in transitioning potential members into their first rehearsal. The individual should be one of the most personable and informative ones in the program. It is also important that this person be present at all rehearsals.

• Section Leader

This person should represent a good blend of high musical ability, accomplishment, and longevity in the program. The primary responsibility of this individual is to ascertain the ability of the potential new member, as well as to lead the section in determining parts, solos, and section balance.

• Prospect Card

This vital data-gathering piece is used to gain information on prospects. Basic information including name, address, phone number and email address should be used, as well as other information, such as primary and secondary instruments played and previous instrumental experience. See example at the end of this chapter.

• Evaluation Sheet

The evaluation sheet is an important tool to gauge every aspect that is important for a potential new orchestra member. Areas of evaluation would include such items as musical ability, spiritual maturity, commitment, and attitude. Although it is the director's primary responsibility to prepare this sheet, it is helpful to gain insight from the section leader on areas such as musical ability.

• Orchestra Guidelines and Structure Brochure

A booklet or brochure that outlines the general guidelines and structure of the church instrumental program is helpful. Areas highlighted might include: ministry philosophy, biblical teaching on worship, a brief description of the different ensembles in the program, attendance requirements, schedule of events for the year, and worship etiquette and dress. Many of these ministry brochures contain a perforated prospect card that can be completed and returned to the director.

The Audition/Evaluation Process

An audition can be conducted over a period of at least two to three rehearsals. One of the most important ingredients of this process is to make potential new members feel at ease from the time they walk into their first rehearsal. As an instrumentalist, walking into the first rehearsal can be quite overwhelming. The New Prospect Greeter, if properly trained, can provide a sort of escort through this initial awkwardness by meeting the new person at the door, helping him or her to fill out an orchestra prospect card, introducing the prospect to the director, and taking him to the section leader for the rehearsal. It is at this time that the actual evaluation period begins.   This can be accomplished with a blend of peer evaluation and director evaluation.

• Peer Evaluation

Peer evaluation is designed to allow the orchestra members to be part of the evaluation, thus giving ownership to the process. During the rehearsal evaluation period, the section leader assesses the new prospect's musical ability. Either place the new prospect next to the section leader, or have the section leader perform a one-on-one evaluation. Peer evaluation should be based on basic musical ability of the prospect, how the prospect will fit into the section musically, and on the applicant's general attitude and spiritual commitment. Also at this time, the section leader informs the prospect as to the three-rehearsal evaluation period. After completing the first two weeks of rehearsals, the director meets with the section leader to determine the prospect's ability to integrate into the group. If this assessment is positive, then the director meets with the prospect either before or after the third rehearsal.

• Director Evaluation

The director evaluation is designed to be a one-on-one meeting with the prospect made before or after the third rehearsal. Although a musical evaluation can be included, the main goal of this meeting is to get to know the prospect. Aside from a musical evaluation there are three key areas to be evaluated: spiritual maturity, commitment, and overall attitude. Spiritual maturity covers areas such as a personal relationship with Christ, spiritual goals, and items that may need prayer. Commitment should be evaluated based on the prospect's schedule and how it relates to responsibility as an orchestra member. The evaluation of attitude is important for such areas as: Is this person a team player? Will he or she be receptive to new members/visitors? Does the individual have a worshipful attitude? Also during this time the prospect should be made aware of expectations as a member of the ensemble. These would include attendance at rehearsals, special projects, and worship services.

Audition/Evaluation Outline

• New prospect calls and/or attends first rehearsal.

• New prospect greeter meets prospect, helps him complete orchestra prospect card, introduces him to the director, and takes him to section leader for the rehearsal.

• Informal meeting with director/section leader explaining three-week evaluation period for prospect to get a feel for the group, and vice versa.

• After two-week evaluation period, the director meets with section leader to determine prospect's ability to integrate into the group (Peer Evaluation). After this evaluation is passed director meets with prospect either before or after the third rehearsal, for evaluation (Director Evaluation). After these steps the prospect is made a new member and, with input from the section leader, is placed in the section.

Conclusion

In conclusion, there are five main factors in determining membership of potential prospects into the orchestra: need, quality of musicianship, attitude, commitment, and spiritual maturity.

1. Need. Will space allow for this person both within the section and the group as a whole?

2. Musical Quality. How will the musicianship of this person affect the group as a whole? How will this person affect the balance of the section?

3. Attitude. Will the person integrate with the group socially?

4. Commitment. Will this be the person's primary church responsibility as a volunteer? Will work/family keep him from rehearsals?

5. Spiritual Maturity. Can the orchestra be an encouragement or vice versa for this person?

By following these steps and procedures, the director should satisfy the need both to fulfill the ministerial aspect of inclusion, and to attain a level of quality control that is so vital to the musical growth and maturity of the orchestra. Beyond the technical and procedural aspects of the evaluation process, prayer by both the group and the director should be the guiding influence in growing any church instrumental program.

Orchestra Prospect Card

Instrument: _____

Date of First Visit _____

Name _____

Email _____

Home Address _____

City _____ ST _____ Zip _____

Home Phone _____

Work Phone _____

Cell Phone *(optional)* _____

Beeper *(optional)* _____

Level of Experience *(Circle one)* HIGH SCHOOL   COLLEGE   OTHER

Have you played in a Church Orchestra before? *(Circle one)* YES   NO

Please return completed card to your orchestra host or director.

Brad R. Matheson is the Minister of Instrumental Music at Roswell Street Baptist Church, Marietta, Georgia. He is also a Contract Consultant for the Music Publishing and Recording Department of LifeWay Church Resources, a division of LifeWay Christian Resources of the Southern Baptist Convention. In addition, he owns and operates the Instrumental Expo conferences which are held nationally each year throughout the country. Find out more about these conferences at www.InstrumentalExpo.com.

CHAPTER 22

Developing an Instrumental Feeder Program

by Carter Threlkeld

The long-term success of any ministry (after God has been pleased to bless it) lies in its ability to feed new participants into the program. An orchestra is not a machine; it is a living body and must be nurtured the same as any other living thing. The best way and the biblical way to feed the church orchestra is through an ensemble ministry! The ensemble ministry can be part of a school of music, which in turn is a part of the overall choral/orchestral program or music ministry.

In the book of 1 Chronicles 23:5, King David assigned 4,000 Levites the duty of praising the Lord with musical instruments "which I made," said David, for giving praise. Moreover, in Chapter 25, David assigned captains (sectional or departmental leaders) over harps, stringed instruments, and cymbals. These were sons of Asaph, Heman, and Jeduthun, and there were 288 of them! They were under the authority of Asaph, Heman, and Jeduthun who in turn, were under King David's authority! Divide 4000 by 288 and you get almost 14, so each of the 288 teachers could have worked with a group of about 14. From this passage, a dynamic biblical pattern emerges for a ministry of music and a **mandate to teach.**

The biblical principle of sowing and reaping is emphasized throughout the Scriptures. Sowing the Word of God is investing one's time and energy into the field where God has placed the believer. The ensemble ministry affords an excellent opportunity for that investment!

How to Begin

The above Scriptures establish the premise that it is spiritually sound to build an ensemble ministry. Faithful, fervent prayer will power the ministry. Assess your talent and leadership. As an instrumental minister, one must decide which ensembles he or she has the resources to begin and commit to empower them with ownership. They will need:

- a director
- an accompanist
- someone to communicate rehearsal/performance information, etc. (secretary)
- rehearsal space, rehearsal time, music stands, and chairs
- music
- a name, a look, a promise Scripture
- performance opportunities
- definite starting and ending calendar dates

Let's discuss these points briefly. The director can be the instrumental minister or someone he or she equips to direct (remember David used 288 of them). Eventually one will assume the role of training directors. Each ensemble director must be trusted as a spiritual leader and example for the ensemble. The instrumental minister may need to assist them with directing techniques, rehearsal skills, and repertoire selection; but in doing this, ministry and effectiveness is greatly multiplied. Carefully pray through the ensemble director selection process.

The accompanist is very valuable in helping the ensemble achieve good intonation and other musical accuracy. If the accompanist is weak, the ensemble will falter. If a strong player is not available, it is better to create accompaniment tracks with an electric keyboard or sequencer. Some directors even prefer this for performances. Younger players are training to participate in the church orchestra, so keep accountability standards high.

The ensemble secretary may simply be a computer if everyone has e-mail, but remember it is crucial to communicate to the parents. There is usually a parent who is gifted in organizational skills that could do a fine job, and may bring other benefits as well!

The rehearsal space needs to be an area that can be arranged before rehearsal time begins, and not interrupted by traffic during the rehearsal. Set a regular weekly time for rehearsal and don't be late. Even if only one person arrives on time, begin and dismiss on time. An accompanist can be helpful in beginning the rehearsal. Music stands, piano, amplifiers, and other equipment should be in place before rehearsal time begins. If players stand during a rehearsal, they are more focused—wind players breathe more efficiently, string players often use better playing form. Obviously, some instruments may not be played while the players stand. The instrumental director should assess each rehearsal, make notes, and be ready to improve the rehearsal next week. Encourage ensemble directors to evaluate and support each other by attending their colleagues' rehearsals occasionally. The students will be motivated to play their best. Repertoire should be at and above the player's abilities. Challenge them! All music should be memorized as soon as possible. This will be difficult at first, but students will learn how to memorize more effectively and easily. The memorized ensemble can perform without music stands, and focus on ensemble balance and musicality. Confident performing prepares young players for the adult church orchestra. The music should be a mixture of hymn arrangements, lively spirituals, and classics. Sometimes a show tune may be used when appropriate. Remember: the music is the highway that these young players must travel to reach their musical goals. Choosing varied, quality repertoire will motivate the players.

Eddie Farguson
Minister of Instrumental Music,
First Baptist Church, Dallas, Texas

Q: What are some basic principles in developing a church youth orchestra?

• "The director should keep both long-term and short-term achievable goals planned throughout the year.
• "The director of a high school orchestra must be able to relate well to teenagers.
• "The high school church orchestra needs to have regularly scheduled rehearsals and periodic worship-leading experiences.
• "The director should lead the young people to grow both musically and spiritually."

The name of the group is very important. It gives the young players a sense of identity and ownership. Along with the name, the group should have a key Scripture verse which serves as a vision statement for their ministry. The group should recite their verses at every practice and shout them out at every performance. Suggested key Scriptures are 2 Corinthians 2:14, Psalm 150, and Psalm 100. A uniform is recommended, and should complement the style of the group, but be dressy enough to make the members look and feel special.

Performance opportunities will come as the group matures. Also make this a matter of weekly prayer at rehearsal time. Most groups begin by playing at nursing homes. This is a wonderful "win/win" situation. The young people bring fresh happy faces and music and will receive a rich blessing for their time. They will learn about worship and ministry in a hands-on classroom. Utilize an ensemble with an appropriate audience who will be receptive to the students' ministry. Wherever the ensemble performs, they should glorify Christ. Print a program that describes the group, and that contains the plan of salvation so that it can be used as a witnessing tool. Proclaim the gospel, and students and director alike will be amazed at the energy and enthusiasm God will pour into the ministry. The ensemble is the perfect tool for reaching out into the community. Partner with other ministries of the church to increase the group's productivity.

Types of Ensembles

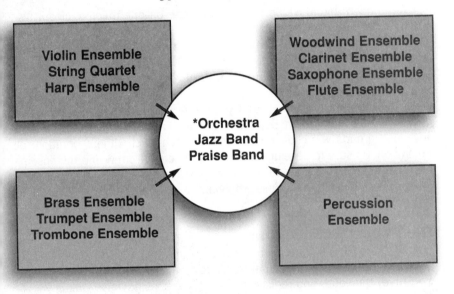

Violin Ensemble
String Quartet
Harp Ensemble

Woodwind Ensemble
Clarinet Ensemble
Saxophone Ensemble
Flute Ensemble

***Orchestra**
Jazz Band
Praise Band

Brass Ensemble
Trumpet Ensemble
Trombone Ensemble

Percussion
Ensemble

*If band or youth orchestra is established, then smaller ensembles can be created from the larger organizations.

Ideas for Ministry

• Combine several ensembles and do a two- or three-day tour of a city. Visit as many nursing homes, hospitals, schools, tourist stops, and prisons as time allows—anywhere one can draw an audience. Celebrate with a fun party at the end of the last day.

• Select an apartment complex and have a block party. Involve clowns, cook hot dogs, draw a crowd, and preach the gospel. Thousands have been saved through these methods.

• Giving thanks for the opportunities. At the end of the semester it is good to take a break to allow time to assess and evaluate the ensemble's progress and direction. Use this opportunity also to have an appreciation lunch or dinner. Show appreciation to everyone involved; recall the humorous and touching moments of the last semester. Give thanks for any victories, those led to salvation, or other reasons to rejoice. Set the date when the group will resume again and give a hint of future goals. Allow them to put the ensemble on their calendar first.

Benefits of the Ensemble Ministry

• **Building Relationships.** Allows the director to impact the personal lives of students.

• **Building a Ministry Paradigm.** Gives young players a platform to experience witnessing and worship leading.

• **Building Confidence.** Teaches stage presence, speaking skills, and interacting with others.

• **Building Musical Skills.** Allows more one-on-one training, clearer listening skills, and more attention to detail.

• **Raising the Musical Proficiency of the Entire Music Ministry.** Influences the choral and youth programs.

• **Creating Groups to Perform for Church.** Ministers to the church family.

As the program grows over the years one will soon need to develop a graded or multilevel system. Beginning, intermediate, upper intermediate, and advanced groups will challenge players at each level without boredom or frustration. Be sure to develop leaders and directors from within the ensembles. Do not be discouraged when older players graduate to upper-level groups. Take advantage of those who want to learn now. In just a short time they will be playing extremely well.

The Praise Band League

Another way to encourage and develop young talent is to create a Praise Band League. This is patterned after the softball league at your church.

• Survey the youth and register them as drums, piano, bass, guitar, vocalist, horn, or violin.

• Divide them into bands.

• Assign them to a "coach." This should be a parent who will organize the practices, provide spiritual leadership, set rehearsal times. Training sessions with the "coaches" should be initiated to teach them how to structure a rehearsal.

• Assign specific choruses to be learned, and encourage each band to write an original piece.

• Have a Praise Gathering. Invite the youth group, other churches, etc. Give awards to each band. Have a Praise Gathering each quarter, at least.

• Invite a worship band to come and give insight and instruction.

• Take the winning band to a recording studio to observe the recording process.

If you are discouraged by the lack of good musicians in your program, don't be. Even though you may have lost some of the older players, take advantage of those who want to learn how. In just a short time they will be playing extremely well and you will have become a part of their lives forever.

Resources for Instrumental Ensembles

Violins and Strings
- *Strolling Strings* (Medium Difficulty), Red McCleod (Neil A. Kjos Music Co.)
- *Sacred Settings* (Easy), Robert Frost (Neil A. Kjos Music Co.)
- *Songs for the Victory Violins* (Medium Difficulty), arr. Carter Threlkeld (Manuscript)
- *Delightful Duets for Young Violinists* (Easy), Various (William & Constance, Sunny Birchard Music, Division of Warner Bros. Music, 1985)

Harps
- *Sounds of the Season* (Christmas Collection) (Easy to Medium Difficulty), arr. Carter/Paula Threlkeld (Manuscript)
- *Hymns and Spirituals* (Easy to Medium Difficulty), arr. Carter/Paula Threlkeld (Manuscript)

Flutes
- "Air" from *Suite in D* (also choir with String Bass), Bach/James Christiansen (Southern Music Co.)
- "Allegro Maestoso" (from *Water Music Suite*), Handel/Linda Badam (Alvy Music Publications, Etc., Inc.; Carolyn Nuessbaum Music Co.) www.flute4U.com
- *Songs for the Flutes of the Spirit*, arr. Carter Threlkeld (Manuscript)

Saxophone
- "When the Saints Go Marching In," Lennie Niehaus (Kendor Music)
- *Hymn Arrangements for Saxophone Choir*, arr. Carter Threlkeld (Manuscript)

Clarinet
- "How Majestic Is Your Name" (Quartet for B♭ Clarinets), Mark Lewis (Manuscript)
- "Come, Christians, Join to Sing" (Quartet), Mark Lewis (Manuscript)
- "Caprice For Clarinets," (Quartet), Clare Grundman (Boosey & Hawkes)
- "O Come, All Ye Faithful" (Trio, Grade 1), arr. Jim Engebreton (Macie Publishing Co.—019-3CL)
- "Amazing Grace" (Trio, Grade 2), arr. Jim Engebreton (Macie Publishing Co.—001-3CL)
- "Little Fugue in G Minor" (Trio, Grade 3), Mozart/Kevin Kaisershot (Grand Mesa Music Publishing)
- "Menuetto from String Quartet, Opus 42" (Quartet, Grade 3+), Hayden/Phillip Hash (Grand Mesa Music Publishing)
- *Yamaha Clarinet Duets* (Easy), John Kinyon & John O'Reilly (Alfred Publishing Co.)
- *Tuxes for Two* (Easy Duets for Clarinet), arr. Christopher Tambling (Mel Bay Publishing Inc.)
- *Easy Classics for Clarinet*, arr. Peter Spitzer (Mel Bay Publishing Inc., 1997)

Woodwinds
- "Irish Tune from County Derry," Frank Erickson (G. Schirmer, Inc., Hal Leonard Publishing—HL50362860)

Brass
- "Praise the Lord! Ye Heavens Adore Him" (Brass Choir), Anita Kerr (Word Music, 1975, B-155)
- "The Lord's Prayer" (Nine Trumpets with Organ), Bob Feller (Manuscript)
- *Brass On Broadway* (Canadian Brass, Brass Quintet Collection), arr. Bob Lowden (Hal Leonard Publishing, 1989, HL50488781)
- *Hymns for Brass* (Canadian Brass, Easy Brass Quintet Collection), arr. Rick Walters (Hal Leonard Publishing, 1990, HL50488754)
- *Book of Favorite Quintets* (Canadian Brass, Intermediate Brass Quintet Collection), arr. Walter H. Barnes (Hal Leonard Publishing—HL50488967)
- *A Canadian Brass Christmas* (Brass Quintet Collection), arr. Luther Henderson (Hal Leonard Publishing, 1988, HL50489978)
- *Christmas Brass,* arr. Camp Kirkland (Gaither Music Corporation—GG 1190)

Other Instruments
- *Two For Christmas* (Unaccompanied Duets – C, B♭, E♭, F/E♭, Bass Clef), arr. James Curnow (Curnow Music Press—CMP0345.00 to CMP0349.00)
- *Christmas Carols For Two*, Collection/Unaccompanied Duets—Flute, Clarinet, Alto Sax, Trumpet, Trombone, (Hal Leonard Publishing—00847192 to 00847196)
- *Christmas Hits for Two,* Collection/Unaccompanied Duets—Flute, Clarinet, Alto Sax, Trumpet, Trombone, (Hal Leonard Publishing, 1991, 00847197 to 00847201)
- *Christmas Duets for All,* Collection/Unaccompanied Duets (Hal Leonard Publishing, 1991)
- *Ensembles Sound Spectacular* (Book 1, Level 1), arr. Andrew Balent (Carl Fisher—05291)
- *Ensembles Sound Spectacular* (Book 2, Level 2), arr. Andrew Balent/Joseph Compello (Carl Fisher—05376)
- *Sounds of Celebration* (Solos with Ensemble Arrangements), arr. Stan Pethel (Daybreak Music, Hal Leonard Publishing—HL08742509)
- *Instrumental Praise & Worship* (B♭, C, E♭, Bass Clef Books—Melody or Harmony with Solos), arr. Fred Bock (Hal Leonard Publishing—BG 0924 to BG 09270)
- *Instrumental Hymns and Gospel Favorites* (Easy Level, C, B♭, E♭, Bass Clef Solos, Duets, Trios with Piano accompaniment), Harlo E. McCall (R. D. Row Music Co., division of Carl Fischer)
- *20 Top Young People's Classic* (Intermediate Level, Tunes for Two), Kevin Mayhow (Kevin Mayhow, LTD)
- *Popular Classics* (Solos, Duets, Trios), arr. John Cacaras (Warner Bros. Publications, 1999)
- *Favorite Wedding Classics* (Solos, Duets, Trios with Piano accompaniment, Flute, Clarinet, Alto Sax, Trumpet), arr. Keith Snell (Warner Bros. Publications, 1992)

- *Favorite Movie Standards* (Solos, Duets, Trios with Piano accompaniment—Clarinet & Trumpet only), arr. Keith Snell (Warner Bros. Publications)
- *Favorite Hymns Volume I & Volume II* (Solos, Duets, Trios with Piano accompaniment—Flute, Clarinet, Alto Sax, Trumpet), arr. Keith Snell (Warner Bros. Publications)
- *Pop Quartets for All* (Playable for any instrument or number of instruments in ensemble—Piano, Flute/Piccolo, Clarinet, Alto Sax, Tenor Sax, B♭ Trumpet/Baritone, F Horn, Trombone/Baritone/Bassoon/Tuba, Violin, Viola, Cello/Bass, Percussion), arr. Michael Story (Warner Bros. Publication)
- "Holy, Holy, Holy" (Easy Level, Duets, Choir/Organ/Conductor, C Flute/Advanced Violin/Clarinet/Trumpet, Alto Sax, F Horn, Trombone/Cello/String Bass/Bassoon, Baritone BC, Tuba, Violin [Oboe], Viola), arr. John Bullock (Belwin Mills Publishing)
- *The Baptist Hymnal,* 1991 (Individual instrument editions, Rhythm, Conductor), Convention Press
- *Christmas Quartets for All; Christmas Duets for All; Sacred Quartets for All; Sacred Trios for All* (C, Flute/Piccolo, Piano/Oboe/Conductor, B♭ Clarinet, Alto Sax, Tenor Sax, Trumpet/Baritone TC, F Horn, Trombone/Bassoon/Baritone BC/Tuba, Violin, Viola, Cello/Bass, Percussion), arr. William Ryden (Belwin Mills Publishing)

Video
- *Instrumental Music Ensembles: Music with a Mission* (Produced by Bellevue Baptist Church), www.bellevue.org

Carter Threlkeld is Minister of Instrumental Music at Bellevue Baptist Church, Cordova, Tennessee. He has served in this capacity since 1983. He directs the Adult Sanctuary Orchestra, Victory Marching Bands, 21 different instrumental ensembles, and is the Director/Administrator of the Performing Arts Center. He is a graduate of the University of Michigan.

CHAPTER 23

Worship Planning with the Instrumentalist in Mind

by Ed Callahan

The potential for a moving worship experience is greatly increased when instrumentalists become part of the worship team. Yet, instrumentalists inherently place new demands on the person planning worship. The worship service that comes to life generally takes prayer, creativity, and much planning. However, the benefits of a dynamic service far supersede the extra work required. Here are just a few possibilities that would add vitality to the worship service:

1. Orchestra prelude
2. Orchestra offertory
3. Orchestra postlude
4. Orchestra and choir, a dynamic duo!
5. Orchestra and multimedia
6. Orchestra and other instrumental groups, i.e., handbells
7. Orchestra and soloists, instrumental and vocal
8. Instrumental ensembles
9. Instrumental soloists

The new dimensions a group of instrumentalists add to the overall worship experience is phenomenal. The new textures are profound, and, when done well, the worshiper is taken to new heights!

For example, instrumental music can easily be used as a prelude to capture the congregation's attention and draw them into an attitude of worship. But even with skilled instrumentalists, there are boundaries that the worship planner should place upon himself when constructing the worship service.

A worship leader should build consistency. Although variety produces freshness, frequent modulation and style changes impede the flow of worship. Too many changes will keep participants from "settling in" for worship. Ron Man has written the following:

"A worship service consists of a variety of elements and parts; the [challenge] is to avoid an awkward sense of repeated starts and stops. To draw an analogy: the cars of a train may have different functions—engine, box car, tanker, caboose—but all are linked together and are heading in the same direction. So also should the various elements of a service have a feel of connectedness; ***the goal should be to minimize unnecessary distractions so that our focus can be on God—the One we have come to worship."*** [1]

The leader should be selective when making drastic tempo changes, sudden modulations, and style changes. Remember: too many changes cause people to abandon the worship train!

Communicating with Instrumentalists

Various forms of communication tools can be used in order to ensure proper understanding of how a worship service is to move along. These include hand signals, verbal instruction, facial expression, conducting, and vocal embellishment. Additionally, most worship leaders utilize a written order of worship much like a coach would use a game plan. This allows everyone to clearly understand the direction in which the team is heading and what plays will assure success. "This coordination will prevent confusion among the people and promote a willingness to be led." [2] The order of worship determines the flow, and a written plan is needed to ensure smooth transitions. From here on the written order of worship will be called the flow sheet. Every team member must know what the flow sheet entails in order to have a successful worship experience. Whenever any change is made, all involved must be alerted. Communication gives each worship participant, including instrumentalists, choirs, small ensembles, and soloists, a genuine sense of being an important part of the worship team.

The Flow Sheet Defined

The flow sheet is the primary written communication tool for all music, media, and platform personnel. The notes on the flow sheet emphasize the fact that these three groups of personnel are crucial to most successful times of worship. Unless all personnel comprehend their worship service responsibilities, unwanted distractions may occur.

This flow sheet should not be a copy of the general bulletin. Instead, it is to be a separate, detailed order of events that must take place before, during, and immediately

> **Dr. Ken Gabrielse**
> **Professor of Music,**
> **New Orleans Baptist**
> **Theological Seminary**
>
> **Q:** Why should instrumentalists be used in Christian worship services?
> **A:** "One of the greatest reasons to use instrumentalists (of all kinds and all varieties) in our worship services is that it allows the people of God to celebrate the recreative act of God in and through the lives of the people playing the instruments. As people are encouraged to use their instrumental ability in leading worship, the church is fulfilling Old and New Testament principles of worship: Old Testament—using instruments in praise (Psalms); New Testament—fellowship (Acts 2:42), which is celebrating God's work in the lives of other church members. (By the way, this is the New Testament principle that allows us to use all of the arts in worship.)"

after any specific worship service. Therefore, the flow sheet is the most important form of communication that tells how the worship service will ebb and flow. It states who is to be involved, when they are to participate, and what they are to do, especially considering that most of the interaction will often take place through a core of "volunteers."

The Importance of the Flow Sheet

While having a written game plan cannot guarantee an inspirational worship service, the absence of a written game plan will most definitely hinder attitudes toward worship. Ron Man has stated, "Flow in a service simply means that the mechanics of the service don't draw attention to themselves, and thus distract from a proper focus on God Himself." [3]

Instrumentalists face challenges unlike others on the worship team. They not only have to be "well oiled" spiritually, but must also interact with the mechanics of their instrument, turn pages back and forth, and at the same time genuinely try to stay in an attitude of praise. There is nothing else like it! A well-planned worship service is "oil" to the instrumentalists. Once they are able to move beyond the mechanics, everyone is blessed because of what the instrumentalists add to the worship service, not only in their spirit, but also in their playing. The flow sheet is a key element in the success of the instrumentalists. It guarantees security and relays to them the importance of their role in the worship experience.

Types of Flow Sheets

There are as many different styles of flow sheets as there are styles of music. However, it is essential to remember that a flow sheet needs to function as it is defined. The best way to arrange essential elements of the worship service is to arrange the location of songs in the order in which they will occur in the service. All words of instruction should be written within the "flow" of the order of worship, void of unnecessary detail.

Locating instructions on one portion of the flow sheet while having the rest of the elements of worship listed on another portion may cause confusion. A cluttered flow sheet is an unnecessary hurdle for instrumentalists.

Those involved in the worship team are usually highly skilled. If they struggle with the readability of the flow sheet, worship will be hindered. This should be avoided! The flow sheet should be written clearly, so the direction of the worship can be easily defined, especially considering the new heights that instrumentalists can bring to a worship experience. This benefit alone should be a mandate for the worship leader to plan well, keeping the instrumentalist in mind.

Nine Essential Elements for the Instrumental Flow Sheet

1. Song title for each song
2. Form changes within each song
3. Transitions from one song into the next

4. Added layers of texture
5. Concert key(s) in which each song is to be played
6. Tempo changes
7. Style changes
8. Lyrics to songs to be sung by the congregation
9. Instrumental features

These nine essential elements are to be considered each time a flow sheet is developed. They are basic to any plan and necessary in order to have successful communication.

1. The Song Title. Each instrumentalist should be able to see what is coming up by just glancing at the flow sheet. Indicate the hymn number followed by the title. Next, write in the corresponding hymn or song file location. This allows the worship leader to develop an accurate filing system. Also, mark the number of times the song is to be played. Write the title in bold, and various instructions in a different font, or highlighted. Make the directions on the flow sheet stand out so they can be read at a glance.

EXAMPLE 1

*Hymn 10 (4) **"HOW GREAT THOU ART"** <u>2x's</u> in B♭; then opt. mod. <u>1x</u> in C

*(The hymn number is taken from *The Baptist Hymnal,* 1991, Convention Press. The number in parenthesis is the corresponding hymn number from *The Hymnal for Worship & Celebration,* copyright 1986, Word Music. Both hymnals are fully orchestrated.)

---

2. Form Changes Within Each Song. Possible changes in the form of a song can include:

1. modulate within a song,
2. begin the song at the refrain,
3. place verses back to back,
4. place the refrain back to back,
5. cut the song introduction (i.e., begin at the vocal line, measure 5, especially when stringing songs together),
6. utilize various "tag" endings,
7. cut the song ending when going straight into the next song.

Most importantly, make note of any form changes within each song. If needed, lay out the song in "storyboard" form, i.e., verse-chorus, verse, verse-chorus, chorus, (v-c, v, v-c, c), or any variety of arrangements. When changing the form of the song make sure that all instrumentalists understand the new form. The ending in Example 2 below was shortened in order to have a more fluid transition into the next song. If all involved do not fully understand the shortened ending, they will continue playing the ending while the worship leader has already started the next song a cappella. Now that would be a joyous occasion!

Changing the form of a song can help give a portion of the worship service a climactic quality. When making several changes within the arrangement of a song, i.e., changing the song form, layering instrumental textures, and modulating, it is best done with a song that everyone knows well, such as "Amazing Grace! How Sweet the Sound," Example 3.

Because the song is familiar to all, more will participate. With that in mind, change the form of "Amazing Grace!" by starting a cappella. Then, add layers of instrumental texture. Next, utilize the technique of modulation, and finally, have the drum kit "push" into the last time with a repeated half-chorus. This technique can add "amazing" heights to a worship experience.

The flow sheet should indicate the changes in song form, and the worship leader must be able to walk the instrumentalists through the modifications during rehearsal time. If a change in form like Example 2 is used in worship, do not create other complex arrangements for that service. Remember: be selective. Don't overuse these techniques.

3. Transitions from One Song into the Next. When writing down the form of the hymn or song, also make note of any transitions from one song into the next. For example, if the next song has an eight-measure introduction, make a note of which instrument needs to lead out during those first eight measures in order to set up the worship leader's vocal line. (See Example 4.) Talk through all transitions with all instrumentalists and vocalists.

One of the most critical transitions takes place when modulation is required between songs. Developing a fluid modulation is another way of adding climax to the worship experience. Again, be sure not to overuse this technique. The Modulation Chart in the back of *Songs for Praise and Worship,* Worship Planner Edition, pages 549-562 (Nashville: Word, 1992), is a helpful tool in planning modulations.

Another example of how to write out a "song-to-song" transition is to spell out how many measures will be between songs and on what measure and beat the change will occur. This is particularly important when a style change is taking place going into the next song. For example, going from a slow $\frac{4}{4}$ meter to a driving $\frac{4}{4}$ is a typical style alteration. In order to make the change fluid, it should take place on beat one of the last measure from which the instrumentalists are transitioning. This sets up the next song without interruption or break in continuity.

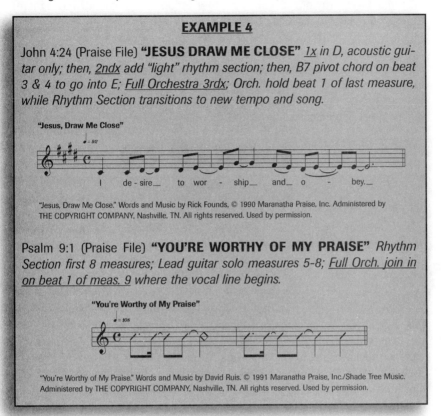

EXAMPLE 4

John 4:24 (Praise File) **"JESUS DRAW ME CLOSE"** _1x_ in D, acoustic guitar only; then, _2ndx_ add "light" rhythm section; then, B7 pivot chord on beat 3 & 4 to go into E; _Full Orchestra 3rdx_; Orch. hold beat 1 of last measure, while Rhythm Section transitions to new tempo and song.

"Jesus, Draw Me Close"

I de - sire___ to wor - ship___ and___ o - bey.___

"Jesus, Draw Me Close." Words and Music by Rick Founds. © 1990 Maranatha Praise, Inc. Administered by THE COPYRIGHT COMPANY, Nashville, TN. All rights reserved. Used by permission.

Psalm 9:1 (Praise File) **"YOU'RE WORTHY OF MY PRAISE"** _Rhythm Section first 8 measures; Lead guitar solo measures 5-8; Full Orch. join in on beat 1 of meas. 9_ where the vocal line begins.

"You're Worthy of My Praise"

"You're Worthy of My Praise." Words and Music by David Ruis. © 1991 Maranatha Praise, Inc./Shade Tree Music. Administered by THE COPYRIGHT COMPANY, Nashville, TN. All rights reserved. Used by permission.

The rhythm section will handle most transitions because they are chordally based and because other instrumentalists might be pausing to turn a page. When placing songs together, it may be necessary to begin the second song at measure 5, 9, 13 or as the vocal line begins. Once the rhythmic pattern is established, the lead guitar player could solo during measures 5-8. This would give the worship leader time to encourage the congregation before coming in on the vocal line, and provide time for the orchestra to get set up for a solid entrance.

Again, most transitions are the rhythm section players' responsibility. Therefore, the worship leader must work with those in the rhythm section, as well as those in the larger group. Instrumentalists, other than those in the rhythm section, need to know specifically when each rhythm section transition is to take place in order to have musical clarity.

The rhythm section can involve drums, bass, various guitars, keyboard, piano, and organ. The foundation of the rhythmic accompaniment begins with the rhythm section. Stuart Townend in his article "The Rhythm Section" states, "If you are taking on the role of music director then you need a working knowledge of the instruments you are directing, and some idea of how to get your team members to make a good sound together. Of the three main 'sections' of your band (or orchestra)—vocals, rhythm section, and solo (or orchestral) instruments—the rhythm section is the foundation of your sound, and is therefore a good place to start."[4]

4. Added Layers of Texture. Build the rhythm section, but do not neglect the rest of the instrumentalists who will be giving the added layers of texture to the overall sound. Adding layers to the texture or "lightening" the texture can construct musical climax or anticlimax of the musical phrase. Doing this builds times of climax into the overall context of the worship experience.

Be aware that some orchestral instruments tend to double certain instruments of the rhythm section. Make sure they interact clearly and the sound does not become messy. When rehearsing, understand which instruments are providing the chordal structure for the song, and which instruments are providing riffs, shorter percussive embellishments, or more legato lines. Know the arrangements and who is providing the different layers and textures. Make notes accordingly on the flow sheet to help the instrumentalists determine which role they are playing in the arrangement of a particular song. Some instruments affect the musical phrase more than others. Also, some instruments color the texture more than others. A good practice when developing texture is to imagine the different sounds instruments make. Ask yourself how that particular instrument's "texture" would sound during a particular song. Certainly a pipe organ sound does not need to be used when the color and feel of the music needs to be in a folk style. However, during a stately hymn a pipe organ has been known to highly augment the worship experience! Practice the art of listening, and imagining different colors, feels, and textures of various instruments in order to enhance the worship experience.

EXAMPLE 5

Hymn 210 (364) **"MY JESUS, I LOVE THEE"** F, *1stx* light acoustic guitar with strings. *2ndx* add piano and WW. *3rdx* modulate to G on beat 3 and 4 and add brass and full rhythm section, except organ. *4thx* stay in G, add organ. Let organ be predominant in the orchestral balance.

The key to utilizing different textures is moderation. In a complete service, there may only be one or two times that layers of textures would be constructed to result in such an augmented worship experience. Consider the time allowed for worship.

5. Concert Key(s). Make note of the concert key(s) for each song and provide each non-C concert instrumentalist with a transposition chart. Place the chart in the three-ring binder or folder. The instrumentalists using the transposition chart will be able to follow along during key changes. Otherwise, they may become frustrated and discouraged. By providing the necessary tools, the instrumentalists will be able to follow along closely. Avoid transpositions further than a whole step up or down. In Example 5, notice the concert keys listed: first, the key of F major; then, the key of G major.

6. Tempo Changes. Note all awkward tempo changes. If instrumentalists tend to push the tempo, make a note for them on the flow sheet. Sometimes instrumentalists have a tendency to push the tempo of the song because they like the feel of the tempo for their particular instrument or section. The worship leader should always determine the proper tempo of any song. He should be sensitive to the congregation's ability to keep up and compromise accordingly. Once the group of instrumentalists has been working with the worship leader for a number of months, it should be able to adjust the tempo when needed, based on the worship leader's vocal line. Not all involved will "feel" the same momentum in worship at the same time. Therefore, trust must be given to the worship leader's sense of tempo, not only of a particular song, but also sometimes of the entire worship service. It's hard for instrumentalists to see the response of the congregation because they have so many mechanics with which to deal.

7. Style Changes. Identify any out-of-the-ordinary style changes. One of the more awkward style changes is going from a rock feel with the snare playing on two and four, such as "Mighty Is Our God," into a straight two-beat style in $\frac{4}{4}$ meter like "Come Into His Presence." In this stylistic transition the tempo has to decrease either gradually over 3 beats, or right on beat one of the next measure. Everyone has to shift together. It is always best to change from a straight two-beat style into  a half-time feel rather than the opposite. The best time to contemplate a style change is during worship planning. Sing and/or play through a worship set before it is "set" in concrete on the flow sheet and introduced to the instrumentalists.

Any duple meter changing into a triple feel, i.e., $\frac{4}{4}$ into $\frac{6}{8}$ or vice versa can be an awkward style change if not given proper treatment. Although certain style changes do not need to be avoided, they should be given their proper respect. It is best to connect duple meter with duple, and triple with triple. The easiest style changes are from fast to slow within $\frac{4}{4}$ meter. At the end of a faster song, use a gradual ritard to "pull back the reins" in order to gently enter the first measure of the slower song.

Sometimes changing the style of a standard hymn can add new life to an overfamiliar "hymn setting."

EXAMPLE 6

Hymn 135 (195) **"NOTHING BUT THE BLOOD"** *Try changing this familiar hymn from a more formal march style into a straight two-beat "jump shout" style. The timing of the change could take place at the beginning of the song or during a double chorus ending.*

---

8. Lyrics. In order to help draw the instrumentalist further into an attitude of worship, type out the lyrics of songs that are intended for congregational singing. This will help the instrumentalist be able to follow the worship leader. Have lyrics available at all times so that instrumentalists will be able to more fully express their worship to the Lord. It is important for the instrumentalists to see the text of songs used so that their worship is more fully expressed. When instrumentalists are not given lyrics, they are being asked to bless others while being robbed of the lyrical expression. Instrumentalists should not be left to "warm the bench" when music is not available for them to play. Having lyrics helps them to take the song to heart.

Example 7 is a complete model of two songs tied together—one new, the other more familiar. This sample includes a Scripture reference, song titles, library file locations, different styles, different meters, different tempis, different textures, as well as form changes, modulations, lyrics, and transitions written out within the flow of each song. See Example 7.

9. Instrumental Features. Make note of any individual instrumental features, i.e., soloists, ensembles, jazz band, praise band, or full orchestra. Through the flow sheet, let all instrumentalists know when special features will occur in the worship order. Well-planned logistics help people get to the right place at the right time.

Other Elements

Although separate details should be given to the media department, and other platform personnel, such as a drama team or a personal testimony, place a general statement within the flow sheet letting the instrumentalists know what will take place. For example:

- Make note of Scriptures to be read, recited, or referenced;
- Note any drama;
- Note any video or Powerpoint presentation;
- Note any prayer;
- Identify the accompaniment for each musical selection that is not congregational, i.e., tape, CD, piano, instrumental ensemble, or praise band.

EXAMPLE 7

1 Thess. 5:18 (octavo orchestration) **"FOR ALL YOU'VE DONE"** E♭ *to F; then, shorten ending by holding beat 1 of measure 105; fade out, then, sing along!*

For all You've done, for all You're going to do;
We give You praise and lift our hands to You;
We give thanks, we give praise, for we know that all things work together for our good.
We give thanks, we give praise for, by faith, we know Your grace will see us through.
We give thanks, we give praise, for we know that all things work together for our good.
We give thanks, we give praise for, by faith, we know Your grace will see us through.

For all those things that we don't understand,
We come by faith and place them in Your hands.
We give thanks, we give praise, for we know that all things work together for our good.
We give thanks, we give praise for, by faith, we know Your grace will see us through.
Even if we stumble, even if we fall,
You will not forsake us; You are King and Lord of all! Lord of All!
  (to F major)
We give thanks, we give praise, for we know that all things work together for our good.
We give thanks, we give praise for, by faith, we know Your grace will see us through.
We give thanks, we give praise, for we know that all things work together for our good.
We give thanks, we give praise for, by faith, we know Your grace will see us through.
  (hold first beat of m. 105; fade out, sing along!)

("For All You've Done," copyright 1997 Integrity's Hosanna! Music. Words and Music by Don Moen, Vocal Arrangement by Jay Rouse, Arranged by Tom Brooks.)

Hymn 330 (202) **"AMAZING GRACE! HOW SWEET THE SOUND"** *1stx in F…a cappella; then, 2ndx piano transition into G add WW & Strings on the pick-up; 3rdx stay in G, add Full Orch. 4thx transpose up 1/2 step to A♭; Drum kit "push" into 4thx. Blow the roof off! Repeat 1/2 chorus for the ending, hold last note for vocal tag.*

Amazing grace! how sweet the sound, that saved a wretch like me!
I once was lost, but now am found, was blind, but now I see.
  (G major, piano/WW/strings)
'Twas grace that taught my heart to fear, and grace my fears relieved;
How precious did that grace appear the hour I first believed.
  (Full Orch.)
Thro' many dangers, toils, and snares, I have already come;
'Tis grace hath bro't me safe thus far, and grace will lead me home.
  (Drum Kit, kick it in!…Read up 1/2 step to A♭)
When we've been there ten thousand years, bright shining as the sun,
We've no less days to sing God's praise than when we first begun.
  (Repeat last 8 measures, and use vocal tag…"Amazing Grace!")
                    [vocal tag=ab, ab, ab, eb]

Beyond the Flow Sheet

Worship that changes people each time they "enter into His courts" takes prayer and planning. When proper prayer and planning has been given to a worship service, flexibility is the result. The flow sheet allows the instrumentalists to relax and enjoy the worship service. Even though minor detours may occur, the majority of the journey is still secure. When instrumentalists know where they are headed, they do not get thrown off course as easily when things are changed.

The question, "Why the sudden change?" is legitimate. The Bible is clear. The Father seeks worshipers who will worship Him in spirit and truth. During worship, there may be times when the worship leader senses that the Father has found some true worshipers and has determined to spend some time with them that they will never forget. When this takes place, flexibility becomes crucial. Here are five options for those moments when the Father has magnified Himself supernaturally:

1. Continue to follow as well as possible.
2. Stop playing and start praying.
3. Let an individual instrumentalist, such as the pianist, carry the moment.
4. Have the rhythm section continue alone.
5. Worship through singing a cappella until the flow of worship coincides with the flow sheet once again.

Forecasting Detours

When the worship service does make a detour, communication must go beyond the flow sheet. The most important instrumentalists to make contact with are the leaders of each section, beginning with the leader of the rhythm section, who is generally the pianist. Next, make quick eye contact with the first trumpet player, woodwind, string, and auxiliary percussion sections if possible. There are different forms of communication that could be used at this point. The most popular are hand signals. For a sample listing of hand signals see *Songs for Praise and Worship,* Worship Planner Edition, pages 456-458 (Nashville: Word, 1992). Other forms of communication could be conducting, clapping, or slight body movements to help indicate the beat or cutoff, such as, nodding the head, tapping the leg, or standing tall until the cutoff. Public or private verbal instruction through a microphone to the congregation, rhythm section, or technical areas is also effective.

The most fluid way to "tip off" the detour is vocal embellishment. Vocally adding to the melody can send a signal that will let the instrumentalists know where the flow of music is heading. Often, this is the best way to keep everyone going in the same direction.

Practical Tips

The best way to hold distractions to a minimum for the instrumentalists is to make the flow sheets available at least one rehearsal prior to the worship service, which generally gives ample preparation time. Photocopy* all music for the instrumentalists and refile after each service—assuming that one original has been properly purchased and remains in the file for every copy made. Provide a three-ring binder containing several clear plastic sheets. Slip all the music, in order, inside the plastic sheets so the instrumentalist can turn the page quickly and with ease from one song to the next.

Divide the three-ring binder in half with an additional sheet, possibly half of a manila folder with the tab outward for ease of grasping. The front half of the binder should be used for the Sunday morning worship service(s). The back half can be used for the Sunday evening worship. Place a copy of the Sunday morning flow sheet in the front pocket of the three-ring binder for the morning service and a copy of the Sunday evening flow sheet in the back pocket for the evening service. Each week the worship leader should spend time trying to commit to memory as much of the flow sheet, including lyrics, as possible.

*For a copy of the brochure, *Copyrights and the Law*, contact Church Music Publishers Association, P.O. Box 158992, Nashville, TN 37215, (615) 791-0273.

Closing Remarks

Valuable worship experiences that the church instrumentalist yields far supersede

---

Darryl One
Conductor/Musical Director
for the Modesto Symphony
Orchestra, Modesto, California

The Transfiguration from Conductor to Worship Leader

• "Learn to worship and become a worship leader. Everyone has their own personal ways to worship, but a leader must worship outwardly and demonstrate a focus on God and glorifying Him.

• "Make conducting automatic. You cannot worship with a good praise chorus unless singing the words are second nature; similarly, you can't lead worship from the podium unless conducting is also second nature to you.

• "Combine the two and become a conducting worship leader; worship outwardly yourself, lead the orchestra where necessary, trust your musicians to help carry the music while you are leading."

---

any challenges that utilizing instrumentalists for worship may hold, and communication is the key that will ensure a successful worship experience for all!

[1] Ronald E. Man, "Flow, Service, Flow" *Church Musician Today,* Vol. 2, No. 10, June 1999, 11.
[2] From *Songs for Praise & Worship,* Worship Planner Edition (Nashville: Word Music, 1992), 462.
[3] Man, 11.
[4] Article #4 by Stuart Townend from WorshipTogether.com.

Ed Callahan is one of the associate pastors at First Baptist Church, Arnold, Missouri. He oversees FBC worship ministries, works with Media Resource Ministries at FBC, and is presently providing leadership for the church's World Missions Ministries. Callahan received his BS degree in Music Education from Southeast Missouri State University, and Master of Divinity degree from Mid-America Baptist Theological Seminary where he is presently working on a Doctor of Ministries degree.

CHAPTER 24

Practical Consideration of the Preservice Rehearsal and Worship Service

by Larry Mayo

There are no scriptural references the music minister can utilize to determine how a church orchestra prepares for a worship service. The Bible gives us little assistance as to the practical matters of architectural accommodation of instruments in a sanctuary, its appearance, or deportment of the instrumentalists. Yet these are pragmatic matters one must consider. If not considered, inappropriate or ineffective outcomes may unintentionally cause harm to the very arena of worship the orchestra was designed to enhance.

Appearance

At some point, the question of the orchestra's appearance must be addressed. There are three possible answers: no uniformity, blazers, or robes. If the visage of the orchestra is not to be homogenous, it should be intentional. The question should be asked, "Why does the role of the ensemble require it to look like the congregation?" If the desire is to have the orchestra be uniform in appearance, but remain distinct from the choir, wearing blazers is the answer. If this were the case, one must decide the required degree of detail (i.e., Must all the men wear the same tie, same color pants? Do the women all wear white blouses? Do the women wear skirts or pants?) A word of warning here: wearing the same "uniform" every Sunday can be confining, especially to the women. Wearing robes unifies the appearance of the choir and orchestra. It is also less restrictive to the Sunday attire of the orchestra members. Care, however, should be given to eliminate the traditional flowing, loose sleeves of the robes by insisting on tailored sleeves (similar to that of a tailored jacket) when ordering robes from the manufacturer. If the orchestra wears street clothes to perform, a dress code that promotes modesty and tastefulness should be adopted.

The Preservice Rehearsal

Mechanical aspects of the preservice rehearsal are critical. Certain basics should be addressed. The rehearsal room's physical setup should communicate that it is prepared for everyone's arrival: the room is properly lit, the temperature of the room is set comfortably, the chairs are in order, the stands properly placed, the percussion correctly set up, and the music folders are on the music stands.

It is important for each player to allot enough time to be prepared prior to the rehearsal. This should include time enough to put on robes or blazers, warm up, and prepare their folders. A specific area should be dedicated to the orchestra players where they can dress. Players should be expected to put on their robes or blazers prior to rehearsal time. Each player should warm up on his or her instrument. If a player does not warm up, he or she will not be able to play at the optimum level or calibrate properly to the tuning process. Ideally the service's worship order is already set up in each musician's folder. (See Chapter 23 and the discussion of flow sheets.) But if this is not possible, each player should be in place early enough to assemble the order of music for the service. Merely showing up by the time the rehearsal begins is not enough. Insist that the orchestra be punctual. Reinforce their promptness by beginning on time.

It is a mystery why some orchestras do not tune. A director loses a valuable opportunity to ensure the musical integrity of the ensemble when failing to tune. The strings appreciate an "A-440" from the piano and a chance to tune without any other instruments playing. Give them ample time. The woodwinds can tune on an "A" or "B♭." If possible, let them tune separately, as well. Give the brass a "B♭" and be careful to not let the brass play too loudly when they tune. Use a tuner, if necessary, to resolve problem intonation. Remind players that if there is a temperature difference between the auditorium and the rehearsal room, they will have to readjust.

If time permits, space is available, and the choir room is sufficiently nearby, the first portion of the orchestra rehearsal (tuning and practicing the orchestra special, if there is one) can take place in the instrumental rehearsal area. This enables the orchestra to concentrate on musical elements without disturbing the choir, or the choir inadvertently interfering with the orchestra. But, if this is not possible, and the entire preservice rehearsal must take place in the choir room, care must be taken to remind the choir politely, from time to time, of the orchestra's need to have a relatively noise-free environment. The discussion of the congregational music should involve both the choir and the orchestra. It is helpful to provide instructions in written form as well as to verbalize how the music will flow in the service. It is even better to mark all the individual parts with highlighter marker and pencil so that the musicians will not have to read an instruction sheet and music simultaneously. Rehearsing the orchestra with the choir in the choir room can be frustrating to the vocalists because they sometimes have trouble hearing themselves over the clamor of instruments. The instrumentalists, particularly the brass and percussionists, should be sensitive enough to keep the volume level down. The orchestra should be permitted to leave the choir room first because of the logistics of transporting equipment and instruments and setting up again in the worship center.

Orchestra Placement

Most church worship spaces were never built to accommodate an orchestra. As a consequence, space for an orchestra must often be creatively contrived, as the architecture will allow. For those churches which intend to build a new sanctuary or redesign existing facilities, a helpful source of information is provided by the Music Educators National Conference—*Music Facilities: Building, Equipping, and Renovating,* written by Harold P. Geerdes. This reference gives established musical guidelines concerning architectural design, recommended space, acoustical schemes, and technical considerations.

There are only a limited number of possibilities available to provide space for the church orchestra. The orchestra can be positioned:

• **between the pulpit and the congregation.** This may require removing some of the front pews. It spreads out the orchestra, creating ensemble problems and requires the musicians to sit sideways facing each other. This either necessitates that the orchestra watch the conductor from the rear or it places the director in front of the orchestra and distanced from the choir. Balance difficulties arise with this set up because the orchestra is closer to the congregation than to the choir. This arrangement also causes problems when dealing with the invitation. Some churches configured with this setup clear the front area by folding up their chairs and moving elsewhere—instruments, stands, and all.

• **between the pulpit and the congregation, but off to one side.** While this option does free the front area for the invitation response, it distances the orchestra even further from the choir. Thus, it further aggravates the problems of the previous option. This particular configuration creates an almost total inability to hear the choir interactively.

• **between the pulpit and choir.** In some churches this may require taking out a few front pews and extending the platform enough to create room for the orchestra. The primary disadvantage of this arrangement is that the proximity of the instruments to the choir causes bleed-over into the choir microphones. Separating the orchestra from the choir just a few feet can yield dramatic reduction in orchestra bleed-over. The advantage of this formation places both the orchestra and choir close together and in front of the director.

- **between the pulpit and choir, but placed in a pit.** This option helps eliminate the bleed-over acoustical problem. Care must be taken here not to make the orchestra pit so deep that the players feel removed or isolated from the worship experience. One drawback to this setup is space limitation; only a certain number of people can be placed in the pit. There is no way to expand the boundary lines. The advice here is to not merely provide space for the current orchestra size, but to anticipate future growth and decide what the desired number of musicians might be.

- **between the pulpit and choir, but elevate the choir loft.** Elevating the choir six to eight feet from the platform can also serve to eliminate microphone bleed-over from the orchestra.

Orchestra Configuration and Microphones

It would be excellent if church worship spaces were designed with acoustical factors in mind. All too often, acoustical considerations are the last things a building committee studies. Many orchestras lack the players to produce a good instrumental balance. In any case, sound reinforcement is a necessary component in many situations. Submixing the orchestra's sound down to a single feed up to the master board is advisable. Rather than depending on a sound technician to produce the desired orchestral sound, some directors prefer to predetermine the best mix. Using this method takes the burden of artistic judgment away from someone who already has to control multiple sound sources. Simplifying the orchestra feed will better guarantee a satisfactory musical experience by, in essence, reducing the sound technician's responsibility to that of determining a single volume control of the orchestra for the "big picture." This system of sound reinforcement is adequate in small church situations, but the larger church will probably want to establish philosophical guidelines about the sound mix. Some songs may require a symphonic mix, while other more contemporary songs may have a rhythm section-driven contemporary mix. The orchestra director may facilitate the work of the technical staff by providing detailed layout sheets, set-up and teardown schedules, and mix sheets and/or scores on every song. If the church retains a professional technical staff, to bypass their mixing judgment would be an affront. Frequent communication and prompt information will facilitate the process. The following factors may be helpful in determining the performance configuration of the orchestra in the sanctuary:

A. Strings

1. In seating the string section on the platform, consider each instrument's angle of acoustical projection.

2. Consider placing a hard surface beneath the string section if the area is carpeted.

3. Use overhead microphones for violin and viola, boom microphones for celli and string basses. Position the microphones so they will not interfere with bowing. There are also clip mikes that are used between the bridge and the tailpiece, or clips that are specifically designed to fit inside the f-holes of stringed instruments. If clip mikes are used, the players should be consulted about the type and the way they are fitted to the instruments.

B. Woodwinds

1. When determining the location of the flute section, consider the angle at which they play in relation to the location of the conductor.

2. Use overhead miking for the flutes. Use clip microphones attached to the underside lip of a music stand for other woodwind instruments. Other options are a floor stand for instruments whose bell points toward the floor (clarinet), and overhead boom stands for instruments whose bell points toward the ceiling (bassoon).

3. Place a hard surface underneath the woodwind section if the area is carpeted.

4. The woodwind section can act as a buffer between the strings and the louder brass and percussion instruments.

5. Place section leaders next to one another if possible.

C. Brass

1. The horn section can act as a buffer between the strings and loud instruments. Because of the angle at which they project sound, the horn section should always progress left to right, first player to fourth.

2. The brass section can act as a buffer between the percussion section and the rest of the orchestra.

3. Locate the lead trumpet player and the lead trombone player near one another. If the trumpet section is placed behind the trombone section, it will help temper some of the trumpet's edge and volume.

4. If the volume level produces problems for the brass section, hang acoustical foam or similar material off the lip of each music stand. The closer the material is to the bell of the instruments, the more effective the decibel reduction.

D. Percussion

1. Place this section in back of the orchestra or on the side, preferably away from the string section.

2. The congregation enjoys watching this section, so make them visible when possible.

E. Rhythm Section

1. Since this group is the heartbeat of the ensemble, it should be centrally located so that all players can hear them easily.

2. It must be stressed that a good drummer is "felt" and not heard. Insist that the drummer watch the conductor and fight the tendency to rush the tempo.

3. If the rhythm section cannot be physically close, consider using a personal monitor system so they can hear one another. Sometimes the speaker cabinets used by guitar and bass players are enough to balance the sound of the orchestra in the worship area. But if the acoustical design of the sanctuary produces uneven results, use a direct box to the orchestra soundboard to feed a more even sound to the room, and have the rhythm players wear open headsets.

Service Etiquette

When an orchestra enters prior to a service, it is helpful to have the chairs and stands already in place. However, from service to service, the specific personnel will change. Get everything in order as far in advance as realistically possible. Try to avoid distracting the congregation with a spectacle of hauling chairs and stands in and out of the orchestra just before the beginning downbeat of the service. With the usual maze of stands, chairs, and microphones in a tightly spaced area, it is difficult for instrumentalists to enter the orchestra area gracefully. Yet the players can come in quietly and deliberately to "set up camp." There should be no playing or warming up after they take their places.

Wonderful things happen when the orchestra plays out its function in worship: the priestly role, as they perform things that cannot be done by the congregation; the role of evangelist, in disseminating the gospel; and the role of worshiper, as they become one with the congregation. It is obvious that the orchestra's musical role is to enable an encounter with God. Just as importantly, the orchestra's collective facial expressions, posture, and listening attitude should also facilitate worship. In this entertainment age, it must be remembered that the orchestra is not the focus of worship but, rather, it is to bring a corporate focus to the sense of worship. This takes unity. Nonmusical things, both small (i.e., eye contact during a sermon) and large (i.e., singing with the congregation when not playing), send out important signals. Ninety percent of the way we communicate with each other is nonverbal. A less-than-modest appearance can be a source of distraction. Careless behavior detracts from the very purpose for which the orchestra is intended. Disinterest in various forms can kill the message that is being musically and verbally proclaimed.

One can never rise in public above what is done in private. Do not enter the sanctuary with under-rehearsed musical elements, worship logistics undiscussed, or rough spots still glaring. Do the homework it takes to produce confidence and competence in musical performance. Rewrite difficult parts, omit certain passages, substitute one instrument for another, "spot-tacet" a player in musical trouble, address every portion of the service just to see that the orchestra is guaranteed a 100 percent chance of having a musical success and that the worship is unhindered. This ultimately does two things. First, the orchestra will enjoy their role in the service. This, in turn, will build morale and validate the efforts they put forth. As well, it will free them to worship unencumbered. Second, the congregation can have confidence in their musical worship. Robert Shaw has been quoted as saying, "God is perfect, therefore we should not offer anything to Him that is less than perfect." This may be overstated, because the human race is fallible. A better revision of Shaw's maxim might be stated, "God is perfect, therefore we should not offer up unto Him anything that is less than our best."

Larry Mayo is Instrumental Music Minister, Rehoboth Baptist Church, Tucker, Georgia. Having served in music ministry since 1976, he has served as orchestra director in the Atlanta area for 17 years. He has earned both a Bachelor's and Master's Degree in music education from Florida State University and a Doctor of Musical Arts Degree from The Southern Baptist Theological Seminary, Louisville, Kentucky.

CHAPTER 25

Programming
and Special Events

by Brad R. Matheson and Billy Payne

Special events and programming can be one of the key ingredients for growth and success in church instrumental programs. Working under the basic premise that quality attracts quality and motivation builds consistency and eventually momentum, programming can be an effective tool in both the gaining and retention of prospects and new members into the instrumental program. Likewise, a well-planned special event such as a concert, mission trip or a recording project can greatly benefit the establishment of an instrumental program. This chapter will discuss how the setting of appropriate musical goals, such as programming and special events, will infuse a degree of excitement into the church instrumental program that will attract quality players and build momentum through motivation and consistency.

The First Step – Ministerial Philosophy

A basic question that each instrumental minister must address is whether or not the ministry interaction is foremost or if the musical quality of the performance should prevail. If an instrumental ensemble is ministering in worship, then the ultimate audience is God Himself, and the heart attitude of the worshiper is paramount. In a natural attempt to "be all things to all people," sometimes musical quality is displaced by the need for inclusion in the ministry setting. One of the more difficult aspects of leading volunteer musicians is trying to develop quality programming while including as many persons in the programs as possible. Some believe that only through higher levels of performance are Christian musicians able to minister more effectively. Programming and special events can motivate players both musically and spiritually while creating an atmosphere of a caring community. Whatever one's ministry philosophy, it is important to understand and take advantage of the long-term benefits received from both programming and special events.

Programming

Although the term "programming" can be very general in its usage concerning the church instrumental program, there are three main objectives that will help to determine programming: quality music, high expectations, and personal ministry. A combination of these three goals, pursued consistently, can create a dynamic, self-perpetuating environment of growth.

Quality Music. One of the most important aspects of programming is the choice of literature. Two guiding principles should be remembered when choosing music. The first guideline is that quality music attracts quality players. Select the majority of the literature to challenge the strongest players. These two principles will not only motivate less-experienced players to grow, but will provide a platform for mature players to feel as though their skills are being developed. Many times the stronger players are willing to mentor the younger instrumentalists. Often, small ensembles and feeder groups can accommodate instrumentalists of varying capacities and interests. Quality literature should be employed regardless of the size of the ensemble or the musical expertise of the players.

High Expectations. There is hesitancy on the part of most church instrumental directors to demand and ultimately achieve high levels of expectations from volunteers within their groups, for fear of alienating either themselves or others. Many musicians have an inherent need for their acquired skills to be fully utilized. For the church orchestra to minister at peak effectiveness, the director must "raise the bar" of expectation both musically and administratively. Accountability structure for attendance, careful adherence to rehearsal times, and correct music in the folders are evidence of a conscientious approach to ministry.

> **"Consistent musical growth in the volunteer church orchestra begins when attendance of regular orchestra membership reaches 85-90 percent."**

Personal Ministry. Creating fellowship is essential to the spiritual well-being of the orchestra. An orchestra will experience koinonia only if the director models servanthood and compassion for the individual members. The more transparency and vulnerability are expressed among the members, the greater the opportunity to meet deep spiritual and emotional needs within the group. This can be achieved through individualized ministry. Meaningful fellowship can be accomplished through orchestra gatherings, retreats, and even concert outings. One-on-one ministry can be developed through handwritten notes and emails, praying for specific needs as a group, knowing member's children's names, and even sending thank-you notes to spouses of orchestra members. Recruiting intercessory prayer teams to support individual orchestra members can bless and encourage those instrumentalists who minister so faithfully.

Promoting the Instrumental Ensemble

If an instrumental group is playing each week, accompanying the congregational singing and the choir, one would assume that the congregation would automatically notice the orchestra's ministry. Surely a former first violinist who happens to sit out in the congregation each week would be compelled to play. This is not necessarily the case. Many orchestra directors have

noticed their enrollments increase after beginning to play orchestra features on a regular basis. Spotlight features for the orchestra will highlight the ensemble's ability to enhance worship through instrumental music.

The instrumental group should be scheduled as often as possible. The prelude or call to worship is an excellent place in the service to feature a church orchestra. The offertory provides yet another opportunity for instrumental music to facilitate worship. A meditative piece will assist the worshiper in spending time before God in quiet contemplation. Instrumental music can speak an emotional language that reaches the heart in a unique and powerful way. Long introductions or interludes in congregational worship songs can also provide a powerful catalyst for emphasizing the message and intent of a congregational piece.

Mime, narration, drama, dance, or reading of hymn lyrics and Scripture during instrumental pieces can greatly enhance the worship experience. An instrumental hymn arrangement can underscore a powerful video or media presentation. Examples of combining media and music would include an original montage of candid photos taken from the nursery set to a children's song or church volunteer photographs projected while the orchestra plays a meditative ballad. The orchestra is heard and promoted in the context of blessing the congregation as they worship. Affirmation and support from the senior pastor and worship pastor for an instrumental ministry can be extremely beneficial in recruiting players.

Special Events

Special events for the church orchestra can be exciting for player and director. These can include seasonal church events such as Easter and Christmas pageants, Fourth of July concerts, orchestra concerts including a "pops" or sacred format, mission trips, and concerts at other churches. Orchestra recording sessions can be one of the most challenging and rewarding special events. As with any event, a great  deal of planning and organization goes into the final product. For our purposes, there are two phases of production for a special event: planning and implementation.

Planning. Of the two layers in planning a special event, conceptual and realistic, the conceptual layer must begin first. The conceptual part of planning is the actual dreaming stage of what the event is to accomplish. If the event is a "pops" or sacred concert, what is the music, mood, or message to be conveyed? If a mission trip is the special event, what does the director want the players to learn? After the concept of the special event is formulated, then realistic planning is needed to finalize the special event. It is very important to begin with what the author calls reverse planning.

Beginning with the event, assess needs such as equipment, transportation, lighting or sound reinforcement, music, promotion, and so forth. After these needs are assessed, organize and develop strategies, timelines, and task lists to accomplish the event.

Implementation. Once the director has conceptualized the event, assessed needs, and developed strategies, implementation of the event should be a scheduled, step-by-step process. After reverse planning, implementation begins as a first step forward. This first step can be the ordering of music, the beginning of rehearsals, or praying for the future event. Each step progresses toward the last note of the last orchestra piece played. One of the most important parts of the implementation stage is to assign or delegate areas of responsibility. Effective management of personnel can help in not only spreading out the workload, but also in instilling ownership of the event to the group.

Concerts as a Recruitment Tool

Concerts provide an extended time period for the instrumental group to minister, both as a seeker event, or an instrumental praise service. Sunday evening services may provide a venue for the instrumental group to perform a "mini" concert of three to five pieces, or a full concert if the time is available. In a concert situation, the setup can be adjusted to give the orchestra prime visibility. Rearrange the stage area to become more symphonic in appearance. If soloists are included, prepare enough floor space center stage to accommodate and accentuate the performance.

Ideas for Concert Planning

• **Several upbeat pieces for every slow piece.** The music for the concert needs to be balanced between upbeat and slower pieces. This change of style will maintain the interest of the congregation. The players, especially the brass section, will also appreciate the balance between lyrical and majestic selections. Many upbeat pieces grouped together can fatigue the players causing the concert to lose tone quality and intensity.

• **Vocal pieces with orchestra encourage audience interaction.** Using a congregational or choral piece can add to the concert as the people become involved in the music. The orchestra can play an orchestral arrangement of a familiar hymn or choral piece and ask the congregation to "join in" singing. Select a piece that makes the instrumental group "shine."

• **A testimony from an orchestra member is always positive.** Include a testimony time where a player in the orchestra explains how he or she came to join the group, how long they have played their instrument, and what the orchestra and Christ means to him or her. This sharing will not only exalt Christ, but will give a personal look to the level of spiritual commitment of orchestra players. The community and fellowship of the church orchestra family is a tremendous draw to unsaved musicians who are accustomed to an environment that is competitive and often highly critical. Many musicians are looking for a place to join a "family" of players.

• **Special piece featuring the pastor, staff members, or local music personalities.** The pastor of the church can be a powerful influence on the congregation. If possible, feature him. If he is not musically inclined, he can be included in a song as a novelty number by letting him play one note or hit a cymbal. Everyone loves to see their pastor in action, and the more staff members you involve, the better!

• **Guest artist.** Featuring a guest musician can add excitement. Instead of using the usual vocal artist, try an instrumentalist. There are many Christian pianists, harpists, violinists, and trumpeters touring as fine soloists who perform with orchestral accompaniment. These people would be happy to sit in with the orchestra and also perform some solo selections. Combining one orchestra with another church orchestra nearby will also promote interest in instrumental ministry. Large community Christian events can be a great way to find prospects.

Mass Church Recruiting Concert

In this concert, use all the names collected as potential orchestra members. Invite anyone to sit in with the mass group. Use nights like this to build the database of prospects. In the weeks leading up to such a concert, find out who has ever played an instrument and could sit in for the night. Other types of "mass" concerts include featuring a particular section, such as the woodwinds, strings, or brass. Using an instrumental ensemble like a jazz combo, a big band, or a woodwind quintet will add a different dimension to the service that the congregation will notice. Avoid using the same orchestra over and over for every service; it will become mundane to the congregation. By using these various ensembles, the instrumental ministry is used in every service, but is not continually the same group.

Music Underscoring to Promote Events

Music is an integral part of life. It's used very persuasively in movies, commercials, stores, and restaurants. With a little imagination, it can be used to help promote church activities, as well. Banquets, pageants, pops or classical symphonic concerts can be presented to encourage and feature other ministries. For example, the orchestra can play a pops concert as part of a Valentine banquet designed to build community in Sunday Schools or small groups. What great reinforcement that would be! Start to see how the instrumental ministry can play a part in the life of church social events. Use the orchestra to emphasize special days by adding underscore. This may require extra writing, but the end result will be well worth it. A few tried and proven ideas include: pastor's anniversary, special guest appearances, and humorous songs for church fellowships.

Themed Events to Orchestrate the Church's Life

Many churches have special events with a particular theme. If the theme is the '50s Era, one could use a jazz combo to play '50s songs during an outdoor picnic. For a men's wild game banquet, a bluegrass band could provide dinner music. A Dixieland band could play for a senior adult banquet. A woodwind quintet, flute ensemble, or string quartet might be utilized for a ladies tea, a wedding, or a funeral. All of these opportunities allow the instrumental ministry program to support the other ministries of the church.

"Equation for Success"

Personalized Ministry

+

High Expectations

+

Quality Music

=

**Orchestra Growth
and Commitment**

Conclusion

In conclusion, there are many benefits to the total program from both programming and special events.

• Quality programming and special events help to retain and attract quality players.

• Programming and special events, if managed properly, can build a tradition and expectation of quality that, in turn, will broaden the ministry of the orchestra program.

• Programming and special events offer a residual effect of enhancing the musical quality of the orchestra during worship services.

• A goal-oriented instrumental ministry can lead to an increase in attendance in rehearsals, special projects and, ultimately, worship services.

Effective programming and special events can have a positive, long-term effect on both the members of the orchestra and the congregation they serve.

Brad R. Matheson is a Contract Consultant for the Music Publishing and Recording Department of LifeWay Church Resources, a division of LifeWay Christian Resources of the Southern Baptist Convention, and Minister of Instrumental Music at Roswell Street Baptist Church, Marietta, Georgia.

Billy Payne is Minister of Instrumental Music, Eastside Baptist Church, Marietta, Georgia, and a freelance writer/composer.

CHAPTER 26

Hiring Professional Musicians

by Jack Wheaton

In most church music ministries there are times when it becomes necessary to turn to the professional musician to fulfill the musical demands of certain sacred literature. In most instances, the church organist/rehearsal pianist is a professional, a person who is dedicated to performing music at the highest standards possible. Usually, these staff members are already members of the current American Federation of Musicians.

The American Federation of Musicians

The American Federation of Musicians celebrated its 100th anniversary in 1996. Today it represents almost 200,000 musicians in the United States and Canada who make their living or avocation performing, writing, recording, or conducting music at a "professional" level.

Douglas Yeo
Boston Symphony Orchestra

Created to help stop abuses of unorganized labor before the turn of the century and the exploitation of the professional musician by management, today the AFM works hard to find employment for its members, improve working conditions, and seek new benefits. In addition, the AFM offers a wide range of support for its members; everything from low-cost instrument insurance to emergency-loan funds for those whose cash flow is temporarily at a low ebb.

What Is a Professional Musician?

Members of the AFM take pride in their work, and are usually a tremendous inspiration to church musicians. A professional musician is one who is able to perform his or her art at a high level, a level of performance, writing, or conducting that would allow them to become a member of any of the top units in the country, from symphony orchestras to chamber groups, ethnic music ensembles, and dance bands. A professional musician:

- arrives promptly
- has the right equipment
- behaves politely and cooperatively
- asks questions when necessary
- sight-reads well
- marks music in rehearsal to ensure an accurate performance
- dresses appropriately
- practices to prepare an accurate, musical performance

Utilizing Professional vs. Talented Amateur Players

True professional musicians are compelled to maintain a high standard of excellence in performance. Some amateur players will be inconsistent in the level of their performance simply because of work-related demands upon their time.

The following guidelines are suggested in working with professional musicians.

• Literature Selection

Be sure that the literature selected for a performance is within the learning capacity of the ensemble. Adding professionals to poorly prepared amateurs will not work. Ninety percent of the preparation should be concluded before the professional players arrive.

• Rehearsal Schedule

Allow enough time to adequately prepare concert repertoire. Clear all facility requests and calendar the combined rehearsals with the added professionals. Communicate this information to the ensemble as early as possible. Allow no excuses for absences during these combined rehearsals. One ill-prepared player can affect the quality of the final product. Remember, the cost of a fine performance takes time, talent, concentration, and energy.

• Vision

No one can sing, play, conduct, or write beyond his or her own musical understanding. If the church ensemble has not studied a professional performance, how can they duplicate it? The director should either play an excellent recorded performance for his ensemble, or have them attend some fine musical performances. It is also important to teach the ensemble germane information about the composer, the musical style of the piece, the compositional elements, and the performance practice of the time.

• Budget

Costs for a symphonic concert should be projected before the event is promoted. Costs may include music rental or purchase, instrument rental, or special sound equipment, technical director costs (lighting and sound), piano tuning and moving, risers, stands, lights, public relations and advertising, publicity, printing costs, hall rental, security, parking, and costs of hiring professional musicians.

• The Contractor

What is a contractor? What does he do? The contractor can be vital in hiring professional players. The contractor will give an accurate budget projection of rehearsal and performance costs, select qualified and experienced players, supervise necessary set-up for a rehearsal or performance, handle any personality conflicts that may occur, discipline the professional for any inappropriate conduct, and work very hard to ensure a great performance so the contractor may return next year.

Establish a friendly rapport with the contractor right away. Discuss any personal anxieties regarding the upcoming performance. Don't hesitate to ask the contractor about the best use of rehearsal time and performance preparation. Ask the contractor about building a rapport with the added professionals— approach and demeanor, correcting them, encouraging them, and so forth.

• The Contract

Be sure to have a signed contract, with a copy for the conductor and the contractor. Be sure all costs have been budgeted for and approved, including an emergency extra rehearsal if necessary. Give the contractor the check or checks (he or she will let the conductor know whether they will payroll the event or the church office will) no later than the evening of the first performance. Never make a contractor or professional musician wait for a check, or have to remind the director that they have not been paid. That is a poor Christian testimony.

Summary

Combining the efforts of amateur musicians and professionals can be the highlight of the year for the singers, players, and congregation. It is also a good outreach opportunity into the community. Because of the media satu-

ration with professional entertainment, the expectations of the average American listener are very high. Bringing professional musicians into the house of God can also be a subtle means of witnessing and of holding up the banner of faith, love, hope, and charity. However, don't try to forcefully convert a guest player. Be faithful to develop a gracious and friendly relationship with guests. The love of Christ has great drawing power.

The most important elements in successfully combining professional musi-
cians are as follows: repertoire selection, rehearsal scheduling, budget, selection of a musical contractor, well-paced rehearsals, proper conduct with professional players, and faithful prayer for God's blessing in ministry.

Jack Wheaton is President of the Musician's Association of San Diego County, Local 325, American Federation of Musicians, and writes commercially for Megatrax Corporation. He serves as Administrative Director of Jazz Studies for the University of Southern California, as well as being CEO for the Grove School of Music, Los Angeles, California. Jack holds a B.A. in Music from the University of Denver, an M.A. from the University of Northern Colorado, and a Ph.D. from the University of North Carolina.

Each year Dr. Wheaton presents a series of lecture-concerts at the Athenaeum Cultural Center in La Jolla, CA. He has authored over 20 books and completed a series of solo etudes for wind instruments.

DOs and DON'Ts

The following is a list of DOs and DON'Ts in handling professional musicians.

DOs

- Start and end rehearsals on time.
- Have all equipment in place, including lights, sound, etc.
- Allow time for tuning, seating, and equipment adjustment.
- Have a printed rehearsal schedule on each music stand along with the conductor's name and phone number.
- Introduce the contractor, concertmaster, and section leaders to your ensemble.
- Learn the names of the professional players and have a seating order list on the conductor's stand.
- Having studied the score for weeks, rehearse the most difficult spots first.
- Encourage all to mark their music..
- Work out the rehearsal schedule with the contractor so that full-ensemble sections are worked on first, keeping the orchestra from sitting idle.
- Allow for a 15-minute break after each 45-minute period. This is mandatory.
- Play through the entire work. Note the rough spots for later drill.
- Tell the musicians what you want; don't make them guess.
- Provide easy parking, a musical instrument storage room, refreshments, and a ready room.
- Require everyone to be in place at least 15 minutes before a performance.
- Remind all about dress, where to park, etc.
- Pray briefly before each rehearsal. Do not change the ministry philosophy for the guest players. Be genuine and caring with the ensemble.
- Thank everyone after the last performance, tell them where they can pick up their checks, and invite the professional to any post-production party or refreshments.
- Take a group picture before the last performance.
- Have a room to which the players can retire during intermission, so they don't have to stand around aimlessly.
- Have modest refreshments in the green room or the hospitality room. Make sure this room is secure at all times so orchestra members can leave personal belongings safely.

DON'Ts

- Don't start late, end late, or ignore required breaks.
- Don't be rude or sarcastic when working with professionals.
- Don't allow any professional musician to be chronically late, inattentive, or rude. Tell the contractor. He will deal with the problem.
- Don't complain about costs in front of the musicians.
- Don't waste rehearsal time talking.
- Don't repeat the same easy-to-play sections; address musical problems that require rehearsal.
- Don't be too self-effacing; phony humility backfires as well.
- Don't express anger or frustration with the professional without first talking to the contractor.
- Don't allow musicians to smoke, drink, or use abusive language on the church campus.
- Don't try to record rehearsals or performances without permission from the contractor.
- Don't talk to the audience before a performance. It's amateurish and ruins the mood.

CHAPTER 27

Rhythm Sections: Nuts and Bolts

by Bob Barrett, David Winkler,
and Julie Barrier

A championship baseball team and a powerful rhythm section share many common strengths. The players share the objectives and vision of the coach. The roles of the players are clearly defined. The successful ball team performs as a unit—the players are completely interdependent. Highly developed systems of nonverbal cues govern the interaction between players. Glorious moments of spontaneity occur when well-trained players respond instinctively during play. Vision, synchronization, interdependence, communication, and improvisation develop dynamic rhythm teams.

How is a rhythm section utilized in contemporary worship? The rhythm team functions as the synergistic drive behind congregational singing. The players may accompany choirs, ensembles, or orchestra. Rhythm sections may underscore drama, congregational readings, or video. Worship planners, leaders, technicians, and players should clearly understand the role of the rhythm section in any given service. The basic purpose of a rhythm section is to keep time, to provide a harmonic structure, and to create a particular stylistic "feel." Rhythm players should play their instruments skillfully, know basic rhythm and harmony, understand a variety of contemporary styles, and play

258

tastefully and sensitively. The mutual goal for any musician participating in a service should be to facilitate worship—to bring people into God's presence.

Rhythm sections usually contain one drummer, one bass player, a lead guitarist, a rhythm guitarist, and a keyboard player. Many rhythm sections also have a synthesizer player and an auxiliary percussionist. When the number of ensemble players increases, the individual improvisation of the players must be carefully limited. The larger the ensemble, the more difficult it is to keep the group tight and cohesive.

Sound mixing of the ensemble is critical to facilitating effective worship experiences. For example, a song in a traditional rock style will have the drums and bass prevailing in the mix. The guitar may have flange or chorusing effects that lend a stylistic flavor to the rock sound. If the rhythm section is accompanying blended worship, the overall instrumental mix should be beneath the voice of the worship leader so that the lyrics predominate. In acoustic alternative worship, the acoustic and lead guitars should be the primary accompanying instruments rather than the keyboard. Sound engineers should consider the median age of the audience when mixing sound levels for the rhythm section. Each player needs sufficient monitor levels to hear the rest of the team.

The roles of each rhythm section player must be clearly defined. In traditional worship, the piano and organ serve as the lead accompanying instruments. In rhythm section-driven worship, the bass player and drummer set tempi and stylistic parameters that govern the roles of the other players. Although the rhythm section generally performs without a conductor, the orchestra that includes a rhythm section is a conducted ensemble.

Orchestrating a rhythm team is much like arranging for any other instrumental ensemble. Allow different timbres of sound to prevail at different times. For example, in a meditative ballad the synthesizer may play a very nonrhythmic chord progression or "pad" to accompany a soloist. This is not a new concept. The baroque recitative was accompanied in a similar fashion. The other rhythm instruments are added to the bridge or chorus of the song to create musical intensity and drive. Each player should know when and how to enter or tacet, and how much or how little to play. For example, the pianist has a clearly defined role when playing in a rhythm section-driven orchestra. If the pianist is playing an orchestral reduction score, places where solo instruments are featured should not be doubled. The piano should also reinforce the rhythmic figures given to the drummer and bassist. Therefore, the pianist reading a rhythm chart with an ensemble should tacet on a solo line, or fill as directed. The electric bass player also holds a very specific role in congregational accompaniment. He or she has the principal responsibility of laying a rhythmic and harmonic foundation for the entire worship team. Even if the bassist is a remarkable soloist, he or she should limit playing fills and solos in worship accompaniment. Worship flow charts should clearly delineate each player's roles in every song. Segues and transitions between songs should also be predetermined for effective musical cohesion. Each team player then feels confident to participate in his or her unique role without interference, competition or confusion.

The Electric Bass

The electric bass player must provide the rhythmic and harmonic foundation for the team. He or she will synchronize rhythmic patterns with the kick drum and snare. The bass player must have a clear knowledge of chord structure and musical harmony. Often, the bass will simply play the root of the chord, or an inversion using the third or fifth. At other times, the bass will fill with passing tones to create a "walking" effect. Composite chords, with one chord in the treble clef and a single note in the bass (e.g. C/D), are quite common in contemporary music. In this case, the bass player should be careful to play only the lower note (in this example, the C), leaving the chord to the guitar and the piano (right hand). The bass player also plays a key role in establishing the basic rhythmic pulse or "feel" of the music. In order to be effective at establishing any particular contemporary musical style, the bassist should be familiar with riffs and rhythmic patterns that characterize mainline contemporary genres. Many educational resources are readily available that contain notated scores, audio tapes, and compact discs delineating these styles. Bass players should also practice with a metronome, a sequencer, or a recording to develop steady rhythmic drive.

Anthony Case
Bass player, Christafari

Q: What are some important considerations for the electric bass player to ponder when he is playing in a rhythm section for contemporary worship?

A: "If Jesus played in a rhythm section for contemporary worship, He would be a bassist because the degree of servanthood is the highest! A bassist's primary role is to serve and support the vocalists and the other musicians. The second consideration for a worship team bassist is to actually worship the Lord as he or she is playing, and that through the music being played. Lastly, be excellent in playing; develop the skills necessary to offer an 'excellent sacrifice' unto the Lord."

The Drums

The principal percussionist in a rhythm section is the drummer, or trap set player. A basic drum set consists of kick (bass) drum, snare drum, two mounted toms, floor tom, hi-hat cymbal assembly, and ride and crash cymbals. The drums and electric bass work closely together in a cohesive rhythm section. Specifically, the drummer will often copy the basic rhythm pattern of the bass player. The role of the drummer is to be the timekeeper of the band along with the bassist, and to establish the unique rhythmic style of the piece. Playing time means maintaining rhythmic integrity while combining with the other players to create a level of energy demanded for the piece. Drummers have the widest dynamic range of all rhythm section instruments. They set dynamic levels for the rest of the ensemble.

If the acoustic environment is very live, an electronic drum set is an excellent option. It allows the sound technicians to control the acoustic environment more carefully. Also, using acoustical material to partially shield the drum's sound waves may facilitate proper balance. If the sound is still too dynamic, there are also varied stick options that will soften the attack on the drum or cymbal surface. Lighter sticks, brushes, or sticks called "multi-rods" or "hot rods" will also give more subtlety to the drummer's attack. One of the most important habits drummers must acquire is listening closely to the bass player, and interacting with him or her effectively as a rhythmic unit. The drummer should fill at points of dramatic intensity, usually during introductions or interludes, or the bridge of the song leading to the chorus. Drum fills at appropriate times will not overpower the singers or inhibit congregational participation. The drummer can also facilitate segues between songs.

Rhythm section drummers should practice regularly to develop fine neuromuscular coordination and independent control of large muscle groups. A constant sense of steady tempo, rhythmic subdivision, and syncopation should be present in a fine trap set player. Drummers should develop ear-training skills to transcribe drum patterns from prerecorded songs. If no auxiliary percussionist is available, the drummer needs to develop basic skills for hand percussion, mallet percussion, and eth-

Duncan Phillips
Drummer, Newsboys

Q: How did you learn to use your instrument as an instrument of worship?
A: "I feel that as a Christian, everything we do should be an act of worship. Being a musician is a natural extension of who I am. Worship is not just an act, but a way of life. The act of the janitor sweeping the church floor is just as sweet to God as the congregation that fills the church. I practice my instrument to improve. As I grow in my walk with God, my playing becomes more and more an act of worship."

Q: What kinds of disciplines do you observe to continue to keep your musical skills on the cutting edge?
A: "Being a musician, I tend to be a musical sponge. Whether I realize it or not, I think I'm constantly absorbing the current musical culture. It's also a great idea to practice your instrument, always thinking creatively. You might hear an idea you like, but once it's filtered through your own creativity it will come out fresh and new. As musicians, we never stop learning."

nic percussion. There are many pedagogical resources listed at the end of this chapter that provide information on auxiliary percussion instruments.

Drummers, guitarists, and bassists often began playing their instruments by ear rather than by note reading. The computer programs listed in the music education sections of this text will facilitate visual note-reading skills for rhythm players. The strength of the rote player is confidence in improvisation and quick memorization.

The Guitar

There are two basic approaches to playing guitar in a rhythm section. In one approach, commonly labeled **"rhythm guitar,"** the guitar keeps a steady beat, either strumming full chords, or playing arpeggiated figures. In the other approach, referred to as **"lead guitar,"** the guitar acts in a more soloistic and improvisatory capacity. Much of the guitarist's sound will depend upon the instrument he uses.

Acoustic guitars come in several types: *classical (nylon string), steel string,* and *twelve string.* These may be amplified using a microphone or internal pickup.

Electric guitars may be either the *hollow-body* or the *solid-body* versions. The tone of the electric guitar can be varied greatly by adjusting the controls on the instrument itself and on the amplifier. The types of strings used can also affect the tone. Heavier gauge strings have a more mellow sound, whereas the lighter strings have a brighter, more "twangy" sound. Lighter strings also bend more easily, which can cause some intonation problems. Electric guitars require amplification, while acoustic guitars do not. The acoustic guitar utilized with other electronic instruments often needs amplification to be heard.

Rhythm guitarists chord or "comp" and reinforce the musical style of the piece. Rhythm guitar players often comp in the range of the piano or synthesizer, so their efforts should be carefully coordinated. The rhythm guitarist and the keyboardist must work in tandem just as the bass player and drummer must constantly interact.

Lead guitarists often play melodic lines, create fills or countermelodies, produce lead melodies, or perform improvised solos. Distortion, chorusing, digital delays, and volume swells can be added to the raw signal of an electronic guitar to modify the sound. Lead guitar sound level and distortion can lend a distinctive flavor to a particular musical style. Lead riffs, or improvised motives, may be based on chordal structures, melodic fragments, pentatonic fills, or rhythmic variations of the basic rhythmic style.

Guitarists, like bass players and drummers, are often eager to receive training in score reading if they began as rote musicians. Guitarists and bass players appreciate working from chord charts that do not have numerous page turns. Scores that include guitar tablature are helpful for young players. Flat keys may often be executed more easily with a capo. Transposition of the score is also an option to assist the inexperienced player. A guitarist should develop the skills of steady rhythm, good pitch sense, careful chord voicing, and improvisation. A guitarist must have a working knowledge of signal processors and amplifiers. All rhythm players need to be able to interact with visual, nonverbal signals. They should be able to see and hear the worship leader at all times.

The Piano

The piano is the only instrument in the rhythm section capable of playing the entire range of the treble and bass clefs. It is also capable of a wide dynamic range with its ability to play soft and sweet or loud and percussive. Expanded voicings on the piano can cover a wider range than any other rhythm section instruments.

The upper range of the piano is bright and can be used to simulate higher pitched instruments such as the flute or violin. This is the register in which most melodies and improvised solos are heard. The middle register (centered around middle C) is where chord voicings offer the most body. This register is more neutral in character, allowing the piano to provide a warm harmonic pad, and give support to vocalists or solo instruments. The lower register has a percussive force that is very powerful and can reinforce certain rhythmic "hits" of the bass and drums. The low register can sometimes present a problem in the context of a rhythm section. Because of strong frequencies (or overtones) that are created when low notes are played on the bass and piano, a muddy effect will occur that will impair the clarity of the sound. The classically trained pianist may find the most difficult adaptation is avoiding too much activity in the left hand. Traditionally trained pianists may often be strong sight readers with good finger technique. Self-taught pianists may often be effective at ear training and improvisation. All pianists may need to learn how to read a chord chart.

The way in which a chord is voiced makes a great deal of difference in the sound or feeling of a particular musical passage. By practice and experimentation, the pianist can learn to choose those voicings that are most pleasing and most appropriate to the style of the music being played. Chord terminology is not always consistent. Chord charts should be reviewed and edited in advance by the pianist or rhythm section leader to facilitate an effective rhythm rehearsal. It is a common practice for rhythm players to add chord tones—sixths, sevenths, etc.—in order to harmonically embellish the music being played. In order to incorporate these notes, two basic rules should be followed.

First, the added notes should always be appropriate to the style of the music. The major seventh chord, for example, is rarely used in country or Southern gospel music, and therefore should be avoided. The major sixth chord can sound trite if used inappropriately. On the other hand, the added ninth (or second) is a neutral sounding chord-tone and can be utilized in a variety of styles.

Craig E. Nelson
Studio Bassist
and recording artist

"No matter what style of music I'm playing, I always try to serve it up as an offering to the Lord that He might find it pleasing. We should always compose, arrange, and perform with Him in mind, bearing witness to others."

The second rule of thumb in adding extra tones to a chord is that the added tone should not clash with the melody of the song. The pianist should listen carefully to the chord embellishments of the guitarists to be sure there is no harmonic incongruity. If a pianist is unfamiliar with contemporary chord voicings, the director could write out those voicings initially until the pianist masters the technique. Many Christian artist folios illustrate contemporary chord voicings for the accompanist. The pianist should also listen carefully to the chord embellishments of the guitarists to be sure there is no harmonic incongruity between the rhythm section players.

Jazz comping for the pianist is a highly technical skill. The chords in the left hand must be carefully voiced, and are often highly syncopated to match the rhythmic feel of the drums and bass guitar. The right hand will fill and improvise while the left hand is playing chords in sync with the rest of the rhythm section. The rhythm section pianist must think like an arranger, not like a soloist.

The rhythm section accompanying worship will occasionally utilize a synthesizer player in addition to, or in place of, the rhythm pianist. When more keyboard players are added to a rhythm section, more coordination is also required. Synthesizers may be used to emulate acoustic instruments such as flute, oboe, clarinet, French horn, clarinet, and bassoon. The keyboard player may also effectively utilize acoustic percussion sounds. Most of the keyboard brass sounds should be used sparingly. If the bass player is not available, a keyboardist may play a synthesized bass line. Electronic keyboards provide many sound colors to facilitate the mood of congregational worship. "Pads" are voices sustained with a wide range of timbres. Pad sounds with delay must be carefully moderated so that waveforms do not carry unwanted harmonic overtones into the next chord. Acoustic sounds like the flute or oboe can provide tasteful solos or countermelodies. Brass and keyboard sounds can add intensity to keyboard rhythmic hits. Strings and vox settings can be layered to create warmth and fluidity to the musical line. Pianists who play synthesizers should have a basic understanding of musical instrument digital interface (MIDI) terminology and sequencing procedures. Synthesizers are also well suited for underscoring prayers, Scripture reading, or making transitions during the service.

The Rehearsal

The key to effective rehearsal technique is clearly defined roles, well-written charts, and adequate spiritual and musical preparation. The obvious prerequisite to an effective team effort is to have all the players at the rehearsal. If players are playing charts that do not have all the parts written out, audio tapes and charts should be provided for the musicians to study before the group rehearses as a team. A master rhythm chart should allow the rhythm section players to play within predetermined boundaries, while everything written for the orchestra members is specific and leaves no room for either spontaneity or improvisation. The only exception is when an instrumental solo is given to one of the instruments, such as a saxophone or trumpet.

Other guidelines for rhythm charts include clearly written title, tempo, and metronome markings, and a clear delineation of the style to be played. Since contemporary music is usually felt in two bar phrases, the chart should be laid out at four measures per line. Writing a double bar line at the end of each thematic section will further enable the musicians to clearly identify where each section begins and ends. Double bar lines bring the eye's attention to the fact that this is the end of one section, and that something new will occur in the next eight bars. Understanding where the thematic sections occur will allow musicians to provide the fills and set ups that may be needed to overlap two sections of a song. Drummers especially need to be able to read the form of a song and recognize, by way of double bar lines, when a new section is about to be introduced. It is the drummer's responsibility to play a fill that sets up each new section. In addition to the double bar line, a chart should be laid out so that each thematic section begins on the left border of the page and ends on the right. Chords should be labeled consistently. Major and minor seventh chords should include "min" or "maj" so that the player does not have to wonder whether the letter "m" is capitalized or not. The use of the triangle and the European 7 can also be confusing. Altered chord tones should be placed in parentheses. For example, an altered dominant should be written as G7 (#11). The more clear and specific the chord charts, the less time will be wasted in the rehearsal. Some additional things to avoid are the double D.S. sign and the double Coda. Musicians can be confused by too many repeat signs and codas. Clearly marked page numbers and measure numbers can also facilitate effective preparation. The most important task of the arranger is to facilitate the successful reading of charts from beginning to end.

Another prerequisite for effective rehearsals is clear stylistic parameters. The bass player and the drummer establish the style of a contemporary piece. If the drummer and bass guitarist are playing their parts correctly, there should be no question as to what style of music they are playing. Assuming that these two key players possess an understanding of various contemporary musical styles, they may be given a simple chord progression and asked to play rock and it will sound like rock; ask them once again to play the same progression as reggae and it will sound like reggae. The same principle holds true whether the style is swing, funk/rhythm and blues, a Brazilian samba, or any other style. If each person possesses a firm understanding of these styles, he or she will have no difficulty producing them—and with no help from the guitar or keyboard. The rhythm section leader should isolate bass and drums to build cohesion and consistency in stylistic approach.

In African and Latin music, the clave is a rhythmic pattern that permeates every style. The clave consists of a syncopated pattern played by the timbalero or the conguero (Latin percussionists), and is embellished by the pianist and the bassist. The clave is rarely played in its original form, but is a rhythmic subdivision that is the basis for the improvisatory part of each player. The inner rhythm of a song will be the key to understanding how to arrange the melodic and harmonic elements of any given contemporary song. For example, two of the key elements in defining funk include a tempo that is slightly slower and less driven, and an accent on the second sixteenth note in a group of four sixteenths by the bass guitarist and the kick drum. All fills and harmonic changes by the guitarist and the keyboardist should be played in the context of the characteristic rhythmic figures, and the specified rhythmic "groove."

The use of simplicity and silence is also a critical part of an artistic arrangement. The listener will complain of the rhythm section sound being too loud when the ensemble is really just playing poorly. The improvisation may not be in the style of the piece, or the players may be taking a soloistic rather than a team approach. A poorly coordinated or unrehearsed team can sound "too loud." God is worthy of the best efforts His servants can offer Him. Musicians should continue to grow spiritually and musically. The rhythm team leader should provide opportunities for the musicians to learn new skills and discover new technology that will enhance their musical offerings in worship.

In Conclusion

Each musician in the rhythm section should focus on what every other member of the band is playing at all times. If each person is going to fully understand his or her own role within a rhythm section, he or she will first need to expand his or her understanding to reach beyond the realm of his own instrument. If a bass player limits his or her understanding to the bass guitar, the bassist is not very likely to coordinate the bass part with the drummer. The bassist will be unable to provide the support and foundation needed by the guitarist and the pianist. If each player focuses on understanding the role of the other instruments in the band, he/she will become more aware of what the end result of every performance should be. This doesn't mean that keyboard players should be required to learn to play the drums, or that guitar players should begin taking piano lessons. Each player should be aware of every instrument and listen closely to what each player is playing. Then, rather than suggest that the other person change what they are doing, the effective team player alters his part to complement the other team members. The leader of the rhythm rehearsal should be respected and followed. Players should be students of beautiful music, listening to successful bands and orchestras and analyzing their strengths. The King of kings deserves the highest and best one can offer Him in worship.

The bases are loaded. It's the bottom of the ninth. Will the team finish the game like a well-oiled machine? A ball game lasts only an afternoon. The stakes are much higher for the worship team. Lives are on the line. A rhythm team's vision, synchronization, interdependence, communication, and spontaneity facilitate powerful worship. God is the audience, and musicians must play with conviction, cohesion, and integrity.

Resources
For Guitar
- *Guitar Praise: Improving Your Ability*, 4-volume video series by Kent Henry
  Available from Kent Henry Ministries, Box 4369, Chesterfield, MO 63006
  Telephone (636-532-7711), www.KenHenryMin.org
- *Contemporary Praise and Worship Guitar*, 3 videos by Paul Baloche
  Baloche Music, 1109 S. Main St., Suite B, Lindale, TX 75771,
  www.Baloche.com

For Electric Bass
- *Essential Styles,* Vol. 1 & 2, By Steve Houghton, Published by C. L. Barnhouse Co. Demonstrates many different jazz and rock styles for bass and drums.

For Keyboard

* *Jazz/Rock Voicings for the Contemporary Keyboard Player*, by Dan Haerle Studio P/R–Columbia Pictures Publications
* *Contemporary Keyboard Styles*, 4-volumn video set, Available from Kent Henry Ministries Box 4369, Chesterfield, MO 63006, Telephone (636-532-7711), www.KentHenryMin.org

For Drums

* *Drums in Worship*, Videos by Mike Kinard (former drummer with The Imperials), LeMar Boschman Ministries, P. O. Box 130, Bedford, TX 76095

For Rhythm Section

* Jazz materials from Jamey Aebersold, 1-800-456-1388 or www.jazzbooks.com
* Bob Barrett's Books-all are $27.95
  Taylor Made Music, 23608 Via Navarra, Mission Viejo, California 92691, (714) 457-1892
  __*Contemporary Music Styles* (accompaniment CD)
  __*Synthesizers In Praise and Worship* (accompanying cassette tape)
  __*Reading and Writing Chord Charts: The Music Director's Guide to Communicating with the Band*

Bob Barrett is Minister of Instrumental Music, Saddleback Church, Lake Forest, California, where he has served since 1991. Bob is the author of three books designed to help church musicians grasp the concepts of contemporary music: *Contemporary Music Styles: The Worship Band's Guide to Excellence; Synthesizers in Praise & Worship: The Keyboardist's Guide to Electronic Orchestration;* and *Reading & Writing Chord Charts: The Music Director's Guide to Communicating with the Band.* Bob studied arranging and composing with Dick Grove in Los Angeles and is currently studying with film composer Jerry Grant. He was also an instructor at the Grove School of Music from 1984–1991. He lives in Mission Viejo, California.

David Winkler is a familiar name in church instrumental music, having been involved in the field since the late '70s. A graduate of North Texas State University, he has served as a pianist, orchestra director, and minister of music in several churches in Texas and Tennessee. Currently, he is a freelance arranger, orchestrator, and editor in Nashville, and maintains an active studio teaching piano and guitar. David attends Judson Baptist Church in Nashville where he conducts the church's instrumental ensemble.

Julie Barrier is Associate Minister of Worship at Casas Adobes Baptist Church in Tucson, Arizona.

CHAPTER 28

Integrating Keyboards with the Church Orchestra

by David Winkler

One of the major differences between the church orchestra and a standard concert band or orchestra is the presence of keyboard instruments: the piano, organ, and synthesizer. While the keyboards add a wonderful dimension to the sound of the church ensemble, several factors must be considered in order to make their inclusion meaningful and useful.

In a typical, traditional church situation, the piano and organ were the only instruments used in past generations. Then, perhaps a few instruments were added, gradually growing into a larger ensemble which could then be called an "orchestra." As the orchestra gains in numbers, the pianist and organist may begin to notice their role changing from that of being the lead instruments to being a part of a larger ensemble. The manner in which they adapt to these changes will greatly affect the overall sound of the church's orchestra.

The Piano

Most orchestrations written for church orchestra, whether a hymn or choral accompaniment or an "orchestra only" piece, include the piano as a part of the instrumentation. In part this is due to the contemporary, rhythm section-based style of music which has become the standard sound for much of today's evangelical church music. In other cases, the inclusion of the piano is simply an acknowledgment that the sound of the keyboard has traditionally been an important part of church music ministry and continues to be an important part of the instrumental grouping.

Many choral arrangements are written by the composer for keyboard first, and the orchestration is added later. Often, however, the music is orchestrated from its inception. It is then recorded with a studio pianist improvising from a master rhythm chart consisting of only chord symbols and some occasional written figures. Afterwards, the publisher contracts with an editor to create a written piano part that is published along with the vocal lines. Sometimes the part will be a condensed score, containing cues for the key orchestral lines. In other cases, the part will be transcribed as more of a "rhythm" part, such as might have been played by the studio pianist when the piece was recorded. Should the church pianist play the part exactly as written, or should the part be altered to fit the need of the moment?

In deciding how much of the written score to follow, the pianist must analyze the part, comparing it to the orchestra score, and keep in mind which instruments are present. A melody line for the flute, for instance, may be included in the piano part. Normally, it should be omitted if a flute is present in the ensemble. In some cases, however, the player may be timid and could benefit from the support of the piano doubling his part. A timpani roll may be cued in the piano part; this also should be left out, unless for some reason reinforcement of the drum part is desired. Sometimes, it may be more appropriate for the pianist to improvise a part, using the chord symbols or the chord structure from the written keyboard score. Usually, a rhythmic-accompaniment part voiced in the middle range of the piano will provide the type of support needed. In all this, the direction of the conductor is a key element in helping the pianist decide how and what to play or not to play. He or she can visualize "the big picture" and take responsibility for the overall sound of the orchestra.

David Meece
Composer, Pianist, Concert Artist

Q: How did you learn to use your piano as an instrument of worship?

A: "As a child, I attended the First Baptist Church in Humble, Texas. My mother directed the children's choir and insisted I be her pianist. I was very young and inexperienced, but my mom was very patient. Over time, she and my piano teacher helped me develop an improvisational approach that I still use today in my concert ministry. As I grew in the Lord, I learned that for those who are willing and obedient, and operate from a pure heart, God will bless even modest abilities in a way that will have a lifelong impact far beyond expectations."

One special point should be made concerning playing the piano when the electric bass (bass guitar) is present. Because of the dominant nature of the sound of the bass, and because electric bass parts are more or less improvised, it is best for the pianist to revoice the left hand parts to avoid playing bass lines which may conflict with those being played by the electric bass. This concept is illustrated in Examples 1 and 2 on the following page. This approach is helpful to both the bassist and the pianist, as each is freer to develop their own parts without overlapping each other's musical ideas. The exception to this principle would occur whenever there are particular bass lines which need to be accented by the piano. These can easily be coordinated by a friendly partnership between the pianist and the bassist, in consultation with the conductor.

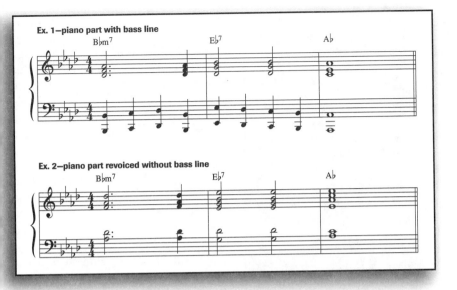

Ex. 1—piano part with bass line

Ex. 2—piano part revoiced without bass line

The Organ

The use of the organ with orchestra requires particular discernment. The organ, as the "king of instruments," is an orchestra within itself. Even the names of some of the stops give this impression: flutes, reeds, trumpets, strings, etc. When combined with a full orchestra, however, the organ can have the potential of covering and muddying much of the instrumental sound unless a careful approach is utilized.

Fortunately, most organists are accustomed to adapting music written originally for piano. When playing with orchestra, this concept should be expanded. Certain parts should be omitted and others reinforced as called for by the situation at hand. Like the pianist, the organist can benefit from consulting with the conductor and referencing the orchestral score to help in deciding what type of part would be most appropriate.

Phillip Allen, organist and orchestra director at Atlanta, Georgia's, First Baptist Church, describes a "three layer" approach to conceiving the organ's place in the music. "The first layer that the listener should perceive," says Mr. Allen, "is the choir, or, for orchestral works, the melody line or solo instrument. The second layer would be whatever accompaniment is under the melody line, be it orchestral, rhythm, or keyboard. The organ," he continues, "by providing the almost subliminal underpinning or 'third layer,' can greatly enhance the total ensemble by giving the piece coherence, helping to fill in the gaps of the chord structures that might be missing due to a lack of instrumenta-

Fernando Ortega
Pianist, Composer, Christian Artist

Q: How do you retool old hymns in a fresh setting? How do you utilize acoustic instruments in a contemporary arrangement?

A: "I look for hymns that are interesting theologically and musically. As a rule, I don't alter the melody or rhythm so that it remains easy to sing for the congregation. If a worship band is to lay the hymn, the rule of thumb is to simplify the chord progression. The challenge is to find chords that support, not distract from, the text. For example, if tension is needed on a certain work, I often add a second to a major or minor chord. An instrumental before the last verse is a fine place to feature an oboe, cello, or violin in an interlude. It gives breathing room to the hymn and provides the congregation with a place for reflection. Again, enhancement of the text is paramount."

tion. Think of the organ as a giant harmonic pot of musical 'glue' that brings together the musical components. There is a definite art to performing this type of function, but the rewards are wonderful!" He sounds one note of caution: "Depending on your acoustical setting, generally the sound of the organ is louder and richer out in the congregation. Always err on the conservative side (i.e., the soft side) regarding choir and orchestra accompanying. The great temptation to 'pull out all the stops' should be subservient to good taste and musical/spiritual sensitivity."

The subject of registration is a key issue to the success of the orchestra/organ combination. Owen Griffin, organist and orchestra director at Hyde Park Baptist Church in Austin, Texas, comments, "Unless it's obviously appropriate, I don't like for the organ to stand out too distinctly during an anthem. Rather, I like to consider it almost to be a 'pad,' depending on the particular texture of the moment. So I go with a very basic registration that includes flutes and strings, adding reeds, brass, and mixtures when more power and attack are called for." Phillip Allen says, "If the style of music is of a more sustained or softer nature, use string stops, softer flutes, and celestes as the foundation of the sound, and avoid the diapasons and the stronger flutes as well as the reeds."

The type of articulation used by the organist is also an important issue when it comes to blending organ with orchestra. Again, Owen Griffin comments, "To keep the organ from sounding too 'muddy' in the more rhythmic passages, I try to play more detached." Phillip Allen adds, "The faster and more rhythmic the piece, the more pedals are avoided, letting the rhythm section drive the rhythm and provide the bass. In such a case, I use articulate stops that speak faster, avoiding stops in the string or flute family."

When can the organ really "let loose" when playing with orchestra? Mr. Allen comments, "Obviously, the organ may dominate the overall sound in the more stately congregational hymns. Also, the organ can really help those 'big endings' of choral works that are not too rhythmic. Finally, find a few pieces of music which feature the organ with orchestra and have fun!" Organ and orchestra combinations will be discussed later in this article.

The organ has served as the basic instrument in church music for centuries. Using a thoughtful and knowledgeable approach, the organ can continue to have an important place even amidst the many changes in the contemporary evangelical church.

Electronic Keyboards

Electronic keyboards of various types, whether they are full-fledged synthesizers, or digital pianos with a few other sounds, have become common in most churches, rounding out the keyboard section. Often an extra pianist, perhaps one with a little more adventuresome spirit, is placed at the keyboard and asked to add a little something extra to the mix of sound. The question becomes, with everything else going on musically, what can be added which will be musically logical and satisfying?

One of the uses of synthesizers with smaller church orchestras is to compensate for the lack of string players by playing string lines. Synthesized string sounds have improved quite a bit over the years, making the use of synthesizers for this purpose more viable. Many published orchestrations now include a "string reduction" part, which combines the several string lines from the orchestra score into a two stave part playable on a keyboard (though in some cases, the part must be reduced further by the player in order to play with only two hands). The manner in which these parts are played will make the difference between a sound that is truly pleasing and that which is not. The player will need to experiment with the sounds available, testing them for tone quality, responsiveness, and volume level. He or she should listen to and imitate the sound of real strings as much as possible. The careful use of a volume pedal, combined with the right touch and articulation, should give a reasonably realistic effect. One other note: If the synthesizer is used in conjunction with string players, special care must be taken in deciding what to play and how best to blend with and support the sound of the live strings.

Depending on the sounds available, the synthesizer can also substitute for other instruments when necessary. An oboe solo, a trumpet fanfare, or a timpani hit played on the electronic keyboard can be a lifesaver on a "slim Sunday." Most late model synthesizers also have excellent mallet percussion sounds that can be put to good use. Few churches, for example, have a marimba, xylophone, or vibraphone (also called "vibes"), but these sounds are some of the most realistic found on modern synthesizers, often having been sampled directly from actual percussion sounds. Latin and other ethnic percussion sounds are also good choices, and can be used effectively, even if there are players present in the percussion section.

What should the synthesizer play if all the instrumental parts are covered? Often an electric piano sound or a "pad" of some sort can provide a nice filler which will complement the piano and other rhythm section sounds. The electronic keyboard can also fill in nicely if the church does not have an organ, or if the church's organ doesn't have a particular sound which may be needed, such as a Hammond B-3 or "gospel organ" sound.

Deciding how a synthesizer is to be amplified is an issue of great importance. The simplest way is to have a combination amplifier/speaker system set up adjacent to the keyboard. A guitar or bass amplifier could be used, though the former will accentuate the high-end sounds of the synthesizer and the latter will bring out the lower end. In recent years, manufacturers have responded to the need of having a system which will accommodate the wide harmonic range of the synthesizer by producing amplifiers especially designed for keyboards (such as the Fender KXA series). This type of system is most recommended. However, an even better effect, depending on the acoustical situation of the performance area, can often be gained by running the sound through the house system. In this case, the sound of the synthesizer should be blended with the sound of the piano and any other instruments that are reinforced. This is especially important if the synthesizer is being used to substitute for or to augment the sound of "real" instruments. If this house system is used as the main sound source, it is still desirable to have a small amplifier or "hot spot" close to the player for monitoring purposes. And one rule of thumb—always have a sound check in order to make sure that the keyboard is coming through the house system and monitor speakers to avoid being unintentionally in "silent mode"!

Considerations Regarding Bass Instruments

One section of the church orchestra that is often lacking in players is the bass instrument section. This would include woodwinds, such as the bass clarinet and bassoon; strings, such as the cello and double bass; and brass—the tuba, euphonium, and bass trombone.

Several explanations could be offered for this dilemma. First, the lower-sounding instruments are usually large, requiring an able body to carry them, as well as a larger vehicle to transport them. They are also generally quite expensive. In many cases, a player may not even own his own instrument, since he may have, in the past, rented or used one supplied by a school. Finally, a psychological factor comes into play here, as the bass instruments almost always play a supportive role, so the player must be content to allow the other instruments to take the lead parts.

Despite the situation described, musically, the bass instruments' role is extremely important, being foundational in nature. It's here that the keyboards can play a vital role. The pianist can assist by bringing out the bass line, adding octaves when necessary. The organ has great potential to provide a lot of bass support to the music. And, bass sounds of various types are some of the most realistic sounds that are available on the synthesizer.

One word of caution: if bass instruments are present in the orchestra but still need some reinforcement from the keyboards, the conductor should see to it that everyone is playing the same bass lines. As noted before, this is especially important if an electric bass is present.

Featuring the Keyboards with Orchestra

In many music ministries, the pianist and organist are the best, most highly trained musicians in the church. Knowing this, why not feature either or both playing with the orchestra in concerto fashion? A number of published arrangements are listed at the end of this chapter, which could be considered for this purpose. It's also possible to create an original arrangement by taking a choral anthem and having the pianist and/or organist adapt the vocal melody lines for their solo parts (as indeed several publishers have done in some of their piano solo collections). Note that in such a case, it will often still be necessary to have another keyboard covering the piano accompaniment part.

Conclusion

Because keyboards are often the "glue" that holds everything together in many church ensembles, it is imperative that communication lines are in excellent order between the conductor and the keyboardists, and between the keyboardists and the rest of the orchestra. Having a clear sightline to the conductor is essential to keeping the tempo consistent. Also, the monitor levels are critical. The keyboardists must be able to hear themselves, the worship leader, the choir, and the rhythm section players clearly. Likewise, the players in the orchestra must be able to easily hear what the keyboards are doing. Take time to talk through the music and other issues with keyboard players so that everyone will understand his or her role in the team.

Lastly, intonation must be addressed. Unfortunately, this is one element of musicianship that is often neglected in church music ministries. First, the keyboards must all be in tune with each other. When the piano is tuned, for instance, the tuner should be able to hear some notes from the organ to see if it is sounding at A-440. In addition, any electronic keyboards used should be adjusted to be in tune with the piano and organ. The orchestra players may then tune to one of the keyboards. And, if an electronic tuner is used to tune to orchestral instruments, be sure that it is calibrated to the same pitch as the keyboards.

Resources

• *Contemporary Keyboard Styles*, 4-volume video series
  Available from Kent Henry Ministries, Box 4369, Chesterfield, MO 63006, Telephone (636) 532-7711), www.Kenthenrymin.org.

Music Featuring Piano Solo with Orchestra

- *Glorious Things of Thee Are Spoken,* arr. Tim Doran (Psalm 150)
- *Joyful, Joyful, We Adore Thee,* arr. B. Payne/R. Kingsmore (Genevox)
- *There's a Wideness in God's Mercy,* arr. David Winkler (Psalm 150)
- *Music by Bruce Greer*—Bruce has produced a number of very nice projects for Word Music, featuring piano solo with orchestral background. Tracks originally produced for choral arrangements were used as the basis for these projects. The published piano solo part and tracks are available (along with a second keyboard part to be played if tracks are not used). Orchestrations were created for these titles as choral projects. Check the publisher catalogs for current titles in print.

Music Featuring Organ Solo with Orchestra

- *Angels from on High,* arr. Phillip Allen (Genevox)
- *Beautiful Savior,* arr. David Winkler (Genevox)
- *Mighty Fortress,* arr. David Winkler (Genevox)
- *Morning Praise,* arr. Winkler (unpublished—available from davidwinkler.com)
- *Our Foundation,* arr. Phillip Allen (Genevox)
- *Take a Stand,* arr. Phillip Allen (Genevox)

David Winkler is a freelance arranger, orchestrator, and editor in Nashville, Tennessee, and maintains an active studio teaching piano and guitar. He attends Judson Baptist Church in Nashville where he conducts the church's instrumental ensemble.

CHAPTER 29

Optional Instrumental Ensembles

by Terry McNatt

Koinonia is a Greek word utilized in the New Testament to describe fellowship. Small groups, or cell groups, can be a great place to teach Christians how to care for each other's needs in community. The second definition of the word koinonia implies that the group is working together toward a common goal. When small ensembles play together to worship God, great fellowship can ensue. Small instrumental ensembles hone the skills of the individual player in unique ways. Because each individual instrument is more highly exposed, the player must be diligent to play in tune with superior tone quality. Ensemble playing teaches players to develop careful phrasing, balance, dynamic contrast, and rhythmic integrity. Additional opportunities for orchestra players to be a part of other ensembles can be provided. Playing in smaller, select ensembles can motivate and encourage players, serving as a reward for their faithfulness to rehearsals and Sunday participation in the larger orchestra. Various combinations of instruments will acquaint the reader with the many options that are available to instrumental players in the church.

The Rhythm Section

One of the most important components of a contemporary church orchestra is the rhythm section. Most instrumental directors consider the rhythm section to be comprised of the following instruments: Piano and/or synthesizer, one rhythm guitar, one lead electric guitar, one electric bass guitar, and drums. These players provide rhythmic integrity, energy, and define the musical style for the larger ensemble. They must create a rhythmic foundation that is clear and solid. The rhythm section is an excellent and versatile small ensemble. One of the best ways to improve the rhythm section is to allow them to play alone. They also provide versatility in accompanying soloists. The rhythm section can play for 10 minutes prior to the evening worship service. This ensemble can play between services if the church is conducting multiple services on Sunday mornings. The rhythm section can also be the primary ensemble for a Sunday morning contemporary worship service. Rhythm section players learn great improvisatory skills from reading chord charts and studying multiple contemporary styles. Please refer to Chapter 27 on rhythm sections for more information.

Praise Bands

Many churches today are making the praise band a regular service ensemble. A typical Praise Band instrumentation consists of the standard rhythm section plus three trumpets, two trombones, two alto saxophones, and one flute. Most publications also provide substitute parts for tenor and baritone saxophone in place of the second trombone part. Several of the major Christian publishing houses have music available that would allow this ensemble to be featured by playing stand-alone arrangements. Orchestrations that are hymnbook accompaniments can be pulled out and used by the praise band, and most of them are quite satisfactory. The praise band is also an excellent group to feature around the church at various banquets or conferences, and other occasions. If the church orchestra can support it, have multiple praise band ensembles and rotate them at worship services and other church functions. The praise band is also an excellent medium to accompany soloists and vocal ensembles in worship. The praise band, the big band, the rhythm section, and the small jazz trio all afford instrumentalists opportunities to improvise creatively, and to play with rhythmic and stylistic integrity.

The Gospel Big Band

Gospel big bands are comprised of the following instrumentalists: two alto saxophones, two tenor saxophones, one baritone saxophone, four trumpets, four trombones, rhythm guitar, bass guitar, acoustic piano, and drums. Gospel Big Band can play services periodically or on a weekly basis. This band is well received by all age groups in the church and provides an excitement and electricity in the worship service that is absolutely amazing! Big band music has the unique distinction of being a musical style that appeals to both senior adults and college students. Because of its broad appeal, it is an excellent way to introduce contemporary musical styles into a more traditional service format. It is best introduced on a Sunday evening or a special event. The most exciting use of the gospel big band is to use it as an outreach ministry to the community. This group can play at malls, housing projects, civic clubs, citywide crusades, prayer breakfasts, carnivals, community fall festivals, and prison ministries. The group is more portable than the larger orchestra. What an opportunity for witness and ministry this provides! The instrumental director can draw a crowd with some standard big band arrangements and, once the crowd is gathered, play some of the many gospel big band arrangements that are available from the publishing houses, share testimonies, and share the love of Christ in the secular community.

Other Ensembles

Christian publishers produce other ensemble music for church instrumentalists. Standard classical combinations like chamber string groups and woodwind quintets are available. Flute ensembles are popular because a church will often have multiple flute players in the congregation. If ensemble players are younger or less-experienced performers, they should have more rehearsals. A clinician can also be really helpful and inspiring to an ensemble. Small-ensemble music is available for duets, trios, quartets, quintets, woodwind choir, and brass choir. These groups can be made up of like instruments such as a clarinet trio, or one could utilize B♭ instruments with various timbres such as one trumpet, one clarinet, and one tenor saxophone. Current ensemble music available is of varying styles and difficulties, so the conductor can customize the music to fit the players. There is considerable music published for woodwind quintet, brass quintet, woodwind choir, and brass choir. The two choirs require a larger instrumentation, and the instrumental director should check the arrangement's instrumentation to be sure that there are players available to cover all of the parts. These ensembles can be used in a number of ways to bring variety to the worship service. For example, ensembles can play for 15 minutes prior to the beginning of worship and between worship services if multiple services are being conducted. Offertory music is a wonderful time to use instrumental ensembles. Small ensembles can play in the church lobby as people arrive on Sunday mornings and Sunday evenings. Again, the objective is to provide more opportunities for players to use their talents in ministry.

Conclusion

The instrumental ensembles discussed in this chapter are certainly not all-inclusive. Ethnic ensembles like Celtic instrumental groups can be highly effective in worship. Other groups can be formed and customized arrangements created to fit the group. Instruments should blend together. A good general rule of thumb—if it sounds good and is appropriate for the service—it works! Instrumental musicians who love the Lord will want many opportunities to use their talents. Many of these opportunities have been discussed in this chapter. The challenge for the instrumental director is to motivate and encourage his players. Small ensembles can provide such a venue.

Terry McNatt is Pastor of Worship and Music at Wallace Memorial Baptist Church in Knoxville, Tennessee. At Wallace, Terry gives leadership in all areas of Worship and Music, directs the Celebration Choir, and gives direction and leadership to the Celebration Orchestra, Praise Band, and other groups. Prior to his call to Wallace, Terry was Associate Pastor of Worship and Music at Germantown Baptist Church. While there, he founded and administered the Conservatory of Music.

CHAPTER 30

The Conservatory of Music: Its Development and Implementation

by Terry McNatt

The Conservatory of Music— Its Philosophy and Purpose

In Colossians, the Apostle Paul exhorts God's people to let the words of Christ dwell in them richly, and he challenges them to teach and admonish each another in psalms, hymns, and spiritual songs. Ephesians 5:18-19 states that the evidence of a spirit-filled life is a melody singing in the heart of the believer. In Psalm 150, the poet commands God's servants to praise the Lord with the trumpet, with harp and lyre, with stringed instruments and pipe, and with resounding cymbals. These fundamental spiritual principles establish a solid theological foundation for developing a conservatory of music based in the local church. The conservatory is a ministry outreach of the local church and should strive to provide the finest musical instruction. Qualified, competent Christian instructors who will incorporate spiritual principles in their teaching and encourage students to develop their God-given talents to their fullest potential must staff the conservatory. The conservatory should seek to provide the finest in musical instruction.

Develop and publish a purpose statement for the conservatory of music. All who read the vision statement clearly understand the conservatory's mission and goals. See a sample purpose statement on the next page.

The Conservatory Board and its Policies

There are many different ways to organize a conservatory board. A conservatory board is more essential than the specific members who participate. An official advisory board protects the ministry and provides a necessary sys-

> The _____ Church Conservatory of Music is a ministry designed to give students from _____ Church, and from our community, the opportunity to receive quality musical instruction with offerings on all wind instruments, strings, percussion, voice, and piano. These private lessons are to provide the student with instruction from a qualified, competent Christian teacher in a controlled Christian environment. Our mission is to train these students to use their God-given musical abilities to honor and glorify the Lord through music.

tem of checks and balances for those involved in the implementation of the conservatory, its policies, and procedures. A sample conservatory board could be comprised of appointed members who would be selected by the overseeing pastor who is responsible for the conservatory. One member would be selected from the finance committee, a second member would be the conservatory administrator, and a third would be the worship pastor or another supervising minister on the church staff. Lay persons on the advisory board who have professional expertise in promotion, public relations, computer technology, or music education can also be of great assistance. The conservatory board should meet quarterly, or as needed, and act on all matters of business that pertain to the conservatory of music.

Publicity and Promotion—Getting the Word Out

The conservatory of music should have a beautifully crafted promotional brochure. This brochure should represent the best piece of printed material that the director can afford to produce. It is suggested that the brochure be typeset and printed by a professional printer who can be responsible for making the brochure's presentation clear, concise, and artistically appealing in every way. The brochure should include the conservatory philosophy and purpose, and all pertinent information concerning curriculum, registration, tuition, and schedule. A detachable application and enrollment form for the registering student should be included in the brochure. Instructions should direct the applicant to complete and return the form to the conservatory administrator. A sample application and enrollment form is included at the conclusion of this chapter.

Church and community advertising are also critical to the successful "startup" of the conservatory of music. The administrator and the conservatory board must determine what publicity avenues are best for the community and utilize those means of publicity. Some suggestions:

1. the church newsletter,
2. ads in the local newspaper,
3. posters to be placed in businesses in the community,
4. Sunday church bulletin inserts,
5. attendance at area band and choral director's meetings where brochures can be distributed,

6. student performances at local malls, schools, and churches.

Remember: the conservatory will only be as effective as its leadership. Develop a quality program and promote it thoroughly and enthusiastically. God will honor prayerful preparation.

Policies and Procedures

Curriculum. The curriculum in the music conservatory should reflect the musical needs and interest of the church and the community. As fine arts budgets for public schools are decreasing, the church has a unique opportunity to develop the musical potential of students in the community. A newly founded conservatory can lose effectiveness by offering too much curriculum too quickly without the resources for effective management. Start slowly and add as needs arise. Suggested starting classes might include piano, voice, strings, percussion, guitar and the basic wind instruments. The program may also offer theory, conducting, organ, Suzuki strings, harp, etc. Classes may also be offered for adults in theory, arranging, or jazz improvisation. Short-term workshops or summer programs can also be effective in identifying and recruiting potential students. The director should remember to start with the basics.

Fees. Fees received for the operation of the conservatory may be deposited into the general fund of the church and are expendable based on a budget that is established and adopted by the church at the same time the annual church budget is adopted. Fees should be voted on and regulated by the conservatory board. It is suggested that the board set up a fee based on a fair rate to pay the instructors, and add $2.00 per half hour of instruction to cover the conservatory expenses such as utilities and administrative fees.

Instructor salaries may also be determined on a sliding scale based upon the experience and the education of the teacher. Set the lesson price based on a competitive rate within the community. Overcharging may prevent

students from taking lessons, and undercharging will make parents skeptical of the quality of the instruction. People expect to pay a fair price. Charge them at the market value and give them high quality instruction. Also study the music and computer technology resources available to enhance and motivate student lessons.

Faculty and Scheduling. Qualified, competent, Christian instructors must staff the conservatory of music. All teachers should fill out an application, submit a resume with references, and undergo an interview with the pastor (minister) who is responsible for the conservatory. The interview process should be thorough. References from previous employers should be checked. It is also highly advisable to have the teacher perform on his or her instrument, as well as submitting a written application. All instructors should read and subscribe to a statement of faith that has been written and approved by the conservatory board. A sample statement of faith is included at the end of this chapter. Lessons should be taught weekly at a time that is mutually agreeable between the instructor and the student. The conservatory administrator should set the schedule based on the times available by the instructor first, and subsequently schedule the students into a lesson time that is practical for all concerned. Lessons can be available in 30 minute, 45 minute, and one-hour blocks. The fees would be adjusted accordingly for the 45 minute and one-hour lessons. Policies concerning makeup lessons should be clearly delineated and parents should clearly understand these rules in advance. Makeup lessons should be offered only if the student is ill or has a death in the family. Notification of the absence should be at least 24 hours in advance except in the case of an emergency. Of course, if the instructor has to miss a lesson for any reason, the student's lesson should always be made up.

The Conservatory Budget

Expenditures primarily involve instructor compensation. Utilities, piano maintenance, special programming such as an arts festival, and guest clinicians may also be expenditures the director would want to consider.

Timothy Kolosick
Professor of Music Theory,
University of Arizona,
and creator of *Explorations,*
music education software

"The following are essentials for establishing a computer lab in Christian school music programs:

1. A notation program—*Finale, Allegro, Encore, Fermata, Sibelius*

2. A sequencer for multitrack playback-making musical sculptures—*Vision DSP, Music Performer, Band in a Box*

3. Training software that will teach basic musical elements like theory and ear training—*Practica Musica, Explorations, Mac-Gamut,* and *Norton* software and book

4. Web access to download music and information

5. Play sounds from a keyboard via midi cabling (orchestral sounds)

Computer technology facilitates active class discussions because interaction must take place to fill in the gaps of knowledge so that the knowledge base is complete. The students become sharers of information, as well as the teacher. The class becomes consumers of information from peers. See your local MIDI product dealer to order."

Excellent computer software is available for budget forecasting and accounting. Instructors are paid based on half hour blocks of instruction. It is suggested that extensive research be conducted in the area surrounding the church to ascertain the proper fees.

Below is an example of a typical fiscal year conservatory budget based on 250 students taking half-hour lessons for the fall and spring semesters at $12.50 per half hour of instruction. This is based on a schedule that includes 12 half-hour lessons in the fall and 16 half-hour lessons in the spring.

Revenues

43% = Fall Semester Revenues

57% = Spring Semester Revenues

100% = Total Projected Revenues for the Fiscal Year

Expenditures

84% = Totals for Instructor Compensation for the Fiscal Year

5% = Printing, Advertising, Brochures, Postage, Stationery, & Envelopes

4% = Equipment and Supplies

3% = Instrument Maintenance: Piano Tunings, Organ Tunings, etc.

3% = Scholarship Monies for Underprivileged Students

3% = Misc. Expenses

100% = Total Projected Expenditures for the Fiscal Year

As one can ascertain from these fiscal projections, the conservatory of music should be a self-supporting financial entity within the overall church budget. The one constant expenditure is the instructor compensation line item. When this line item is calculated, the remainder of the annual revenues represents what monies are available to offset conservatory expenses. One strong suggestion: make the conservatory financially independent. Do not overextend the budget. Start conservatively and, as God blesses, there will be additional monies to expand the budget. Church finance committees love ministries that are self-supporting.

Payment Plans. It is strongly suggested that tuition be collected at the beginning of each semester of instruction. Parents tend to be more committed to getting students to the lessons if the tuition has been paid in advance. A suggested payment plan is as follows:

1. $15.00 one time annual registration fee to be paid with the application
2. Half of the semester tuition to be paid on or before the semester begins
3. The balance of the semester tuition to be paid 30 days later

Most people can fit these payments into their family budget. Remember, parents are much more faithful to see that their students make their lessons if they have already paid for them. A lesson-by-lesson or month-by-month payment plan is much more difficult. Make the payment plan fair and then be consistent in its implementation. Payments may also be arranged on a Web page.

Conclusions

Following are some typical sample forms, contracts, and letters that should be helpful examples of how to get started with the conservatory of music. Some conservatories may also want their faculty to provide a statement of faith.

Adapt the forms to the church's needs:
1. Conservatory Brochure Application & Enrollment Form
2. Sample Conservatory Letter for Returning Students
3. Instructor Employment Application
4. Instructor Contract

May God bless the efforts of all who reach out to the church and to the community to provide quality musical instruction in a God-centered environment!

Key factors to remember:
1. Hire instructors who are qualified, competent, and Christian.
2. Publicize the conservatory effectively.
3. Set fees that are fair, yet competitive.
4. Make the conservatory a self-supporting entity within the church budget.
5. Operate the conservatory as a MINISTRY because that is exactly what it is!

Terry McNatt is Pastor of Worship and Music at Wallace Memorial Baptist Church in Knoxville, Tennessee.

_____ Church Conservatory of Music

APPLICATION and ENROLLMENT for (please check one):
_____ Fall   _____ Spring   _____ Summer Semester

Date_____ Date of Birth_____
Student's Name_____
Street Address_____
City_____ State_____ Zip_____
Home Phone_____
Student's School_____ Grade_____

If student is living with parents or guardian, please complete:
Parent's Name(s)_____
Home Phone_____
Business Phone(s) (Dad)_____ (Mom)_____

The annual registration fee of $15 must accompany this form. Make checks
payable to _____ Church, and mail the form and check to:
_____ Conservatory of Music,_(address, City, ST, Zip)._

Instruction Available _(Check One)_

___Flute	___Trumpet	___Cello
___Suzuki Flute	___Trombone	___Bass/Bass Guitar
___Oboe	___Baritone	___Classical Guitar
___Clarinet	___Tuba	___Piano
___Bassoon	___Percussion	___Voice (age 15 & older)
___Alto Saxophone	___Violin	___Music Theory
___Tenor Saxophone	___Suzuki Violin	___Kindermusik
___French Horn	___Viola	___Jazz Master Class

How many years of previous instruction have you had in the area checked above?
_____

Length of Lesson _(check one)_
___30 minutes   ___45 Minutes   ___1 Hour

Day of the Week Preferred _(1st and 2nd choice)_
___Monday   ___Tuesday   ___Wednesday   ___Thursday

Returning Students Only

Current Teacher_____
Previous lesson day and time_____
Request teacher/time change? ___**Yes**   ___**No**
If yes, to which teacher/time?_____

Sample Conservatory Letter for Returning Students

Dear Conservatory Members and Parents of Members,

We are so thankful that each of you has been previously enrolled in the _____ Church Conservatory of Music. God has blessed us in an unbelievable manner with wonderful students and fantastic teachers! This year promises to be another great opportunity for us, and we look forward with great anticipation to Fall Semester.

Last year was a fabulous year for us with over <u>100*</u> students taking lessons during the year. Your faithfulness as students and parents and the expertise of our faculty played two very important roles in making this <u>ninth</u> year a smashing success. How wonderful it is to see how the Lord is working to develop our Conservatory to be among the finest anywhere in the country.

It is now time to sign up for lessons for Fall Semester. Enclosed are two copies of our brochure, one for you and one for you to share with a neighbor or friend. The application attached to the brochure is for you to detach, complete, and return to the Music Ministry offices with your registration fee of $15.00. We will begin scheduling for Fall semester on <u>Monday, August 2</u>. In order for you to receive priority scheduling, we must have your application form and your $15.00 registration fee returned to us on or before <u>Monday, August 2</u>. Adhering to this deadline ensures your placement for Fall, and every effort will be made to accommodate you with the days and times for lessons that you prefer. Please remember to complete the box at the bottom of the form to indicate your teacher preference for the new semester. We want to schedule you at the same time and day from this past Spring, if at all possible, and if this works for you. New students to the Conservatory this Summer need to complete the day and time of lesson section of the brochure, and will be assigned a time before any other new students to this Fall's Conservatory are scheduled.

One thing—help us please: If any of you do not plan to re-enroll with us this fall, please return the application form with the name of the student on the form and write "NOT RETURNING" in the upper right hand corner.

Parents and students, please observe the <u>August 2</u> deadline. We want to help you with your busy schedules by scheduling lessons that are as compatible with your lives as is possible. Help us to help you by completing and returning the application form and registration fee today! We are anticipating a record semester enrollment of over <u>600</u> students this Fall and we want to take care of you first! Get these in today and help us to work toward assigning you a "premium" time and day for your lessons.

Thank you for your support of the _____ Church Conservatory of Music. We look forward to serving you again in <u>2002-2003</u>! God Bless You!

_____,

Associate Pastor of Worship and Music

Underlined information indicates places in the letter you will want to supply information that pertains to your particular situation.

Instructor Employment Application
_____ Church Conservatory of Music

Date _____ Date of Birth _____

Name _____ SS# _____

Address _____

City _____ St _____ Zip _____

Phone _____ Marital Status _____

Church Affiliation _____

Your Employer _____

Work Address _____

Work Ph _____

Spouse's Name _____

Employer _____

Name, Age, and Sex of Children

_____

_____

_____

Educational Background: (Please give in reverse chronological order)

School	From	To

Areas of Certification

Degree	Major	Date Awarded	School

Previous Two Employers, Addresses, and Phone Numbers:

_____

_____

Have you ever been convicted of a crime? (Excluding Traffic Violations)
Yes No
If yes, please explain:

List Three References: (One Personal, One Spiritual, and One Musical)

Name _____ Phone _____

Name _____ Phone _____

Name _____ Phone _____

Instructor Contract for the
_____ Church Conservatory of Music

September _____ Through _____

THIS CONTRACT is made and entered into on _____, by and

between _____ Church, Inc., and _____.

Witnessesth: _____

WHEREAS the _____ Church Conservatory of Music is desirous of securing the services of the above named Instructor; who in turn is desirous of providing said services; and

WHEREAS the _____ Church Conservatory of Music and the above Instructor wish to enter into a written contract specifying the obligations of each party as it regards to said contractual agreement;

NOW, THEREFORE, for and in consideration of the mutual obligations contained herein, the undersigned parties do hereby agree and contract as follows:

1. _____ Church does hereby secure the services of the above named Instructor to serve as an Instructor of:

   _____

   at the _____ Church Conservatory of Music. The Instructor accepts the terms of this contract, and agrees to carry out the policies and the duties set forth by the Conservatory of Music.

2. The Instructor agrees to abide by the rules of the Conservatory related to teaching policies, Christian behavior and influence, and agrees to conduct himself/herself in accordance with the teachings of the Bible for followers of the Savior. Accordingly, the Instructor has signed and does subscribe to the Statement of Faith of the Conservatory as approved by the Church. Violation of this provision shall constitute a breach of contract and shall be grounds for termination of services.

3. The Instructor shall not undertake, participate in, or support any action, verbal or otherwise, which is intended to harm, injure, harass, or insult any other person on the grounds of race, color, or national or ethnic origin. Violation of this provision shall constitute a breach of contract and shall be grounds for termination of services.

4. _____ Church shall pay the Instructor as compensation for services rendered pursuant to this contract during the term, hereof, a predetermined sum _____ for each 30 minutes of instruction given in the Conservatory each week. The Instructor's check shall be mailed on the 15th day of each month, and on the last working day of each month. Two conservatory Instructor meetings are held each year. The Fall Semester meeting is held the Tuesday after Labor Day. The Spring Semester meeting is held the Tuesday in January prior to the first week of lessons for that semester. Attendance at these two meetings is manda-

tory. $50.00 from your compensation as an Instructor is earmarked for these two meetings. Failure to attend either of these two meetings for any reason will result in a $25.00 deduction in pay to be reflected in the first check issued at the beginning of the Fall and Spring semesters. As you are a professional instructor and not an Employee of

_____ Church, Inc., the church has no payroll tax obligation. The Instructor will receive from the Church a Form 1099 at the end of the calendar year for your personal Income Tax purposes.

5. In the event that the Instructor has to be absent from lessons that he or she is scheduled to teach through the Conservatory, it shall be left up to the Instructor to set up a day and time to make up this lesson with the student. In the event that a student notifies the Instructor or the Music office as to illness, death in the family, or an unavoidable conflict that shall be deemed reasonable by the Instructor and the Conservatory Administrator, every effort will be made to schedule a make-up lesson for the student. After-school work conflicts by the student will not be considered a reasonable conflict; therefore, no make-up lessons will be scheduled to cooperate with the student's work conflicts.

6. In the event of the Instructor's discharge, resignation, or death,

_____ Church's obligation for payment of compensation, installment thereof, shall cease as of the date that the services of the Instructor are terminated.

7. _____ Church shall have the right, at its option, to terminate this Contract or declare it breached by the Instructor, and to suspend or dismiss the Instructor for his or her incompetence, insubordination, neglect of duty, failure to maintain his or her weekly schedule as it pertains to the Conservatory, violation of any ordinance, or failure to carry out any provision of this Contract.

8. The Instructor shall have the right to terminate this Contract after giving thirty (30) days written notice to the Conservatory Administrator, in which case the provisions of Number 6 of this contract shall apply.

I, _____, agree to the terms and provisions of this contract, and my signature below seals this contract as binding between

_____ Church, Inc., and myself.

_____   _____
Instructor   Date

_____   _____
Associate Pastor of Worship and Music   Date

_____   _____
Conservatory Administrator   Date

CHAPTER 31

Literature Selection

by Camp Kirkland

Appropriate literature selection is a challenging and rewarding task for the instrumental music minister. Not only does he or she have to consider the musical and technical resources of the ensemble, but also the spiritual and emotional climate of the worship service. The conductor usually bases the selection of literature on four principal criteria:

- size or instrumentation of the group
- musical aptitude of the players
- worship styles of the congregation
- musical and spiritual goals of the worship leadership team

The task of literature selection is rewarding because it is a highly creative process and can greatly motivate the instrumental ensemble. Poor selection techniques can frustrate and defeat players, or inhibit the effectiveness of the ensemble in leading worship.

Size and Instrumentation of Group

The size and instrumentation of the group should be a primary consideration because no matter how outstanding the arrangement, the piece will not be performed effectively if the players are not available to make the arrangement sound full. For instance, a lyric setting of a hymn featuring woodwinds and strings will not facilitate worship if there are not enough mature players in the section to produce warm tones, beautiful legato lines, and sensitively shaped phrases. Young string players may not be able to play high, melismatic passagework in higher positions and maintain proper intonation. Brass players who do not practice regularly will struggle with majestic fanfare or jazz-oriented arrangements that keep the brass playing continuously in the upper range. Church arrangers often score the brass less judiciously than symphonic arrangers, so the brass parts must be carefully edited and the section assignments should be made so that players do not get overtired and lose tone quality and range. Scoring for a smaller ensemble is even more critical, because the group needs to sound full. In a smaller group, each individual player is more exposed, so the orchestral parts should be carefully edited to match the abilities of the individual players. Another player who is more confident and mature might double an insecure solo player. Instrumentation affects music choice more if the music is for instruments only. Music that accompanies choral or congregational singing is not so exposed. A critical consideration in orchestral accompaniments is that the arrangement not overpower the choir or the congregation. If the instrumentation competes rather than enhances the setting of the text, the arrangement should be simplified. If the arrangement is mundane and provides no additional emotional impact to the listener, then the arrangement should be embellished with tasteful percussion writing, beautiful solo countermelodies, or motivic rhythmic enhancement. Consult Chapter 3 on instrumental arranging for more suggestions.

Musical Aptitude of Players

Players in a church orchestra should be able to perform successfully with a limited number of rehearsals. Many instrumental groups perform weekly, so a large amount of literature is required to support a service. Professional symphonies usually have several rehearsals to perform a two-hour concert. Church orchestras have listeners who are accustomed to hearing professional recordings and, yet, church orchestras do not have the luxury of multiple rehearsals for a single service. The instrumental conductor wants the ensemble players to succeed, so the level of music selected should be challenging enough to engage the mature player and simple enough to avoid frustrating the less-experienced player. Often a group is composed of musicians with a wide range of competency. Each part should be examined for editorial detail that will facilitate the musical interpretation of the piece (brass articulations, dynamic markings, bowings, etc.) and musical interest that will excite the player. For example, playing whole notes on every piece will not motivate a young high school string player. The instrumental conductor should select some pieces to challenge his or her ensemble, and some pieces that will easily be mastered. Mixing this combination of challenge and success is an important part of rehearsal planning, as well.

Worship Styles of the Congregation

The selection of musical styles utilized in worship is a philosophical issue that should be prayerfully considered by the entire worship production team.

The styles of music utilized in a service speak an emotional language that will target different audiences. This topic is discussed in detail in Chapter 42, the contemporary worship trends section of this book. If an offertory or prelude is the precursor of the pastor's sermon, then the pastor should give input as to the mood and impact the piece should make before the sermon. When the conductor has the freedom to choose his or her instrumental selections within acceptable limits, then a variety of styles should broaden the instrumental ensemble musically. The music styles that will reach the target audience in a congregation should be utilized whenever possible. An instrumental conductor observes which styles the ensemble most enjoys and plays the best, as well.

Musical and Spiritual Goals

As a pedagogue, the instrumental conductor will also want to improve the playing technique of the ensemble. Balance, intonation, rhythmic accuracy and effective sight-reading can all be taught effectively in the rehearsal of appropriate literature. Certain pieces may be selected that will challenge the musical growth of the players in specific areas. Settings of Scripture, hymns, or devotional texts may be chosen by the conductor to facilitate the meditation and worship of the players and congregation. Often devotional meditations may be derived from the lyric of a hymn setting that is being played.

God may send dedicated, accomplished soloists to a church to greatly enhance worship. The conductor may want to feature a guest soloist with the ensemble. Consider the Christian commitment of the featured performer as well as his or her musical ability. Many arrangements are available that feature a solo instrumentalist, or small ensemble with orchestra. An orchestra can also play a choral accompaniment and utilize a soloist or small ensemble on the parts written for solo or choir.

Occasionally, secular classical literature may be used in a service when the piece would underscore a Scripture reading or meditation. Classical literature may also underscore powerful sacred video clips. The conductor should again consider not only the musical taste of the congregation, but also the musical aptitude of the instrumental group.

Many sources are available to procure sacred instrumental music in a variety of styles with varying instrumentation requirements. Some publishers of church instrumental music are listed below.

Instrumental Music Resources

"Sacred Instrumental Published Music List," available from the Christian Instrumentalists and Directors Association. See David E. Smith Publications
(Many publishers have demonstration recordings available on request.)

• Allegis Publications (dist. by Lillenas) Kansas City, MO, 1-800-877-0700
www.lillenas.com
Allegis Orchestra Series: Silver (Easy), Gold (Moderate), Platinum (Advanced)
Praise Band, Brasscapes, Windscapes

- AnderKamp Music, Nashville, TN, www.anderkampmusic.com
  Brass Quintets

- Barncharts Music, Modesto, CA, 1-888-577-6963, www.barncharts.com
  Cool charts for Praise Bands

- Brentwood-Benson Music, Brentwood, TN, 1-800-846-7664
  Strike Up the Band Series (Carmichael), Brentwood Jazz Orchestra
  (McDonald), Continental Orchestra Collection

- Camp Kirkland Productions, Jacksonville, FL, 904-260-8313
  "Seven Plus" Series

- Carol Press, Charleston, SC, 1-800-942-7407
  Brass and Church Orchestra

- Claude T. Smith, Olathe, KS, 913-541-9422, www.ctspubs.com
  Band and Orchestra

- Coral Key Productions, Inc., 3933 Northwest Hwy,
  Dallas, TX 75225, (214) 860-3914
  Orchestra

- David E. Smith Publications, Deckerville, MI, 1-800-OSACRED,
  www.despub.com
  Various solos, ensembles, concert band, string orchestra for church
  and school instrumentalists

- Franton Music, Memphis, TN, 1-888-202-2238
  Solos, Ensembles, School Music

- Gaither Music Co. (dist. by WORD), Anderson, IN, 1-888-324-9673
  www.gaithermusic.com
  Camp Kirkland Christmas Brass, Sanctuary Symphony Series,
  Fanfare Preludes, others

- Genevox Music, Nashville, TN, 1-800-436-3869
  Celebration Orchestra Series (Advanced Level)
  Jubilation Orchestra Series (Easy Level)
  Power Praise for Worship Band Series
  Various solos and ensembles
  Camp Kirkland Instrumental Series
  Instrumental Hymnal
  John Gage Orchestra Series
  Solo Celebration Series
  Exaltation Series
  Rhythm +4 Series

- Hal Leonard, 414-774-3630, www.halleonard.com
  Band, Orchestra, and Ensembles

- Hinshaw Music, Inc., P. O. Box 470, Chapel Hill, NC 27514

- Hope, Carol Stream, IL, 1-800-323-1049, www.hopepublishing.com
  Various pieces
  "Ensemble Music for Church and School"
  Doug Smith's 4+Brass and Woodwind Ensembles

- Integrity Music (dist. by WORD), 1-800-533-6912, www.integritymusic.com
  Classic Christmas Brass

- James Curnow Music Service, Nicholasville, KY, 606-885-3696
  Brass Ensemble
  Band and Orchestra arrangements (many by James Curnow)
  at various performance levels

- Jenson Publications (dist. by Hal Leonard Publications), Milwaukee, WI,
  414-774-3630
  Music by Jim Curnow and Claude T. Smith

- Les Stallings Music Group, Brentwood, TN
  Brass Quintets, Ensemble, Various others

- Lillenas, Kansas City, MO, 1-800-877-0700, www.lillenas.com
  "500 Hymns for Instruments," various solo pieces
  (See Allegis Orchestra Series)

- Lorenz, Dayton, OH, 1-800-444-1144
  Doug Smith's Brass Ensembles

- Matterhorn Music, Contact Rick Powell, 813-831-0500
  Rick Powell "Assurance" Collection

- Mel Bay, 1-800-863-5229, www.melbay.com
  Various pieces

- Pathway Music, Cleveland, TN
  Brass and rhythm charts

- PRISM Music, Franklin, TN, 1-800-326-8987, www.prismmusic.com
  Prism's Light Orchestra Series, Various Arrangers
  Gloryland Band Series, Camp Kirkland
  Praise Band, Jim Gray

- Psalm 150 Publications (dist. by Theodore Presser), 610-525-3636,
  www.presser.com
  Church Orchestra, "Five or More" (Churchestra), various ensembles

- Robert King Music Sales, North Easton, MA, FAX ONLY, 508-238-2571
  Brass literature

- Ron Cobb Copy Service, Franklin, TN, 1-800-955-1730
  Camp Kirkland's Benson Brass Series
  Don Marsh's Treasury of Hymns and Solid Brass Series
  various others

- Salvation Army, Des Plaines, IL, 847-294-2000, www.salvationarmy.org
  Brass and more

- Shawnee Press, 570-476-0550, Delaware Water Gap, PA,
  www.shawneepress.com
  various pieces

- Temple Sounds Publications, Contact Omar Allen,
  Tallahassee, FL, 850-562-2625
  Orchestra, Gospel Band

- Tempo Music, Leawood, KS, www.tempomusic.com
  various products, including a contemporary church orchestra series

- Theodore Presser, King of Prussia, PA, 610-525-3636, www.presser.com
  Woodwind ensemble pieces

- Volkwein Bros., Pittsburg, PA, 1-800-553-8742
  Phil Norris band arrangements

- Washington Music Ministries, www.washingtonmusic.org
  various solo and ensemble pieces for small to medium size groups
  by Bob Walters.

- Willow Creek Music, 1-800-570-9812, www.willowcreek.com
  Praise Band

- WORD, Inc., Nashville, TN, 1-800-876-9673, www.wordmusic.com
  Sunday Sounds Series (Easy Arrangements)
  Coronation Series (More Challenging Arrangements)
  Brass Ensemble Music
  Instrumental Hymnal
  Songs for Praise and Worship Orchestrations

Much Music Is Available; Be Selective!

There are many resources for previewing music before purchasing. Many publishers offer demonstration tapes, CDs, Internet downloads, and/or sample scores to assist instrumental leaders. Check each piece carefully for:
1. the instrumentation you need,
2. the style which would be most appropriate,
3. the difficulty level,
4. the upper range limits of the instruments,
5. whether improvisation is required in rhythm section parts,
6. performance time, and
7. general musical character.

Camp Kirkland is a composer, arranger, and clinician. He has been a church orchestra director for 17 years, in addition to being a high school band director, and college band director/instructor of low brass/professor of music theory. He has published over 1000 works.

CHAPTER 32

Creatively
Complementing
the Vision Statement
of a Church

by James E. Helman

A local church must examine the claims of Christ and determine God's leadership for the local congregation. A vision statement is a carefully crafted, concise, memorable sentence that incorporates the principal values of an organization. For the church, these statements often reflect the Great Commission passage in Matthew 28. Eugene Peterson interprets the passage this way: "Jesus, undeterred, went right ahead and gave his charge: 'God authorized and commanded me to commission you: Go out and train everyone you meet, far and near, in this way of life, marking them by baptism in the threefold name: Father, Son, and Holy Spirit. Then instruct them in the practice of all I have commanded you. I'll be with you as you do this, day after day after day, right up to the end of the age'" (Matt. 28: 18-20, MES).

This author's church has massaged the message of Christ this way to form its vision statement:

"To introduce people to Christ and help them grow to be like Him."

© North Phoenix Baptist Church

The vision statement is simple. It is easy to remember, and intriguing in its application to instrumental leadership. In this instrumental minister's inter-pretation, it means involving instrumentalists in evangelizing through music ministry in the worship services. It is challenging to consider the perspective of the unchurched person visiting the worship service who attends out of curiosity or at the invitation of a friend. The minister must seek to discern how the ministry of the church can impact his or her life and bring healing, salvation, and restoration.

Challenges of evangelizing the unsaved are best addressed by pondering how the church service *wouldn't* make a strong impression. Imagine the non-Christian who suffers through some poorly performed musical presentation, and feels he is pressured to give his money to support such an effort. "All they ask for is money!" he harrumphs to himself, echoing the hue and cry throughout the walls of any church any Sunday. Or see him distracted by the pomposity of a presentation that excels in orchestration, yet fails to lead toward Christ's glory.

"Introduce people to Christ..." Imagine now the possibilities in a sim-ple and well-rehearsed offertory playing softly, as pictures from the recent youth mission trip light up the screen. How about a video collage of happy children blessed by the gift of Vacation Bible School this past summer? Is it possible to show the visitor *how* the gifts of church members make a differ-ence in the lives of people? Creativity can build a bridge between capturing his attention and demonstration that kingdom work is indeed *worth* his attention. Ensure that the observer is impacted emotionally so that music and accompanying media can stir his soul.

How is the vision statement applied to the new Christian filling a chair in the church orchestra? She is faithful to be there week to week, yet she has little idea of what draws her to attend. Are the waters of her spiritual growth muddied by sloppy organization that wastes her time during rehearsal? Lost music and lingering rehearsal start times can hinder her musical and spiri-tual experience.

"Introduce people to Christ..." Advance preparation is imperative and exemplary of Christ Himself. In little things, one can lead this young lady toward a deepening understanding of the standard of a life committed to Christ. Similarly, what does the conductor who insists on speaking in a con-descending way to the instrumentalists convey about Christ? His ego hinders his example. Complex worship plans and quick decisions to modulate on the spur of the moment can cause musical frustrations that hinder the worship of the player and the participant. While the wrong notes go whizzing by, one feels there should be some disclaimer in the bulletin explaining that the orchestra has to sightread a chorus in a new key since it was more impor-tant to make a direct musical seque from the choir special. Proper planning can avoid such musical catastrophes. A Christ-like instrumental leader disciples the young Christian in the orchestra and challenges the player's musical talents while refusing to push beyond his or her musical capabilities.

The second part of the Great Commission passage, and consequently the vision statement, deals with spiritual growth to be more like Christ. What can the instrumental ministry do to implement this mission?

"Help them grow to be like Him..." For many instrumentalists, orchestra is much like a Bible study small group, providing the bond of fellowship whereby a person grows in camaraderie with other Christians. People are already busy. Without providing a place that treats the instrumentalists to an enjoyable experience, recruiting skills will be taxed—constantly replacing those that are dropping out. A rehearsal begun by sharing prayer requests and finished with a brief Bible study shared by one of its own members is a good start. Both the hearer and the presenter are better for the time spent, as well as encouraged by the complement of great music in the rehearsal. It is a worthy goal to close an evening with a rehearsal hall echoing with the sound of laughter and teeming with smiles of satisfaction.

A moving piece in worship becomes a ministry when members exercise their own leadership abilities by sharing the results of their personal growth with others. If the instrumentalists are excited about their presentation and fellowship together, it is contagious to the listening congregation who observes a group of growing Christians utilizing their gifts to God's glory! Through Christian community, authentic worship, and powerful testimony, players are introducing others to Christ and many are growing to be more like Him.

James E. Helman is the Minister of Instrumental Music and Prayer Center Coordinator at the North Phoenix Baptist Church, Phoenix, Arizona, since 1979.

CHAPTER 33

Developing an Orchestra Handbook

by John G. Gage

An orchestra handbook is one of the best ways to communicate instrumental ministry policies and procedures to orchestra visitors and members alike. The development process itself helps leadership and officers solidify policy and answer potential questions, and allows leadership to say things once in written format, rather than repeating information verbally to new members. The handbook should be creatively presented and user-friendly. It should communicate church policies in a clear and kind voice. The handbook can foster vision for the orchestra and help set the tone for the season.

A handbook should be mailed to each first-time visitor with a personal letter, explaining the membership policies (for instance, attending two rehearsals as a guest and then setting up a time for an audition, prior to being assigned a folder and a "seat"). The handbook should explain everything else a potential member would need to know about how the ensemble functions and what is expected from membership, and should include a listing of orchestra members and birthdays, officer and section leader names and phone numbers/email addresses, and names of church staff members with corresponding office phone numbers/email addresses.

When designing a handbook, the following sections should be included:

• **A letter of welcome and affirmation from the senior pastor**

There is nothing that will enhance the credibility and growth of an instrumental ministry as much as pastoral affirmation and appreciation. This is one way that the pastor can express his gratitude to ensemble members for their commitment, faithfulness, and contribution.

• **A letter of welcome and challenge from the minister of music/music director**

It is easy for players to feel used and even abused, especially in a large, active, and visionary music ministry. The handbook allows the minister of music an opportunity to cast a vision to the players, helping them see the big picture, the eternal benefits of their ministry, and his or her gratitude for their involvement.

• **A letter of welcome from the orchestra director, if different from the minister of music**

A word of welcome, the director's personal expectations for orchestra members, and gratitude for player commitment is very appropriate. Policies that can be found elsewhere in the book should not necessarily be restated, but a personal, warm word will reap the benefit of players who know and share the director's passion for ministry and excellence.

• **Membership requirements**

Steps to membership (come as a visitor a time or two, play an audition, etc.) and how well a person should be able to play in order to make a positive contribution to the group's ministry should be included. Something as nebulous as "an average high school ability" will give them an idea that if they've played oboe for six months in middle school, they may not be ready for the demands of this ensemble.

• **Service responsibilities**

How often the group plays (every week, every other Sunday night), special seasonal programs where their involvement is anticipated—anything that will give the prospective member an idea of the required commitment should be stated. Also included here can be a brief description of WHAT is expected in a worship service...accompanying the choir and congregational singing each week, playing an offertory twice per month, etc. Also, does the orchestra stay on stage through the entire service or is there a time during the service when they can be seated with their families? Do they play at the conclusion of the service or just at the beginning?

• **Appropriate service dress**

Players need to know the standard of worship leadership attire or they won't be able to meet it. In this section the prospective player discovers whether ties and jackets are required for the men, if jewelry is allowed (in a church with a television ministry this could be an important issue), whether perfume and aftershave are allowed, etc. What they aren't told, they can't be expected to know.

• **Service and Sunday involvement**

In this area, multiple service responsibilities can be explained: If there is more than one morning service, does everyone play both services? Are there first and second service teams? Does the same group play in the evening service? Does the group play every week?

• **Accompanying soloists and ensembles**

If the ensemble accompanies vocal soloists or ensembles, they will need some direction on volume, style, dynamic contrast, etc. When a soloist or vocal group is utilizing trax, and the orchestra is on stage, they need to be reminded to focus their attention on the performer(s) in order to help direct congregational attention to the point of action.

• **Rehearsal schedule**

Times, places, length of rehearsal, everything a prospective member will need to know to coordinate their schedule with that of their family should be included. Promptness can be emphasized here.

• **Rehearsal etiquette**

What is allowed in the way of talking, moving around, etc? It could be stated that if the noise level prohibits effective rehearsal with an individual or section, it is too high. It can also be recommended that latecomers enter doors to the REAR of the ensemble, so they aren't as distracting. Players should be told, *in love*, what is expected and what the consequences of infraction are, if any. With a primarily young group, stricter guidelines and more severe consequences may be necessary.

• Absence procedures

Whatever the method of keeping track of attendance, it should be defined in this section, as should expected attendance percentages. One hundred percent should be expected except for illness, business, family emergencies, etc. The player should be reminded here that allegiance is not to a church, director, or pastor—it is to the Lord and He deserves his or her wholehearted effort.

• Child care

Child care is very important. Players need to know ages that will be provided for, where to take their children and pick them up, and if there is any cost involved. If there is cost, the church or music ministry budget should cover it. In a church with a preschool minister or director, THAT leader should be asked to write this section.

• Library information

May folders be taken home? Are there separate performance folders and rehearsal folders? Are individual selections numbered or are the rehearsal folders arranged in rehearsal order for each rehearsal? Do the players have any obligation in refiling music (or collecting it) when finished with a selection? Pertinent library-related information should be given, including location of folder racks, etc.

• Other groups

Are there small ensembles (flute quartet, brass quintet, etc.) in which a person could be involved? If so, how do they pursue them and what are the membership/participation requirements? Who leads those groups? When do they rehearse?

• Officers

This portion of the handbook should contain a description of each office. The qualifications and requirements of the people who will fill these offices should be enumerated. All nomination and election procedures should be defined. The responsibilities of section leaders should be included. A list of officer and section leader names and phone numbers/email addresses should be included. A current orchestra member roster BY SECTION, with phone numbers and addresses should be included.

Member permission should be requested and granted before publishing addresses and phone numbers. Some people with sensitive jobs (law enforcement, etc.) don't want that information distributed, and the director must be sensitive to their desires. If they request that such information be omitted, publishing their name under the appropriate section and placing "unpublished" beside it should be sufficient.

• Birthday roster, BY DATE

Birthdays should be listed January through December by the month. Members should be encouraged to refer to this list on a regular basis and to remember the birthdays of fellow members with a card or a phone call.

• Church staff members and their positions

New members may not know all of the church staff members. This is valuable information to include, even for older members, especially as staff personnel changes.

The last section of the handbook, including member listings, officer listings, birthdays, etc., should be prepared as a pullout, so that next year when the officer / section leader / member sections are updated the entire handbook doesn't have to be replaced—only the pull-out section.

The booklet can either be prepared in an 81/2" x 11" format bound with a spiral binder (NOT stapled), or the same size paper folded in half and stapled. However it is done, it should be attractive, the printing straight on the page, the design on the cover attractive and centered, the cover paper colorful and heavy enough (67 lb. card stock is thick enough and will go through a copy machine), and excellent in quality without being excessive or opulent. If a graphic artist is available, she should be asked to help design a logo unique to that ministry. At least every other year the officers should evaluate the contents to ensure that the handbook remains current and correct. Policies and procedures occasionally change, and those adjustments need to be reflected as soon as possible. The more involvement the officers have in developing and evaluating policies and procedures, the greater their sense of ownership and the greater their desire to help the director "enforce" the guidelines they have helped establish.

Throughout the handbook the reader should sense the director's heart of affirmation and encouragement, and not see just a list of rules and expectations. When guidelines or policies are violated, the handbook should be the standard that is used in correcting guilty parties, but love, forgiveness, and restoration should also be clearly expressed. Guidelines that have become obsolete or unnecessary should be changed. Overall, the handbook should be a vehicle for effective communication and should be designed to save extra work, not create it.

An orchestra Web page can also be an excellent information source for prospective players.

John G. Gage serves at Valley Baptist Church, Bakersfield, California. His responsibilities include developing and directing an adult orchestra, a big band and two youth orchestras, arranging for each group, and teaching trumpet in the Valley Academy of Performing Arts. John earned a Bachelor's of Music Education from John Brown University, Siloam Springs, AR, and a Master's in Church Music from Samford University, Birmingham, AL.

CHAPTER 34

Budgeting and Fund-raising

by Eddie Fargason

A director should have a budget designated for any continuing instrumental program. Designing a budget is not always a pleasant task, but it is essential that a director keep track of his expenses while using God's money wisely.

Just as with one's own personal financial record, a budget tracks resources, as well as expenditures in a particular fiscal year. A budget may consist of numerous categories, based upon the size of the church and the needs of the organization. The following is a suggestion of categories that may be adapted according to each individual situation.

The first step is to decide what amount the budget needs to be. Think of any expenses that may already exist for a particular year. Take into consideration the following:

1. General operations: office supplies, copy costs, music folders
2. Music: including new music to purchase or rent, commissioned arrangements
3. Consulting and contracts: fees of professional musicians for special events, substitute players, guest clinicians or conductors, graphic program designers
4. Printing and postage

5. Instrument maintenance and repair: strings, drum heads, piano tuning, etc.

6. Instrument purchase: larger instruments such as hanging chimes, mallet percussion, harps, etc.

7. Sound equipment for orchestra: microphones that are utilized especially for strings, earpieces, monitors, etc.

Short- and long-term purchases need to be considered separately. Short-term items might include repertoire for Sunday services and special events, storage boxes, and music folders. Long-term goals may include large instrument purchases; sound equipment; computer technology for mixing, recording, composing and arranging; scanners; copy machines; digital cameras for promotion or media enhancement; standard symphonic repertoire for the orchestra library; touring cases for the transportation of instruments and equipment. A major event such as a tour or recording project should have its own itemized budget.

Fund-raising is important in providing money for nonbudgeted items. Sometimes the director may want to schedule events or take trips that are above and beyond the feasibility of the annual budget. This is where a fund-raiser may make the event possible. Traditional fund-raisers would include candy sales, bake sales, or car washes. Other fund-raisers have the potential of earning more money.

A gigantic, churchwide garage sale comprised of donated items from the congregation can provide a larger profit return. The sale of appliances, furniture, clothes, televisions, stereos, computers, boats, and cars are all items that can bring a significant profit. These items should be collected and stored for several weeks—possibly at a vacated store or warehouse. Rent the storage space, display the items carefully, and promote the garage sale heavily. Depending on how many items are collected, the potential return can be several thousand dollars.

Another great fund-raising idea is to have an auction. This can be very successful in more affluent churches and neighborhoods. The auction can be combined with a dinner for the participants. Donated items can come from the following sources: furniture stores, home improvement stores, sporting goods, gift certificates from restaurants or service-type businesses, sports franchises and sports memorabilia. The more diverse the auctioned items, the wider audience the auction may draw.

Another successful way of raising money is through a sporting event like a golf tournament. People who play golf will flock to play in a tournament if it is advertised and promoted well. Although this is not something every church may want to attempt, a golf tournament can be a high-profit event. For example, if someone in the church is a member of a country club, he or she may be willing to investigate the possibility of hosting a tournament at his or her club. Charity tournaments may be held on the day the country club is closed to the public. By doing this, there will not be any interference from people who are not in the scheduled charity tournament. Usually country clubs are closed on Mondays. The golf tournament works like this:

1. An entrance fee needs to be agreed upon. Each person entering the tournament may receive a 50 percent tax deduction for the entrance fee. The

reason for the 50 percent reduction is that half of the entrance fee goes to the country club for the facilities and the dinner that follows the tournament; the other half of the entry fee goes to the church or charity organization.

2. Corporate or individual sponsorships could be set up as follows:

Gold. The Gold Level of sponsorship is $2,500 and includes four players (with dinner included), a tee box sign, a sponsor's gift, and anything else donated to sponsor for giveway, and perhaps then tickets to another church event on the calendar.

Silver. The Silver Level of sponsorship is $2,000 and includes two players (with dinner included), a tee box sign, and a sponsor's gift—perhaps eight tickets to another church event.

Bronze. The Bronze Level of sponsorship is $1,500 and includes two players (with dinner included), a tee box sign, and perhaps six tickets to another church event.

Each country club may require a minimum number of people to play, but this can be determined by contacting the club. The potential for this fund-raising event is anywhere from $15,000-$30,000, depending on how many people are playing. Such an event is also an easy and fun way to make money with relatively little effort.

Another idea for a fund-raiser event is a dinner/concert. Before the concert, sell tickets for a nice dinner that perhaps ties in with the theme of the concert. Valentine's Day is a great time to provide an opportunity for church members to bring their seeker friends to a beautiful dinner and an entertaining evening. After the dinner, everyone moves to the place where the concert is held. Hopefully this would take place in the same building, such as the church or maybe a concert hall with a space for dining. The cost of the tickets would exceed the actual cost of the meal so that a profit could be made. This event would be a good opportunity to utilize patrons who would contribute enough to cover the actual cost of the event so that all tickets sold would be profit. A dinner/concert would be an enjoyable occasion in which the whole church could be involved.

The possibilities for raising funds for a particular cause are endless. One is only limited by his creativity and should make use of whatever avenues and facilities or opportunities he has in his community.

The Lord will lead and guide as one seeks to design events that are not only worthwhile and rewarding for those who contribute, but also for those working to make the event happen successfully. Money is not an end in itself, but through careful budgeting and thrifty use of God's money, one can be successful in raising money to be used for effective Christian ministry.

Eddie Fargason is Associate Minister of Music and Orchestra Director for First Baptist Church, Dallas, Texas. A graduate of The University of Texas at Austin with a BA, and a MM in music theory and composition, Eddie is a composer and arranger who currently directs the Sanctuary Orchestra (adult), Chapel Orchestra (high school), and oversees all instrumental areas of the church, including handbells. He is also the General Manager of the Criswell Music Press, a music publishing division of Criswell College.

CHAPTER 35

Officers
and Section Leaders

by John G. Gage

In Exodus 18, Moses was overworked and underpaid—in a word, burned out! His father-in-law, Jethro, observed the frustration, long hours, and never-ending tasks. He made a suggestion to Moses which revolutionized his ministry to the nation of Israel. Jethro's suggestion also provides justification for having orchestra officers, regardless of the size of the ensemble.

"The work is too heavy for you; you cannot handle it alone. Listen now to me and I will give you some advice...select capable men from all the people—men who fear God, trustworthy men who hate dishonest gain—and appoint them as officials...have them.. bring every difficult case to you; the simple cases they can decide themselves. That will make your load lighter, because they will share it with you. If you do this and God so commands, you will be able to stand the strain, and all these peoples will go home satisfied" (Ex. 18:18-23, NIV).

Having officers accomplishes several tasks:

• **It lightens the director's load.** It frees the director from being over-committed and ineffective.

• **It allows the director to focus on the right priorities.** Ministers need to protect their personal spiritual preparation time, their time to minister to individuals, adequate service preparation time, etc. Others could oversee some duties which will free up quality time for the important tasks of ministry.

• **It gives the orchestra a sense of ownership.** As players are utilized according to their giftedness and desire, they assume more responsibility for rehearsal behavior, planning, evaluation, and faithfulness. The more the players are empowered, the less the director has to "enforce" the rules and guidelines because the leadership team has been a part of the process of establishing the policies and procedures. The instrumental minister needs to place as much responsibility as possible in the hands of the lay leadership, developing in them a positive attitude of pride and teamwork in the organization and accomplishments of their ensemble.

• **It develops leaders.** Meet with the orchestra president often. Share calendar information, performance ideas, spiritual concerns, organizational ideas, and other items for his or her feedback. Ask him or her hard questions: about the director's effectiveness, ministry, and possible insensitivities; about the direction of the group, the spiritual climate in the group, and other musical or programming concerns. Regular and honest times of evaluation and dreaming between the orchestra president and the instrumental minister can stimulate genuine leadership qualities and deep, loving fellowship.

Certain office positions may be **elected,** and others may be **appointed.** Elections are not popularity contests; they are really more of a consensus nomination process than anything else. The officer year begins in September and is begun with an orchestra retreat in late August, at which time officers for the current year are announced. The process of officer elections must commence four to five weeks prior to the fall retreat. First, everyone in orchestra receives a listing of potential officer *positions* and the responsibilities and requirements for each office. They are asked to pray over the list and see if God brings any specific name to mind as they pray. The ideal is to fill each position with persons whose personalities, background, and giftedness uniquely qualify them for that position. Following is a list of recommended officer positions and the responsibilities and requirements of each office.

President
Responsibilities:
• Meets with the director on a regular basis to evaluate procedure, policy, efficient operation, future needs, and spiritual climate of the orchestra
• Presides over all orchestra and officer business meetings
• Is constantly sensitive to the spiritual "temperature" of the orchestra, and to specific and individual needs of its members
• Oversees and assists in the effective operation of the other officers and their responsibilities
• Is ultimately responsible for orchestra set-up for rehearsal, and performance, in tandem with the stage crew chairperson
• Acts as a liaison between the orchestra and the director, and between officers and the director
Requirements:
• Member of the church
• Faithful in attendance
• Respected as a leader, both musically and spiritually

• Must exhibit an attitude of spiritual maturity, optimism, creativity, encouragement, and commitment

Vice-President/Devotional
Responsibilities:
• Assumes presidential responsibilities if necessary
• Assists in developing the spiritual maturity of the orchestra through evaluating and overseeing rehearsal devotionals and discipleship opportunities
• Keeps abreast of prayer needs and other orchestra member needs, advising the director as necessary, and oversees the distribution of benevolence funds for flowers or other appropriate expressions in the event of bereavement or hospitalization
• Assists in the development of an orchestra evangelism strategy
Requirements:
• Member of the church
• Spiritually mature and respected as both a spiritual leader and one who can maintain a confidence
• Faithful in attendance

Vice-President/Social (and assistant)
Responsibilities:
• Plans social activities and events for the orchestra to foster brotherly love and a spirit of unity
• Recognizes orchestra members' birthdays on a regular basis, creatively, and in a manner in keeping with the orchestra philosophy and guidelines
• Greets orchestra visitors and makes sure they have been introduced to the orchestra secretary and to others in the visitor's section
• Keeps the orchestra bulletin board up-to-date with information, commendations, honors, birthdays, pictures of events and personnel, and any other pertinent and informative material
Requirements:
• Member of the church
• Friendly and loving, with a heart for people
• Faithful in attendance

Secretary-Treasurer
Responsibilities:
• Makes sure attendance records are completed accurately for each rehearsal and performance and gives them to the music secretary
• Greets all orchestra visitors and has them complete a visitor's card—introduces visitors to the orchestra and gives completed card to the director
• Assists in compiling the information on the member's card after the visitor has auditioned for the director or section leader
• Oversees meeting benevolence needs; taking periodic offerings to replenish budget funds used for benevolence; collecting and accounting for tape sales, clothing sales, or other financial needs as necessary

Requirements:
- Member of the church
- Faithful in attendance
- Above reproach in integrity
- Must work well with people, friendly, and outgoing

Stage Crew Coordinator
Responsibilities:
- Verifies that setup is correct for rehearsals and Sunday services and supervises teardown when necessary
- Oversees loading and unloading on road trips, verifies tour arrangements and logistics

Requirements:
- Member of the church
- Faithful in attendance
- Leadership qualities
- Knowledge of or capacity and desire to learn how to set up electronic keyboards, drums and amps; understands trailer weight distribution.

Each of the offices listed above is a **nominated** position. In addition, selected **appointed** positions are recommended. Appointed positions include section leaders, section leader chairperson, and librarian. Since these positions require specialized skill, it is advisable to appoint the person to each position who demonstrates the greatest amount of qualification for these particular offices. Below are the qualifications and responsibilities for these positions.

Section Leader Chairperson
Responsibilities:
- Facilitates communication of section leaders; makes sure that all attendance reports are in at each rehearsal
- Represents section leaders at officer meetings

Section Leader
Responsibilities:
- Takes attendance at each rehearsal and performance and reports it to the orchestra secretary
- Makes certain the section has every part covered for each performance and rehearsal
- Leads her section musically
- Assists in assigning seating for the sections
- Assists in assigning solos for the section

Librarian and Assistant Librarian*
Responsibilities:
- Assists in filling rehearsal folders and performance folders

- Assists director during rehearsals in the case of missing, wrong, or incomplete parts
- Makes certain all music is refiled correctly after use

Requirements:
- Member of the church
- Must have 6-8 hours minimum per week that can be given to orchestra library work
- Teachable spirit and willing to work behind the scenes

*Both of these positions require a knowledge of transpositions and ranges and a keen attention to detail, as well as several hours per week in filling and emptying performance and rehearsal folders, and in filing.

Prayerful consideration of each office position, and prayer that the *right* person is selected for that year to fill that position is essential.

The next step is to give orchestra members a nomination ballot they may take home, pray over, complete, and return. Two spaces are given for each office, so that each member may nominate a first and second choice for each.

After the ballots are returned, the **current officers** compile the results, listing the number of nominations each person received for each position. The current president asks the person who received the most nominations for president if he is willing and able to serve. If the answer is positive, that person is the nominee for president for the next year. If the response is negative, the person with the next highest number of nominations is contacted and asked if he or she is willing and able to serve. This happens for each position, with the person currently holding the position asking the potential nominee if he or she is willing to fill that position for the coming year, and continuing through the list of nominees for that position until someone agrees to serve. Ask that everyone in the orchestra pray in advance about his or her personal willingness and ability to serve in any capacity for which he or she might be nominated, knowing that the orchestra has been seeking God's will for the right person to be nominated for each position.

What if a *current officer* has the greatest number of nominations to serve in that capacity again the next year? That person is asked in the officers' meeting, where the nominations are tabulated, if he or she would be willing to serve in that capacity again. If the answer is yes, he or she is the nominee of choice. If the person declines, the person with the next highest number of nominations for that position is asked to serve.

A suggested guideline is that **no one person can serve in the same office for more than two consecutive years**. This assures that there are no monopolized positions, and it also gives a new flavor, personality, and giftedness to each position at least every two years.

When the new slate of officer nominations is complete, the orchestra assents via a vote of affirmation, since the orchestra members have nominated their choice for each office, and each nominee has agreed to serve for the next year. This avoids unnecessary contention.

A miniretreat should be scheduled after new officers are selected to review responsibilities, the director's expectations, and an evaluation of the past and vision for the future. These times can be invaluable both to evaluate and to plan, and to bond the new group of officers into a team. Carefully communicate expectations and goals:

Officers and Section Leader Goals

• A personal, growing, meaningful relationship with God

• Behavior befitting a Christian, both onstage and offstage

• Zero tolerance for gossip, backbiting, and the willful damaging of another orchestra member's reputation

• A positive, optimistic, affirming attitude

• Promptness and regular attendance at all orchestra rehearsals and services

• A welcoming attitude toward all visitors and new members, whether in their section or not

• Support of the pastoral staff, both onstage and offstage

• Conflict resolution dealt with privately, directly, and quickly

• A spirit of confidentiality

• Time utilized in the officer position viewed as an investment, not an expenditure. The leadership team needs to see the big picture of worship leadership, evangelism, and orchestra family life, and not see involvement as an annoyance or interruption of regular routine. (However, all Christians need to balance regular priorities of family, vocation, school, and orchestra responsibilities, and not forsake other important matters.)

• Honest communication with the director, including constructive criticism. The lay leader and minister should relate in mutual honesty and love.

However the selection process is conducted, and regardless of how the officers function, follow Jethro's advice and select capable men and women to assist the instrumental director in the leadership duties for the ensemble. The lay leadership will grow, the instrumental director will grow, and the ensemble will reap the benefits.

John G. Gage serves at Valley Baptist Church, Bakersfield, California. His responsibilities include developing and directing an adult orchestra, a big band, and two youth orchestras, arranging for each group, and teaching trumpet in the Valley Academy of Performing Arts.

CHAPTER 36

Communication

by John G. Gage

Music ministry leaders must effectively communicate with their players. A leader must not only communicate detailed plans, but also his or her vision for ministry. Effective communicators must take nothing for granted and must use multiple methods of transmitting information. Communication also implies receiving information and being available and accessible to one's team members for input and dialogue.

There are many ways to communicate effectively and creatively.

• **Use humor.** People tend to remember what amuses them. Whether it is a funny way of saying something, a skit with funny costumes, a clever video, or making fun of oneself in order to make a point, humor is effective.

• **Have orchestra section leader phone/email the members.** If communication needs to be reinforced, section leaders can inform their people. Retreat registration, uniform sales, rehearsal time changes, last-minute schedule adjustments, and urgent prayer requests are all excellent opportunities to utilize lay leadership to inform players. As with all volunteers, one should not abuse the time of section leaders. Their ministry should be reserved for urgent situations.

• **Consistently repeat event promotions.** Special events should be promoted for several weeks and in various ways. In the event of a banquet, retreat, away concert, or other special event that requires 100 percent participation, the orchestra president, the director, and other key leaders should encourage players to be involved. The more often an event is mentioned, the higher the percentage of positive responses.

• **Write letters and cards.** Though postage budgets can be prohibitive, the best method of communication is a group mailout, especially when a written response (officer ballot, commitment form, etc.) is needed. A quantity of information can be mailed. For example, written correspondence works well at officer election time, before major Christmas concert(s), and other major special programs.

• **Create a weekly newsletter or Web page.** This can be a primary method of communication, and one that is very well received. Each "epistle" should be colorful, contain some cartoons or interesting clip art, and full of interesting and informative bits of information, including the rehearsal order for that particular rehearsal. Utilizing a newsletter can assist players in double-checking their music folders, BEFORE rehearsal begins, to assure they have everything they need. Absentees enjoy receiving the newsletter with a personal note. Letting players know that they are missed and giving them the latest information demonstrates concern and compassion.

In the weekly publication to the orchestra, utilize the **METRIC** system of communication:

Motivation. Offer a Scripture verse, a thought about the role of a worship leader, a devotional thought or quote from a recognized Christian author, or a historical perspective of the use of instruments in the Bible.

Encouragement. Recognize player birthdays, special recognitions or honors one may have received, an especially good presentation on a choir accompaniment or orchestra special the preceding week, etc.

Thanks. Express gratitude for outstanding individual effort, their faithfulness, the playing (or singing) of a solo the previous week, etc.

Reminders. Keep members informed of prayer requests, dates to remember, special events, library instructions, appropriate Sunday dress, group policy and procedures, sign-out, etc.

Information. Provide new calendar dates for players, extra rehearsals, schedule, new policies, special orchestra needs, various other dates, times, and places.

Challenge members to a greater level of commitment, to bring their friends to rehearsal, and to understand the message to be conveyed through the special by studying the lyrics to Sunday's anthem, etc., that is provided.

The director may be unable to include every one of these items each week, but within every two-three week period, all six of these devices should appear. Players can work together most effectively when they are well informed.

John G. Gage serves at Valley Baptist Church, Bakersfield, California. His responsibilities include developing and directing an adult orchestra, a big band, and two youth orchestras, arranging for each group, and teaching trumpet in the Valley Academy of Performing Arts.

CHAPTER 37

Developing and Maintaining a Music Library

by Ruth Gage

One of the important ingredients of an effective instrumental music program is developing and maintaining an efficient music library. This will impart to the players a sense of value as they realize conductor preparation, productive use of rehearsal time, less stress and anxiety when performing, and stewardship of the resources God has provided for the ministry.

There are several basic library needs:
- A place that is appropriate for filing the music
- A large workspace (It is beneficial if this is close to the rehearsal room.)
- File cabinets or shelves for storage
- A rack or cabinet for holding the rehearsal folders
- Rehearsal folders (These usually may be obtained from a local music store at no charge.)
- Storage envelopes and supplies (a numbering stamp, a church or school stamp, stamp pad and ink, magic markers, a three-hole punch, tape, and scissors)
- A spiral binding machine with binding combs to bind conductor's scores, and other large documents

Preparation

The first step in organizing a library is devising a system of cataloging and filing each selection. Some groups file all music in consecutive numerical order. Others have a more detailed filing system using prefixes before each number.

Sanctuary **O**rchestra: **SO**100, **SO**101, etc.

Youth **O**rchestra: **YO**100, **YO**101, etc.

Jazz **B**and: **JB**100, **JB**101, **JB**102, etc.

Ensembles: **E**100, **E**101, **E**102, etc.

Solos: **SL**100, **SL**101, **SL**102, etc.

A list of titles should be compiled, including:

- the **composer's name**
- the **arranger**
- whether the piece is **instrumental only** or **an accompaniment** for the choir
- the **grade** or **difficulty level** of the piece
- the **publisher**
- the **ensemble** that will use the piece
- the **instrumentation**
- the **theme** or **subject**

Cards should then be filed or a computer database constructed from that information.

The list should be printed alphabetically, numerically, and topically. This will assist the conductor in planning for rehearsals and performances. The repertoire list should be updated regularly.

As new music arrives, it should be cataloged with the appropriate number before being copied and distributed. The number is usually stamped on the top right-hand corner of each piece if there is enough room. A church or school stamp can be included on the bottom of each piece. Most arrangements give permission to copy enough parts for the purchasing ensemble. This is particularly true if only one part per instrument is provided with the arrangement. If permission is not given, the publisher should be contacted and permission requested and granted before copying. The publisher should also be contacted if the arrangement is changed or adapted in some way.

It is important to keep a set of the originals. These should be marked or stamped in red or some color other than the copies. Some groups file these separately from the duplicated copies, which prevents the originals from being distributed by mistake.

After copies have been made of the new arrangement, the library number should be stamped on the top right-hand corner of the storage envelope, with the title on the top left-hand corner of the envelope, and the arrangement is then ready for filing or distribution. The envelopes can be filed in boxes on a shelf or in file cabinets. They should be filed numerically, making them easily accessible.

Seasonal musicals may best be filed in clearly labeled storage boxes placed in an area that may not be as easily accessible. Special event arrangements are used less frequently, so they may be filed separately.

Rehearsal

1. At least one folder should be provided for every two people in sections with smaller instruments such as clarinet, flute, trombone, and trumpet; one folder for each player in sections like cello, French horn, tuba, and other larger instruments. Percussion will probably need a folder for timpani; one for bells and chimes; and one for suspended cymbal, tambourine, and other non-pitched instruments. (If just one player is available, timpani and suspended cymbal are the most critical parts to have covered. If there are parts for both to play simultaneously, a player from another section may be asked to cover the suspended cymbal part.)

2. Players should leave their rehearsal folder in the storage rack after each rehearsal. This gives the librarians access to organize the folders for the next usage.

3. Players should not be allowed to take rehearsal or performance folders home with them, but extra parts may be provided for personal practice. A "request form" may be provided where each player can select the titles they would like to take home, and it may be prepared for them prior to the next service or rehearsal. Some players may want to receive copies of all music, others may desire one or two specific, especially challenging titles, and some may not be interested in any practice copies.

4. Every instrument should have all pages of every tune for rehearsal in their folder.

5. Every instrument should have a part for every piece in their folder.

6. Every instrument should have a correctly transposed part for every piece.

7. Special care should be taken to make sure that each folder receives the correct part. An alto sax player with a tenor sax part or a trombone 1 player with a trumpet 1 part wastes valuable rehearsal time and is frustrating for the affected musicians. The librarian should be well versed by the director as to which parts can be played by other instruments and which cannot. For example, a baritone can easily read a tenor saxophone part, but should not be given a bass clarinet part.

8. Each selection should be placed in a specific order: either alphabetically, numerically, or in a rehearsal order. All folders should be prepared and stored in a folder rack or some type of cabinet with each instrument labeled for easy access for rehearsal and performance.

9. The music should be taken out of the folders once it has been used and filed in score order or folder order, so that the next time that piece is used it is a simple matter to distribute it correctly.

Performance

The main objective in preparing the music for performance is to make it as convenient as possible for the players. The less "hassle" before and during the service or concert, the easier it will be to focus on the presentation of the music.

1. It seems to work better to have the music placed in three-ring binders. This makes it easier to move from one piece to another in worship packages. In compiling these pieces, preparation should be made for unhurrried page turns. The music can be taped to make page turns smoother. If the part does not have rests at the end of the page, the first two pages can be placed side by side to minimize page turns.

2. When purchasing a hymnal orchestration, a book should be purchased for each stand. If two violins share a stand, then just one violin book needs to be purchased. If four violins share two stands, then two books will be needed. **Books should be purchased even if the arrangements are copied for performance binders.**

3. These folders need to be cleaned out and refiled on a weekly basis. It takes only a short time to empty and refile music regularly. If it is left, it will accumulate in a very short time to become a major task, pieces will not be easily accessible when needed, and parts may be misplaced or defaced.

Some directors prefer to have conductor's scores filed separately from the arrangements in a designated file drawer; others allow the score to be filed with the arrangement. Either option is satisfactory, and is predicated on director preference.

The director should attempt to find and train lay personnel to handle the many library needs as a ministry. If someone is willing to invest time in this area, it will cause rehearsals to flow more smoothly, will ultimately save many precious hours of rehearsal time, and will give the accurate impression that players are valued and worthy of the investment of adequate preparation time.

Ruth Gage serves as Instrumental Ministry Secretary, music copyist, and head instrumental music librarian at Valley Baptist Church, Bakersfield, California, where she also is in charge of the church publication ministry. Ruth earned a Bachelor's in Elementary Education from John Brown University, Siloam Springs, AR, in 1970. Married to John Gage the same year, she has served alongside him in music ministry since that time. In 1982 she helped develop one of the first church orchestra libraries and orchestra folder systems in the country.

CHAPTER 38

Using Technology to Enhance the Instrumental Program:

Computers, Multimedia, and Video

by Larry Brubaker

Advancements in technology and the integration of computers, multimedia, and video into our lives have become almost commonplace. Any instrumental program can be enhanced, whether large of small, with the tools of technology. Computers can be used for writing music, recording digital audio, interactively teaching musical skills, and controlling elements of a performance and many other useful applications. Multimedia and video have great potential for embellishing instrumental performances. The following is a list of ideas for applying the tools of technology.

Computers

Writing music with a computer program has become a standard for the music industry. The software is referred to as notation software. Score pages can be created with multiple methods of input, such as with MIDI keyboards, computer keyboards, note recognition with a microphone, or even a scanner copying existing music and converting it into editable music. Making corrections and changes to the score, creating new transposition parts for any instrument, and printing quality parts on a laser printer make notation software an important tool for any instrumental program. Learning curves vary with notation programs, but most basic functions can be mastered within a short period of time. Standard professional notation programs are recommended, so that compatibility with others is increased and files can be shared more readily.

Recording audio with a computer as digital audio is a method of recording that is replacing the linear, magnetic tape method, like an audiocassette. There are two forms of digital audio—linear and nonlinear. Linear digital audio is when the audio signal is converted to digital information and stored on a digital tape. Examples of this are DAT, ADAT, and DA-88 formats. Nonlinear digital audio is when the audio is converted to digital information and stored on a random access media, such as a computer hard drive, a compact disc, or a mini-disc format. Nonlinear media allows for instant access to any part of the recorded audio without waiting for a tape to rewind or fast forward to the selection. MIDI samplers are also examples of nonlinear player/recorders that recall digital audio, triggered by a MIDI controller.

Nonlinear Media Uses

Using a computer to record multiple tracks of audio can be a valuable tool in an instrumental program. Making recordings of groups for musical evaluation can be very helpful to the director and the players. Recording projects for fund-raising or other purposes can be done affordably with a computer. Productions using click tracks, MIDI sequences, and/or prerecorded audio are a natural fit for the computer. All of these uses require some special equipment and software to maximize the potential.

Multitrack recording with a computer requires special hardware, but the cost of such equipment can be surprisingly affordable. Here is a basic list of requirements:

1. Computer with a current, fast processor
2. At least a 17" monitor
3. A special digital audio card that will allow multitrack recording, a minimum of eight channels of audio simultaneously in and out
4. Special digital audio recording software that works with the digital audio card. Software that integrates a MIDI sequencer with the digital audio is highly recommended.
5. At least one large hard drive, in addition to the computer's main hard drive, that is compatible with the digital audio card and software
6. Mixing board, microphones, and speakers for listening
7. A UPS (uninterrupted power supply) for the computer *(very important)*

Most digital audio software packages will allow you to mix together more tracks of audio than you can record at one time through the audio card, depending on the computer's processing power. For instance, an audio card that will input and output only two channels at a time could be used to make a multitrack recording of any number of tracks with multiple overdubs. The limitation is that on playback, the output will only have two channels available. Having at least eight channels of input/output is preferable.

In live performances that require prerecorded audio to synchronize with live music, computers can make this happen much better than previous methods using linear audio. This nonlinear method provides instant access to any location on the track (great for rehearsal), as well as near-instant start times during the performance. Digital audio software that incorporates MIDI sequencing with digital audio allows for click tracks to be created with the sequencer and the digital audio to be played with the sequence. The musicians listen and play with the click track while the computer plays the audio in synchronization. Here is a step-by-step procedure that illustrates how to create this type of synchronized track.

1. The sequence is first created with measures that match the music and has all the correct tempos and tempo changes programmed.

2. A MIDI keyboard track is created on the sequence for reference when recording the digital audio.

3. Audio tracks are recorded onto the sequence. This can be anything you need for the performance that must be prerecorded, such as vocals, instrument parts, or even count tracks for the director to assist him or her with directing the song through difficult tempo changes, etc.

4. In addition to digital audio tracks, MIDI tracks can also be added to the sequence to play any MIDI module for drums, strings, percussion, and so on.

5. In the live setup, at least the director (and possibly other players) needs to hear the click and any other tracks used to keep with the sequence. The computer operator starts the sequence on cue and everything plays together.

It is important that the computer used for performance is reserved for this use only so that software conflicts are minimized. Using an uninterrupted power supply (UPS) on the computer is an absolute must for reliability.

Another idea for creating sequences would be using the score from a notation program, saving the file as a standard MIDI file (SMF), and importing the file into the sequencer program. By assigning MIDI instruments to the various score parts, the sequencer can play the score as a reference track when recording other audio tracks.

Click tracks and sequences can be made to match an existing recording, such as a CD track, by recording the music as digital audio into the sequencer and then adjusting tempos and measures in the sequence to match the recording. Other audio can then be added, if needed, and the sequence can be used with a click and a live group.

Multimedia and Video

The creative use of multimedia and video during live performances is limited only by the imagination and resources of the director. Many facilities have large image magnification screens that would allow for visual presentation during musical performances. Presentation slides can be used to display the text of an instrumental piece being performed to enhance the congregation's worship experience. Video footage that complements the mood of an instrumental song would be another possible use of the visual technology. When live video cameras are available for image magnification, well-rehearsed close-ups of featured players adds immeasurably to the effect of the performance.

Larry Brubaker is the Minister of Instrumental Music at Prestonwood Baptist Church, Plano, Texas.

The
Christian School
Instrumental
Music Educator

CHAPTER 39

Christian School Bands

*by Jeff Cranfill, Jim Hansford,
Max Cordell, Mel Wilhoit,
and Mark Bailey*

The band director is the leading advocate for instrumental music in the Christian school. With limited amounts of money, students, space, and periods in the school day, the director must be able to justify to the administration, school board, guidance counselors, faculty, parents, and students why music is more than a frill; he must be able to verbalize the reasons why the band program should be included in the regular curriculum of the school. The primary difference between Christian school music education programs and public school programs will be in philosophy. In the public schools, music is taught primarily as a valuable and worthwhile art form that reaches the heart as well as the head. Many references to the nonmusical benefits of music (discipline, cooperation, concentration, thinking skills, etc.) are often pointed out, as well. Although all these things are worthwhile reasons for having music in the schools, they do not address the divine origins of music and how it has been so greatly used by God from Bible times to the present. Psalm 150 commands God's people to use music to praise Him. In Psalm 33:3, the writer instructs musicians to play skillfully to the Lord. In order for people to praise God skillfully with instruments as Psalm 150 proclaims, they must be taught. Instrumental classes provide the means for discovering and developing God-given musical gifts for His glory. The great composers, conductors, and performers of tomorrow are the students of today. If Christian schools do not send out skilled musicians to be the next generation of music leaders and teachers, then future church music ministries will suffer. Students should be held accountable by the director, and encouraged to the high calling of playing for God's glory. The director should see his or her responsibility as twofold: he or she is called to be a conscientious minister to the students, and a responsible educator. The Christian school band program can also be a means of evangelization—presenting the gospel at concerts, and being a light to the world by participation in musical events with public schools. Christian school bands should strive to be salt and light to the community by having students that play and conduct themselves exceptionally well—to the glory of God.

Benefits of Having a Band Program in Christian Schools

Instrumental classes provide hands-on, practical applications of musical concepts. In band classes, students experience vivid examples of how God created instrumental music to impact human emotions. Students will develop a love of quality music as they study and play in band class. Participation in music ensembles is part of a well-rounded musical life, filling the human need for community, and providing a venue for musically talented students to develop their God-given gifts.

An overwhelming amount of existing research shows a strong, positive correlation between the study of music and academic achievement of students. Music also helps to reinforce essential academic skills: analysis, concentration, persistence, listening, cooperation, and teamwork. Howard

Gardner's theory of multiple intelligences lists music as one of the seven. Recognizing the existence of a separate musical intelligence has profound implications for music teachers and learners, including justifying music training for all school children.

Along with musical skills and information, band classes in the Christian school are fertile ground for building character in band students. Students need the responsibility, determination, persistence, diligence, delayed gratification, and patience that are necessary in learning to play an instrument well. These character traits will serve students well for the rest of their lives.

An instrumental director should always be Christlike in interacting with the students, even when strong discipline is required. Band students should know that their director is deeply and sincerely interested in their well-being. Numerous opportunities for ministry will occur, and the Christian school band director must be sensitive to these situations and react accordingly. A director should pray for the students regularly, and during band devotion times encourage them to share prayer concerns in their lives. Having the band pray together as a corporate body will provide strength and unity to the entire program.

School bands help to provide live, student-produced music for school or community functions including concerts, chapel services, parent/teacher meetings, graduation, church services, and athletic events. One strong motivation to develop skilled musicianship is that most colleges will offer sizable scholarships to students who demonstrate these musical skills. The time and money invested in a student's musical training can bring a multitude of rewards.

Lack of funds, qualified teachers, time constraints, and space limitations are excuses that many Christian school administrators use for eliminating an instrumental program. The instrumental music teacher should be a strong advocate for supporting and justifying the validity of a band program in the school. Musical involvement can last for a lifetime!

Motivation

Students may enter band class for any number of reasons—some lofty and some quite ordinary. Whatever their reason for joining, it is the responsibility of the band director to meet the students where they are motivationally and to encourage them to want to improve their musical skills. The director must lead students from being interested in joining the band to voluntarily and consistently striving to meet the set standards for the band class. Instrumental music classes depend on the quality participation of every member in class. External motivators can be used effectively in the early stages of band classes, but the goal is for the students to be internally motivated to consistently give their best effort. Diligence and perseverance are required when learning to play an instrument well.

Colossians 3:23-24 addresses motivation as follows: "Whatever you do, work at it with all your heart, as working for the Lord, not for men, since you know that you will receive an inheritance from the Lord as a reward. It is the Lord Christ you are serving" (NIV). God is worthy of man's best efforts. Band members should do their assigned work to the best of their ability. Much wisdom is needed to meet the needs of all students and to know the best ways to encourage their progress, both musically and spiritually.

Show interest in the lives of students outside of band activities. Go to their games, plays, and other extracurricular activities. Students will be much more willing to work if their director has been available to his or her students.

The director should set high standards for student work and behavior, and those standards need to be communicated clearly and often to the students. They must know that the assigned work is worthwhile. Set goals and present challenges to the band. Difficult assignments give students the opportunity to rise to the occasion, particularly when the assignment presents a challenge just beyond what they can presently do. As students work and accomplish goals, they will be willing to take on more challenges. Success breeds success.

Band students must enjoy their work and their leader. The atmosphere in the band class needs to be focused and well ordered. Vary teaching techniques as much as possible, always seeking innovative ways to present the same concepts. If the band setting is boring or oppressive, students probably will not remain long in the program, and they will accomplish little. Run an organized and efficient class/rehearsal. Students must feel that their time will be well used.

Each person in the band class depends on the other students to learn their music and complete their assignments. The class can only move on to new material when everyone learns the present material successfully. The class must function as a team, with each person doing what it takes to get his or her music learned. Grades can be external motivators in the band class. Some students will be more likely to do what is required if there is a grade attached to their work.

The director should build clear concepts and establish models for musical excellence. Recordings of good musicians performing quality repertoire should be played for the students. Rather than just telling them how to play a particular passage or style, let the students hear an outstanding soloist or ensemble. These aural models can assist students in setting high standards.

Friendly competition can be used in the form of chair auditions. The purpose of the auditions/contests is to motivate the band members to learn their assignments completely and to give each student an opportunity to play individually for the director. In performing groups, chair auditions and challenges exist to help motivate players to improve. Auditions are discussed later in this chapter.

In the early years of band, requiring students to document their practice time for a grade can develop regular practice habits. The purpose of the practice journal is twofold: it reminds the band members to practice, and it can show the students how indispensable regular practice is to their musical growth. Consider requiring young band students to practice at least five days per week for at least 20 minutes each day. The students reinforce information assimilated in class when they practice at home. Practice journals can be graded in class weekly to see that enough practice is being accomplished. It is important that parents be required to validate the practice log by signing it. This ensures that some parental supervision is being accomplished at home.

Provide extra opportunities for musical growth. Use solos and ensembles wherever possible. Encourage students to participate in church orchestras, clinic bands, and community bands, and to audition for All-State Bands. Private lessons will also help students play better and enjoy playing more.

Students are often more motivated when they feel a sense of ownership in the group. Let students be involved as much as possible in the operations of the band—such as taking attendance, leading in prayer, giving devotions, managing equipment and uniforms, and taking care of the band room. Students who are good players can assist weaker players.

Awards for achievement and service in band are appropriate and very beneficial. Publicly recognize efforts and achievements that are valuable to the band program. A yearly band awards banquet is great for building morale and motivation.

The director can develop awards or use national awards that are available, such as the John Philip Sousa Award. If possible, allow the students to vote on who should receive certain awards. Some possible band awards might include a Director's Award for the best all-around band member, a Band Letter, Most Improved Player Award, Most Outstanding Musician (one per grade), or a Character Award that honors certain character traits demonstrated by an outstanding student.

Discipline

During the band class, the time should be spent learning music. Any behavior that distracts from the task at hand must be dealt with immediately in love and firmness. Make sure that the students know what is expected of them, and the consequences of failing to meet those expectations. In order to be effective, discipline must be consistent. When students know that the director will not settle for less than their best, they will be more likely to work diligently. Effective discipline has:

1. the authority that makes it advisable to obey. Correct offenses with consistency and fairness.

2. the wisdom that makes it reasonable to obey. Students should understand what is expected and why. Expectations must be reasonable.

3. the love that makes it desirable to obey. Students must know, respect, and trust the director, and the director must reciprocate that esteem and trust.

Praise admirable efforts and accomplishments publicly. A positive class atmosphere is conducive to a good work ethic. Correct or discipline students in private as much as possible. The goal of discipline is to encourage self-discipline, not cause embarrassment. However, a group rebuke may be appropriate on occasion.

Curriculum Development and Program Structure

Instrument pedagogy and teaching methods in Christian schools are the same as in most any teaching situation. The goals of music educators as stated by the National Association for Music Education (www.menc.org) should be known by the director, and the teaching objectives of the band program must be designed and structured around them. Practically all programs of quality start with a good recruitment program in the spring, a good working relationship with a music dealer, a thorough digestion of a method book for two or three years, along with a good mixture of quality concert music. A graded band program in a K–12 school might be structured as follows:

- Beginning Band: 1st year (4th or 5th grade)
- Elementary Band—2nd year (5th or 6th grade)
- Middle School—Grades 6 - 8
- Junior High School—Grades 7 - 9
- High School—Grades 9 - 12
    Training Band *(for beginning or less-experienced high school players)*
    Concert Band *(auditioned high school performance group)*

Beginning Band Students should not be grouped on a daily basis with experienced players. It is extremely difficult to meet the educational needs of both beginners and experienced players in the same class. Those with experience will become bored and it is likely that many will drop out of the program. Poor instruction during the first six weeks of a beginner's history can be the single most limiting factor in the student's playing career. Eldon Janzen, in his book *Band Director's Survival Guide* (out of print but available from Janzen), gives four reasons why beginners drop out after the first three months of study:

1. lacks necessary musical apitude
2. receives poor instruction
3. child's time and energies are too diversified
4. lacks encouragement by the parent

This trial period is critically important and it behooves the band director to work diligently to capture student interest during this beginning stage.

Since it is a scheduling impracticality to have separate classes for each instrument, the next best option is to group students by instrument family: woodwinds, brass, and percussion. The method book chosen for class instruction will determine the skills and information learned and the sequence in which it is presented. Today there are an abundance of excellent and visually attractive beginning band method books using state-of-the-art technology, including compact discs with each instrumental book. Choose your method book carefully and be prepared to supplement if needed. Following are recommended goals for the first-year player:

- Proper assembly of the instrument
- Correct posture
- Proper hand positions
- Well-produced tone quality (embouchure and tonal concept)
- Understanding of proper breath control and support
- Three basic articulations: regular, *legato,* and *staccato*
- Rhythmic reading—whole notes through eighth notes, plus dotted quarter and eighth notes, and cut time
- Scale proficiency within the range of notes covered

Percussion students should play snare drum, timpani, beginning mallet percussion, bass drum, and cymbals, along with being introduced to the care

Middle School Bands should utilize a mixture of technical exercises and full band arrangements. These advancing students should address the following skills:

- Improving tone (flutes and oboes should be adding vibrato)
- Increased range
- Technical dexterity (motor skills of fingers and tongue)
- Rhythmic accuracy and playing more complex rhythm patterns; accurate subdivision
- Increased endurance on the instrument
- Learning all 12 scales, and some of them two octaves (depending on range).
- Increased ability to play independent parts
- Double tonguing for flutes and brasses
- Blend and balance (should be carefully addressed with maturing tone)

> **High School Band Students** should be mastering the following skills:
> - Mature tone development in all ranges
> - Control and dexterity
> - Excellent intonation
> - Interpretation of style and dynamic control
> - Sensitive musical phrasing
> - Increased endurance
> - Effective blend and balance
> - A working knowledge of basic musical terms
> - Scales in all keys, major and minor, two or more octaves, at faster tempi

and use of other auxiliary percussion. Instruction books on basic rudiments should be included the first year, and supplemented with additional snare drills as the percussion players improve.

Sight-reading should be included as early as possible, at an appropriate level for the group. The more reading done, the more proficient and confident the student will become. The most important concept for any instrumentalist is good tone. At all levels, tone production should be a major part of the curriculum emphasis. Playing in tune is closely related to playing with a good tone. Discussions on intonation can be incorporated as soon as the students consistently play with a good sound.

As the students learn more notes and gain more musical independence, the director can include full-band arrangements, whether from the book or as separate pieces. With full-band arrangements come great opportunities to introduce music theory, form, and music history. Band classes do not often permit long discussions of these issues, but they can be woven into the curriculum very effectively. It is recommended that the reader consult the Robert Garofalo book, *Instructional Designs,* mentioned in the list at the end of this chapter. MENC also has several publications dealing with the comprehensive musicianship approach in the rehearsal hall.

Hopefully high school players have also learned about the responsibility, diligence, patience, and persistence necessary to learn to do anything well. High school is also when student leadership becomes very important to the motivation of the band. Remember: as students get older they will not necessarily get musically wiser. It is the director's responsibility to set high standards and nurture and encourage his students to aspire to those high artistic goals.

Assessment and Evaluation

If musical objectives are important enough to teach, and if this teaching results in observable student outcomes, measurement is possible and necessary. Band students at all levels need evaluation from the teacher. Evaluation is the process of making judgments based on collected data, and measurement is the process of collecting that data. The best measurement tools available to the instrumental music teacher are the ears of the students and the teacher. Quality teaching depends on objective measurement, and two vital components of that are diagnosis and prescription.

A variety of measurement tools are available to the instrumental teacher, one of the simplest being the rating scale in the form of the checklist or additive scale where the list contains a series of statements that the teacher rates as accomplished satisfactorily or unsatisfactorily by the student. This system

works especially well with scales, assigned sections or exercises from a band method book or a concert work, or any technical performance challenge. Points may be awarded for each accomplished task. Students may also be given points based on the quality of the performance, rated on a scale ranging from poor to superior (for example, poor-1 point; average-3 points; superior-5 points). Other testing options include a variety of teacher-constructed exams, such as multiple choice, fill-in-the-blanks, and matching tests.

Teachers should report musical achievement regularly to the students and their parents. A simple letter grade is usually insufficient. Proper reporting should include an evaluation of performance skill, a diagnosis of the problem areas, and some assistance or advice to encourage improvement. A separate form to report instrumental achievement in addition to the regular academic report card is advisable. The bottom line is that student achievement is a reflection on the overall success of the instrumental program. It is also advisable that class attendance and subjective assessment of attitudes be reported separately and not included as part of the achievement grade. Attendance should not be the primary source of the grade in an instrumental class. It is risky, at best, to insinuate that showing up for class is really more important than what is being learned and demonstrated musically.

The grading system needs to promote desired behaviors and discourage undesirable behaviors. Grades can be effective communicators of progress in band classes. Always have the system of assessment approved by the administration, and be sure that the system is consistent with school policy.

For elementary or middle school band, each student earns a daily grade which includes both subjective (the teacher's personal discretionary judgment) and the objective (measured by testing in a just and equitable manner against a standard). The average of his/her daily grade becomes the student's grade for the term.

Playing Tests, Exams

Since the main goal of band classes is learning to play an instrument, playing tests/auditions are necessary and should occur frequently. As with any other tests, playing tests should include an assignment to be performed later, either in class, privately for the instructor, or by recording it for later review by the teacher. Measurable objectives should, at least, include the following:

- Purity of tone
- Correct notes
- Accurate rhythms
- Proper articulation
- Appropriate dynamics
- Proper phrasing
- Progress (in some cases)

With beginning band, a regular reporting procedure more often than the semester grade report will pay valuable dividends to your program and keep the students and parents apprised of the observable progress of their children. Design appropriate musical and instrument technique objectives by which you can measure each student's progress. Grades should clearly reflect specific achievement levels based on these objectives.

The nature of this chapter does not permit more in-depth discussion of assessment but this writer encourages the reader to review Chapter 7 in the Stanley Schlueter book, *A Sound Approach to Teaching Instrumentalists,* as listed in the resource list at the end of this chapter.

Scheduling

In the elementary and middle school band classes, the more often the class meets, the more progress the class will make. With chapel sessions one day a week, elementary band could meet three days per week for 35 or 40 minutes for each class. Some directors endorse 40 minutes, five days a week, as optimum for a band rehearsal. The larger the class, the longer the time needed to effectively work with them. One possible method of keeping band students from missing academic class time to come to band, and to give the elementary classroom teachers some break time, is to have general music class and the band class meet at the same time. All of the students in that grade would then choose between the two classes. The same idea can be applied in middle school, where middle school band and middle school chorus meet the same period. Often the schedule does not have enough slots to put them in different periods. If the middle school operates on a period schedule, then middle school band and chorus would probably need to meet five days per week.

By high school, the schedule can hopefully afford to put band and chorus during different periods, five days per week. A high school training band class can meet some other period, also five days per week. In the high school, if a block schedule is in place, request a first period that meets 50 minutes each day and is not on the block plan. Periods two through seven could meet every other day for 90 minutes. This plan has worked well for some and provided the time needed to instruct the students. (An outstanding book by Richard Miles and Larry Blocker addressing block scheduling, music classes, and the inherent problems and solutions is listed in the resource list at the end of this chapter.)

In many Christian school settings, the same students often participate in many different activities, including music, athletics, student government, missions groups, etc. In most situations, schedule extra rehearsals for high school band and ensembles before school rather than after. With fewer students to go around, schedules that accommodate as many activities as possible, without conflict, encourage students to be involved without having to choose between band and other interests.

Many times, the high school band and chorus classes are the largest classes during the school day. They are also the classes that have the greatest dependence on having enough students enrolled. Encourage the school guidance counselor to include band and chorus classes in working out student schedules. With growing demands for credits toward graduation and the increased popularity of block scheduling, music classes often depend on help from the guidance counselor to have enough students.

Instrumentation

Beginners/Elementary Band Students should select an instrument with the guidance of the instrumental director. All too often, a student will choose whatever instrument is popular, rather than what they are physically suited for or what the band needs to fill instrumentation needs. There needs to be a balance of all these factors in determining which instrument a beginner will play.

Oftentimes beginning band classes in Christian schools are fairly small, even with a large percentage of students per grade level in band. Regardless of class size, a balanced instrumentation is always desirable. Christian schools often have the challenge of a large turnover in the student body from year to year. Develop an instrumentation chart for each grade to help decide where the recruiting effort needs to be for beginning classes. Try not to overload a section with any one instrument so that balance is likely to be maintained in years to come, hopefully even with attrition.

Beginning band classes usually include the following instruments:

- Flutes
- Clarinets
- E♭ Alto Saxophones
- Trumpets
- French Horns in F
- Trombones
- Baritones
- Percussion
- Electric Bass (Some band method books include this.)

If the students and equipment are available, consider beginning students on "color" instruments (French horn, tuba, double reeds, low woodwinds). Directors must not depend on gaining these players from other schools or waiting a couple of years to secure players. Plan ahead.

Middle School/Jr. High Band. Middle school is a good time to switch students to other instruments, at the discretion of the director, to complete the instrumentation of the middle and high school bands. Switching to another instrument can be discussed with the individual at the end of the preceding school year, and students learning new instruments can get summer lessons to prepare them for the next school year. Reassigning instruments can be particularly helpful in filling holes in instrumentation left by students who are graduating or transferring, or to balance overloaded sections of the band. Compatible choices for instrument transfers include the following:

- trumpet to baritone or tuba,
- saxophone to oboe or bassoon,
- flute to oboe or bassoon,
- clarinet to bass clarinet,
- trumpet to French horn.

High School. Ideally, a graded band program from elementary through high school can plant and grow a fairly balanced instrumentation in the high school band. An acceptable instrumentation might look as follows:

- Piccolo (1)
- Flutes (6-8)
- Oboes (1-2)
- B♭ Clarinets (8-10)
- Bass Clarinets (1-2)
- Contra alto and/or contra bass clarinet (1)
- E♭ Alto Saxophones (3-5)
- Tenor Saxophones (1-2)
- E♭ Baritone Saxophone (1)
- Trumpets/Cornets (6-8)
- F Horns (3-5)
- Trombones (4-6)
- Baritones/Euphoniums (2-3)
- Tubas (2-3)
- Percussion (5-6) [snare drum, bass drum, cymbals, mallets, tympani, auxiliary instruments]

Typical bands might be as follows:
- small band (30-35 students),
- medium sized band (40-55 students),
- large ensemble (60+ students).

For pep bands or marching bands, a slightly different instrumentation is required. Several of the flute players could play piccolo (if instruments are available). Double reeds and lower clarinets would probably play clarinet, one of the saxophones, or even percussion.

Instrument Substitution. Many, if not most, Christian school bands are small in number and usually have a limited instrumentation. Much of the band music available today accommodates groups with more limited instrumentation—alto saxophone cues for French horn, trombone, baritone, tenor saxophone, all doubling, and convertible bass lines which include any bass instrument in the band.

The director may consider approaching students to change to other needed instruments, or announce that a particular instrument is needed. Students are often the best recruiters—just by word of mouth among their fellow students. Be willing to start beginners in any grade, if at all possible. With tutoring from the director before or after school, or private instruction from a qualified teacher, a willing student can become a contributing player in a surprisingly short time. Pianists can be quickly converted to many of the percussion instruments. A synthesizer, or even a piano, can fill in many missing parts.

Literature Selection

Christian school bands have the freedom and privilege to draw from a great wealth of music, both sacred and secular. To be sure, one mission of the Christian school band program is to help the school family to know and love great sacred music. Settings of sacred music of all styles and time periods should be includ-

ed in band rehearsals and performances. Another mission of bands in Christian schools is to raise a standard of quality music in the school and community. Great secular music should also be included in the work of Christian school bands. All of God's creation declares His greatness (see Psalm 19:1). Since God created music, and God created composers of music, then He is glorified when groups play great music well. There is a great body of band literature that contains original works for band, song arrangements, transcriptions, marches, and much more. Directors should use every appropriate tool available to teach band students to play, understand, and love God's artistry in music.

Selecting literature for the band and other organizations in the instrumental music department can be a difficult task at times. Although a great deal of music is available, the following criteria must be kept in mind.

1. Is the music available and in print? Sometimes directors will hear a piece on an old promotional recording from another group and, upon investigation, find the piece is out of print. Marching band tunes particularly go out of print rather quickly. Selections can sometimes be borrowed from other schools or a custom arrangement can be made. More and more championship bands seem to be using custom arrangements. Sometimes a search on the Internet can produce results. J. W. Pepper (www.jwpepper.com) has a discussion group that one can log onto for requests such as this. Other resources will be listed at the end of this chapter.

2. Does the selection fit the band? The director of band and choral groups must know their students' strengths and weaknesses in order to select appropriate literature. Consider carefully the range of the parts, the tempo of the notes, the instrumentation required to perform the piece authentically, the key relationships, the complexity of the rhythms, the length of the selection (endurance could be a problem), and the overall musicianship required to perform the piece. This is not to say that everything must be currently within the grasp of the group before a selection is chosen. There are times when a director will choose to introduce a piece to present new challenges.

Most Christian schools will not have the good fortune of a well-balanced instrumentation, which may require some editing and minor rewriting. The director or arranger must use common sense and good judgment, however, when editing parts. The goal should be to write a weak or missing part into another instrument that has a similar sound or timbre and plays in the same range. For example, baritone and trombone parts can be easily interchanged, horn and sax parts can be interchanged, and the muted trumpet can replace the oboe. If one is missing percussion players, other instrumentalists will often be glad to give up their instrument to occasionally play a bass drum, mallet, or auxiliary part. Rudimentary trained percussion players should normally play snare drum parts, however.

Music can often be slightly simplified without doing damage to the piece. One must be careful and sensitive not to cross the ethical line of copyright infringement and negate the original intent of the composer or arranger. Ultimately, the director must decide if the advantages of editing a work outweigh the option of finding a more appropriate work for the ensemble. Directors should consult publishers about excessively edited pieces in order to avoid copyright violations.

Many sources are available for obtaining appropriate band repertoire. Most state band organizations have a required music list that must be used for a festival. Festival literature lists are excellent in locating what the experts believe to be high-quality music for bands. The Christian Instrumentalists and Directors Association has a listing of sacred instrumental music that is published every few years. (Contact David Smith: despub@greatlakes.net.) Directors will also find a wealth of material at state and national music conventions such as the National Association for Music Education or regional band and orchestra clinics. Distibutors of instrumental music have catalogs available from multiple publishers. Pay particular attention to the books for beginners and intermediates that are collections of previously published single works. These are a good value for the money. Music may be ordered from some companies "on approval." This is a very valuable service since the most expensive music is the music bought but never played. Directors should try to get on the mailing list of as many publishers as possible to receive free promotional recordings. These are invaluable in hearing the new music and making judgments before ordering. State music associations have graded music lists for their festivals, a valuable resource of titles that have been selected by a committee as literature of artistic merit. *The Instrumentalist* magazine gives a review of new music each month and occasionally will feature an article analyzing a standard or contemporary band work of varying difficulty levels. The Eileen Fraedrich book on elementary band directing, listed at the end of this chapter, has superb chapters on elementary band music and solo and ensemble recommendations, as well as many other relevant subjects.

When selecting and purchasing music, directors should have some good warm-up and technique books in their libraries to prepare embouchures and help with sight-reading skills. (For additional information regarding literature and musical merit please refer to the Conducting chapter (Chp. 2), and also consult the resource list at the end of this chapter.)

Organization and Administration of a Band Program
Audition Procedures

The placement of students in "chair order" in an ensemble can be formidable to the students, but is often necessary to distribute parts fairly. Unless a director wishes to rotate parts and have no chair placement system, it will be necessary to hear the students play and assign parts based on ability. The reason for this is rather simple. Generally, the first parts are higher and more technically challenging, so the stronger, more-mature players will likely be assigned those parts.

Younger groups can be placed at the beginning of the year by simply having everyone play an exercise from the method book or other assigned piece. All like instruments should have the same music. The director can then post a list of the seating order but should explain that all parts and people are important.

Students should always feel that there is an opportunity to move up in the section. Post a challenge sheet and set up a system for challenges. One should consider a mandatory waiting period between challenges so that students aren't challenging every day and wasting valuable class time. Another possibility is to have a certain day set aside for challenges, or not have challenges at all and just reseat every couple of weeks if the director observes a change in playing ability. Sometimes it is advisable to have a piece where the lower chair musician plays the higher part and the first chair musician plays the lower parts. In beginning band, it is often wise not to have chairs at all.

If a director uses pieces where each instrument group is on the same part there is really no need for chairs. More-advanced beginner music usually has parts, however, and the director must devise a way to distribute them. In the advanced groups, seating should be set based on final exams at the end of each semester. Students should feel that their seating is based on ability rather than just seniority. The opportunity should be given to challenge, but it should be an after-school or class evaluation, not a public kind of show down. The advanced students should understand that at festivals, competitions, concerts, etc., no one really cares who's first, second, or third. The judges want to hear all the parts and experience a good ensemble sound. Distribute strong players throughout the section for proper balance. Lower parts normally need more players for proper balance. The pyramid concept of balance is utilized as follows: two first clarinets, three second clarinets, and four third clarinets.[1] Remember: Proper balance and blend is the key to good intonation.

It is generally beneficial to hear students new to the school play before assigning them to a band (unless they are beginners). Sometimes the number of years that a student has been playing in the band does not always indicate his or her ability. Listen to the child play and place him in the appropriate group based solely on his or her ability.

Recruiting and Retention

The lifeblood of the band is recruiting and retention. There will always be some attrition from year to year. In fact, research shows that only about one-half of the students who start band in the sixth grade will remain in the program through graduation. The key to success is to minimize the impact of these losses by having a strong feeder program. In most Christian schools the band director will teach at all levels from beginners through high school and therefore will be able to control his own feeder program.

Generally, all beginners should be given an opportunity to join beginning band with a few exceptions. If the director begins band in the 5th grade, the 4th graders should be given a musical aptitude test to determine their ability to discriminate pitches and rhythms. The Selmer Music Guidance Survey has been used for many years as an indication of basic music skills of prospective band recruits. Although it can give some guidance as to how a student may perceive pitch or discriminate between rhythm patterns, it is not a valid, long-term indicator of serious musical aptitude. One interested in testing at this level must consult the tests of Edwin  Gordon and other recognized scholars. Scholarly research shows that musical aptitude and strong academics are the most valid predictors of long-term success in the school instrumental program and beyond. One must strive to encourage and recruit students who tend to fit this profile without excluding other students who demonstrate a strong interest and a seriously cooperative spirit. Many fine band students come from a background of average academic performance and musical talent but love the band and contribute greatly to its success. Many of these students will serve on local school boards in the future and may help determine the success or failure of school music programs. A positive band experience for these students is vital to the health of our profession and to the arts in general. Another aspect to consider is discipline. Students who struggle with self-control will have trouble being successful in a band class. A high level of personal discipline and self-control is mandatory for a beginning band student. Disruptive behavior makes beginning band class and other effective ensemble rehearsals impossible. Students who fit this profile should be given a minimal amount of time to control themselves or be encouraged to find an activity, other than band, that they enjoy.

The beginning program must be promoted heavily. Elementary music teachers should begin familiarizing the students with the instruments as early as the second grade, and flutophones, recorders, or other appropriate pre-band instruments can be introduced in the third and fourth grades. This will often spark an interest in the students and give them a feel for playing wind instruments. A concert by the advanced band or a visiting group for all 4th, 5th, and 6th graders will further generate interest. A great motivational tool is to have students conduct while the band plays a march. The students love it and the audience has a good time watching all the odd variations. A flyer should be given to the 5th- and 6th-grade students advertising a meeting for parents and students in which students can try out the instruments. The flyer also includes an enrollment form that the students can return to their teacher. Near the time of the concert (within a day or two), it is good to test the 4th graders with a musical aptitude survey and determine who should receive an invitation to join next year's 5th-grade band. In addition to the concert, it is a good idea to bring each grade into the band room and give a demonstration with the current beginning or intermediate band, or show a promotional video, several of which are available through instrument manufacturers.

At the evening recruitment meeting for the students and parents, have a short concert by the current beginning band and then share with parents the opportunities in the band. Explain to the parents about the rental program ("rent to lease") that is made available by many local music stores, and answer any questions that they might have. Although no one should be forced to use a specific dealer, and several reputable companies should be invited to display instruments, it is a good idea to develop a special business relationship with at least one dealer. Dealers will often give practice cards and folders at no charge and provide other perks throughout the school year. Never consider accepting a commission on instruments sold to your students. Not only is it unethical, it can provide the groundwork for legal problems. After an explanation of the program, students should be given an opportunity to play on the instruments. Make a special effort to really promote the instruments that the ensemble needs and say less about the more popular instruments that students will naturally select. Use students from the advanced band or college students to assist in the selection process. The director should look at the child's mouth and teeth, the size of his or her hands and arms, and keep an eye on instrumentation when making suggestions to the students. If a child has trouble getting a sound after several attempts encourage him or her to try something else. All prospective drummers should be tested for rhythm recall and coordination with the hands and feet. Students who cannot play back simple rhythm patterns should not be allowed to start on percussion. Students should submit a form signed by the parents if they wish to be in the band, and then submit a list to the office for scheduling. The school should supply larger instruments such as the French horn, baritone, and tuba. If a band particularly needs low brass, consider having the school purchase several trombones and rent them out for a flat yearly fee. Students who cannot afford an instrument will sometimes play a school instrument and become a fine asset to the program.

Keeping students in band is often a greater challenge than initially recruiting them. Once a child has enrolled in band, it is the responsibility of the director to make the class fun and exciting so that the child has a desire to continue. Some creative motivational techniques are to play enjoyable music with the students, to schedule frequent concerts for the students to observe, and to treat the students kindly and with respect. One should have lots of positive contact with the parents and try to resolve scheduling problems with the guidance counselor. Meaningful rewards, such as band letters, medals, trophies, and scholarships (for summer study) help students feel that they are appreciated and needed.

One word of caution is in order about retention. All directors feel a certain personal loss if one or more of their better students announce that they are not going to be in band anymore. In many cases, the director has been the sole musical pedagogue for these students. Although a director may feel a keen sense of loss, directors are paid to do a job, and if they have done it to the best of their ability such situations should not be taken personally. Building good instrumentation and planning for attrition from the beginning band on up will prevent bands from being debilitated if they lose their only tuba or French horn.

Developing Student Leadership

The school band program provides fertile ground for developing student leadership. These positions should be clearly spelled out in the band manual that is made available to every student on the first day of class. Each advanced band should have, as a minimum, the equivalent of a president, vice-president, and secretary. These students, often called the band council, serve as student representatives of the band and assist with such tasks as fund-raising, roll checking (always verify and double-check for legal reasons), maintaining bulletin boards, cleaning the rehearsal hall, and so forth. Meetings should be held regularly with the officers to get their feedback as to how things seem to be progressing with the band. Being open to hearing student perspectives makes for a healthy student-teacher working relationship and ensures the student leaders that their opinions are vital to the overall operation of the band. Other jobs where students can assist include: librarians, publicity managers (how about a band Web page?), section leaders, equipment managers, stage setup crew chiefs, and after-performance cleanup. (Sample job descriptions appear at the end of this chapter in the section titled "Band Organization.")

A leadership class should be held in the spring in which all section leaders learn the principles of leadership. Topics covered can deal with peer relationships, marching fundamentals, music fundamentals, reading a drill chart, and conducting. These sessions help students become assistant directors and enable them to assist with sectionals and drill sessions. There is an outstanding leadership and motivational speaker who is available to give workshops to school band members. Dr. Tim Lautzenhauser is a former college band director who has developed a superb program of leadership and motivational lectures and activities that relate well to the school-band world. He stays very busy with his speaking engagements and must be scheduled far in advance.

The drum major of the marching band holds the most influential position of student leadership in the band. He or she must be thoroughly trained before taking over this responsibility. There are numerous camps available during the summer to train drum majors. All interested students should have some training sessions during the leadership classes. Students should be required to direct the band, demonstrate outstanding marching skills, and demonstrate teaching skills as part of the audition process. The drum major can serve as the student conductor for concert season, or other interested students can be recruited. The student conductor position can serve as a great training ground for aspiring directors and can provide a substitute conductor when the director has to miss a class and a nonmusician is hired as a substitute teacher for the day.

Seating Arrangements

Setup for the band will depend greatly on the kind of space that is available. With beginners it is recommended that they be spread out so instrument cases can be left at the chair and the director can supervise instrument assembly at the beginning of class and disassembly at the end of the class period. Young students congregating in an instrument storage area to replace instruments can result in damaged equipment and discipline problems. Also, with beginners there should be ample room for the teacher to walk through the setup and observe students and make on-the-spot corrections. Often in this situation, a simple seating arrangement with the chairs in two or three straight rows will suffice. If the beginning band class is so large that a traditional semicircular setup is required, then leave a few aisles through the seating arrangement allowing freedom of movement by the teacher. Do not immobilize yourself on a stool behind a podium for the duration of a class.

There are numerous seating arrangements that are practical for the middle school or high school band. Each director must develop an arrangement that is suitable for his or her use, based on the specific instrumentation available. In general, the flutes, clarinets, and oboes tend to be grouped toward the front; the saxophones, trumpets, trombones, baritones, and tubas near the middle and back; with the percussion normally being placed behind the band. Horns can be placed near the middle of the setup or at the outside on the conductor's left with bells pointing toward the audience. The director's concept of balance and blend play an essential part in the desired or preferred seating arrangement. On the next page are some typical seating arrangements.

Equipment Needs and Strategies for Procurement

Obtaining instruments and equipment can be a great challenge. The more developed the band program, the more instruments and equipment needed. Administrators must be made aware of the continuing needs of a growing instrumental program. A marching band program, even in a small school, can require an immense investment in instruments, equipment, and uniforms. Frequently, school executives do not have a clear understanding of the requirement for annual maintenance on instruments and the expendable nature of certain percussion accessories. A program for regular replacement and repair must be in place to maintain instrumental equipment at an acceptable playing level.

Most band students should purchase their own instruments. Flutes, clarinets, alto saxophones, trumpets, trombones, and snare drums are available for rental from most music stores, with rent being applied to the purchase price. Some schools provide the larger, more expensive, or "color" instruments (piccolo, double reeds, bass clarinets, tenor and baritone saxophones, French horns, baritones, tubas, Sousaphones, mallet instruments, possibly marching percussion, and timpani).

All band classes need additional equipment, as well. Chairs for each player should permit proper playing posture and position. Music stands are essential, and available in a wide price range. Folding stands are inexpensive, and may be a good option for beginning programs if budget constraints are a reality. Sturdy music stands (black stands) are more expensive, but will last for many years with proper care. For large classes

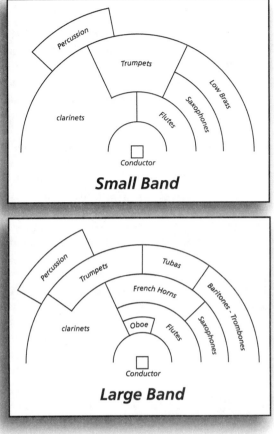

Small Band

Large Band

(groups with more than 2 rows) the director will need a podium (platform) on which to stand. A standard podium of about 3 to 4 feet square and 7 to 10 inches high will suffice, depending on the size of the ensemble.

All band equipment and instruments should be permanently labeled as band property. Complete and accurate inventories, including the serial numbers of school instruments, should be maintained. The purchase of instruments and equipment should be planned to meet the eventual needs of the band program as it grows. Keep instruments, equipment, and rehearsal facilities in good condition. High deductible fees may discourage instrument insurance by the school, but the parents of band students should consider registering student instruments against theft or damage on a homeowner policy.

The first school instruments likely to be needed for purchase are orchestra bells, a bass drum, and a suspended cymbal. Crash cymbals, timpani (26" and 29"; then add 23" and 32" respectively), xylophone, chimes, and other percussion instruments will be eventually needed. The instrumental director should develop a good working relationship with a local music store. When store owners know that the director will send business their way (rentals, purchases, and repairs), they are likely to give discounts or set up payment plans on new instruments for the school instrumental program.

Occasionally, purchasing new instruments is not possible, especially when beginning a school program. Music stores and catalog music companies often sell used instruments. Quality used instruments can be less expensive and of higher quality than economy-line new instruments. Check the classified ads in area newspapers and music journals for good values in purchasing needed instruments. Pawn shops, flea markets, and yard sales can also be good sources for instrument purchase. The band director, a qualified private teacher, or a skilled instrument repairperson should examine the used instrument and approve the purchase. With the approval of the administration, publicize the needs of the band program to the school family. People may have instruments at home that they will loan or donate to eager band students. Another potential source for used instruments is local public school systems. At times, public schools may have surplus instruments they may be willing to sell or loan. Do not be afraid to buy instruments in need of repair, if they are repairable.

Support for the Band Program/Communication with...

Parents. Band parents must be kept well informed as to what is happening in the band program as a whole, as well as reports of how the band student is doing in class. Since many band students are dependent on parents for transportation to rehearsals and performances, make sure the parents know what is planned well in advance. Often students will wait until the last minute to notify parents,

which at best causes stress in their family, and at worst will cause the student to miss a rehearsal. Student discipline, attitude, or musical problems are more effectively solved with parents and teacher working together. For that to happen, there must be good communication between parents and the director.

Keep all communication as positive and optimistic as possible, even when making needs known. Broadcast the successes and accomplishments of the band students often. Keep a positive attitude about the program yourself. The rest of the school and community need to know all the positive things concerning the band program.

Administration. The band program will only prosper to the degree that the school administration supports the program. Keep the principal well informed of the band's activities. When needs arise, go to the principal with ideas and proposals to meet the need, and always be prepared to provide persuasive justification. Do your homework and have your requests in some type of priority order with accurate cost estimates. The director's ideas will be more readily adopted when the administration knows of his or her commitment to the prosperity of the entire school, rather than just the band program. Nothing can set a more conducive atmosphere for a postive meeting with the principal than having the reputation of being a team player.

Faculty. Keep lines of communication open with other faculty members. All of the teachers are working together to educate students. Do not take students out of other classes for band events except on rare occasions when absolutely necessary. If a student needs to miss another class for a band event, communicate to the teacher well in advance, and ensure that the students follow up on any missed assignments. Show support to the faculty for other school programs. Communicate to the faculty also that the band members must attend band class. Band is a hands-on participation class, a team effort, and progress depends on having all of the students present. When problems arise, communicate with the other teacher or the administration. Always refrain from criticizing other teachers, students, administrators, or parents in front of the students.

School Staff. When the band needs help from the school office or custodial staff, respectfully communicate the needs well in advance. Always show gratitude for the assistance of other faculty and administrators. There is a great deal of work for the school support staff, and your congenial and appreciative attitude will go a long way in establishing an affirmative relationship with school staff personnel.

Parent/Booster Organizations

A booster club can be one of the greatest assets to a band program. The booster club not only functions as a fund-raising organization, but as a parent support group for band trips and activities. The band booster club should be organized with a constitution and bylaws that outline the purpose and structure of the organization. Most booster clubs have a president, vice-president, secretary, and treasurer. To be an official tax-exempt organization, some states will require the group to complete some legal paperwork and register through the office of the Secretary of State. The organization should carry a separate account (two-signature requirement is advisable) at a local bank. Accurate financial records should be kept, and a complete accounting of transactions should be made available to the school on a monthly basis. An annual audit by a third party is recommended.

The parents who attend the booster club meetings provide a pool of people who can help with fund-raising projects, concessions, chaperoning trips, bus driving, stage and field setup, refreshments, uniform assignments, and many other jobs that would be nearly impossible for the director to do alone. Advertise the meetings at least a week in advance and send notices home with the band students. The booster meetings can be used to inform parents of special needs and projects, and can also be an avenue for the children to perform. Have a different band perform at each booster meeting and watch the attendance swell! At the meetings there should be a reading of the minutes, a treasurer's report, old business, new business, and items to effectively administrate the business of the organization. Normal parliamentary procedure should be followed. The director should review the upcoming schedule and activities. If possible, there should be some type of entertainment and refreshments, and the meetings should be kept under an hour and be conducted in a positive, enthusiastic manner. Try not to limit the discussion to the activities of the advanced band or marching band, otherwise the beginning and intermediate parents will not feel the need to attend.

One important function of the booster club is the handling of miscellaneous money. Money that the director collects for trips, uniform cleanings, shoes, band shirts, etc., should be put into a special account and carefully recorded. Always encourage the parents to send checks, not cash. The band director should log in the money and then give it to the booster treasurer for deposit as soon as possible. Try not to store money in the band office. Use the school's safe or get a safe for the band. The treasurer should be a trusted parent with some bookkeeping skills. He or she should be able stop by the band room often to pick up money and leave checks if bills need to be paid. Funds disbursement should be made at the direction of the full booster organization or the officers. Some items will be a yearly expense that will be normal and will not require full club approval. Items that the director wishes to purchase that are not a routine expense should be approved and voted on by the booster club or at least approved by the officers. This would include the purchase of uniforms, instruments, charter bus transportation, etc., all of which can require a large expenditure of funds. Parents are usually willing to give the director whatever the club can afford, but they appreciate being informed since they have contributed to the raising of the money. The treasurer must be apprised of the balance and not write checks if funds are not available. Funds for long-range projects, such as uniforms, should be set aside in an interest-bearing account until needed. The exact procedure for disbursement of funds should be outlined in the booster's constitution.

Budgeting

The assessment and administration of a complete band program falls squarely on the shoulders of the instrumental director, regardless of the size of the department. There are times that an administrator will not be open to allocating specific funds to support the music program, but the wise director will research and plan an annual budget to submit to his respective principal. It is prudent to prepare an annual budget to help the administrator realize he is dealing with a band or orchestra director who understands fiscal matters and the necessity of thorough financial planning. It has been this writer's experience that top administrators in charge of fiscal planning for the district appreciate a five-year plan showing what expenditures are needed to provide for instrument replacement and program growth.

Occasionally, administrators must be educated concerning the fact that the band (music) department should be funded just like every other department in the school. They must realize band is a valuable educational experience that benefits not only the students involved but also the school district and the local community. The instrumental director can become a powerful advocate for arts education as part of the curriculum and should do the proper research and preparation in order to justify and support that advocacy. There is abundant research supporting arts education and music as part of the standard curriculum. Any attempts to apprise an administrator of the importance of music in the schools should be done with diplomacy and sensitivity. There are times that the director may be asked to go before the school board to present the case for funding. Until the respective administrator and the school board fully understand the significance of arts education, it is unlikely there will be substantial financial support for the instrumental program.

Some school districts charge an extra fee for band, though the best option is to have expenditures included in the total school budget. Capital expense money should be considered for new or replacement instruments and uniform purchases, and student activity accounts can often be used for bus transportation and other expenses necessary for trips to away games and various competitions. Programs with a strong booster organization often utilize this group to subsidize funding, although it is a dangerous precedent having the booster club do fundraising to provide the majority of financial support to the instrumental program.

A typical annual budget might include the following items:
- **Supplies** (office, recording, minor repair items, oil, reeds, band awards, etc.)
- **Equipment Purchases** (new and replacement instruments; uniforms, stands, recording and video equipment, computers, office equipment, and expendable items—heads, sticks, flags, etc.)
- **Services** (piano tuning, instrument repair, office equipment repair)
- **Travel** (meals, lodging, fuel, buses)
- **Music** (marching arrangements, pep band, concert, solo/ensemble, jazz, teaching materials)
- **Audition and Entry Fees** (honor bands—district, regional, state; solo contests, band contests)
- **Recording and Videotaping** (taping rehearsals, contests, performances, compact discs)

When preparing the annual budget do not forget that professionals such as your music dealer and the local instrument repairperson can be of great assistance to you. Also, be well aware of school policies regarding requirements for obtaining bids on capital expenditures. Even if you have an approved budget, know the formal procedure for requesting a purchase (purchase order) and abide by those guidelines. It is to your benefit to have a good reputation with those who process the purchase orders and pay the bills.

Fund-raising

Most schools will require some fund-raising to meet the needs of the band. One trip to a state teachers' convention will provide many fund-raising ideas.

Band calendars, Christmas tree and poinsettia sales, citrus sales, concessions at football games, candy, catalog sales, donation cards, discount cards, and a host of other items and ideas have all been used by bands with varying degrees of success. Even in schools that do not allow fund-raising, directors should seek permission to conduct a limited fund-raiser or scholarship program to assist students who need to raise money for trips, since this is the only way that some families will be able to afford expensive tours. Also consider charging a uniform rental fee, which covers the cleaning of the band uniform and helps offset transportation expenses for the marching band.

There is a viable alternative to fund-raising sales and that is the option of direct solicitation of funds from community businesses and individuals, a method many school districts have found highly successful. Before considering this approach it is advisable to get approval from the principal and ascertain there are no school district policies preventing this alternative. Obtaining approval of the school district is essential before embarking on any fund-raising campaign. If dealing with finances and figures are not in your comfort zone, then request the assistance of a band parent who is in this type business. Many band parents and booster club members will have valuable contacts in the community and should be invited to serve on a steering committee. Obvious people to consider should include bankers, attorneys, accountants, and school administrators with the hope that some will be former band members or parents of former band members. These folks can carry a very positive message of what band did for them or for their children. For more in-depth knowledge about direct solicitation, this writer recommends you consult an article in the 1996 issue of *The Instrumentalist* by Marcus Neiman, a fine arts and corporate funding consultant from Ohio.[2]

Handbooks

Maintaining high standards in band class takes great effort on the part of the director, the students, and the parents. Students and parents should know from the beginning what will be expected from them as band participants. Goals, standards, director expectations, grading policies, and a band calendar should be included in a student handbook and presented to band students at the beginning of the year. All student behavior and performance throughout the year can be evaluated by the standards presented in the handbook. Dates for concerts, performances at athletic events, parent-teacher meetings, trips, festivals, etc., should be publicized early. Students and families are involved in many activities, and if the band program is to be a part of their schedules, it must be planned as far in advance as possible. Included with the handbook should be a detachable form for the parents to sign and return. The form affirms that the parents have read, and support, the material in the handbook.

Keep these letters on file for the school year. If some problem arises and a student is corrected for a violation of band policy, the letter affirms that the parents (and students) knew in advance what was expected of them.

Publicity

When publicity is needed for recruiting or for special events, be creative. Always clear publicity ideas with the administration in advance. Make use of all the appropriate resources available to get the word out:

- students—word of mouth,
- announcements over the school public address system,
- announcements in school newsletters,
- church bulletins/newsletters,
- bulk mailouts to the school family,
- band mailing lists of school and community people interested in the band,
- posters on and off campus,
- ads or stories in local newspapers, and
- local radio and television public service announcements.

As the band's image improves, expectation and anticipation for the next performance is built, and the reputation of the band program grows.

Chapel Services

The band can be an effective part of chapel services. This provides the band students with the opportunity to lead in worship by accompanying corporate worship, playing special music, and even providing soloists or small ensembles. Instrumental music can add dimensions of energy and power to worship.

Playing in chapel and other school assemblies is beneficial also because it keeps the band and its work visible to the administration, faculty, student body, and parents. Be sure to schedule chapel performances with the director of the chapel program. Allow time for setup and warm-up before the services, but be careful not to remove students from other classes too frequently or for too long.

Community Performances

Outstanding bands should not be kept a secret! Performances outside the school can be a great public relations tool for the Christian school and a positive image builder for the band program. Performing at the away football games is a good start if a school has a marching band. A local Veterans Day or Christmas parade is also a great public relations tool. Playing in local churches, rescue missions, or nursing homes can be another outlet for Christian service. Local malls may allow bands to play during the Christmas season. The benefit of playing community events is that a donation to the band will often be given, although this should not be the primary criteria in the decision to accept performance opportunities in the community.

Bands that travel on tour have great opportunities for community concerts. A trip to Washington. D.C., can be the highlight of the school year. Contact the district congressman about arranging a performance on the Capitol steps.

Q: What is the value of band clinics and festivals for the Christian school band?
A: "Contest preparation demands more thoroughness and detail on the part of the ensemble than for other performances. Peer encouragement is a great motivation. The students see the evaluator's comments. The students can be proud of their work, and it gives them a sense of joy and satisfaction in their progress.

"Band clinicians are beneficial because reinforcement from another voice and another personality helps to communicate significant musical principles to players. Sometimes a different approach will clarify a concept to a student."

Tour companies that work with bands have information as to where concerts can be held in most major cities. Major theme parks have some type of performance venue for bands, and there is the added benefit of getting to visit the park after (or before) performing. Though the outdoor venues are often attended mostly by the chaperones, they do leave a lasting impression on the students. How many people can say that they gave a concert with the U.S. Capitol or with the New York skyline in the background? (Further information on touring is included in Chapter 40.)

Concerts/Festivals/Competitions

Many Christian school music programs have developed dramatically over the last 10 years or so and have gained the respect of both public and private schools. In Florida, several Christian schools are scoring high and making superior ratings at both marching and concert events. These achievements are helpful for the Christian school because it promotes the ministry of the school in the community.

Instrumental directors hold several divergent philosophies about competitions. The least stressful competitive environments are the festivals in which all bands can win by receiving a superior excellent rating. Here the band is in competition with itself and a set standard of excellence. It should be emphasized that the goal is improvement from year to year. An "excellent" rating for a band that made a "poor" or "fair" rating the year before would be a great accomplishment. These festivals are beneficial and should be a part of every accomplished band program.

Festivals that feature numerical scores and winners can be a real challenge for the students and create a lot of excitement. The very fact that students realize that their placement may depend on their practice, effort, and attention in class is a great motivation. The director should emphasize, however, that the students are not to belittle their competitors. A first place simply means that one band may be better (according to three judges) than the other participating bands in the same division on those particular selections. The director should avoid declaring his band the "state champion" or "national champion" when it is often a fact that many fine bands did not participate.

Festivals sponsored by tour companies are quite popular and can be entered for comments, ratings, or placement. Look at the tour cost carefully and consider if a "festival only" entry fee might be more economical. The band can save some money by arranging its own meals and lodging. Major cities such as New York, Washington, and Chicago may require the aid of a tour company to get the most out of the sight-seeing opportunities and save the many phone calls necessary to arrange everything. These companies also know contacts for performance opportunities within the city. Other competitions may be sponsored by the Christian school organization of the state. (In Florida, the Florida Association of Christian Colleges and Schools has a statewide Fine Arts Competition each March. The winners in the various areas are eligible to go on to the American Association of Christian Schools National Competition held annually at Bob Jones University.) The national competition is a great time of spiritual and musical challenge. It is exciting to hear groups from across the country and get a sense of how one's ensemble compares on a national level. Local schools often sponsor marching competitions as a fund-raiser. These are usually nearby and are somewhat friendlier than the high-powered competitions sponsored by groups like Bands of America (BOA). Again, keep in mind that one is only as good as one's competition. A trip to BOA would give the conductor a better idea of his ensemble's proficiency level with a national perspective. Smaller bands should pick marching competitions that have a class for smaller bands. Prepare the students for the big bands and help them understand that God expects His servants to do their best with the resources He has given them. Always work for good blend, balance, and intonation on the field or on the stage.

Bands must begin preparing for the festivals early. Conductors should choose the music several months in advance and set up a schedule of rehearsals and sectionals to perfect it. Always make sure that deadlines and fees are paid on time and that transportation and chaperoning responsibilities have been assigned. Doing a pre-festival performance (even with judges) is an excellent way to help prepare the students for the experience of competing.

Concert Attire and Protocol

"Clothes make the man" is an old saying that describes the significance of first impressions. Now while it is not true that a person is what they wear, how a person or a group looks makes a big impression in this visual age. Apparel for performances—concert attire—is important because it serves many purposes. Concert apparel can help an ensemble establish a group identity. Wearing a particular outfit identifies a student as part of a group that is unique from all others and helps provide a sense of belonging that is crucial to many students. Concert attire also contributes to an important sense of esprit de corps, or group spirit. Group members are often asked to sacrifice valuable time, energy, and cash to perform in a musical organization. Confidence is necessary and is part of the reward for many students who make those sacrifices. Parents and friends experience the same sense of pride and fulfillment when they see their offspring on stage or in the group photo, clearly delineated because of the group's concert attire. Proper concert attire should reflect a standard of dress appropriate to a performance. Students do not always have the judgment and discretion necessary to dress appropriately.

How does one select appropriate concert attire? Criteria should include appearance, style, flexibility, versatility, and practicality. One of the most important considerations in purchasing concert attire is how the attire will be used. Important questions to ask include:

1. What types of programs will the group present during the year? For an instrumental group, this could include marching, concert, school assembly/chapel, or church worship services. Some programs will be performed on school property where dressing for concerts is easy; other programs will be away from school where changing clothes might be more difficult. The performance attire should "travel" without getting wrinkled, and should be easy to clean. Performing groups play in many different venues. Therefore a director must choose multiple uniforms or one outfit that can be adapted to many different situations.

2. What about players who perform in multiple groups? In most school programs, some players will be in choral and instrumental groups. An outfit that is easy to change would facilitate the student who needs to change quickly to perform in another ensemble.

3. What are the options of adapting a basic outfit for different types of programs? Can a basic uniform be simple enough to wear for a casual school assembly, yet be accessorized (with ties, sashes, vests, coats, hats, etc.) for formal concerts?

4. What about the availability of the uniform in multiple sizes?

5. Is the uniform durable enough to be reused the next semester or next year as the personnel changes? Unless students purchase their own attire to fit themselves, the director must keep buying various new coats and pants for the upcoming season. Although one size won't fit all, how adaptable are parts of the concert attire to varying human sizes?

6. What are the weather or environmental considerations under which the group will perform? If the players are uncomfortable in their uniforms, they will not give their best performances.

Individual cost for a band or orchestra uniform is a primary consideration. Costs for uniforms are varied. Some uniforms are expensive but can be used or easily adapted to off-field programs such as a concert or worship. Band uniforms are usually colorful, stylish, and generally versatile. They are the most expensive option, however. Uniform suppliers are easily located on the Web. Typical formal concert attire for a non-marching group would generally include tuxedos for men and long black dresses for women. At the time of this writing, a basic tuxedo with pant, coat, shirt, tie, and cummerbund can be purchased for $150 from several national suppliers. Women's formal dresses cost $50 or more. By shopping carefully, one will find some disparity in pricing. Sometimes a local tuxedo or formal-wear shop will offer discounts for large orders.

Although basic black always looks impressive in formal concerts, many schools or churches simply do not have groups where this type of dress is appropriate or practical. A simple concert attire could include a tuxedo shirt for a man and a white blouse for a woman coupled with dark pants or skirts. This still looks nice and is much cheaper. The use of colorful vests over white shirts or blouses can often add interest and variety to a group's visual appeal; and vests are quite versatile. A good possibility for many groups is the use of knit pullover shirts (variously called polo or golf shirts), in short or long sleeves that can be worn by both sexes. These come in almost any color, and the group name or logo can be ordered at a nominal price and affixed to the shirts, providing a very nice informal type of attire that will work for many occasions. These shirts are very flexible for various occasions when combined with khaki skirts or pants or even "dressy" jeans. If funding for concert attire is completely nonexistent, colorful sweaters are a tasteful option for a Christmas concert.

Don't forget to factor in uniform maintenance. Does the attire require expensive dry cleaning or is it washable? Is it susceptible to food stains that students will invariably obtain? How easily does it wrinkle? Some fabrics look great but require ironing with every reuse, and that's not very practical: think polyester or a polyester blend!

The purchase price of the uniform must be a consideration. Cost factors must include who pays for the outfits and to whom they belong. In many groups, students purchase their own uniform unless it is a multiple hundred-dollar band uniform (in which case there is often an annual but nominal rental fee). If students purchase their own attire, the group outfit should be standard enough in style so that new outfits in successive years will closely match the old ones—or the purpose of uniformity is defeated. Standard tuxedo dress is popular because it is so timeless.

7. How many seasons (years) can one expect to use a particular uniform? Because it is unreasonable to expect one's members to purchase a new outfit every year, purchase something that will work for several seasons. Factored over three or four years, the initial investment of $150 is actually quite reasonable. The cost of concert attire should not be a barrier to participation for students who come from families that already sacrifice financially to send their students to a private school. The best scenario would be to have the cost of concert attire subsidized in the music budget or through the Boosters Club.

Group Protocol/Stage Etiquette

Protocol involves how one acts in certain situations, especially those of a public nature. Do not take for granted that students have a clear idea of what proper behavior entails. The best way to help them is to write out procedures in advance for acceptable and expected behavior. Although this is a very informal age, certain formal or standards of concert etiquette should be kept in mind and communicated to the students.

The group and its members should always present a positive visual appearance that does not detract from the music or from the group's testimony. One will need to collaborate with the administration and spell out guidelines in advance for concert etiquette where it relates to personal appearance. But if the director has visual guidelines for concerts that go beyond general school policy, problems should be anticipated before the first concert is performed.

Specific concert etiquette should generally reflect the nature of the program—some are quite formal while others are not; some are worship services and should be presented as such. If the group can logistically be seated and in place before the program begins, this is desirable as instrumental group entrances and exits are awkward by nature because of the need to adjust chairs, instruments, and individuals, in general. If possible, be in place and ready to play; and that includes tuning ahead of time.

There are generally three playing positions for seated instrumentalists:

1. Rest position involves the instrument in a resting position. This is usually indicated when the conductor stands beside the podium (or beside the music stand if no podium is present). The director will probably have to decide ahead of time which direction and at what angle some resting instruments should point; percussionists will need some assistance in how to hold sticks or their equipment.

2. Ready position follows when the conductor mounts the podium or steps behind the conductor's stand. This generally involves all instruments coming to an upright position (a vertical orientation) with the bell or base of the instrument resting on the player's lap. This will also need instruction to produce visual uniformity.

3. Play position results when the conductor raises the baton. Only those instruments that play immediately should bring up their instruments. [Hint: do not move to the ready position until the percussionists have had time to change equipment and retune the timpani.]

After a musical selection, the audience may applaud. In a formal concert, the conductor (both male and female) should bow. Start the bow by rolling the head forward and follow immediately by bending at the waist allowing the upper torso to relax with a curved back. An effective bow can be accomplished by bending at a 30- to 60-degree angle. A spouse or a trusted colleague can assist one in refining his or her bow. Do not keep a stiff back and be certain not to look at the audience during the bow. The arms should remain relaxed at one's side while bowing. The inexperienced conductor should practice bowing to appear comfortable when in front of an audience. After the conductor bows, soloists should be recognized where appropriate. The conductor should turn to each and extend an arm in the soloist's direction. The soloists should stand and smile. Group bows, especially with music stands and instruments present, seem awkward and cumbrous. Unless the soloist has performed a concerto or a major solo, an acknowledgment and a big smile from them is appropriate. At certain points in a concert, the entire group may be acknowledged. Motioning toward the group and directing the audience's attention to them can accomplish this. If the director wishes to stand the group, probably after the final selection within each major section on the program, he or she should motion to them to rise. One should rehearse group bows ahead of time so that it is also visually appealing.

In the orchestral tradition where the group is primarily strings, it is proper and important to acknowledge and shake hands with the concertmaster/mistress. This tradition has generally not carried over into the band world; however, there might be an occasion to shake hands with the principal clarinet or flute in a guest conducting situation.

If the conductor or soloist leaves the stage and applause continues, he or she should return to the stage immediately to acknowledge it. Don't wait around backstage wondering what to do—don't hesitate to return to the stage to accept the thanks of the audience.

On occasions where the concert is not so formal—as in a school assembly for example—a simple nod of the head and a mouthed thank you toward the audience may suffice. That may also be appropriate for some softer selections in a formal concert where the applause is restrained; a deep bow is simply not appropriate there.

Applause in worship services is a different matter. In those instances, a group should not be performing for public recognition but for the glory of God. When applause occurs, a bow is not appropriate. In general, attempt to direct the congregation (not audience in this case) to focus on God and do not do anything extra to call attention to self. If some recognition is necessary, a simple nod of the head will suffice to signal thank you. It is important that directors educate students that they are not "performing" at a worship service but offering their musical gifts in ministry for God's glory. This can be conveyed both verbally and nonverbally by how the director conducts him- or herself in worship (including the careful use of terms such as "audience" and "congregation").

Unfortunately, the dividing line between worship and entertainment is not always clear. School concerts will probably have a mix of sacred and secular selections (hopefully grouped together) that again blur the line between worship and entertainment. In a concert setting, however, acknowledging performers is proper.

It is also important to remind your performers what to do when they are not playing. Where should they look during solos or while the choir is performing? Remind them that while they are on stage, someone is always looking at them—even if they are not performing. There should be no talking, chewing gum, doing homework, or any other activity. Cell phones should never be brought to a performance stage. All attention should be directed to the performing group.

Another important part of concert etiquette is the public acknowledgment of all who have sacrificed to make the program a success but do not get to bow before an applauding crowd. Parents who have sewn costumes, made props, transported people and equipment; the secretary or wife/husband who typed the programs; and the custodial staff who had better be on the director's list for Christmas cards and thank-you notes. School administrators and staff should also be thanked. Acknowledgements can be made in a printed program or given orally at the concert. A personal thank you from the director encourages volunteer helpers and reminds musicians that they are not the only stars, although they get all the public applause. Remember that a servant's heart, not fame, is what lasts throughout eternity. And in this age when fame is a major goal of the world's musicians, spiritually-minded directors can be very effective if they model an attitude of humility and Christlike service.

In the rare instance during a performance that some major mistakes or minor disasters occur, do not react in any way to magnify the error. Most of the audience will not even know the difference. Professional musicians make mistakes, but they do not falter—they continue with grace.

Remember that creating musical sounds is not enough—presentation is also critical. Take the time to rehearse and properly prepare an ensemble so that the performers and the audience alike will be blessed.

Marching Band

A marching band in a Christian school should be considered if a school has a football team and the enrollment is sufficient in the band program. The marching band requires a great deal of time from both the students and director. The extra time demands required of the director should be expressed to the administrator of the school and the director should be properly compensated with a salary supplement. A school may want to begin with simply a pep band in the stands for the first year. This will help the students get a feel for the football atmosphere and the excitement that is generated at these games. Once the administration understands the financial obligation required of supporting a marching band program and the commitment is made to

move forward, the school must begin purchasing marching percussion equipment, uniforms, and color guard equipment. These items are very expensive with a single band uniform often costing over $300. The time line required in procuring this equipment and the uniforms must be substantial since designing, ordering, and obtaining uniforms can take a year, depending on what time of year the order is placed.

An intensive program of training should start in the early spring on the marching percussion equipment. Playing multiple bass drum parts is unlike anything seen in concert band. Quad players require special training in moving from drum to drum and most snare parts are of far greater difficulty than in concert music. Younger or less experienced band members, or even talented students from the general school population, can often be recruited to play cymbals or the auxiliary instruments since these instruments tend to be less taxing. It's good to have one or two mallet players on the sideline (often called the "pit") to add color to the percussion parts. The color guard can consist of flags, rifles, sabers, or a variety of other interesting items limited only by director creativity. A trip to a drum corps exhibition or competition during the summer can give a director numerous ideas on the use of the color guard. Also, the local educational television station (PBS) will likely broadcast the Drum Corps International (DCI) finals in August where the top corps in the nation compete. Students should be encouraged to view this presentation either in small groups or as a band, together with the director.

Recruitment for the marching band should begin in March or April with letters, posters, telephone calls, etc. A letter of intent should be given to students to find out if they plan to march. Be honest in telling students that marching band requires some summer practices and after-school rehearsals. Expect the students in the top concert band to march unless a valid reason is given for not doing so. Sometimes students have work conflicts or they lack transportation. Gentle pressure usually works the best, though some students will choose volleyball, football, or cheerleading over the band. Encourage even the athletes to stay in the band and help with the concert season. They may change their mind about marching later on in their high school careers. The summer practices are very important to championship programs and usually produce excellent results. One successful formula is to practice once a week for four or five weeks during the summer. Two weeks before school have a band camp at school that lasts from 8:00 a.m. to 12:00 noon. Where the climate is extremely hot it might be advisable to schedule outdoor rehearsals in the evening. This schedule allows the band to have a good part of the show learned before school even starts.

Color guard tryouts are usually held in late April or early May. A good deal of promotion should precede guard tryouts. One technique that has been quite successful is to have each physical education class become a guard class for a day or two, to actually experience using the equipment. Directors should begin a search in the winter for a guard instructor who will abide by the standards and rules of the school. The ideal would be a current faculty member who has performed or taught in the past. A faculty member may also be willing to learn by attending a summer flag camp. Bringing a Christian color guard instructor to the school for a summer camp is an excellent alternative to sending the team off to a secular camp. The guard captains then do most of the instructing during the year with an adult supervisor. The ideal situation would be to have an adult who can both supervise and teach the routines. Make sure that any sponsor or instructor is paid. The amount given to part-time coaches is usually a good guide for the fair amount of compensation (assuming the coaches are paid and the time commitment is equivalent). The school should cover this expense, if at all possible. Otherwise it must be raised through fees or fund-raising.

The music in the marching band must be selected early. If using stock arrangements, order the music and have the students read through it in rehearsal during April or May. Once a final decision is made on the music and the personnel is set, the show is ready to be written. Many directors now have shows written by professional drill designers and arrangers. One reason for this is the abundance of marching competitions that put as much emphasis on show design and music, as on its execution. If a director feels incapable of writing a visually appealing show and selecting music that has good general effect, then the band has little chance at marching competitions. Most professionals are able to write the drill on computer using the Pyware 3D program or other similar charting programs. They can send to the customer not only the drill charts, but a video of the drill, allowing the band to view the show before starting marching rehearsals. Many directors have learned to use these programs themselves and save the expense of hiring a designer. Directors must have the time, energy, creativity, and computer know-how, however, to write the show. They must also be able to devote ample time in the summer to this project. The result can be quite satisfying. The marching band in the Christian school can be a great public relations tool and a source of pride for the students. Band directors must decide if the personnel, funding, and commitment from the parents and administration are adequate to accomplish the task.

Band Organization

In order to be a representative of the total program all officers must be members of the marching band.

I. Band Officers (elected) and Duties
A. President
1. Presides at all band meetings and band council meetings
2. Upholds the highest traditions and spirit of the band
3. Assists with uniform and instrument inspections
4. Assists with fund-raising
5. Reports to the director any problems or suggestions
6. Serves as a bus chairman, checking roll
7. Appoints committees for special events or projects

B. Vice-President
1. Assumes all duties of the band president when necessary
2. Assists with fund-raising
3. Serves as a bus chairman, checking roll
4. Serves as rehearsal hall monitor (inspecting shelves, folio cabinet, etc.)

C. Secretary
1. Assists in attendance by taking lists to the office
2. Records minutes of band council meetings
3. Assists in record keeping during fund-raising and trips
4. Sends sympathy and get well cards
5. Records practice hours

D. Class Representative
1. Selected by members of each class to be the spokesman for that class and reports to the director
2. Assists in cleaning band room
3. Builds spirit and assists in fund-raising for his or her class

II. Band Officers (appointed) and Duties
The director appoints these officers. Students interested in these positions should make written requests to the director who will select or, if necessary, have a vote to help determine the best people.

A. Drum Major
1. Instructs in basic marching fundamentals
2. Assists in maintaining good discipline in the marching band
3. Assists in marching band inspections

B. Librarian and Assistant Librarian
   1. Responsible for the music library and all music—filing, cataloging
   2. Distributes and collects all music, filing it away in score order and making notes of missing parts

C. Stage and Equipment Manager
   1. Responsible for the arranging of the chairs and stands for each concert
   2. Supervises loading of equipment on buses. Should work closely with percussion section leader and vice-president. Aids in the lining of the football field, loading of drum major stand, getting rehearsal aids to the field, etc.

D. Publicity Manager
   1. Directs and devises publicity for the activities of the band, including newsletter articles, bulletin boards, and annual scrapbook.
   2. Develops Web page (use an adult to help)

E. Band Council
   1. Comprised of the band officers and director.
   2. Meets at least once a month to discuss band projects and problems

F. Section Leader/Field Assistants
   1. Assists in teaching and rehearsing all marching band shows (normally the best players in the senior class). They must have a thorough knowledge of marching fundamentals, drill teaching techniques, and be respected for experience in the marching band.
   2. Conducts sectional rehearsals when asked

G. Symphonic Section Leader
   1. Normally the best player in the section, but consider experience and seniority

H. Color Guard Captain
   1. Appointed on the basis of experience, leadership ability, and skill

Conclusion

Running an effective band program is challenging and time consuming, but for the director it can be very rewarding. The opportunities to train these young people to use their talent for Christ is a great blessing, particularly when they continue as musicians in their churches or as music majors in college. The rewards are tremendous!

Resources

- *A Sound Approach to Teaching Instrumentalists: An Application of Content and Learning Sequences,* 2nd ed., by Stanley L. Schleuter (New York: Schirmer Books, 1997)
- *The Art of Elementary Band Directing,* by Eileen Fraedrich (Ft. Lauderdale, FL: Meredith Music Publications, 1997)
- *The Band Director's Companion,* by James Middleton, Harry Haines, and Gary Garner (San Antonio, TX: Southern Music Company, 1998)
- *Band Director's Survival Guide,* by Eldon A. Janzen (Out of Print but available

from the author at 1485 Sunset Place, Fayetteville, AR, 72701, 501-443-5132)
- *Block Scheduling: Implications for Music Education,* by Richard Miles and Larry Blocker (Springfield, IL: Focus on Excellence, 1996)
- *The Complete Instrument Reference Guide for Band Directors,* by Richard Williams and Jeff King with Derrick Logozzo (San Diego, CA: Neil A. Kjos Music Company, 2001)
- *The Complete Marching Band Resource Manual,* by Wayne Bailey (Philadelphia, PA: University of Pennsylvania Press, 1994)
- *The Creative Director: Alternative Rehearsal Techniques,* 3rd ed., by Edward S. Lisk (Fort Lauderdale, FL: Meredith Music Publications, 1991)
- *Improving Intonation in Band and Orchestra Performance,* by Robert J. Garofalo (Ft. Lauderdale, FL: Meredith Music Publications, 1996)
- *Instructional Designs for Middle/Junior High School Band,* by Robert J. Garofalo (Ft. Lauderdale, FL: Meredith Music Publications, 1995)
- *Instrumental Music Teacher's Survival Kit,* by Randy Navarre (Paramus, NJ: Parker Publishing Company, 2001)
- *The Instrumentalist,* The Instrumentalist Company, Northfield, IL
- *Rehearsing the Band,* by John E. Williamson, Kenneth L. Neidig, ed. (Cloudcroft, NM: Neidig Services, 1998)
- *So...You're The New Band Director: Now What?* by Phillip C. Wise (Oskaloosa, IA: C.L. Barnhouse Company, 1996)
- *Teaching Music Through Performance in Band,* by Richard Miles, ed., Eugene Corporan, Ray Cramer, Tim Lautzenhauser, et. al., Vols. I, II, III. (Chicago: GIA Publications, 1997, 1998, 2000). CDs of cited works are available.
- *Teaching Techniques and Insights for Instrumental Music Educators,* revised, by Joseph Casey (Chicago: GIA Publications, Inc., 1993)
- *Techniques of Marching Band Show Designing,* by Dan Ryder (Austin, TX: Dan Ryder Field Drills, 2000)

[1] Francis McBeth coined the term "pyramid" in his 1972 book, *Effective Performance of Band Music,* to describe a concept of balance which basically states that voices sounding successively higher frequencies require proportionately less effort to balance those below them. Simply stated, lower frequency instruments (tuba, bassoon, bass clarinet, etc.) must play louder to balance the higher frequency instruments (flute, oboe, trumpet, etc.), or in the clarinet section there should be more people playing the third clarinet part than the first. This concept of balance applies within each section as well as between sections and families of instruments.

[2] Marcus L. Neiman, "Fund-raising Without Fruit," *The Instrumentalist,* Vol. 50, No. 11 (July, 1996), 36-40.

Jeff Cranfill is Associate Minister of Music at First Baptist Church, Snellville, Georgia.

Jim Hansford is Professor of Music, Director of Bands, and Coordinator of Instrumental Studies, Oklahoma Baptist University, Shawnee, Oklahoma.

Max Cordell (B.S. Music Ed., Bob Jones University, M.M.E., University of Georgia) is a faculty member at Trinity Baptist College and directs the Trinity Baptist Church Orchestra. He is a member of many organizations, including MENC National Conference and the National Band Association.

Mel Wilhoit is Chair of the Music Department at Bryan College in Dayton, Tennessee, where he teaches courses in music history, music education, instrumental music, and fine arts. He has written for *The New Grove Dictionary of American Music, American Music Journal, International Trumpet Guild Journal, The Hymn, American National Biography,* and *The Guide to United States Popular Culture.* He has directed and adjudicated many choral and instrumental groups. In addition to being Music Critic for Chattanoogan.com, an on-line newspaper, he also serves as Minister of Music in the Chattanooga area.

Mark Bailey is an Associate Professor of Music at Lee University in Cleveland, Tennessee. He holds the Doctorate in Music Education from the College-Conservatory of Music at the University of Cincinnati, Cincinnati, Ohio. Dr. Bailey has directed the Lee University Symphonic Band for the past 13 years and has toured thoughout the United States and internationally. The ensemble has developed a reputation for excellence in music and ministry. Dr. Bailey is presently the President-elect of the Christian Instrumentalist and Directors Association.

Band Letter Award Requirements

In order to earn a Band Letter, band members must fulfill the following during one school year:
1. Must be in grades 8-12.
2. Perform in at least 5 football games.
3. Attend band camp.
4. Perform in a least 4 concerts in the Symphonic Band (other than football).
5. Maintain an "A" average in band over a period of one school year (as of the awards banquet). This does not necessarily mean all As, only an A average.
6. Demonstrate a willing spirit fitting for Christian service.
7. Successfully complete one of the following:
8. Perform a solo or in an ensemble in a chapel service, concert, or festival.
9. Play from memory all 12 major scales and arpeggios. Percussionists will play the rudiment sheet (front and back) from memory.

Sample Elementary or Middle School Band Grading System

Band members earn a daily grade, and these grades are averaged to determine the final grade. The daily grade will include playing assignments (A, B, C, D, F) and bringing instrument, music, and pencil to class.

A = Present with instrument, pencil, and music, prepared to play the assignments for the day. On Mondays, having a complete, signed Practice Journal.
B = Present with all materials; few problems playing the day's assignments.
C = In class without pencil, or not demonstrating that the assignments are learned. On Mondays, an incomplete or unsigned Practice Journal.
D, F = In class either without proper materials, or with major problems playing the day's assignments.
0 = Present without music or instrument. Some directors also believe the amount of private practice should be reflected in the grade.

Sample High School Band Grading System

For high school band students, the grading is more complex. The three main aspects of band student behavior are:

Participation—Their work in class, having their instrument, music, pencil, paying attention, and on task in class.

Preparation—Learning assigned music and being prepared to play it when assigned.

Attendance/Punctuality— Being present and on time at rehearsals. Band students begin the grading period with a grade of 100. Infractions of class policies and procedures causes grade reductions; extra credit projects earn bonus points.

• **Every band member** begins each quarter with an A+ 100 (minus final exam). Points are subtracted for a lack of preparation, punctuality, or participation.

• **Playing a solo** or participating in an ensemble in chapel, a concert, or festival will earn an "A" for the final exam. There will be a final exam each semester for those who do not play a solo or in an ensemble each semester.

• **Semester averages** will be determined as follows:

Preparation, punctuality, and participation (point total) = 90% of average

Final exam = 10% of average

• **Point System Information**

Points will be added or subtracted from grade as per information posted under Point Assignments.

Point totals will cover 9 weeks. Point totals will be renewed at the beginning of each quarter.

Point Assignments

Points subtracted from grade average:

✔ Unexcused tardy -2
✔ No music at rehearsal -2
✔ Insufficient/improper equipment -2
✔ Not prepared to play assigned music -2
✔ Delaying rehearsal -1
✔ No pencil at rehearsal -1
✔ Chewing gum in rehearsal -1
✔ Leaving instrument or music at school -1

Excuses

Excused absences from a rehearsal must be requested and arranged with the director at least 48 hours in advance (excluding emergencies).

Excused absences from a performance must be validated by a note from the parents at least two weeks in advance (excluding emergencies).

Any absence/tardy that is not properly excused is unexcused.

✔ Unexcused absence from any rehearsal will result in lowering of final semester grade by 4 points.

✔ Unexcused absence from any performance will result in lowering of final semester grade by at least one letter grade, and possible dismissal from the band.

Honors Credit

Many students, especially those in advanced level courses need to keep their cumulative grade point average as high as possible. In an effort to keep college-bound honors students enrolled in band classes, consider adding a band honors program. Work with the administration and the guidance department to set up honors credit for qualifying high school band students. By doing extra work in band, students can earn honors credit in band, with the honors grade in band having a greater weight in the overall GPA (an A might be 4.5 instead of 4.0). Requirements and procedures for an honors program are included here:

Music Honors Program

Band and chorus classes may be taken for honors credit. The purpose of this program is to encourage students to develop their God-given musical talents, and to reward the students for efforts above and beyond the regular group requirements.

Application Process. Students applying for honors credit must pick up an application from their director. The director will then set up an audition with each student.

Auditions. Audition requirements include:

1. Instrumental—Any 3 scales (for snare drum, any 3 rudiments*, open, closed, open). Vocal—Vocalises
2. An exercise or etude that demonstrates technique*
3. A solo of the student's choice*

*Student should ask director or private teacher for assistance in selecting above materials.

Interviews. Upon acceptance to the honors program, each student will have an interview with the director. The student will fill out a contract at the beginning of each grading period. The contract will list the materials that the student will prepare and perform individually for the director during that quarter, as well as recital and other activities/projects.

Quarterly Requirements. Honors students are to maintain exemplary participation in the performing groups. Problems with improper attitudes or low grades in the class may prohibit honors credit. In order to earn honors credit for a music class, the contracted work must be successfully completed during that quarter. Materials to be completed by the student include:

1. Technique exercises
2. Etudes or vocalises
3. Solos
4. Preparation time (number of hours per week)
5. Music from class (band, chorus)
6. Participation in one honors recital (one per semester)
7. Optional—Concert attendance, research or music theory project

Honors Recitals. All honors students will participate in at least one recital per semester (18 weeks). There will be one recital each quarter, and all Honors students must attend both recitals. Recitals will be at the school and dates will be published at the beginning of each semester. Parents and friends are encouraged to attend.

Music Performance Honors Program

Name_____ Grade _____

Phone No. _____

Performance Group _____Director _____

Grading Period 1   2   3   4   Year _____

MATERIALS:

A. Technical Study_____

B. Etude_____

C. Repertoire_____

D. Preparation Time per Week_____

E. Repertoire of Group (band, jazz, etc.)_____

F. Honors Recital Selection(s):_____

G. Project: Research, Theory, Concert Attendance, Listing Project

_____

Due By: _____   Initialed: _____

Music Honors Listening Project

Title of piece_____

Movements _____

Composer's full name _____

Composer's country of origin _____

Composer's dates _____

Who is performing the piece? _____

Write a paragraph or two describing each piece/section/movement.
Your description should include:

1. Key—major, minor, or something different
2. Instrumentation—large group, chamber group, solos, etc.
3. Tempos—fast, slow, moderato, does it change in the piece?
4. Style—marcato, legato, march style, etc.
5. Mood—light, heavy, happy, sad, serious, humorous, etc.
6. Outstanding features—solos, difficult technical spots, etc.

Lastly, answer the following for the complete piece:
Do you like the piece? Why? or Why not?

CHAPTER 40

Christian School Instrumental Ensembles

by Mark Bailey, Jim Hansford, and Mel Wilhoit

Solo and Small Ensembles in the Instrumental Program

Small ensembles, often called chamber ensembles, are an important component of an effective instrumental program. Instrumental directors often overlook the smaller groups in favor of the larger organization. However, the small ensemble can provide musicians with critical listening skills, more attention to musical detail, and more confidence in an exposed performance environment. Instrumental programs are probably conceived of as being organized around a large ensemble experience—even though the "large" ensemble may boast only 25 players. While this is natural, because the vast majority of literature is composed for the traditional band or orchestra, solos and small ensembles within the instrumental program can be invaluable.

Five Reasons to Initiate a Solo-Ensemble Program

1. It works well as a "start-up" method for developing a band or orchestra program. Consider beginning the quest toward the ideal concert band by building on the foundation of a brass and a woodwind ensemble that can be combined once both groups have achieved sufficient instrumentation.

For those with orchestral aspirations, begin with a small string group to build a larger performance group.

2. It provides players with musical and technical challenges that may not be possible in the larger unit. Typically, the more advanced first chair players will feel underchallenged with the literature that the larger group is performing. Solo/small ensembles provide one means of keeping the best students interested, challenged, and growing.

3. There exists a wealth of quality literature available for myriad instrumental combinations, as well as solo performances. It would be a tragedy not to expose students to this superb musical outlet.

4. Employing smaller forces provides the flexibility of programming for solos or ensembles. It is much easier to prepare a small group on short notice for music specific to a particular assembly, banquet, or special program. In fact, such forces are almost tailor-made for such occasions. In addition, the performance space requirements, travel considerations, and other logistical challenges are more easily solved in the context of a small group.

5. It serves as a laboratory to improve pitch awareness, listening skills, precision and clarity, tonal concepts, and balance and blend.

When a director enters a new school, he or she may be unable to begin a full band or orchestra with sufficient instrumentation the first year. The small ensemble experience is demanding for each individual player. Tuning, balance, nuance, clarity, and confidence are required in a small group, even more than in the larger unit.

A wider variety of styles may be utilized in small ensemble literature. Students need to be exposed to the abundance of quality literature written for diverse instrument combinations. Bright students can be motivated by a faster rehearsal pace and more challenging literature. Students learn confidence and mature tone production when forced to take a leading role in a small ensemble. Bad playing habits are magnified in a small group, so a sensitive player will find the small ensemble a fertile environment to grow musically and rise to the challenge. The interaction between student-musicians in a small ensemble can reinforce teaching concepts that the director seeks to teach band students in the large group setting.

Perhaps the best way to begin small ensembles is to think in terms of standard combinations for the available literature. The following combinations are fairly standard and hold the potential for a reasonably wide variety of published literature on various levels of difficulty.

Flute Ensemble—From trio to flute choir; lots of options here, some requiring piccolo or alto flute.

Woodwind Quintet—Flute, clarinet, oboe, bassoon, French horn. Although this is the standard classical woodwind chamber ensemble, this combination is difficult for the average band to have a capable oboe, bassoon, and horn player. (Substitutions do not often work well with this highly idiomatic literature.)

Saxophone or Clarinet Ensemble—Trios, quartets, quintets, sextets, and septets in various combinations.

Mixed Woodwind Ensemble—The challenge here is that a larger ensemble (such as an octet) requires a bassoon and/or bass clarinet; without them, such groups are handicapped.

Brass Quartet/Quintet/Sextet—A wealth of literature is available on all levels for almost every combination. The quintet medium of two trumpets, horn, trombone, and tuba (or bass trombone) is the chamber music standard for brass instruments. Listen to the Canadian Brass Quintet at any CD store to hear this medium at its most commercially successful. Books of their arrangements are available from medium to difficult.

Brass Ensemble—A wealth of literature is also available. There is no standard instrumentation for ensembles larger than quintets, but they usually necessitate a tuba.

String Quartet/String Orchestra—The quartet is the standard classical chamber ensemble consisting of two violins, one viola, one cello. Expand the number of these instruments and add string bass to produce a string orchestra. Music for this ensemble is prolific, and readily available.

Mixed String Ensemble—Finding music for odd combinations of strings (such as four violins, one cello, and one bass) is more difficult.

Percussion Ensemble—This is a growing area of highly creative literature with unlimited instrument combinations. Attend a performance or review a video of the group Stomp to gain an awareness of the vast array of possibilities.

Jazz/Big Band Combinations—Lots of possibilities ranging from duos and trios (with or without keyboards) to the standard "big band" instrumentation of four to five saxes, four trumpets, four trombones, string/electric bass, drums, keyboard.

Keyboard Ensemble—An overlooked, but exciting, possibility, especially combining electronic and acoustic instruments. A small, but growing, amount of literature is available.

Guitar Ensemble—An important outlet for developing reading skills and general musicianship; literature must often be adapted from other sources; good performance opportunities for players with otherwise limited outlets.

Solos with Strings—Lots of literature, usually more classical or traditional, for a multitude of wind or string instruments with small string ensemble. (Vivaldi composed lots of concerti for such forces, including some for mandolin).

Before initiating a program of solo or small ensembles into the curriculum, a number of issues should be addressed. Will this be a regularly scheduled class or an ad hoc group that performs as the need arises? If it meets regularly, scheduling and credit requirements are two important issues. If one cannot find a successful meeting time that is relatively free of competition from activities that will regularly deplete the group, it probably should not qualify for academic credit. But if it does meet the same criteria as attendance, outside of class requirements, and supervision, it might well qualify for academic credit—probably as an elective. The issue of supervision must also be considered. Will the group be conducted or coached by a regular teacher or will it be student-directed to some degree, especially if it is rather small, such as a trio or quartet? Student-led ensembles, periodically supervised by the instructor, can be a fertile training ground for future performers, conductors, and educators.

Perhaps the biggest issue for the small ensemble is the selection of literature. While there is much secular music available for many of the combinations listed above, sacred music appropriate for Christian school programs or worship services is more limited. To find what is available, consult a combination of publisher catalogs and Web sites. Catalogs are more user-friendly in some ways because one can view an abundance of information at a glance.

As a creative conductor, one can solve some of the problems of instrumentation (not having the right instruments for the published parts) through substitution of parts. In general there are three principles to observe in substituting parts:

1. A substitute part must be in the same clef as the original. (Treble clef baritone players with range restrictions can play bass clarinet parts, but bass clef baritone players cannot.)

2. A substitution must be in the same approximate range. (Treble clef baritone players can play tenor sax parts but not clarinet parts; flutes can play oboe parts but they won't carry well when the original is written on the staff where the flute tone has little projection.)

3. Substitutions must reflect equal technical abilities. (Trumpets can't play clarinet parts with fast arpeggiation, and trombones can't play bassoon or cello parts with those same demands.) One possibility for substitution, of course, is the keyboard, especially an electronic one that can duplicate some sounds. It's a practice that goes back to the Baroque period with the ever-present harpsichord filling in for any missing parts or instruments. It requires experimentation, and it doesn't always work well, but does provide an option when the director owns a great piece for woodwind quintet but has no bassoon.

Another issue related to the larger subject of ensembles pertains to entrance requirements. Will there be auditions or will you demand a certain level of competency? As a general rule, the smaller the group, the closer players need to be to the same technical and musical levels. Where there may be a large range of abilities in a band, this won't work well in a brass quartet with one player per part. The advanced players will definitely get bored waiting for the lower intermediate players to learn the music, and can be discouraged with the performance quality. Of course, one will rarely get everyone playing on the same level, but the disparity can't be too large in a small group.

Another related, and sometimes controversial, area involves the issue of whether one will require membership in the larger performance group as a prerequisite for small ensemble participation. In general, it is suggested the answer be affirmative. Without that requirement, there is a tendency for better players to skip the large group and perform only the more challenging music of the smaller ensemble. This results in various problems. First, one loses the best players who are certainly needed to provide musical quality in the larger group. Second, if the best players can bypass the regular band, group spirit is negatively affected with the feeling that only the lesser players are left in the band. In the long range, exempting better players from playing in the larger group doesn't teach much about

doing music for ministry's sake where, in the average church orchestra, there is a large range of abilities. Ultimately, the Christian director is trying to educate his or her students to play for God's glory and others' enjoyment, as well as their own fulfillment. The younger musicians need the models and leadership provided by the more mature players.

In some cases, certain players may want to bypass the larger group because of the style of literature. These players want to play jazz or big band and don't want the more traditional fare of the concert band. Don't exempt them from the band; they need exposure and experience playing both (guitars possibly excepted).

In many ways, soloists and ensembles are very economical. If one already has an instrumental program, the instruments and needed equipment are already present. The conductor simply needs to purchase music. When developing a program from scratch, it is still an economical approach. Include music for solo/ensemble in the music budget, because even ensemble music can be moderately expensive.

Although the larger instrumental ensemble is often more impressive visually and even aurally, the use of solo/ensemble experiences can provide added breadth and depth to the instrumental program. Perhaps the greatest challenge is that the small ensemble is very labor-intensive and usually needs a director's expertise and leadership. Small ensembles are well worth the effort!

Touring with an Instrumental Ensemble
Goals and Objectives

The establishment of a strong rationale for the purposes of touring a Christian school ensemble is essential before determining the type of touring one will do and the locations for these trips. First and foremost, the purposes for touring should be:

1. to promote the ministry of the gospel, and
2. to provide for the educational needs of the band students.

Tours should not be done for social reasons, purely promotional reasons, or to merely promote the "spirit" of the ensemble. Although this often occurs when making trips, it should be secondary to the primary purposes of the group. A good way of thinking about any Christian venture is to ask if it fulfills the following four charges that Christ gave His disciples:

1. **exaltation**—ministry of praise and worship,
2. **evangelization**—winning the lost to Christ,
3. **education**—the training of individuals to do Christian work, and
4. **edification**—support and encouragement of other believers.

Instrumental ensembles have a powerful potential role in fulfilling all of these goals. Instrumental music was central to worship in the Old Testament (Psalm 150, 2 Chronicles 5: 11-14). Colossians 3:16 commands us to "teach and admonish one another in Psalms, hymns, and spiritual songs." Each one of these four purposes can be accomplished through the instrumental ensemble and specifically through touring church and school ensembles.

The goals of the group will help to establish where tours should occur. Obviously, a good place to start is other church schools. Weekend trips to other churches are also a strong possibility. A trip that can meet with wonderful success is a mission trip to other countries. Good educational trips include performing at concert festivals and community cultural events. For church schools, these purposes can coexist. A well-scheduled tour can be conducted to churches, schools, and other venues. These opportunities will present themselves to most groups as the director develops outside contacts and as the group grows in maturity and reputation.

For Christian schools and churches, touring provides a means of fulfilling the Great Commission. Music has the ability to speak to many hearts that cannot be reached through the spoken word alone. This is especially true of excellent instrumental music performed under the anointing of the Holy Spirit. As the director selects the repertoire, he takes into consideration those who will be listening to the group's performances. A well-organized tour repertoire will include excellent concert band works, but should also include selections that will speak to the heart of the listener. Thankfully, many compositions are now being written on hymn tunes and popular gospel songs that can speak to audiences. Also, the instrumental director should not be afraid of using vocal solos, media, narration, and other means to portray the gospel message. One idea that promotes good will between the visiting team and the host church is to accompany the host church choir. This allows for interaction with the church, as well as being an excellent demonstration of what an instrumental program might add to the worship of their church. Standard band and orchestra literature may also be included in tour programs. Nevertheless, remember that when performing on tour, the audience or congregation must always be taken into consideration. The key is creativity in programming. If the director is willing to be creative and sensitive to the leading of the Holy Spirit, a group can have an outstanding musical tour experience.

With every school ensemble, the musical development of each individual must be the focus of the ensemble. Tours for the church school group are an excellent means of extrinsic motivation initially, and can be a very important means of intrinsic motivation eventually. They should serve to help motivate the player to musical excellence. This has been an important focus of public schools as they have developed marching and concert bands. Students have a desire to play their instruments and play them well. Directors should build on this desire. However, much care must be taken that the tours not become the focus of the ensemble. Whether in church or school, the focus must be on the development of musicality of the individual and not just the performance itself. If ever a director needs the wisdom of Solomon, it is on this point. Much budgeted money in public schools is allocated to marching bands that work on eight minutes of music for half the year. Church school ensembles, both touring and nontouring, should avoid this trend.

How to Get Started

There are several essential elements that must be considered in establishing a successful touring ensemble. First and foremost is administrative support. The administration must understand why the group is touring and be willing to support their efforts. In many cases, administrators will support the idea, but will not provide the funds. Before beginning, the director must have an idea of the types of costs that will be encountered.

There is always an initial cash outlay for any instrumental ensemble, whether performing primarily for local functions or tour. A touring ensemble must account for several essential elements, which always encounter finances. For the touring ensemble, these include:

- **Equipment**—instrument stands, music folders, large instrument cases, keyboard cases, percussion cases, sound equipment cases
- **Transportation**—instrumentalists, equipment
- **Meals and Lodging of Membership**
- **Miscellaneous Costs**

Equipment that is transported for most tours will include instruments (often including amplifiers and other electronic equipment in the modern church instrumental ensemble), stands, and music. Although this is obvious, the means by which this equipment is transported from place to place is a very important concern. It only takes one accident with a valuable instrument that is not transported properly to convince the director of this need.

Larger instrumental ensembles should rent, or if possible purchase, a boxed truck for this purpose. The space in the truck can then be organized to safely transport all equipment. The director should also be concerned with travel cases and other means of protecting equipment. Drumheads are particularly susceptible to damage if not properly protected. Before beginning any tour, the director should take inventory of all equipment used and how the equipment will be transported. A good librarian and the proper transportation of music and the accountability of folders are another concern.

Transportation of membership is another vital concern. Most directors have found that if comfortable transportation for the players is provided, other problems are eliminated—charter buses if possible. Although the cost may be higher, the bus company will provide important safeguards such as insurance, maintenance of vehicles, and other important legal ramifications. This allows the director to focus on other important aspects of the tour.

Group lodgings and meals must be planned well in advance. The types of touring done will dictate how this must be arranged. If the tour is a ministry tour to churches, host churches can provide much of this. The essential element is having a clear ministry focus for the ensemble and letting the church know the needs of the group. Many churches enjoy seeing young people minister in different ways and are excited and pleased to provide for these needs. Tours to churches that are in driving distance from the band's school or church can be very profitable in many ways. Do not underestimate their value in ministry.

Other tours may necessitate obtaining housing at motels or other suitable facilities, as well as budgeting meals for the group. Travel agents can be helpful in making these arrangements. Often they can provide discounted motel rates and, sometimes, packaged deals for groups. Usually, it is less expensive per person for a large group to travel than single individuals. This is particularly true regarding airline costs and motel expenses. Travel agencies specialize in arranging tours for church groups. It is important to make use of a travel agent when arranging trips. The director can also contact corporate offices of hotel-motel chains to obtain group rates.

If planning an overseas trip, it is important to make contact early and often with nationals in the country where one will tour. A local contact overseas will often know much more about anticipated needs of the group. If it is a ministry trip, it is important that contacts have caught the vision of what might possibly occur through the ministry of the ensemble. Successful concerts overseas are dependent upon the organization provided by the leadership organizing the tour in the country to be visited.

Be sure to be aware of unexpected costs, which can occur on any tour. A corporate credit card from the school or church can be useful. This includes (among a multitude of other things) emergency vehicle repairs, instrument repair, unexpected medical costs if someone in the group becomes ill, road tolls, and other possible financial needs. Have forms to show for tax exemption, and complete housing lists for motels and church hosts. When traveling abroad, check for special visa requirements, as well as the amount of departure taxes to leave a foreign country. Also consider tips and other travel expenditures with large groups.

Other Considerations

When considering church tours, bands must anticipate many unusual set-up options in order to perform effectively. Because of this, plenty of advance time must be allotted before a concert or service to set up, adjust sound, and adequately prepare. Also take into consideration the multitude of different acoustical problems that may present themselves. An excellent sound technician touring with the ensemble can be a tremendous asset in these situations. Remember: the group has worked hard to prepare the music. One of the director's responsibilities to the ensemble is to assure the group can hear when playing and be adequately heard by the listeners.

Legal considerations must always be followed before making any trip. Most states require a release form signed by the parents of students under 18 to allow them to travel with the group. This is extremely important, not only for the director's sake but also for the student. If the student were to become ill away from home, it is the director's responsibility to see that the student receive proper medical attention. It is also the director's responsibility to make sure that all vehicles have proper insurance, especially liability insurance. Check with a lawyer in the state to make sure all legal considerations have been anticipated.

Conclusion

Taking a band or orchestra on tour takes a great deal of work, time, and planning, but the rewards of touring can outweigh the problems. First, every venture should be undertaken through prayer. Consider the original premise: "What are the purposes for beginning a touring ensemble?" If the Lord has provided the vision, it is the director's duty and purpose to follow the vision he has been given. This can be particularly true for any ministry trip, especially mission trips.

Mark Bailey is an Associate Professor of Music at Lee University in Cleveland, Tennessee.

Jim Hansford is Professor of Music, Director of Bands, and Coordinator of Instrumental Studies, Oklahoma Baptist University, Shawnee, Oklahoma.

Mel Wilhoit is Chair of the Music Department at Bryan College in Dayton, Tennessee.

CHAPTER 41

Cooperating with the Other Arts

by Mel Wilhoit

For a music teacher, cooperation with other arts programs in the school or church is both a philosophical and a practical necessity. Although the possibility of sharing scarce resources of funding, time, space, and personnel may initially appear to be a negative factor in developing a program, a look at the bigger picture may reveal that, in the long run, students are actually better served. Take an interest in and be supportive of the choral program, the art department, the drama group, and increasingly, the area of dance, because they all have intrinsic merit and value; they also attract many of the best instrumental students. Together with music, all of the creative arts are God-given gifts that reflect His image.

Besides these philosophical issues, there are a multitude of practical reasons for developing a close working relationship with other fine arts teachers. All fine arts disciplines enhance the understanding, reception, and enjoyment of music. This present age is primarily a visual one, but music is basically aural; visual media can greatly enhance a musical concert. In understanding and cooperating with the other arts, musicians will become more effective.

Consider the possibility of combining at least a few selections on an instrumental program with the visual arts. For example, there are several instrumental works that directly describe works of art (Mussorgsky's *Pictures at an Exhibition*); others are highly programmatic and suggest a visual component (Copland's many pieces originally composed for ballet such as *Appalachian Spring*). It is increasingly easier to scan artwork into a computer and project it onto a large screen while the ensemble is performing. (One will probably need to darken the performance space for the audience to see the screen, and this will likely require stand lights.) Project artwork done by the students in the school that can creatively coordinate with some of the band or orchestra's musical selections. Parents and friends will come to view the artwork of their children. For a chapel or worship service, the musical selections can be an underscore for a Scripture reading or biblical monologue. There are many religious videos that can provide a worshipful focus for a classical piece. Artistic banner processionals can be utilized with instrumental worship music. As a general rule, combining an instrumental music program with other fine arts departments results in a better crowd and introduces new people to the arts.

Combining instruments and choral music is excellent, and countless selections for band and chorus or orchestra and chorus are available. Many beautiful instrumental pieces are beautifully danced. There are probably several students in the school studying classical ballet or various forms of modern dance. Be sure to provide the dancers with a recorded copy of the music—at the correct speed—so they can work out and practice their routines before the two groups are combined. Make sure to plan enough rehearsal time for the dancers to get accustomed to a live rendition which may vary considerably at times from the earlier recording. This combination of live music and dance can be highly effective and very appealing. Any special lighting effort available should be considered to enhance the performance.

Combining instrumental forces with the drama department to present musicals or other dramatic stage works takes extra effort, but is generally very appealing and highly popular with students and parents alike. In general, one cannot use the entire band or orchestra because the instrumentation varies from musical to musical and is often so difficult to combine with the stage action that a smaller group works best—and is less likely to overpower the  singers. Rehearsing the traditional Broadway musical is often highly frustrating because most selections are not available with full scores that identify what instruments play what notes. Generally, there is only a "piano-conductor" part (almost identical to the vocal-choral score) that provides only basic cues and often does not correspond to the player's parts. The parts are frequently poorly edited in terms of rehearsal letters or even correct notes. In the end, however, all the work and frustration usually pays off, and it becomes a superb educational and musical experience for the students.

The synthesis of performing resources provides additional benefits. Arts instructors can often pool limited budgets to purchase or rent materials or services otherwise unavailable separately. Sharing performance venues and dates can often facilitate competing schedules. Sharing performance dates also aids many groups who simply do not have enough music to fill a complete program. By combining the various creative arts into one or two programs, a more interesting, varied program and a larger crowd will result. Some logistical and staging problems can ensue, however. Cooperation may entail educating one's colleagues about its shared benefits, as well as teaching the students to appreciate all of the arts.

Mel Wilhoit is Chair of the Music Department at Bryan College in Dayton, Tennessee.

What's Next?

CHAPTER 42

Wave of the Future: Contemporary Worship Trends

by Julie Barrier

Instrumental worship leaders wield powerful, life-shaping tools in their hands. Musical language crosses cultural boundaries and generational lines. Experiencing authentic worship can draw the God-seeker to thirst for the undeniable presence of God. Instrumental worship leaders and planners must utilize the medium of music to reach hearts. To impact one's culture, the Christian instrumental conductor should identify the target audience of his or her surrounding community. The palette of musical timbres, rhythms, and styles provide the conductor with dynamic options for underscoring Scripture, enhancing lyrics, and developing powerful instrumental preludes and offertories. What does worship in the new millenium look like?

A lone crooner sits center stage with his acoustic guitar. The candlelit sanctuary is decorated with liturgical symbols. Communion elements are prepared and displayed. Worshipers echo the soloist's heart-wrenching chorus in unrhymed, uneven meter. A hush falls over the congregants. Clearly, the presence of God is here. Freeze the frame.

The orchestra plays a triumphant fanfare. The mass choir and tenor soloists join in thunderous cadence. Worshipers leap to their feet and clap in rhythmic affirmation. The excitement is contagious. Surely, the presence of the Lord is in this place. Freeze the frame.

The stage lights pulse in sync with an aggressive drum fill. The lead guitar and keyboardist hit a catchy riff to introduce a praise chorus. Six highly polished ensemble singers invite the congregation to join the celebration. God is exalted with rhythm section, mellow saxophone solo, and a slick video presentation. Freeze the frame.

Which of these worship models typifies the leading worship trend in today's American churches? The answer is—all of the above, and other assorted scenarios not described as well. "Cutting edge" worship demands asking new questions. When the Samaritan woman questioned Jesus about worship, He gave her a penetrating reply. She wanted to talk about logistics instead of content: "Our fathers worshiped on this mountain, but you Jews claim that the place where we must worship is in Jerusalem" (John 4:20, NIV). The Son of God replied with startling truth: "a time is coming…when the true worshipers will worship the Father in spirit and in truth, for they are the kind of worshipers the Father seeks. God is spirit, and his worshipers must worship in spirit and in truth" (vv. 23-24, NIV).

Spiritual worship is difficult to define but unmistakable when encountered. God manifested His presence in a cloud as Solomon consecrated the temple in Jerusalem. The presence of the Lord was so awesome that all activity ceased. Sally Morgenthaler, in her book *Worship Evangelism,* identified four essentials for genuine worship:

- nearness—sensing God's manifest presence;
- vulnerability—opening oneself up to God;
- knowledge—centering on worshiping Christ; and
- interaction—participating actively in a relationship with God and others.[1]

The balance between spiritual and emotional connection (relevance) and theological integrity is essential. Nearness and vulnerability affect emotional experience. Knowledge affects the understanding of God as revealed in Scripture. Response in the other three areas produces intimate interaction.

Sensing the urgency of worship must precede the planning of worship content. America is now in the post-Christian era. In September 1999, seven Texas teenagers were massacred as they attended a "See You at the Pole" rally to pray for their school. The war for souls is escalating. Worship in a contemporary setting should prepare Christians to be lean, mean, fighting machines. Bringing people into the presence of God is not fluff or hype. Worship is the lifeblood of survival in post-Christian society. It can stem the tide of darkness and pour healing oil into America's wounds. David lamented in Psalm 73 about how evil men pervaded and prospered in his culture. But, he said in verse 17, "I entered the sanctuary of God; then I understood their final destiny…. Whom have I in heaven but you? And earth has nothing I desire besides you. My flesh and my heart may fail, but God is the strength of my heart and my portion forever" (Ps. 73:17, 25-26, NIV). King David, in those short verses, captured the true essence of relevant worship—that God is enough.

Ken Medema, Christian Artist

"Many of the trends of worship over the last 20 years seem to be narcissistic; that is, What will I get out of it or who can we attract with the latest, hippest, and most contemporary presentation? Worship given as an offering to God will never rely on style or formats, but will radiate human passion and will experience fire from heaven. Worship is the authentic sharing of our whole selves—the praise, the confession, the agonies, the laments, the longings, the yearnings, and the celebrations. As I travel, I have seen both, and it has nothing to do with the age of the congregation or building."

Vital biblical worship transforms. When David entered the throne room of the Almighty, his worldview was forever altered. Obstacles seemed smaller. Playing fields were leveled. Incredible joy and wonder filled the heart of a king who knew all the world's offerings. David left the sanctuary with power for strong, vital, abundant living.

Worship is critical to the believer's spiritual health and endurance. So why is worship style such a point of contention in churches? Understanding spiritual and sociological dynamics help answer this question. Today's American church struggles over the issue of contemporary worship because the American church is struggling to survive at a foundational spiritual level. Christian sociologist George Barna, in *The Second Coming of the Church,* prophesied with alarm that "the church in America must...turn itself around and begin to affect the culture, rather than be affected by it."[2] In a Gallup poll conducted in May 1999, 62 percent of Americans believed that religion as a whole was losing its influence on American life.[3] Laodicean apostates loom at the church doors and American clergy scurry to avoid their approach. Relevant worship styles and forms are touted as cures for flagging congregations. Worship ministers and planners must look beyond the methodology and address the core issues before them.

Charles Colson, in *Against the Night,* predicted this struggle a decade ago. He decried an insidious moral relativism and hedonism, which would sap the strength of God's people.[4] The problem begins with the American dream. It is man-centered rather than God-centered. "For as he thinketh within himself, so he is," wrote Solomon, the wisest of the wise (Prov. 23:7, NASB). Christians in this country have swallowed the poison of American egotism, and it is sapping away spiritual vitality.

This American malady might well be described as "the incredible lie of the American pie." The confection is continually sliced and served by secular media and slick society. Such deception contaminates churches.

The first lie is **"Consumer Christianity"**: church exists to meet personal needs and make life easier. Worship based on cheap grace implies that coming to God need not change anyone. Paul wrote in Romans 12:1: "I urge you, brothers, in view of God's mercy, to offer your bodies as living sacrifices, holy and pleasing to God—this is your spiritual act of worship" (NIV). God's beneficence is only one aspect of His character. He is also to be exalted, feared, and obeyed. Many contemporary worship songs elevate the Creator to His rightful place and inspire awe and obeisance. Life-changing consecration is the essence of encountering a Holy Creator. In the music video, *Consume Me,* D.C. Talk illustrated this mandate for radical discipleship. The robotic citizens of this allegory bowed under the autocratic hand of their captors and were compelled to wear oxygen masks in a world where no masks were needed. One brave soul could live no longer under such bondage. He ripped off his mask, and prepared to die. To his amazement, he breathed freely and easily. His peers gasped in horror as the life-support system was torn from his face. Then, shocked and emboldened by his survival, they removed their masks. The prisoners then walked strongly and confidently away from their tormentors and crossed a bridge which led to a new and better land.[5] This powerful picture of regeneration inspires an all-consuming radical discipleship. Worship demands man's highest and best.

The second heretical lie served up with a smile is **"Casual Christianity"**: American Christians now select the truths of their choice at the buffet table of life. This brand of worship uses feel-good songs to assuage a compromised conscience. Moral relativism needs no biblical standard—and syncretism drains the Word of God of its power. Spiritual truth takes a backseat to emotional hype. Worship songs, which reaffirm Christian theology, are needed to address a biblically illiterate culture. George Barna states that 52 percent of Americans are functionally illiterate.[6] American worshipers not only ignore their Bibles, Allan Bloom writes that most American adults seldom read at all.[7]

The third piece of American pie is **"Conceited Christianity"**: narcissism impairs one's ability to see God. The Almighty is demoted to genie status as He is implored to supply needs and provide contentment. Spiritual selfishness affects worship when God's agenda for His people is ignored and replaced with narrowly focused needs and preferences. Christian leaders skirmish over worship semantics and lose the battle for souls.

The fourth seductive slice is **"Instant Christianity"**: the value of living for unseen rewards is implausible to many American Christians. Worship must lift the worshiper to a higher realm. Biblical faith is about living beyond the here and now for the hereafter. Educators used to evaluate students on their intelligence quotient, or I.Q. The child with the right brainpower succeeded in school. Today, school psychologists and counselors use another significant measuring stick, the emotional quotient, or E.Q. Emotionally mature children can defer present pleasure for future rewards. Sometimes God defers earthly blessings for heavenly crowns. True worship transports the believer to the throne room. Paul emphasized this in Philippians when he wrote, "I want to know Christ and the power of his resurrection and the fellowship of sharing in his sufferings, becoming like him in his death, and so, somehow, to attain the resurrection from the dead" (Phil. 3:10-11, NIV). African spirituals focused on the life hereafter and lifted oppressed men and women up from sorrow and slavery. Many popular Russian Christian choruses identify with the sufferings of Christ. Worship that teaches prosperity theology will not satisfy the hearts of committed Christians who follow Jesus at any price.

The last sliver on the heretical Christian pie plate is, **"Cloister Christianity"**: others are excluded from worship for any number of reasons. For example, some American Christians withdraw out of fear. Teens face gang wars and drug lords at school. Their parents struggle with broken marriages. Children suffer in abusive homes. Government officials are often untrustworthy. Rather than suiting up for the conflict at hand, many American Christians sit on the couch and dream of happier, more secure days. Occasionally they congregate in dwindling fortresses and lob "gospel grenades" into enemy territory. Other Christians refuse to open the doors of worship to outsiders because they feel that their own worship experience will be hampered or altered. However, Jesus said, "when I am lifted up from the earth, [I] will draw all men to myself" (John 12:32, NIV). Intimate worship reaches the culture and reveals the wonder of Christ.

Sociological solutions must also be explored to answer the question: "Why is contemporary worship such a point of contention in today's churches?" Churches agonize over musical issues, and the debates are highly charged with emotion. Relevancy in a society that reinvents itself every three to five years is hard work. Paul knew the challenge of communicating Christ to a god-less world. The apostle cried, "I have become all things to all men so that by all possible means I might save some" (1 Cor. 9:22, NIV). Secular advertising moguls know more about what Americans think and feel than do many Christian leaders. Worship leaders are called to be shepherds; they must know the needs of the sheep and speak "sheeplish." Information about the worshiper in the pew and the unchurched people in the surrounding community is easier to obtain than ever before. Demographic information may be obtained from local government or tourism agencies. Bookstores and Web sites have materials and statistics on societal trends and popular belief systems. Church leaders must face their congregations and ask three basic questions.

1. Who comes to church?
2. Who should be there?
3. Who came and did not return?

Who comes to church? Since the average pastor has a tenure of four years or less, knowing the people is a challenge. Pastor Paul spoke lovingly

George Barna, Barna Research Group

Q: What are some changes to anticipate in worship in the new millenium?
A: "Communications styles will change: music will be more narrowly targeted to the audience's preferences (i.e. blended music will be passé), preaching styles will use language and methods that reflect the target audience, and the means of conveying announcements will be modified to fit the audience.

"A different atmosphere will emerge in which people dress casually, there is more time for authentic interaction, and the dominant focus of the time together will be personal connection with God rather than taking care of business.

"There will be continuity of content as worship leaders coordinate the content of the music, the sermon, prayers, and liturgy to provide a seamless flow of unified wisdom. That continuity will extend from week to week as worship leaders plan more comprehensively what they are doing and where they want people to go in terms of spiritual growth."

DEFINITION OF THE GENERATIONS*

Generation	Current Age (2002)	Birth Years
Seniors	76+	Pre-1926
Builders/Peacemakers	57-75	1927-1945
Boomers/Pathfinders	38-56	1946-1964
Busters/Pacesetters	18-37	1965-1984
Blasters/Millenialists	under 17	1985-2004

*From *Boiling Point,* George Barna and Mark Hatch (Ventura, CA: Regal Books, 2001), 56. Statistics are from the U. S. Census, 2000.

GENERATIONAL POPULATION*

Generation	Millions of People	% of Population
Seniors	31 M	11 %
Builders/Peacemakers	52 M	18 %
Boomers/Pathfinders	75 M	26 %
Busters/Pacesetters	68 M	24 %
Blasters/Millenialists	59 M	21 %

*From *Boiling Point,* George Barna and Mark Hatch (Ventura, CA: Regal Books, 2001), 56. Statistics are from the U. S. Census, 2000.

to his little flock in Thessalonica: "But we were gentle among you, like a mother caring for her little children. We loved you so much that we were delighted to share with you not only the gospel of God but our lives as well, because you had become so dear to us" (1 Thes. 2:7-8, NIV).

Great worship songs describe the place where believers met God, or they take worshipers to the place where they can encounter God. Craig Ludrick trains pastors in third-world countries. There was little food or water at a Rwandan refugee camp where several hundred African pastors gathered. Disease and death were everywhere. Persecution was intense. Yet the worship was incredibly powerful. The men sang, "You can take away my wife, you can take away my children, but you can't take away my Lord."[8] Why did the worship speak so powerfully to those pastors? The content of the songs focused on their own life issues. Even though the criteria for developing worship in first- and third-world countries are radically different, the need to reach the hearts of the worshipers at the point of their needs is essential in any cultural setting.

Different generations have different life issues. Seniors, the power-builder generation, were born pre-1926. A mother-raised generation, these individuals became the bright, rational problem-solving people that turned this country into one of the most powerful nations in the world.

The **Peacemakers**, or **Builders,** were born between 1927 and 1945. Peacemakers developed a keen sense of humanity and a tender social consciousness. The oppression of world wars brought forth among them a manifestation of pluralistic attitudes, public service, and the civil rights, women's, and environmental movements.

The **Pathfinders,** or **Boomers,** were born from 1946-1964. They were the indulged and protected generation. They turned a nation inside out, calling for more inward-centered focus. Individuals were more important than the community and the good of the masses. They explored, tested, risked, and investigated.

Pacesetters, or **Baby Busters,** were born from 1965-1984. Generation X, as they are often labeled, view themselves as self-reliant, realistic nonconformists. They are pragmatic, streetwise survivors.

Blasters or **Millenialists,** born between the years of 1985 and 2004, will grow up in a world stressing more values, more structure, and more protection.

These generational descriptions are all generalizations, yet in order to be relevant, the caring worship leader should be a student of people's backgrounds and life issues.[9]

A good worship leader must also consider the practical needs of the varying groups in his midst. For example, consider the seniors. Lyrics to contemporary choruses are usually displayed on a video screen. Older adults with vision problems and sensitivity to light are often unable to read the words on the screen. When lyrics are also printed in big print on a bulletin or handout, worship is greatly facilitated. Consider that senior adults often have difficulty with interference learning. Too many sensory elements can be overwhelming. Careful pacing of video and audio elements in a worship service can eliminate the stress of change in many situations.

Even an issue as basic as more sitting than standing during worship is crucial to seniors but irrelevant to millenialists. Logistical elements must be analyzed for their effect on all groups of worshipers.

One prime example of worship conflict is the senior adult who complains about the loudness of the mix of a contemporary worship band. An understanding pastoral leader looks past the initial criticism to the life issues involved. Very often the aging adult loses upper hearing partials. The lower partials of a drum or electric bass will overwhelm the high partials of the singer's voices. There are different areas of a sanctuary that are acoustically less "live" than other areas. A slight change in mix for a service with a predominance of seniors may make an enormous difference in their attitude toward contemporary worship music, whatever the style.

Conversely, busters often processed the pain in their young lives by escaping into their rooms and listening to music. If the level of the church music is not intense, the musical experience is not cathartic to the gen-x listener.

**Bill Bryan
Dean of Student
Internships, Perkins
Theological Seminary,
Dallas, Texas**

Q: What traditions in your denomination helped to formulate contemporary worship trends today?
A: "The United Methodist Church is uniquely blessed in its worship heritage. The grandparents on one side of Methodist worship were English cathedrals, and the other grandparents were North American brush arbors. Both high worship, centered in sacraments, and free worship, centered in preaching, are our heritage."

Therefore, when the young worshiper comes to church, if the music lacks intensity and volume, it also lacks emotional impact.

Builders often complain about changes in worship. Sensitive pastoring means hearing the hurt behind the complaint. Builders may be losing their health, their influence, and their support system of peers at a frightening rate. They look around at the world and scarcely find anything familiar. If their hurt is addressed, the anger will often dissipate.

Of course, it goes without saying that good worship leaders know the musicians in their midst. Wise worship leaders must cultivate and utilize the unique gifts of the Christian musicians that God sends to the church. If anointed instrumentalists and singers are featured in worship, the church will attract others with the same passion and giftings.

Music therapists relate a simple truth: people often prefer the musical style that was in vogue during the time they first fell in love. In the same way, most Christians prefer the church music in style when they first received Christ. Sensitive worship leaders recognize that music is a powerful emotional language. It speaks with a heart-cry that surpasses words and transcends relational barriers. The church leader who knows the congregation well is best able to focus with clear-cut and accurate worship service planning on specific needs among the flock.

Who should be there? Who lives in the surrounding community? Several questions must be pondered. Can the church reach all four generations at once? What will that look like? Can it even be done? God wants outsiders enfolded into the Kingdom. In order to reach them, the worship must be relevant. How was the gospel made relevant at Pentecost? The people saw the transforming, supernatural power of God at work as the Holy Spirit came in power on the lives of the disciples. This means dealing with the issue of change. Then they each heard the gospel in their own language. The Word does not get more relevant than that.

Relevancy in worship implies change, and change is always painful. It's hard to change plays on a third-down situation in a close NFL game without telling the other players on the team. Changing the pay structure or retirement plan at a business without telling personnel can spell disaster. Changing the sides of the bed at night without telling a spouse means trouble. If change is so painful, why try to change? Because Jesus gave a commission to reach the world—to go and make disciples. The world is changing by the day and morphing by the minute. New computers are practically obsolete while still in their boxes. Brian McLaren in his book, *The Church on the Other Side,* cites Ken Blanchard's analysis of change in five phases. The **simplest changes** are the result of growth in knowledge—a shift in rational thinking. The **second level of change** is a change in attitude with its emotional impact. The **third level of change** is even more radical—it is behavioral change. The **fourth level of change** is organizational change—a change that requires an enormous amount of effort and pain. The **fifth level of change** is the kind of metamorphosis that requires all of the other four levels of change to occur simultaneously. A radical change in worship is a fifth-level change that impacts the congregation on all levels. Those changes must be made thoughtfully and carefully.[10]

Considering who should be there means understanding the great gulf between modernism and post-modernism. From the Age of Enlightenment, rationalists taught that if man could just become smart enough, he could create an efficient utopian world that would bridge all races and cultures. The tall-mirrored skyscrapers in every major city in the world are monuments to modernistic rationalism. The goal was to standardize and perfect, to find all the right answers through science and technology. Post-modern architecture illustrates the radical break with the past. It breaks all the old rules. Post-modernistic busters say to their predecessors, "We've seen your institutions, and your enlightened marriages. We've seen technology rise, knowledge increase, and we are not impressed. The more we know, the more unanswered questions we have. We're looking for authentic relationships that work! What does organized religion have to offer us?"[11]

Answering the philosophical questions of the new generation is critical. Leonard Sweet wrote in *Quantum Spirituality in a Post-Modern World*:

"The missionary expansion of the gospel today is as much generational and chronological as it is geographical. In the same way, Jesus entered into the culture of his day in complex ways; in the same way Paul in front of Areopagus presented the gospel to the Athenians by quoting two of their own poets (Epimenides and Aratus of Crete): so the church is to be a dialoguing fellow-traveler with culture, exhibiting a critical but not unfriendly relationship to history."[12]

Contemporary church worship leaders now face a daunting chasm. A major world-view shift is occurring in this new millenium. A monumental change like the one from modernism to post-modernism occurs only about once every 500 years. The chasm separating these two views is still small. Any determined church can still cross the chasm and be in position to change and adjust to a post-modern contemporary culture.

> **Toby McKeehan**
> **Lead singer, DC Talk**
>
> "One thing we don't feel is covered enough in Christian music is songs about human relationships. Most songs are about the vertical relationship, our relationship with an awesome God. But sometimes I think we miss the mark. I believe a human relationship is our faith played out in everyday life. I believe that's where we can truly see where we are spiritually. Our human relationships will tell us how our relationship is with the Father."

Unfortunately, churches have very little time to cross the chasm. Very soon the gulf will widen to the point that a modern church will always be modern and thus irrelevant in a post-modern world. At that point, it will be difficult for a modern church to say anything significant to a post-modern contemporary world.

The shift from rationalism to post-modernism may be illustrated by two worship songs.

"Jesus is the answer for the world today
Above Him there's no other, Jesus is the way.
Jesus is the answer for the world today
Above Him there's no other, Jesus is the way." [13]

Notice how this chorus is modernism-crafted. It contains symmetrical structure, even lyric scansion, and predictable harmonic resolution. Notice that it teaches Jesus has a formula to be followed to find all the answers. This is the essence of modernism. People must come to Christ by the same intellectual formula. Traditional church language and culture are quickly adopted. Project-oriented, isolationist modernists saw the rise of Bible churches, highly structured behavioral codes, and very specific biblical parameters.

Modern church leaders did a good job of teaching biblical content—but did not always communicate how to develop relational, experiential answers to the issues of life. Paul said, "Knowledge puffs up; but love builds up." Evangelical theology has always dealt with two basic approaches to biblical truth: "What am I to believe and how am I to behave?" The relational purpose of truth asks the question, "What is in this truth that shows me how to have a deeper relationship with God and with others?" Until the church deals with man's first crisis—his aloneness (Gen. 2)—it cannot address man's second crisis—his fallenness (Gen. 3). Intellectual truth tends to divide mankind in his Pharisaic pride and arrogance. Relational truth opens hearts and brings men together. Post-modernists cry out for genuine, relational Christianity.

Hear are the lyrics to a popular post-modern chorus:

"Lord You have my heart, And I will search for Yours.
Jesus take my life and lead me on.
Lord You have my heart, And I will search for Yours.
Let me be to You a sacrifice.
And I will praise You, Lord. And I will sing of Love come down.
And as You show Your face, We'll see Your glory here." [14]

This song begins in plaintive minor tones, with uneven lyrical scansion. It changes from minor to major mode between verse and chorus. Most of all, it makes no assumptions, but sees a relationship with Jesus as a journey, a search. It implies progressive revelation. Finally, it ends with a powerful declaration of unity—"we'll see your glory here."

Both songs are biblically based but they address different issues. These two songs represent a huge paradigm shift in the way to do church. A paradigm is a set of parameters for problem solving. Sensitive, innovative leaders recognize when the rules have changed and standard operating procedures no longer apply. Churches that prepare for the post-modern future must remember three things. First, no paradigm lasts long. Second, the people who succeeded in navigating the current paradigm will have the most trouble transitioning to the new paradigm. Finally, a bold innovator, someone totally outside the organization, is best able to successfully determine the new paradigm parameters. [15]

Who came and did not return? The wise pastoral leader determines who is coming and going in the congregation and reacts accordingly. For example, displeased seniors complain loudly before finally deciding to leave. Boomers and Busters tend to show their disapproval with silence. If their needs are not met, they do not complain. They just do not come. They are absent by the millions.[16]

What does powerful, authentic, life-transforming worship look like in the new millenium? Time will tell! Will God manifest His presence in the same way in every church and culture? Of course not! Worship will be as creative and diverse as the Creator God Himself! Eclectic is the watchword for the future. Ethnic diversity, multiple service formats, multigenerational leadership, even cyber services will mirror the niche-market mentality that is the wave of post-modernism.[17] The challenge for church worship leaders and planners and instrumental music directors and arrangers is to maintain biblical integrity while achieving cultural relevancy. When Jesus said He wanted His followers to worship Him in spirit and in truth, He was deadly serious. Churches that will transform lives will present the Logos-God as He truly is and will be as spontaneous as the wind of the Spirit.

By better understanding worship trends in the church today, we hope to meet the needs more completely of those who are already worshiping, those who attend our churches but do not worship, and those who do not yet know the Lord. Successful church instrumental leaders in the new millenium will seek to provide the best worship resources for a changing and diverse worship community.

[1] Sally Morgenthaler, *Worship Evangelism: Inviting Unbelievers into the Presence of God* (Grand Rapids: Zondervan Publishing House, 1999), 93-121.

[2] George Barna, *The Second Coming of the Church* (Nashville: Word Publishing, 1998), 55.

[3] George Gallup, Jr., "Gallup Social and Economic Indicators," May 1999. www.gallup.com/poll/indicators

[4] Charles Colson, *Against the Night* (Ann Arbor: Servant Publishing Company, 1999), preface.

[5] DC Talk, "Consume Me" from *Supernatural,* Words and Music by Toby McKeehan, Michael Tait, Kevin Max, and Mark Heimermann, 1998 (Blind Thief Publishing/Fun Attic Music).

[6] Barna, op. cit., 55.

[7] Allan Bloom, *The Closing of the American Mind* (New York: Simon and Schuster, 1987), 35.

[8] Quoted by Craig Ludrick, November 1997. Used by permission.

[9] Tim Celek and Dieter Zander, *Inside the Soul of a New Generation* (Grand Rapids: Zondervan Publishing House, 1996), 30-36.

[10] Brian McLaren, *The Church on the Other Side* (Grand Rapids: Zondervan House, 2000).

[11] Neil Howe and William Strauss, *13th Gen: Abort, Retry, Ignore, Fail* (New York: Random House, 1993).

[12] Leonard Sweet, *Quantum Spirituality: A Postmodern Apologetic* (Dayton: Whaleprints, 1994), 2.

[13] "Jesus Is the Answer," (André Crouch and Sandra Crouch) © Copyright 1973 Bud John Songs, Inc. (ASCAP). All rights administered by EMI Christian Music Publishing. Used by permission.

[14] "Lord, You Have My Heart," (Martin Smith) © Copyright 1992 Thankyou Music (ASCAP/PRS). Administered worldwide by worshiptogether.com songs except for the U.K. and Europe which is administered by Kingsway Music. Used by permission.

[15] Joel Barker, *Paradigm Principles* Video (Minneapolis: Charthouse International, 1996).

[16] Tom Beaudoin, *Virtual Faith: The Irreverent Spiritual Quest of Generation X* (San Francisco: Josey Bass Publishers, 1998), 37.

[17] Sweet, op. cit.,12.

Julie Barrier is Associate Minister of Worship at Casas Adobes Baptist Church in Tucson, Arizona.

Appendix

RANGE AND TRANSPOSITION CHART

The ranges below indicate the most extreme notes possible in black notes (●) and more moderate suggested ranges in open notes (O). Notes in parenthesis indicate that the instrument must have a special key or attachment to be played. Sounding transpositions are indicated at the right of each example.

PICCOLO - 8va higher

FLUTE - as written

OBOE - as written

ENGLISH HORN - perfect 5th lower

CLARINET IN B♭ - major 2nd lower

BASS CLARINET IN B♭ - major 9th lower

BASSOON - as written

SOPRANO SAXOPHONE IN B♭ - major 2nd lower

ALTO SAXOPHONE IN E♭ - major 6th lower

TENOR SAXOPHONE IN B♭ - major 9th lower

BARITONE SAXOPHONE IN E♭ - 8va & major 9th lower

HORN IN F - perfect 5th lower

TRUMPET IN B♭ - major 2nd lower

TENOR TROMBONE - as written

EUPHONIUM - as written

BARITONE - major 9th lower

BASS TROMBONE - as written

TUBA - as written

20" TIMPANI - as written

23" TIMPANI - as written

25-26" TIMPANI - as written

28-29" TIMPANI - as written

30-32" TIMPANI - as written

ORCHESTRA BELLS - 2 8ves higher
(glockenspiel)

CHIMES - as written
(tubular bells)

HARP - as written

PIANO - as written

GUITAR - 8ve lower

VIOLIN - as written

VIOLA - as written

CELLO - as written

DOUBLE BASS - 8ve lower

INDEX

A

A soprano clarinet, 87
Abelardo Albisi of Milan, 71
Abraham, 17
Adjustment screws, 82
Against the Night, 377
Age of Enlightenment, 383
Ahaz, 15
Air attacks, 130
Allen, Phillip, 271
Altissimo register, 91f
Alto flute, 71
Alto clarinet, 87
Amati, 102
American Association of
  Christian Schools
  National Competition, 349
American Federation of
  Musicians, 254
American scrape, 75
Amos, 23
Amplifiers, 274
  Fender KXA, 274
Anhydrous lanolin, 153
Animal horn, 21, 113
Aoyama, 209
Appearance, uniform, 242
Apperson, Laura, 189
Aratus of Crete, 383
Arco, 102
Armstrong, Gerald P., 138,
  145
Arranging, 52
  adding emotion, 60
  adding variety, 60
  form, 54
  for instruments, 52
  necessary tools, 53
Articulation, 99, 131
Arts programs, 388
Arundo donax, 100

Asaph, 222
Asor, 23
Asymmetrical meters, 38
Attire, podium, 47
Audiation, 40
Audition process, 218, 326
Auditioning players, 217
Aulos, 22

B

Bach, 118, 135
Bade, Christopher, 64, 86, 99
Bailey, Mark, 323, 358, 363,
  371
Balance, 244
Ballet, 389
Bamboo cane, 100, 107
Band council, 339, 357
Band director, 323
Band program, 324ff
  administration, 336
  assessment of students,
    329ff
  auditions, 336
  beginning students, 327
  benefits, 324
  boosters, 343
  budgeting, 344
  classes, 331
  chapel services, 347
  community performances,
    347
  equipment needs, 340
  evaluation of students,
    329ff
  fund-raising, 345f
  grading system, 330
  handbooks, 346
  high school students, 329
  middle school students,
    328

  organization, 336, 356f
  playing tests/exams, 330
  recruiting and retention,
    337
  resources, 357
  seating arrangement,
    340f
Bands of America, 349
Banners, 389
Baritone oboe, 83
Baroque music, 83, 119
Baritone horn *(see
  Euphonium),* 138, 194
Barker, Joel, 385
Barna, George, 14, 377, 378
Baroque trumpet, 119
Barrett, Bob, 258, 268
Barrier, Julie, x, xi, 213, 215,
  258, 268, 375, 385
Bass clarinet, 56, 86, 97ff
Bass flute, 71
Bass horn, 146
Bass joint, 100
Bass oboe, 83
Bass viol, 196
Basset horn, 87
Bassoon, 56, 79, 97, 100ff,
  194
  care and maintenance, 103
  intonation, 100
  problems, 101
  purchasing, 102
  reeds, 100
  resources, 103
  writing for, 101
Batter head, 157ff
Beats, divided, 39
Beaudoin, Tom, 385
Beecham, Sir Thomas, 31
Beethoven, Ludwig van, 120
Bell trees, 168

Bells, 21, 57, 165
Benge, 135
Benny, Jack, 173
Benson, Warren, 49
Berlioz, Hector, 28, 105,
120, 127, 135, 146
Biblical worship, 13ff
Blocker, Larry, 331
Bloom, Allan, 378
Bluhmel, Friedrich, 119
Bocal, 100f, 103
Body language, 47
Boehm, Theobald, 65, 86
Boiling Point, 380
Boismortier, Joseph, 103
Bolero sticks, 157
Bongos, 58, 169
Bore, 128, 139, 142
Bore oil, 81, 93
Bow, 176, 181, 188, 191,
193, 197, 199f
Bowing techniques, 182, 199
Blanchard, Ken, 383
Blazers as uniforms, 242
Braces, 68, 129
Brahms, Johannes, 120
Brass, 52, 56, 63, 112
configuration and place-
ment, 246
volume level problems, 246
Brass quartet, 55
Brazilian samba, 266
Bridge, 173, 181, 191, 193
Bridge keys, 79
Brubaker, Larry, 319, 321
Brushes, 159, 166
Bryan, Bill, 382
Budgeting, 304ff
Buescher "Aristocrat," 108
Buffet, 94
Buffet, August, 86
Bugler, 121
Bulow, Hans von, 28
Bundy, 108
Buttons, 98, 199
Buzz(ing), 114, 120, 129, 138

C

C clarinet, 87
Cabasas, 58, 169
Callahan, Ed, 230, 241
Camac, 209
Capo, 263
Caravan, open-chamber
mouthpiece, 109
Carpal tunnel syndrome, 197
Case, Anthony, 260
Castanets, 58
Cataloguing, 316
Celek, Tim, 385
Cello, 59, 97, 100ff, 111, 117,
190
care and maintenance, 193
intonation, 192
playing techniques, 191
purchasing, 192
resources, 195
tuning, 191
Celtic harp, 205
Chalkos, 20
Chalumeau register, 86, 91f
Character building, 324
Chimes, 58, 164, 165
Chin rest, 173, 188
Chord charts, 264
Chord pads, 58
Chords, labeling, 265
Chorus, 384
Christian Instrumentalists
and Directors
Association, 335
Christian school bands,
323ff
beginning students, 327
curriculum development,
327
discipline, 327
Christian school ensembles,
380
ensembles, various, 381
Christianity,
casual, 378
cloister, 378

conceited, 378
consumer, 377
instant, 378
Chromatic passages, 207
Chromatic tones, 52
Church, American, 377
Church Music Publishers
Association, 241
*Church on the Other Side,
The*, 383
Cierpke, Timothy H., 190, 195
Clarinet, 55, 64, 79, 86, 117
breath support, 88
care and maintenance, 93
characteristics of, 87
embouchure, 88
equipment, 89
family, 86-87
hand position, 89
history of, 86
intonation, 91
misuses of, 93
playing technique, 88f
purchasing, 94
reeds, 90
registers, 91
repairs, 93
resources, 95
tuning, 91
uses of, 93
Clarino, 119
Clarion register, 91, 92
Clarion trumpet, 86
Classical period, 119
Claves, 169
Cleaning snake, 117, 143,
153
Cleveland, 108
*Closing of the American
Mind, The*, 385
Col legno, 182
Collins, Ernie, 149
Color guard, 354, 357
Colson, Charles, 377
Communication, 313f
tools, 231

with instrumentalists, 231
with band parents, 342
with faculty members, 343
with school administration, 342
Community performances, 347
Competitions, 348
Computer labs, 283
Computers, 319
Computer software, 283
Concerts, 251, 348
  attire, 48, 349
  budget, 255
  contractor, 255
  ideas for, 252
  stage etiquette, 351
Conducting, 27ff
  baton, 30
  choral, 44ff
  cueing, 35ff
  downbeat, 32ff
  fermata, 34ff
  instrumental, 44ff
  mirror, 37
  mixed meters, 38
  phrasal, 37
  posture, 29
  preparatory beat, 32ff
Congas, 58
Conguero, 266
Conical tubing, 139
Conn, 118, 135
Conservatory of Music, 280
  application form, 286
  board, 280
  budget, 283
  curriculum, 282
  faculty, 282
  fees, 282
  instructor contract, 289
  instructor employment, 288
  letter to returning students, 287
  policies, 282
  publicity and promotion, 281

Contra-alto clarinet, 87, 97
Contra-bass, 196
Contra-bass clarinet, 87, 97
Contra-bassoon, 100
Contractors, 255
Cook, Gary, 168
Copyright, 53, 55, 316, 335
Copyrights and the Law, 241
Cor anglais, 83
Cordell, Max, 323, 358
Cornet, 123
Cork, 70, 106, 143
Cork grease, 80, 93, 143, 163
Counterhoop, 159
Countermelody(ies), 54, 55, 57, 78
Cowbells, 169
Cranfill, Jeff, 52, 61, 323, 358
Crash cymbals, 58, 166
Crescendo roll, 163
Crook, 100, 119
Cross-sticking technique, 162
Crouch, André, 385
Cues, 35ff
Cyber services, 385
Cymbal, 20, 24, 166
  hi-hat, 260
  ride and crash, 260

D

Dampening, 163
Dance groups, 388
Darken, Eric, 162
David, 17, 23f, 376
Dealer, music instrument, 108
Denner, Johann, 86
Détaché, 182
Dickinson, Edson, 104, 111
Diddle approach, 162
Digital audio, 320
Discipline, 327, 337
Divided beats, 39
Donut, 98
Double bass, 97, 196
  intonation, 197
  playing technique, 198, 199

purchasing, 201
range, 199
recruiting players, 202
resources, 203
Double-reed instruments, 74, 100
  suppliers, 103
Double tonguing, 67, 93, 151
Drama group, 388
Drum, 20
  kick bass drum, 260
Drum Corps International, 354
Drum major, 339, 356
Drum sets, 58, 260
  electronic, 261
  sticks, 261
Dulcimer, 23
Duncan, Jon, 13, 25

E

Eclectic, 385
Edwards and Shires, 135
Electric bass, 202, 259, 260
Electronic keyboard, 264
  in church orchestra, 273
  intonation, 275
  players, 259
  resources, 275
Electronic tuner, 101, 115, 207
Embellishments,
  percussive, 236
  vocal, 240
Embouchure,
  baritone horn, 141
  bassoon, 100
  clarinet, 88
  euphonium, 141
  flute, 66
  French horn, 114
  oboe, 74
  saxophone, 107
  trombone, 129
  trumpet, 120
  tuba, 148
End pin, 191, 200
English horn, 74, 83, 100

Ensemble,
  accompanist, 223
  brass quintet, 279
  benefits, 226
  Celtic, 279
  ethnic, 279
  flute, 279
  how to begin, 223
  instrumental, 277
  ministry, 222, 225
  performance opportunities,
    224
  promoting, 250
  resources, 226-229
  types of, 225
  woodwind quintet, 279
Epimenides, 383
Ethnic diversity, 385
Etiquette, Podium, 47
Euphonium, 138, 146
  care and maintenance, 143
  characteristics of, 138
  mouthpiece, 142
  purchasing, 142
  resources, 144
  tuning, 141
Evaluation process, 219
  peer evaluation, 219
  director evaluation, 220
Evaluating players, 217
Evangelism, 213, 297, 323
Evil spirits, 21
Expectations, 249

F

F-holes, 173, 181, 186
Farguson, Eddie, 224, 304,
  306
"Fear" factor, 64, 171
Feast of Trumpets, 22
Festivals, 348
Feeder program, 222
Feeder groups, 249
Fermata, 34ff
Fibercane reeds, 90
Fills, 262

Fine tuners, 173, 181, 191
Fingerboard, 174, 192
Fingernail technique, 206
Flipping method, 163
Floor peg, 98
Flow sheet, 171, 231-240,
  243, 259
Fluegelhorn, 123
Flute, 22, 55, 65
  breathing exercises, 67
  care and maintenance, 70
  embouchure, 66
  family, 71
  history of, 65
  intonation, 69
  lubrication, 70
  misuses of, 69
  playing technique, 66
  problems, 68
  purchasing, 70
  repairs, 70
  resources, 72
  tonguing, 67
Flutter tonguing, 67, 151
Folders, 317
Fox, 102
Fraedrich, Eileen, 335
French bow, 197, 201
French cymbal, 166
French horn, 55, 57, 101,
  110, 112, 113
  care and maintenance, 117
  embouchure, 114
  history of, 113
  intonation, 115
  mouthpiece, 114
  playing techniques, 113-117
  purchasing, 118
  resources, 118
  tuning, 115
  uses, 117
French scrape, 75
Frets, 192
Frog, 177
Frozen valves, 118
Fund-raising, 304ff, 343, 345f

G

Gabrielse, Ken, 231
Gage, John G., 63, 112, 300,
  313, 307, 312, 313, 314
Gage, Ruth, 315, 318
Gallup poll, 377
Gardner, Howard, 324
Garofalo, Robert, 329
Geerdes, Harold P., 244
Generations, definition of, 380
  Baby Busters, 381
  Blasters, 381
  Boomers, 381
  Builders, 380
  Pacesetters, 381
  Pathfiners, 381
  Peacemakers, 380
  Seniors, 380
German bow, 201
Germanic cymbal, 166
Girdler, Jeffrey H., 113, 118
Glissandi, 69, 102, 117, 129,
  135, 206f
Gordon, Edwin, 40
Gospel Big Band, 278
Grading system, 330
Grand concert harp, 204
Great Commission, 297, 385
Green, Elizabeth, 29f, 43
Griffin, Owen, 272
Grip,
  French, 161
  German, 161
  matched, 157, 165
  traditional, 157
Guidance counselor, 332
Guiros, 58, 169
Guitars, 259, 262

H

Haithcock, Michael, 28
Halil, 21, 74
Hand-in-bell technique, 114
Hand slide, 133
Hand slide brace, 131
Handbook, orchestra, 300

Hansford, Jim, 27, 51, 146, 154, 323, 358, 363, 371
Harmonics, natural and artificial, 178f, 198, 198, 206
Harmony, 63
Harp, 22, 24, 204
  Celtic/Irish, 205
  care and maintenance, 208
  characteristics of, 207
  playing technique, 205
  purchasing, 208-209
  resources, 210
  tuning, 207
Harris, Patricia, 209
Hatch, Mark, 380
Haydn, Franz Joseph, 123
Hazozerah, 21
Heckel, 102
Heckelphone, 83
Helicon, 146
Helman, James E., 297, 299
Heman, 222
Hezekiah, 15
Hindemith, Paul, 105
Holton, 118
Holy place, 21
Holy Spirit, 15, 17, 382
Honegger, 105
Horn, 21, 24,
Horn rips, 57
Howe, Neil, 385
Huff, Ronn, 53
Humidifiers, 82, 181, 188
Humidity, 82, 181, 188, 207
Hummel, Johann Nepomuk, 123
Humming method, 163

I

Ictus, disappearing, 37
Inside the Soul of a New Generation, 385
Instruments,
  in the Bible, 20
  in worship, vi
  purchase/rental, 342

selection of, 332
Instrumental director, responsibilities, 139
Instrumental ministry, 19
Instrumental music ministry, vii, ix
International Phonetic Alphabet, 46
Intonation,
  bassoon, 100
  cello, 192
  clarinet, 91
  double bass, 197
  flute, 69
  French horn, 115
  saxophone, 107
  trumpet, 122
  tuba, 150
  viola, 187
  violin, 173f
Isaiah's "dialogue," 16

J

Jacobs, Arnold, 149
Janzen, Eldon, 327
Jazz ensembles, 105
Jeduthun, 23, 222
Jeremiah, 22
Jericho, 21, 113
Jeroboam, 14
Jeté, 182
Jethro, 307
John the Revelator, 16
Jones, James, 93
Josephus, 20
Joshua, 113

K

Karajan, Herbert von, 31
Kathros, 23
Katterjohn, Michael, 156, 170
Keilwerth, 108
Kelim, 18
Keren, 21
Key cups, 106
Key oil, 80

Keyboard mallet instruments: 155, 164f
Keyboard players, 259
Kiefer, Michael, 126
King, 108, 118, 135
Kinnor, 22
Kirby, Steve, 155
Kirkland, Camp, viii, ix, 52, 61, 291, 296
Kithara, 22
Kithros, 23
Klose, Hyacinthe, 86
Koinonia, 277
Kolosick, Timothy, 283
Krause, Charles A., 146, 154
Kroener, 102

L

Latin music, 266
Latin percussion instruments, 168
Lautzenhauser, Tim, 339
Leadpipe, 122, 148, 151
LeBlanc, 94
Legato, 182
Leinsdorf, Erich, 40
Leonard, Richard, 18
Levine, Sam, 68
Levitical law, 15
Library, 315ff
Librarian, 310
Ligatures, 90, 95, 107, 109
Lip tension, 115
Lipping, 115, 142, 151
Liszt, Franz, 28
Literature selection, 249, 255
  for bands, 334
  for orchestras, 291
  resources, 293ff
Louré, 182
Ludrick, Craig, 380
Ludwig, 163
Lugs, 157
Lully, Jean-Baptiste, 28
Lyon & Healy, 209
Lyre(s), 22, 24

M

McClure, Carol, 204, 211
McDonald, Valorie, 193
McKeehan, Toby, 383
McLaren, Brian, 383
McMinn, Lauren, 181
McNatt, Terry, 277, 279, 280, 285
Mallets, 161, 164, 166, 168
Man, Ron, 230, 232
Maracas, 169
Marcato, 182
Marching band program, 340, 354ff
  color guard, 354
  marching percussion, 354
Marimba, 273
Marimba mallets, 166
Mark tree, 155, 168
Martellé, 182
Martin, 108
Martin, Ralph, 17
Massenet, Jules, 105
Matheson, Brad R., 217, 221, 248, 253
Matthews, David, 78
Mayo, Larry, 242, 247
Measurable objectives, 330
Meditation, 124
Meece, David, 270
Mehta, Zubin, 50
Megaphone, 21
Melding, 37
Memorizing music, 224
Mena'an'im, 20
Mendelssohn, Felix, 28
Meters, changing, 38
Mezillot, 21
Meziltayim, 20
Microphones, 245f
Middle Ages, 65
Miles, Richard, 331
Milhaud, Darius, 105
Military bands, 105
Mims, Lloyd, 196, 203

Ministry,
  ensemble, 222
  investment, 213
  personal, 249
Minstrel, 23
Modernism, 383
Modulation chart, 234
Monitor, 259
Monteux, Pierre, 31
Moosemann, 102
Moral relativism, 378
Morgenthaler, Sally, 376
Morley, 209
Morris, Patricia, 71
Moses, 119
Mount Zion, 24
Mouthpiece,
  clarinet, 90, 95
  bass clarinet, 97
  euphonium, 142
  French horn, 114
  saxophone, 108-109
  trombone, 128, 129
  trumpet, 122
  tuba, 148, 151
Moyse, Marcel, 65
Mozart, Wolfgang A., 87, 103
Mpengo, 81
Mueller, Ivan, 86
Multigenerational leadership, 385
Multimedia, 321
Multiple-service format, 385
Multitrack recording, 320
Musette, 83
Music Educators National Conference, 244
Music therapists, 382
Mute,
  tuba, 152
  bucket, 135
  cup, 135
  straight, 135
  waa-waa, 135
Myall, Celeste, 172, 184

N

Nahilah, 22
Natural trumpet, 119, 121
Nebel, 23
Nebuchadnezzar, King, 23
Neck strap, 97, 100
Neiman, Marcus, 346
Nelson, Craig E., 264
Newsletter, 313
Newspaper ads, 108
Niche-market mentality, 385
19th century, 119

O

Obbligati, 55
Oboe, 22, 55, 74, 100
  care and maintenance, 79
  embouchure, 74
  family, 83
  history of, 74
  misuses of, 79
  playing technique, 76
  problems, 75
  purchasing, 83
  range expectations, 76
  reeds, 75
  repairs, 82
  resources, 84
  tone holes, 80
  tone production, 74
  tonguing, 75
  tuning, 77
  uses of, 78
Oboe d'amore, 83
Officers, 307ff
One, Darryl, 241
Open strings, 174, 198
Ophicleide, 146
Orchestra,
  bass instuments in, 274
  budgeting, 304ff
  configuration, 245
  feeder program, 222
  fund-raising, 304ff
  handbook, 300ff
  officers, 307ff

placement, 244
pit, 245
prospect card, 221
service etiquette, 246
Web page, 303
Orchestra bells, 164
Orchestration, 55, 269
Organ, 269
  articulation, 272
  Hammond B-3, 274
  in church orchestra, 271f
Ormandy, Eugene, 31
Ortega, Fernando, 272
Overtone series, 128
Overtones, 263

P

Pa'amonim, 21
Pads, 70, 82, 95, 106, 143, 153
Paradiddles, 162
Paradigm Principles, 385
Paradigm shift, 384
Paul, apostle, 377, 379, 383
Payne, Billy, 248, 253
Pedal harp, 204
Pedals, 162, 207
Pentecost, 382
Pep bands, 333
Pepper, J. W., 334
Percussion, 20, 57, 63, 155, 156
  accessories, 166
  configuration and place-
    ment, 246
  resources 169-170
Pesanterin, 23
Phillips, Duncan, 261
Philosophy,
  ministerial, 217, 248
  open door, 217
  process, 217
  product, 217
Piano, 263, 269
  in church orchestra, 270
Piccolo, 56, 71
Piccolo trumpet, 123
Pipes, 22

Piston valves, 143, 152
Pizzicato, 102, 182, 194, 197
Post-Christian era, 376
Post-modernism, 383ff
Praise Bands, 278
Praise Band League, 226
Praise Gathering, 226
Pratt, Samuel O., 208
Prausnitz, Frederik, 45
Près de la table, 206
Professional musicians,
  171, 200f, 254ff
Programming, 249
Prokofiev, Sergi, 105
Psallo, 18
Public domain, 53
Public school music
  systems, 64
Puchner, 102
Purchasing an instrument
  (see individual instrument)

Q

*Quantum Spirituality in a
  Post-Modern World*, 383

R

Ram's horn, 21, 113
Range chart, 386
Rascher, Sigurd M., 111
Rationalism, 383f
Recruiting,
  church members, 213
  concerts, 252
  instrumental owners, 214
  professional players, 214
  recent graduates, 215
Recruitment, 213, 251
Reed suppliers, 84
Reeds,
  bass clarinet, 97
  bassoon, 100
  clarinet, 90, 95
  oboe, 75
  plastic, 107
  saxophone, 107, 109

Reggae, 266
Register key, 93
Rehearsal,
  definition of, 48
  orchestra, 243
  preservice, 242
  room, 243
  schedule, 255
  space, 224
Reinhardt, Donald S., 121
Remley, Jon S., 74, 85
Remley, Rececca Danner,
  65, 73
Renaissance, 65, 119, 190
Repertoire, 224
Resonite, 89
Reynolds, H. Robert, 48
Rhythm and blues, 266
Rhythm chart, 265
Rhythm section, 52, 235, 258
  configuration and place-
    ment, 246
  ensemble, 277
  piano, 263
  purpose, 258
  make-up, 258
  rehearsing the, 265
  resources, 267-268
  use in contemporary
    worship, 258
Ricochet, 182
Ridenour, Tom, 91
Riffs, 236, 262
Rim, 114
Rim shots, 159
Robes, 242
Rock stop, 201
Rolls, drum, 158, 165
Root, Denise, 116
Rosin, 181, 188, 193, 197
Rotary valves, 134, 150, 152
Russian bassoon, 146

S

Sabbeka, 23
Sabian, 166

Sachs, Curt, 23
Sacks, Oliver, 13
Saltando, 182
Salvi, 209
Sanctuary orchestra, 24
Sax, Adolphe, 104, 106, 109
Saxophone, 104, 117
  alto, 105, 110
  baritone, 105, 111, 194
  characteristics of, 106
  embouchure, 107
  family, 105
  history of, 104-105,
  intonation, 107
  mouthpiece, 108-109
  purchasing, 106
  reeds, 109
  resources, 111
  soprano, 105
  tenor, 105, 110
Scholarship programs, 346
Score memorization, 43
Score study, 40
Scripture references,
  to use in worship, 18
Seating arrangement, 340
Secco staccato, 102
Second Coming of the
  Church, 377
Segler, Franklin, 17
Selmer, 94, 108
Selmer, Mark VI, 108
Selmer Music Guidance
Survey, 337
Sendry, Alfred, 20
Selah, 24
Sequencers, multitrack, 283
Serpent, 146
Sewing machine oil, 80
Shakers, 169
Shalishim, 20
Shalosh, 20
Shank, 122, 128, 151
Shapparu, 21
Sharpening lever, 205
Shawm, 22

Shifting, 174, 187, 198
Shofar, 21, 113
Sh'minit, 23
Shreiber, 102
Sight reading, 328, 336
Silicone spray, 163
Sims, W. Hines, 18
Single tonguing, 67
Sistrum, 20
Slatkin, Leonard, 44
Sleeve adaptor, 128
Slide grease, 117, 153, 163
Slide position chart, 131
Slurs, 93, 102, 130
Smearing, 129
Smith, Douglas, 119, 126
Smith, Martin, 385
Snake brush, 122
Snare drum, 58, 156, 260
  care and maintenance, 159
  parts of, 156-157
  playing technique, 157
  problems, 159
  purchasing, 160
  tuning, 158
Snare head, 157, 158
Snare release lever, 159
Snare sticks, 166
Software, 283
  notation, 319
  Pyware 3D, 355
Solomon, 376, 377
Soprano clarinet, 87
Soprano flute, 71
Sound baffles, 112
Sound box, 204
Sound post, 173, 193
Sound technician, 245, 387
Sousa, John Philip, 146
Sousaphone, 146
Special events, 248, 253
  implementation, 251
  planning, 251
Spenser, Dan, 136
Spiccato, 178, 182, 199
Spiritual awakening, 13

Spiritual maturity, 220
Spit keys, 143
Spohr, Ludwig, 28
Springs, 70, 82
Squeezing, 178
Staccato, 102, 182, 199
Stage crew coordinator, 310
Stalter, Timothy, 47
Steward, Bruce, 25
Stewardship, 19
Sticking, 157, 165
Stocking, 132
Stolzel, Heinrich, 119
Storyboard, 233
STP, 153
Straight trombone, 127
Straps, 166
Strauss, Richard, 67, 105
Strauss, William, 385
Stringed Instruments, 22
String bass, 97, 101, 147, 151, 194
Strings, 52, 58, 63, 171
  configuration, 245
  placement, 194
Strings, nylon, 208
Strings, soft-core, 181
Strings, steel, 181, 193
Strobe, 207
Student conductor, 340
Sul ponticello, 182
Sul tasto, 177
SuperSlick, 132
Suspended cymbals, 58,
  159, 166
Suzuki, 175
Swanson, 209
Swanson, Carl, 208
Sweet, Leonard, 383
Synagogue, 17
Syncretism, 378
Synthesizer, 171, 259, 265,
  269, 334
  in church orchestra, 273
Synthesizer string reduc-
  tion, 60
Szell, George, 31

T

Tablature, 263
Tail piece, 173
Tambourine, 20, 58, 167
Tapping method, 163
Technology, 319ff
Teflon™ tape, 94, 163
Telemann, Georg Phillip, 103
Temperature, 82, 181, 188, 207
Tension, body, 130
Tension rods, 157, 158, 159
Terry, Terry C., 171, 185, 189
Tessitura, 55
Textures, 55, 236
13th century, 20
13th Gen: Abort, Retry,
  Ignore, Fail, 385
Threlkeld, Carter, 222, 229
Throat tone register, 89, 91,
  92
Timbales, 58, 169, 266
Timpani, 57, 151, 155, 160
  care and maintenance, 163
  mallets, 166
  parts of, 160
  playing techniques, 161
  purchasing, 163
  tuning, 162
Tof, 20
Tonguing,
  flute, 67
  oboe, 75
  trombone, 129
  tuba, 148-149
Tours,
  acoustical problems, 387
  ensembles, 384
  group lodging, 386
  overseas travel, 387
  release form, 387
  repertoire, 385
  transportation, 386
  travel agencies, 387
  unexpected costs, 387
Townend, Stuart, 235
Training directors, 223

Transposition chart, 237
Transitions, 234
Transpose, 117
Transverse flute, 65
Tremolo, 102, 182, 194
Triangle, 167
Trills, 69, 79, 93, 102, 194
Triple tonguing, 67, 151
Trombone, 56, 100, 110,
  112, 117, 121, 127, 194
  arranging for, 134-135
  bass, 111, 128
  care and maintenance, 133
  characteristics of, 127-128
  embouchure, 129
  history of, 127
  mouthpiece, 128, 129
  mutes, 135
  playing technique, 130
  problems, 132
  purchasing, 135
  resources, 136
  slide, 130ff
  straight, 127
  tonguing, 129
  valve, 128, 146
Trombontine, 132
Trout, Jerry, 348
T'ru'ah, 22
Truax, Bert, 121
Trumpet, 22, 24, 56, 119
  changing pitch, 120-121
  family, 122-123
  history of, 119
  intonation, 122
  mouthpiece, 122
  natural, 119
  Piccolo, 123
  resources, 125
  use of, 124
Tuba, 57, 111, 112, 160, 194
  bass, 147
  care and maintenance, 152
  double bass, 147, 151
  embouchure, 148
  history of, 146

  intonation, 150
  mouthpiece, 148, 151
  playing techniques, 147-148
  purchasing, 152
  resources, 153
  stands, 148
  tenor, 147
  tonguing, 148-149
Tuning,
  cello, 191
  clarinet, 91
  euphonium, 141
  French horn, 115
  harp, 207
  oboe, 77
  timpani, 162
Tuning gauges, 161
Tuning pegs, 173, 191
Tuning slide, 115, 133, 150

U

Ugab, 21
Underscoring, 253
Unger, Ruth Shelley, 100, 103
Uniforms, 242, 350

V

Valentine Emergency Pad
  Repair Kit, 94
Valve,
  oil, 143
  slides, 151
  springs, 143
  string, broken, 117
  tone tuning, 116
  triggers, 134
Valve trombone, 128, 146
Valves,
  frozen, 118
  piston, 143, 152
  rotary, 134, 152
Vaseline, 143, 153
Venturi, 89
Venus (W & W Harp Co.),
  209
Vibraphone, 273

Vibraslap, 169
Vibrato, 68, 78, 187, 192, 199
Vic Firth General, 157
Video, 321
Viennese cymbal, 166
Vintage saxophones, 108
Viola, 59, 117, 185
  care and maintenance, 188
  characteristics of, 185
  intonation, 187
  playing techniques, 186
  purchasing, 189
  repairs, 188
Violin, 55, 58, 172,
  care and maintenance, 181
  characteristics of, 173
  playing techniques, 173-178
  purchasing, 180
  resources, 183
  uses of, 178, 180
Virtual Faith: The Irreverent
  Spiritual Quest of
  Generation X, 385
Vision, viii, 213, 255
Vision statement, 297
Vito, 108
Vivaldi, 103

W

Wagner, Richard, 28, 146
Wainwright, Geoffrey, 16
Wall, Robert F., 86, 96
Walter, Bruno, 31
Water slide, 115
Web site, 303, 313
Weber, Carl Maria von, 103
Webber, Robert, 16
Wheaton, Jack, 254, 256
Wheel bearing grease, 117
Widow's point, 120
Wiley, Fletch, 124
Wilhoit, Mel, 323, 358, 363,
  371, 372, 373
Willbanks, Scotty, 110
Williamson, Bob, 213, 215, 216
Wind chimes, 58, 168

Winds, 21
Wing joint, 100
Winkler, David, 258, 268,
  269, 276
Woodwinds, 52, 55, 63, 64
  configuration and place-
    ment, 246
Workshop, 215, 282
World-view shift, 383
Worship,
  characteristics of, 14-17
  contemporary, 377
  cutting edge, 376
  definition of, 14
  leader(s), 13, 124, 375, 381
  model for, 14
  new millenium, 375
  order of service, 231
  planning, 230
  relevancy, 382
  role of orchestra, 246-247
  Scripture references to
    use in, 18
  service, elements of, 231
  style changes, 231
  team, 232
  use of instruments, 17
  Worship Evangelism, 376
Wye, Trevor, 71

X

Xylophone, 164, 273

Y

Yamaha, 94, 102, 108, 118,
  135
Yanagisawa, 108
Year of Jubilee, 21
Yeo, Douglas, 127, 137
Yobel, 21

Z

Zander, Dieter, 385
Zelzelim, 20
Zildjian, 166
Zither, 23

Scripture Index

OLD TESTAMENT

Genesis
2 384
3 384
4:21 22

Exodus
18:18-23 . . . 307
19:6 21
19:13 21
28:33-34 21

Leviticus
4:7, 18, 25 . . . 21
12:2 15
23:24 19
23:23-25 22
25:9 21

Numbers
10 119
10:2 22
29 19

Joshua
6:5 21

1 Samuel
10:5 18
10:22 18
16:16, 23 23
18:6 20

2 Samuel
6:5 18
6:5 20

1 Kings
1:39 22
1:40 22
10:12 23

2 Kings
3:15 23
9:13 22
11:14 22

1 Chronicles
13:8 18
13:8 24
15:16, 28 18
15:16 20
15:16-24 24
15:19 20
15:28 21
15:28 24
16:4-7 24
16:42 18
16:42 20
23:5 222
25 222
25:1 20
25:1-7 24
25:3 23
25:5 21

2 Chronicles
5:11-14 vi
5:11-14 . . . 368
5:13 20
29:26 18
30:27 15

Nehemiah
12:36 18

Job
21:12 18
30:31 22

Psalms
3:2 25
5 22
6 23
12 23
19:1 334
33:2 23
33:3 323
43:4 22
50 vi
57:8 23
71:22 22
73: 376
73:17 376
73:25-26 . . . 376
81:2 23
81:2-3, ... 18
81:3 21
92:3 18
92:3 23
98:5 22
98:6 21
98:6 24
100 224
137:2 22
144:9 23
147:7 22
149:3 22
150 224
150 280
150 323
150 368
150:3-5 18
150:3 21
150:3 23
150:4 ix
150:5 20

Proverbs

23:7 377

Ecclesiastes

1:9 53

Isaiah

5:12 18
5:12 22
6. 14
6:1-3 16
6:5 16
6:7 16
6:8 16
6:9 16
6:11 16
30:29 22

Jeremiah

48:36 22

Ezekiel

26:13 23

Amos

5:10-12 15
5:21-23 14
6:5 18

Daniel

3:4-6 24
3:5, 7, 10, 15 . . 19

Zechariah

14:20 21

NEW TESTAMENT

Matthew

9:23 22
23:27 14
28:18-20 . . . 297

Luke

7:32 22

John

1:3 19
4. 14
4:20 376
4:20-21, 23 . . 14
4:23-24 376
12:32 379
17. 213

Acts

2:42 231

Romans

8:26 viii
12:1 19
12:1 377
15:9 18

1 Corinthians

9:22 379
10:31 19
13:1 20
14:7-8 19
14:15 18
15:52 19

2 Corinthians

2:14 224

Ephesians

5:18-19 280
5:19 18

Philippians

3:10-11 378

Colossians

3:16 vii
3:16 368
3:23-24 325

1 Thessalonians

2:7-8 380
4:16 19
5:18 239

Hebrews

10. 14
10:19-25 14

James

1:5 52

Revelation

8:2, 6 19
18:22 19